# Epistemology, Economics, and Ethics

# Epistemology, Economics, and Ethics

## A Practical Philosophy of Prehistoric Archaeology

---

Konrad Ott

ROOTS • Studies • RS | 04

ROOTS Studies, Vol. 4

Series editors: Eileen Eckmeier, Martin Furholt, Lutz Käppel, Johannes Müller
Associate editor: Andrea Ricci

Published by Sidestone Press, Leiden
www.sidestone.com

Imprint: Sidestone Press Academics
This book has been peer-reviewed. For more information see www.sidestone.com

Layout design: ROOTS/Tine Pape and Sidestone Press
Copy editing and proofreading: Eileen Küçükkaraca, Kiel
Cover design: Petra Horstmann, Kiel
Cover image: after E.C. Harris: Principles of Archaeological Stratigraphy (London, San Diego 1979). An example of layer and feature interfaces with numbered layers. Available at: https://de.m.wikipedia.org/wiki/Datei:InterfacialLines.jpg.

DOI: 10.59641/v9144yh

ISBN 978-94-6427-081-5 (softcover)
ISBN 978-94-6427-082-2 (hardcover)
ISBN 978-94-6427-083-9 (PDF e-book)

ISSN Print: 2950-2373
ISSN Online: 2950-2381

Published with funding of the Deutsche Forschungsgemeinschaft (DFG, German Research Foundation) Germany's Excellence Strategy – EXC 2150 ROOTS – 390870439.

# Preface of the series editors

As the outcome of overarching, interdisciplinary scientific research efforts within the Excellence Cluster 'ROOTS – Social, Environmental and Cultural Connectivity in Past Societies' at Kiel University, we are pleased to present the fourth volume of the publication series **ROOTS Studies.** This book series of the Cluster of Excellence ROOTS addresses social, environmental and cultural phenomena as well as processes of past human development in light of the key concept of 'connectivity' and presents scientific research proceeding from the implementation of individual and cross-disciplinary projects. The results of specific research topics and themes across various formats, including monographs, edited volumes/proceedings and data collections, are the backbone of this book series. The published volumes serve as a mirror of the coordinated concern of ROOTS researchers and their partners, who explore the human-environmental relationship over a plurality of spatial and temporal scales within divergent scientific disciplines. The associated research challenges revolve around the premise that humans and environments have interwoven roots, which reciprocally influence each other, stemming from and yielding connectivities that can be identified and juxtaposed against current social issues and crises. The highly dynamic research agenda of the ROOTS Cluster, its diverse subclusters and state of the art research set the stage for particularly fascinating results.

The new book in the **ROOTS Studies** series is a result of an intensive collaboration between philosophy and archaeology. The author presents his reflective thoughts not only on epistemic processes and theoretical investments with new approaches to the hermeneutic assessment of archaeological sciences but also to their role in the reconstruction of history. From a philosophical point of view, the study, which provides a view over millennia and in societies of very different character, becomes accessible and also contributes to philosophical questions.

The editors of the **ROOTS Studies** series would like to take the opportunity to thank those colleagues involved in the successful realisation of the fourth volume. We are very grateful for the detailed and well-directed work of the ROOTS publication team. Specifically, we thank Andrea Ricci for his steady support and coordination efforts during the publication process, Petra Horstmann for the preparation of the cover design and Eileen Küçükkaraca for scientific editing. Moreover, we are indebted to the peer reviewers and our partners at Sidestone Press, Karsten Wentink, Corné van Woerdekom and Eric van den Bandt, for their support and commitment to this publication.

Kiel, November 2023
*Eileen Eckmeier, Martin Furholt, Lutz Käppel, Johannes Müller*

# Contents

# Preface of the author

I am not an archaeologist. I studied philosophy and history and took some graduate courses on the history of mentalities in medieval times, as the Latin West came into closer contact with the Byzantine, Islamic and Mongol empires. In philosophy, I took an interest in the philosophy of history. It seemed to be divided into the analytic epistemology of academic history and speculations about the fate of humanity within its history. From 1988 until 1990, I wrote a PhD thesis on the origins and the discursive logic of history. The thesis wished to combine the genealogy and epistemology of history. Thus, I studied the origins of German historism, such as Herder, Humboldt, Droysen, and Dilthey, as well as modern analytical epistemologies of history as found in Danto, Dray, Rüsen, and Acham. One of my many questions at this time was about the presumptive credibility of historical narratives that are composed of single propositions backed by sources.

After my thesis, I should have continued with the philosophy of history as a theory of historical discourse, but, for better or worse, my interest shifted toward the emerging field of environmental ethics which became the focus of my academic career since the 1990s. In this period of time, my historical interest was satisfied by lectures on the history of nature conservation. When I changed universities from Greifswald to Kiel, however, I took up contact with archaeological research at Kiel, especially with the Graduate School "Human Development in Landscapes". Some years later, Johannes Müller persuaded me to contribute to a funding proposal for a CRC "Scales of Transformation". The idea was to bring archaeological research and philosophical reflection into close contact in order to conceive an anatomy of historical transformations in the periods under study. The funding proposal was approved and sometime later even the ROOTS Cluster of Excellence was established which includes the "Reflective Turn Forum" with a focus on theory formation in archaeology and history. It took me some years to explore this vast and dynamic field but my expertise remains limited. In many respects, I see myself as an educated amateur who tries hard to overcome popular images and prejudices about the remote past and the discipline called "prehistoric archaeology". Readers may detect all my shortcomings and biases.

My first and general impression from a series of lectures, conferences, meetings, articles, and books which I experienced and studied before and within the years of the recent pandemic was the following: Archaeologists always consume theories from the social sciences and humanities, including philosophy, but they often do so in an arbitrary mode. Quite often, a theoretical investment has a philosophical background which remains rather obscure. If this diagnosis is reasonable, a philosopher must consider how to overcome such a situation. How might philosophy contribute to make theoretical investments in prehistoric archaeology more explicit and more convincing? To answer this guiding question requires that one takes a step from first-order theory to second-order meta-theory. Generally, philosophy as meta-theory intends to offer groundworks which guide scientific research without curtailing it. The meta-theoretical approach which I am proposing belongs to the camp of transcendental pragmatism which forces scholars to become reflective on the theoretical investments they wish to make.

My second and more specific impression was that the lines between empirical analysis and explanation, on the one hand, and normativity, ethics, and even politics, on the other hand, are often blurred in prehistoric archaeology. Theoretical investments in prehistoric archaeology often have value-laden and prescriptive connotations, suggestions, and underpinnings. Following Max Weber, I wish to separate epistemic rigor and normative engagement. Separation is not denial. In this volume, parts 1 and 2 are epistemic, part 3 prepares a normative outlook on the Anthropocene from a historical perspective, while part 4 is explicitly ethical. Ethics is taken as a reflective normative enterprise which focuses on environmental concerns in the Anthropocene.

With support from Kiel University, which granted me a sabbatical in winter 2022-2023, I was enabled to compose this book out of many notes and excerpts that were written over a decade. The result is far from being perfect. As readers shall realise, there are still some rather incomplete and even fragmentary subchapters. Since the epistemology is about conceptual scaffolding on a theoretical ladder, the readers may and should wish to become active and joyful participants in the common enterprise of conceptual scaffolding.

Research for this book was conducted and financed in the context of the 'ROOTS' Cluster of Excellence (project number: EXC 2150 ROOTS – 390870439) and the Collaborative Research Centre 1266 'Scales of Transformation: Human-environmental Interaction in Prehistoric and Archaic Societies' (project number: 290391021), both of the German Research Foundation (DFG).

The book is dedicated to the 'ROOTS' Cluster of Excellence and to the CRC 1266 'Scales of Transformation', especially (in alphabetic order) Vesa Arponen, Tim Kerig, Johannes Müller, René Ohlrau, Henny Piezonka, Artur Ribeiro, Laura Schmidt, Chiara Thuminger, Mara Weinelt, Maria Wunderlich, and Dana Zentgraf.

A special thanks goes to two referees for many helpful comments and to Eileen Küçükkaraca for a close and rigid proofreading.

Konrad Ott
Wackerow and Kiel, autumn 2023

# Introduction: What the book is all about

This book is an outcome of the ongoing inquiries that are being performed by the Reflective Turn Forum (RTF) within the Cluster of Excellence 'ROOTS' and the theoretical cluster A1 within CRC 1266 'Scales of Transformation' at Kiel University. Both research programs constitute the *context of discovery* of the book. The *context of justification* is the overall epistemic community in archaeology, prehistory, and ethnoarchaeology.

In a system of science that turns to multi-author, peer-reviewed articles, it appears outdated to write a monography. A book, however, contributes better to the current theoretical demands of prehistoric archaeology (PA), because books can presume to have theoretical substance and provide grounding (in a Kantian sense). The unavoidability of theory in PA has to be recognised. There is, however, a highly diversified world of theories and concepts circling in archaeological articles, books, and presentations. This multitude indicates a need for reflections about how archaeologists and historians may find common epistemic ground without falling prey to arbitrary theoretical colonialism. "Theoretical colonialism" means to impose theories top-down onto PA that may have merits in philosophy, cultural disciplines, social science, biology, *etc.*, but are worlds apart from archaeological practices and research. Theories should stay close to epistemic practices of specific disciplines. Modifying a Kantian statement, one can argue that theories and concepts without empirical topics are empty, but empirical work without concepts and theory is blind.[1] We do not just want, but *must* have both. As the book argues, the "death of theory" is not an option.[2] Bintliff and Pearce (2011) regard theory as coming close to ideology. Although I agree that PA stands in danger of becoming "ideologised" (whatever the meaning), such danger is not a sufficient reason to avoid theorising.

The following book is divided into four parts. The *first part* deals with the epistemology of PA. The *second part* adopts a specific theoretical approach, historical materialism, in order to substantiate the claim that humans have been economic agents since prehistoric times. This part is also concerned with the implications of economic ways of human lives. *Part 3* presents a Hegelian argument why the Anthropocene has deep origins in the Neolithic transformation. *Part 4* deals with ethical topics about how historically and morally enlightened humans may cope with the troublesome situation of the full-fledged Anthropocene within a transformation to sustainability.

The *first part* continues the tradition of "*Historik*" (= epistemology of history (EH)) under a transcendental-pragmatic approach. The term "pragmatic" indicates that doing science is a common enterprise being performed by epistemic communities (Stegmüller 1980; Ott 1997). The Kantian term "transcendental" indicates that any epistemic disciplines rest on sets of presuppositions and theoretical investments. Both sets can and should be reflected. Such reflection is performed in epistemology. Therefore, part 1 deals with *theoretical investments* (TI). Reflections upon presuppositions and theoretical investments in PA are close to the tradition of EH. Prehistoric archaeology must be grounded in archaeology (seen as epistemic practices), profiting greatly from natural sciences, but remaining history. The first part is an epistemological "groundwork" in a Kantian sense. Methodologically, it relies on the idea of an epistemological "ladder" (Hawkes 1954) on which different theoretical investments are to be located. As we shall see in part 1, the metaphor of a "ladder" will be augmented by conceptual "scaffolding" (Chapman and Wylie 2016, see also Routledge 2021). PA scholars perform scaffolding while climbing an epistemic ladder. Philosophy prevents "free climbing".

The first part makes room for different conceptual and theoretical investments in PA and it, finally, facilitates critical claims about past-past- and past-present-connections. It also provides room for criticism against "ideologies". The approach gives due respect to the positivistic side of archaeology, but it enables and motivates controlled hypothesis formation, interpretation, modelling, theoretical investments, and even some speculation. The logic of speculation is analysed as abductive reasoning. The first part shows that historical theories fly at different altitudes and it intends to become specific about so-called *middle-range theories* (MRT).

The transcendental-pragmatic EH combines a liberal spirit with an epistemological pressure to substantiate specific theoretical investments for specific purposes in PA. By doing so, it sheds light on the interdisciplinary affair between the natural sciences, the social sciences, and the humanities within PA.

1 Concepts are either fundamental categories, specific definitions (terms), or are embedded in theories. Since many concepts play functional roles in specific theories, and since there is a plurality of theories, a comprehensive and unified terminology in PA is utopian. Moreover, some concepts, such as "power", "urbanism", "colonialism", *etc.*, may be essentially contested in the sense of Gallie (1955). See part 1.

2 See contributions in Bintliff and Pearce (2011). I will return to some topics in part 1.

The philosophical idea of the overall book is also presented in the first part. This idea is my basic theoretical investment. It can be stated as follows: *It must be supposed that humans at any time in history have had reasons to act.* The emic side of human life is full of reasons R at any time t. The concept of reason is presupposed in concepts such as "intentionality" (Ribeiro 2022), "capability" (Arponen *et al.* 2016) and "agency" (Graeber 2001; Johnson 1989; Dobres and Robb 2000; 2005). It is possible to speculate on past reasons (abductively) and to "understand" them. If so, past and present humans are united under a transcendental category: *the lifeworld of practical reasons.*[3] In PA, however, such past reasons cannot be inferred directly from the material record. The material record, however, gives some evidence for hypotheses about presumptive reasons that past agents might have had.[4] The operation called "understanding" refers in an abductive and "speculative" manner to such reasons.

Theories in PA presume to have some explanatory power. The explanatory power of PA theories is different from causal determinism (Arponen *et al.* 2019b) even if humans always act under specific boundary conditions. Boundary conditions are full of pressures, challenges, incentives, risks, *etc.* that humans must cope with. They are, in part, environmental and climatic conditions which can be reconstructed by palaeoecology and palaeoclimatology. Theoretical investments in PA presume explanatory power according to standards of modern scientific rationality. Theoretical investments also allow for hypothetical past-past- and past-present-connectivities. The artificial term "connectivity" indicates that present people, for some reasons, correlate a) present states of affairs with past ones or b) correlate different past states of different periods. Results of connectivities are connections. A "*past-past*"-connection may, for instance, reconstruct the transition from the Neolithic to the Bronze Age or the transition from the Western Roman Empire to early medieval kingdoms. A "*past-present*"-connection correlates the historical past with some aspect of present or recent times.[5] While the former remains within the logic of history, the latter induces specific methodological problems, as historians are not experts for present societies. They are enlightened citizens at best, but they are never devoid of biases and prejudices. "Past-present"-connectivities are always close to the "all-too-human" (Nietzsche) inclination to look into history for political and moral support as: "lessons from history". I do not wish to revitalise naïve "*historia magistra vitae*", but keep its grain of truth in a reflective manner.

History has been always politicised and this holds true for PA as well. Archaeology was, for example, a political science under National Socialism.[6] While in recent years PA has become a global affair (Mizoguchi and Smith 2019; O'Brien 2006), many projects are still conducted under the aegis of national politics (Brück and Stutz 2016). Since archaeologists should not be forgetful about how archaeology has been politicised, epistemology must integrate critical reflections on each and any past-present-connectivity. By doing so, we shall make archaeologists aware that many contemporary social science theories smuggle

3 The concept of "lifeworld" was coined by Husserl (1936/2012) and it plays a crucial role in the *Theory of Communicative Action* (Habermas 1981).

4 Underlying this idea is the position that the material record of the past is not a direct reflection of past behaviours, like a photograph of past activities. To read more on this, see Binford (1981) and Schiffer (1985) on the Pompeii premise.

5 In times of the Covid pandemic, the history of infectious diseases attracted attention (Krause-Kyora 2022; Fouquet 2022).

6 See Schulz (1934); Engel (1942).

implicit values, morals, justice, and politics into PA. Social science theories are often value-laden and many concepts (such as power, inequality, stratification, exploitation, decadence, urbanity, and conflict resolution) have moral connotations and political suggestions (Wylie 1985). This is especially true if specific theories presume to overcome contemporary repugnant ways of thinking (neoliberalism, patriarchy, colonialism, Euro-centrism, populism, *etc.*). Quite often, it is argued that one must adopt a specific theory T in order to overcome repugnant ways of thinking. "Overcoming X" supposes that a theory T is "better" than another one in normative respects. Such a "betterness" relation is located at the tricky intersection of epistemology, morals, and politics. Here, I wish to continue the legacy of Max Weber to become aware of the fine-grained lines that separate history from morals and politics (Ott 1997, chap. 3). Past-present-connectivities must be aware of such lines.

The *second part* of the book presents a specific theory with presumptive explanatory force, namely *historical materialism*. Historical materialism (HM) is, however, to be distinguished from political Marxism which shaped the real history of the 20th century and still attracts many scholars in PA. Current debates about inequalities, property rights, global trade, variants of capitalism, *etc.* are distinguished from the HM perspective as it is adopted here in the second part. I emphasise "*historical*" in HM. HM adopts and transforms two Marxian ideas: First, theories (including concepts, models, and categories), which can explain structures and functions of modern economic systems (such as liberal market capitalism), might also shed light on the archaic origins of economic life. Persons who are sceptical about this presupposition should try to falsify it. In *Capital*, however, Marx argued that an economic analysis of capitalistic modes of production must start with elementary economic units as biology analyses the structure and function of cells. Marx adopted the concept of commodity ("Ware") as a "cellular" unit of economic analysis. Commodity production, however, is specific to a modern market economy. With respect to PA, HM must start with different elementary categories.

I start my HM analysis with the category of surplus. As Graeber and Wengrow (2021, 128) argue, the notion of surplus raises philosophical and "almost existential" questions. In contrast to animals, humans "invariably" produce more than they need:

> *"We are creatures of excess, and this is what makes us simultaneously the most creative, and most destructive of all species" (Graeber and Wengrow 2021, 128).*

This dramatic statement is an anthropological investment which motivates a closer look on surplus as one basic economic category.

This second part discusses why and how economic life, *as such*, emerged in the Neolithic. For better or worse, humans have been economic agents since then. For humans, economic reasons have been and are an essential parcel of the overall portfolio of reasons. The second part is concerned with foraging, surplus, storage, husbandry, seeds, division of labour, exchange, trade, waste and other economic activities which emerge in correlated, dynamic, and spiral-like ways within and beyond domestic modes of production. This second part adopts a "classical" materialistic narrative of the agricultural ("Neolithic") transformation with a focus on the emergence of economic life as such. The HM line of reasoning does not suppose a specific modern economic theory (as standard micro-economics), but it hypothetically consumes different current economic theories (household economics, natural resource economics, institutional economics, *etc.*). Economic theories are devices for specific theoretical investments in PA. Finally, the second part demonstrates how and why economic life increases both wealth and inequalities among humans at different speeds and locations, but it imposes neither the figure of "*homo oeconomicus*"[7] nor modern egalitarian morals onto the past. This second part has been written in an a-moral spirit. It wishes to avoid the many accusations and the demonisation of modern market-based capitalism which has filled libraries since centuries (see Rousseau, Babeuf, Proudhon, Blanqui, Marx, Lenin, and Mao).[8] It also takes a critical stance against the ideals of original communism (part 2, section 2.4).

The *third part* supposes both previous parts. It makes a (risky) "past-present"-connectivity arguing that the Anthropocene, which now has become the predicament of our species on Planet Earth, originated in the Neolithic. This part follows ideas put forth by Ruddiman (2007; 2014) and Scott (2017), but, in a genealogical sense, it also follows Horkheimer and Adorno (1944/1947). Key is the song from Sophocles' tragedy "Antigone" which praises the achievements of human inventiveness that were already existent in an ancient human way of life. Ancient humans had knowledge about crucial achievements that were made in prehistoric times, paving the ways into the Greek state of civilisation, including its economies.

Those (striking and even praiseworthy) achievements, as the argument claims, dialectically eclipse under modern "Baconian" conditions (science, technology, and industry) from being "qualities" which are "good to have" into ever increasing quantities, such as in shipping, trade, urbanism, agriculture, husbandry, fisheries, *etc.,* which produce devastating side-effects on natural environments and biotic diversity. This eclipse into ever more increasing quantities ("expansion", "growth") was favoured by dominionistic attitudes and by instrumental modes of rationality (Horkheimer and Adorno 1944/1947; Horkheimer 1947). It finally resulted in the "Great Acceleration" after 1945. Such an eclipse terminated in a global ecological crisis within a "full world" (Daly 1996). Early globalisation (1400-1600) and the industrial revolution (1760-1900) exhibit some technological and intellectual markers ("spikes") on this transformative route.

The third part also wishes to coil the archaic "thin" and the modern "thick" Anthropocene (Scott 2017). It views the "Anthropocene" as a diagnostic and analytical, not as a moral concept. The deep roots of the Anthropocene explain the long-lasting and widespread inclination to material growth that is paradigmatic in the Western way of life. This past-present-connectivity, however, casts doubts on many moral-political recipes of how to overcome the troubling situation of the Anthropocene. Most recipes underrate the ties that bind humans to an attitude of "more" (surplus, expansion, growth, and power). Since stocks of capital and their accumulation are part of this logic of "more", it is not helpful to replace the term "Anthropocene" by the term "capitalocene".[9] By recognising the deep roots of the Anthropocene, the intellectual bars are set higher for the quest of how a sustainable post-growth society might be institutionalised in decades to come.

The book ends with an *ethical part 4* that is devoted to a quest for sustainable and resilient ways to institutionalise a globalised society on different scales.

---

7 This model figure of perfect egotism does not represent social realities of human lives.

8 For an overview, see Künzli (1986).

9 Liberal market capitalism is not the greatest problem within the Anthropocene since liberal capitalism has, according to Schumpeterian theories (Aghion *et al.* 2021), much intrinsic potential for renewal by creative destruction within "long waves". Capitalism and markets can flexibly adapt to environmental regulations being legislated by democratic governments. Therefore, the re-naming of the Anthropocene as "capitalocene" brings no intellectual progress.

Ethics is seen as a reflective mode of moral reasoning. Part 4 addresses the question what, if anything, might PA, HM, and the genealogy of the Anthropocene contribute to a "good" Anthropocene for the present time (Boivin and Crowther 2021). PA may show that humans have some aversion against being forced (Graeber and Wengrow 2021). Ethics can turn such aversion into the idea of human freedom. PA may also show that the difference between hierarchical and heterarchical societies often matters, but it cannot show why one should prefer heterarchies over hierarchies. Ethical principles are not to be found in history or in any imagined "golden" age. They must stem from the project of modernity itself (Habermas 1984). I shall rely on a) discourse ethics which emphasises commitments of arguing, b) a concept of deliberative democracy, c) the universe of discourse in environmental ethics, and d) the concept of "strong" sustainability which can be linked to different fields of environmental policy making. Conceptionally, I combine a "thin" moral universalism with a "thick" historical memory function which points at the particular sides of ethical life ("*Sittlichkeit*", Hegel 1821/1970, see Ribeiro 2021). History cannot substantiate ethical principles, but it may contribute "lessons" indicating whether past practices might be helpful to realise principles. The ethical logic of such past-present-connectivities is made explicit. Some topics and strategies are outlined with a special focus on land-use practices, restoration, and adaptation to climate change. Part 4 does not end in despair. It ends with hopeful outlooks to "cultural" practices such as gardening, tilling the soil, restoring natural environments, morally decent husbandry, recycling of waste and the like. These past-present-connectivities may be inconvenient truths since they demonstrate that sustainable ways of human life often are less comfortable than the ordinary urbanised Western modes of life. Connectivities between the prehistoric past and the present must focus on problem-solving without writing, without money, and without state. Dealing with the dialectic of system and lifeworld (Habermas 1981), I finally oppose the claim made by Graeber and Wengrow (2021, 519) that we are "stuck in just one social reality". The final part also opens a route for PA to go public and disseminate its findings.

*To sum up in a nutshell*: The reflective turn (RT) is a theoretical *idea*, the epistemological ladder/scaffold is a meta-theoretical epistemological *method*, HM is a substantial *theory* about roles and functions of economic life, the *hypothesis* about the origins of the Anthropocene is an eye-opening past-present connectivity, while *ethics* shall provide practical orientation for a "good" Anthropocene. Being an ethicist by profession, I shift most moral reasoning to part 4. Some implicit ethics is present within other parts. Part 1 relies on ethics of epistemic honesty (Ott 1997). Part 2 resolves HM from political Marxism. Part 3 is close to Hans Jonas (1979) and his "ethics of fear".

# Part 1: Epistemology: Scaffolding on a ladder

## 1.1 Ethics, reflection, and transcendental pragmatics

Any scientific enterprise should be reflective. Such a "*should*" can be grounded in the ethics of science (Ott 1997). If so, any discipline should reflect upon its epistemic practices (as methods, technologies, suppositions, standards of discourse, hypothesis formation, argumentation, modelling, *etc.*). In the philosophy of science since the 1980s, there was a move away from a unified general epistemology, which often took physics as an "ideal" model of "objective" science, to *specific* epistemologies of single disciplines. This part endorses the move to specific epistemologies, focusing on prehistoric archaeology (PA). It also takes interest in the epistemology of cultural anthropology (= ethnology) (see Sperber 1989), because the knowledge of cultural anthropology is often consumed in archaeology by (contested) way of analogies. We will come back to the problem of analogical reasoning in PA (part I, section 1.11) arguing that critical analogical reasoning is unavoidable in PA (Wylie 1985). PA can be generally defined as a discipline that "is focussed on the study of human activity through the physical evidence which survives to be analysed" (Ramsey 2023, 1).

General epistemologies remain important as a methodological framework of discursive falsification and a corroboration of scientific claims (Popper 1934; Habermas 1981). Any substantial scientific claim must be able to undergo procedures of rejection and criticism, but also justification and confirmation. Such procedures are discursive practices that are performed by scientists and they rely on different methods. If there is some unity of the natural sciences and the humanities, it is based upon the methodic and performative practice of reasoning (= arguing) about *validity claims*. If so, special attention must be given to claims and justifications within PA. Claiming combines findings, data, interpretation, hypothesis, modelling, explanations, and some theory. Claims constitute epistemic discourse because they allow for "yes" or "no". Epistemic disciplines establish specific standards of reasoning ("state of the art"). Denials, contradictions, and rejections are essential for discourse. This is true for PA as well.

Reflection is always reflection *upon* a matter at stake. As such, reflection should be distinctive as epistemic matters within PA are not homogeneous. Moreover, reflection is ongoing. Once having been opened, it cannot be stopped at any specific epistemic point. *Reflection proceeds*. Such a procedure takes a route: "*method*" in the original sense of the Greek term. The reflective and distinctive route can be structured by a "ladder" and it shall provide some insights why *specific sets of concepts* (SC) are required by the idea of doing "good" PA. Epistemological reflection upon essential requirements is a *transcendental* approach as it asks under which conditions and requirements "good" history and archaeology become possible. Since scientific enterprises are seen as "praxis" (Ott 1997), the overall epistemological approach can be termed "*transcendental pragmatics of PA*". Under this approach, some categories and concepts are essential ("*must*"), while other theoretical investments are permissible ("*can*"). On reflection, the line between "must" and "can" might be drawn.

This approach exploits a Kantian idea. Kant argues that concepts without data (Kant: "*Anschauungen*") are empty, while data without concepts is blind.[10] This holds true for PA. The archaeological materials are empirically given findings ("*terminus a quo*"), while past human life (in a broad sense) shall be addressed via different *sets of concepts* that are organised in models and narratives ("*terminus ad quem*"). On our methodical route, we shall, by way of reflection, identify *sets of historical and archaeological concepts which can be arranged as a kind of ladder*. The "ladder"-idea is adopted from Hawkes (1954) and Smith (1955).[11] Hawkes (1954) distinguished four steps: a) technology, b) subsistence-economy, c) social and political institutions, and d) religion. Stepwise, reasoning becomes more speculative: "easy", "fairly easy", "harder", "hardest". This results in an "anti-climax: the more human, the less intelligible" (*ibid.*, 162). Hawkes presents this riddle and moves to other topics.

Smith (1955) argues in line with Hawkes that the archaeological record "*underdetermines some processes to a greater extent than others*" (Perreault 2019, 146). Smith (1955) draws sceptical conclusions from underdetermination. We should concede that knowledge in PA is to some degree conjectural, but we should, however, not fix in advance "insuperable limits" (Smith) of what can be known about the past.

The transcendental-pragmatic conceptual ladder (TPCL) allows for many conceptual and theoretical investments (TI). It is grounded in solid archaeological scientific positivism (remote sensing, excavation, materials, findings, dating techniques, collections, and reconstruction) and it peaks in past-present-connectivities and anthropology. TPCL has empirical roots and speculative tops – *and*

10 "[...], *so daß weder Begriffe, ohne ihnen auf einige Art korrespondierende Anschauung, noch Anschauung ohne Begriffe, eine Erkenntnis abgeben können*" (Kant 1781, B 75). [English translation]: "[...] *so that neither concepts without intuition corresponding to them in some way nor intuition without concepts can yield a cognition.*" [Translation available at: https://plato.stanford.edu/entries/kant-judgment/supplement1.html; last accessed: 6 December 2023].

11 The "ladder" model has a long tradition in the medieval arrangements of different disciplines and arts.

*rightly so*. The TPCL approach is liberal with respect to the manifoldness of theoretical investments, but it is rigid as it requires justification why specific investments are made.[12] Anthropology is present right from the scratch as archaeologists detect human fingerprints and it terminates in modes of self-reflection upon an undetermined ("free") way of human life.

The TPCL is based on a *historical* attitude which might be stated as follows: History should try to come as close as possible to previous ways of human life. From a historical point of view, archaeological materials point to past societal life being the "*terminus ad quem*" of historical research. Here, the distinction between the *etic* and the *emic* perspective is important. Both terms denote a scientific perspective. As Pike (1967, chap. 2) writes: "The etic viewpoint studies behavior as from outside of a particular system [...]. The emic viewpoint results from studying behavior as from inside the system." In contrast to the comparative etic perspective, the emic perspective is "culturally specific" (Pike). The emic perspective "results" (Pike) from studies "as from inside". The historian, however, never has been "inside" the collective under study. If so, how can we understand the emic viewpoint as a result? I argue that the emic viewpoint makes sense if and only if "emic" dimensions of previous lives are presupposed. The historian always remains an observer whose observations may ideally "result" in hypothetically taking the role of specific participants of past collectives. Within TPCL, the "emic" ("as from the inside") is a transcendental idea.[13] Only few historians would hold that understanding previous ways of human life necessarily requires written sources. Under such a requirement, historical understanding would be impossible in PA. This argument is not valid. Even if there were written sources, they might have been produced by a small elite, while the emic side of ordinary life of most ordinary people would nevertheless remain obscure (Moreland 2001; Sauer 2004). In most parts of history, the emic side of life is also represented in material culture (buildings, textiles, food, vessels, weapons, coins, *etc*.). Via material culture one can "reconstruct" past societal life and, moreover, (try to) "understand" previous lives. The operation called "understanding" will be explained in some detail here in part I, section 1.7 with respect to agency, intentionality, and reasons.

Even if there is distance in time, historians can (try to) come close to former ways of human life. Old theories believed that "coming close" must rely on capabilities such as "empathy", "feeling the inside" or "taking the role of the other". The implicit (folk)-psychology of this approach is highly contested in the epistemology of the humanities. I wish to demonstrate that coming close to the past relies on theoretical investments, not on empathy. The better the explanation, the closer the understanding.

In PA, one has to accept that the most interesting topics cannot be represented within the empirical records, because they could not remain.[14] In particular, all the performative aspects of prehistoric human life could not remain and are gone. Speech acts, rules, habits, emotions, rituals, experiences, beliefs, dreams,

---

12 The "ladder" has similarities with the epistemological concept of scaffolding in Chapman and Wylie (2016). "Scaffolding" is intended to make "data work as evidence" (*ibid*., 6). I shall return to the relation between the "ladder" and the "scaffold".

13 To exploit Pike's parallel between the study of language and culture: Whoever studies a foreign language "from outside" may wish to become a native speaker.

14 Of course, many practices do not remain even from times when there are written sources. The daily life and the beliefs of ordinary people might not have been represented in the writings of the ruling elites, whereas the beliefs of a miller around 1600 CE have been represented, in contrast, in the sources of the inquisition which made the victim speak. See Ginzburg (1979).

jokes, hopes, sexual and nursing practices, gender topics, *etc.* are paradigm cases of what is not left. How did humans communicate? What kind of speech acts did they use? How did knowledge spread in oral cultures? Which responsibilities (commitments, duties, and loyalties) did prehistoric humans attribute to each other? Which beliefs and convictions did they hold about the "world" they lived "in"? What kind of moral status did they give to roles and to patterns of interaction? How did these humans evaluate things and actions? What reasons did past humans hold? How did they perform and experience childhood, play and games, sex and gender, maladies, aging, and mortality?[15] How did they experience pleasure and pain, desires and dreams, anxieties and anger? *What was it like to be a prehistoric human?* Positivists may state: "*Ignoramus, ignorabimus* – let us avoid speculation about ancient ways of life!" What, however, exactly is "speculation"?

After a plea for scientific positivism in archaeology, Kristiansen (2014, 27-28) surprisingly makes room for epistemic utopia. This is worth quoting since it indicates a peculiar dialectics between positivism and speculation within PA. According to Kristiansen:

> *"My own unfulfilled dream is that one day we shall be able to release the sounds of prehistory: talking, music, etc. stored in some mysterious way in the atomic pottery and metal* [...]. *Innovative research is fostered by dreams about what the past was like and how we can find new ways to get to know about it, and secondly what we can learn from it in the present."*

Kristiansen's dream remains positivistic as it hopes for storage of life's expressions in materials. Such hope is in vain, but the dream makes good epistemological sense. Imaginations may stimulate research ("context of discovery") and they also motivate past-present-connectivities. Kristiansen supposes the very possibility of "learning from the (remote) past". This remark supposes that not all human wisdom is fully represented in our contemporary bodies of knowledge. Learning from the past implies a) that something has been lost and forgotten on the long pathway to modern times, and b) that it remains possible to identify forgotten knowledge. The abstract opposition of material positivism and speculative (= conjectural) dreaming should not be the final epistemic constellation in PA. TPCL wishes to overcome this opposition stepwise.

The TPCL approach presumes not to impose a specific theoretical doctrine upon PA. It rather wishes to *enable* archaeologists to reflect upon their conceptual investments. With some assistance by theorists, archaeologists should be enabled to perform, control, correct, revise, and criticise concept and theory formation in archaeology. This is the general *epistemological* idea of a *reflective turn* (RT) in the philosophy of PA.

The general *philosophical* idea stems from a theory of communicative action (Habermas 1981). It can be stated as follows: *It must be supposed that humans at any time t in history have had reasons R to act.* The emic side of human life is full of reasons. If one, for instance, assumes the practice of festivities as quite common among humans, there must be numerous reasons to celebrate: weddings, funerals, worshipping, potlaches, *etc.* In PA, such reasons cannot be inferred directly from the material record. The material record gives some evidence at best. The operation called "understanding" refers in an abductive and conjectural manner to presumptive reasons that humans might have had. Theories in PA presume to

15 See Rappe (1995). Rappe's approach is based on Schmitz's phenomenology of embodied experiences.

have some explanatory power with respect to "*erklärendes Verstehen*" ("explanatory understanding"; Max Weber 1921/1972, 3-4). Some theoretical investments are devices to detect the reasons which past humans might presumably have had. Archaeological findings both suppose and indicate reasons. They give evidence for past reasons. Theoretical investments also allow for hypothetical past-past- and past-present-connectivities. If so, past and present humans are united under a transcendental category: *the lifeworld of human reasons*. The lifeworld-focus is centred on practical reasons, not on cosmologies and world-views.

The TPCL approach is an epistemological approach that must, however, be aware of *ontological commitments*. Concepts and categories are lingual entities that have reference points outside language (Kellerwessel 1995). Since concepts must be construed and debated, I also dub my approach on concept formation as "*realistic discursive constructivism*".

Before presenting this TPCL approach in detail, I wish to present some reflections which are mandatory in order to locate TPCL in the epistemic field of archaeology and history. By doing so, we can, on reflection, identify some essential sets of concepts which shall become first scaffolding steps on the ladder.

## 1.2 History and archaeology

Archaeology deals with human history (Ribeiro 2018). Since anatomically modern humans (*Homo sapiens sapiens*) entered the planetary scene roughly 250,000 years ago (Olszewski 2020), there is, strictly speaking, no *pre*-history. Since then, there is human history on a long and slow onset that we call the "Palaeolithic". Let us take a brief look on the origins of the term "prehistory". The term "*Prähistorie*" is used by Droysen in his "*Historik*" (1882/1974, § 22) as a periodical term defining a historical period before writing. Probably, Droysen adopted Ranke's statement:

> *"Die Geschichte beginnt erst, wo die Monumente verständlich werden und glaubwürdige schriftliche Aufzeichnungen vorliegen" (Ranke 1922, 2).* [English translation Ott]: *"History first begins when the monuments become understandable and credible written records exist."*

We should not follow Ranke, as Droysen and even Jaspers (1955) did. On conceptual and epistemic grounds, it does not make sense to start human history with the existence of writing. This would deny the historicity of all oral cultures. Droysen implicitly denies his own Ranke-like definition as he speaks of "historical insights" being grounded in materials:

> *"Alles und jedes, was die Spur von Menschengeist und Menschenhand an sich trägt, (kann) von der Forschung als Material herangezogen werden. Und eine Fülle von historischen Erkenntnissen* [...] *erwächst uns aus derartigen Materialien" (Droysen 1882/1974, 38).* [English translation Ott]: *"Anything and everything that bears the trace of the human spirit and the human hand (can) be used as material by researchers. And a wealth of historical knowledge* [...] *emerges from such materials."*

Strictly speaking, archaeologists should avoid saying that they are doing "prehistory".

Some terminological notes are appropriate here. The term "archaeology" is ambiguous (Müller 2016). It can be used as a *methodological* or as a *periodical* term.

From a methodological perspective, there can be archaeology at any time in history. Archaeology *as a method* refers to a broad scope of epistemic practices that deal with the material dimension of human history. It encompasses different types of on-field data-recovery practices (including excavations, core-drilling, field-walking, aerial reconnaissance, geophysics, *etc.*) as well as a vast arsenal of scientific methods carried out in laboratories, and other practices such as experimental archaeology. This scope should not be reduced to excavations. In field work, the methods are applied at sites. The concept of a site has been determined by Sanjuán (2005). I adopt his definition of a site as a spatially defined and functionally significant grouping of material remains of human activities developed in the past. The broad scope of methods can be applied to slave prisons in the U.S. (see Müller 2017) as well as to pop-culture sites, such as Woodstock, where one finds the remnants of sex, drugs and rock-n-roll. "Classical archaeology" deals with works of art and architecture in ancient times when there are written sources as well. The same holds for "biblical" archaeology. Here, "archaeology" is a methodological term ("archaeology-M"). Archaeology is also often used as a periodical term, denoting human history before writing had been invented ("archaeology-P"). As a periodical term, archaeology would thus stretch from the Palaeolithic to ancient times. It comes to an end at different time periods in different regions. This comes close to the German wording "*Ur- und Frühgeschichte*" (= UFG). The conventional and worldwide established periodical term is "prehistory". "Prehistory", however, suggests that writing is constitutive for history. It draws an arbitrary line between past societies on the basis of one particular kind of source. Its "scripto-centrism" denies the historicity of oral cultures. As we have seen, the origins of the term "prehistory" in Ranke and Droysen are flawed. If one wishes to avoid the term "prehistory", one may propose the term "archaic history" as a translation of UFG. But such a terminological move may create new irritations and confusions, because some individual periods are specifically termed "archaic". Another solution would take "archaeology" as a periodical term which denotes the same periods in human history as "prehistory" and "UFG". This solution comes at the price that archaeology-M and archaeology-P are not strictly separated. A pragmatic solution would permit the further use of the term "prehistory", if and only if it is understood as a non-literal and purely conventional "*terminus technicus*". The best solution for this terminological problem seems to be "*prehistoric archaeology*". This solution comes close to concept formation in Eggert (2012). "Prehistoric archaeology" (PA) conceptually combines the periodical dimension with the focus on material residues, and it stays close to the established terminology. "Prehistoric archaeology" denotes a discipline. If I refer to past human lives, I prefer to speak of "archaic ways of life" since "prehistoric life" seems to be a contradiction in terms.

PA starts with hunter-gatherers (Kretschmer 2015), it encompasses complex foragers, the agricultural ("Neolithic") transformation, the Bronze Age, the Iron Age and it gradually shifts into ancient history. By definition, PA has fuzzy borders and it ends at different times in different regions. Clearly, the "lithic" terms stemming from the 19th century should not overrate the role of materials in societal life, although the use of metals may have caused the transformation to the more violent epochs of the Bronze Age and the Iron Age. Personally, I would like to overcome "lithic" parlance.

But how shall historical knowledge emerge from materials if it should reach beyond the presentation of cleaned and dated materials in archives and collections? How can archaeologists squeeze past societal life from residual materials? This basic epistemological problem is at the core of any philosophy of PA. As far as I can see, cognitive archaeology has addressed these questions.[16] From a logical point of view, there are *materials* that refer to *practices* which are embedded in a specific *way of human life*. Without such reference points, the material would not count as something historical. If archaeologists deal with waste, they suppose a practice called "disposal" that is connected to production and consumption. The same holds for cleaning and litter. A theory of the material record is given by Perreault (2019). I assume an "underdetermination" of the archaeological record as an epistemological premise.

The concept "*way(s) of human life*" will be used often. It may emphasise the particularities of specific collectives, but it does not exclude commonalities and similarities among different ways of life being qualified as "human". The term "way" refers to the fact that humans have to perform their life practically (Plessner 1928/2011). Here, I see myself in line with the motive in Graeber and Wengrow (2021, 9) to model past humans as full-fledged practical, embodied, intelligent, creative, and even playful beings.

An epistemology of PA is to be located within the tradition of theories of history ("*Historik*"), but it should take a profile of its own. Generally, history is based on research, it results in narratives, *and* it consumes theories. Note that the "and" can indicate different logical relations. Any true propositions can be combined to an endless series: "2+2 = 4" *and* "Whales are mammals" *and* "Napoleon was defeated in the battle of Waterloo" *and* "Konrad was born in 1959", *etc.* A philosophy of PA must give the "and" between theory, narrativity, and research another meaning: "*correlation*". Correlations are intrinsic relations between elements forming specific epistemic patterns ("constellations"). Historical narratives are full of constellations and correlations (see part 1, section 1.11).

## 1.3 Basic suppositions and distinctions

A basic distinction within the concept of history holds between "the past" ("*Vergangenheit*") and the epistemic practices of historians ("*Historie*") (Marrou 1973). This distinction separates ontology from epistemology. We distinguish "*history-as-past-times*" (h-P) from "*history-as-an-epistemic-discipline*" (h-E). Doing history correlates h-E with h-P. H-E refers to "past events". Historical propositions implicitly claim to refer correctly to a reference point in the past. If so, *truth-orientation is among the basic epistemological presuppositions of PA.* The proposition "the settlement S was abandoned at t" is true if and only if the settlement S was abandoned at t (Tarski 1944/1977). True propositions can be integrated either in established bodies of historical knowledge or new truth requires a revision of established knowledge. The longer historical research is performed, the less likely major belief revisions become. The epistemic practice of how to coherently integrate new insights into established knowledge is reflected in coherent-oriented theories of truth. Agreement among historians establishes the consent-approach of truth finding. A comprehensive theory of historical truth might be a synthesis of correspondence, coherence, and consent aspects. It must entail a concept of historically credible narratives. I suppose truth-orientation in PA, but will not

16 See contributions in Overman and Coolidge (2019). This volume presents the recent achievement in cognitive archaeology.

present a full-fledged theory of truth in history.

There is no epistemology in history without *ontological commitments*. The past has a peculiar ontological "existence" with respect to time. Since the past is "gone", existence is non-existent and must be reconstructed from sources. I will not present an ontology of the past, but keep reflection alive. As convenient shorthand, we can say that history is *the past in as far as historians know it* (Marrou 1973).

As Arthur Danto (1965) claims, history is dialectical as the past is, *ontologically*, completely fixed (= determined) and, *epistemically*, infinitely open to new research questions.[17] The past is both (ontologically) fixed and (epistemically) inexhaustible. Our attitudes to and interests of past events may change, but the events themselves are "petrified". This implies that we cannot correct or "heal" history-P by history-E. All past events that we may (from our moral point of view) perceive as atrocities, victimisation, and cruelties are beyond change. We may demolish the monuments of slave-holders, but we cannot liberate past slaves – not even by apologies and reconciliation processes.[18]

The Kantian insight holds that any empirical science must presuppose both time and space for history. As new approaches to philosophy of time indicate (Klein 2009), there are several components of a general basic time structure. There was "a time before/after x". A basic order "a happened before/after b" constitutes an infinite sets of time spans (temporal intervals) which can be scaled up and down (from days to millennia and to geological time spans) (Robb and Pauketat 2013). The order relation implies that event a precedes or follows event b. The past precedes the present – always. History, with transcendental necessity, must use a complex and flexible *set of time-related concepts*. This points to epistemological problems, for example, in dating, "squeezing" time in narratives, and in prior-later determinations where time mixes with causality. This points at the importance of precise dating methods in archaeology because such methods determine "before/after" relations in prehistory which are crucial for explanations. "Timing" belongs to the positive side of PA. Ideal is a preciseness of dating. Dating techniques in PA have made great progress (see section 1 in Pollard *et al.* 2023). Research on ancient DNA and dendrochronology may count as further examples.

A second distinction holds between *natural and human history*. Natural history is done in geology, geography, palaeo-climatology, palaeo-ecology and similar disciplines. Natural history supposes the deep times of Planet Earth, as discovered by geologist Lyell (Gould 1987). I define natural history before humans as pre-history. The history of the family of early hominids (for an overview see Foley 1995; Olszewski 2020, part 2; Flannery 2018 for Europe) still belongs primarily to natural history that is governed by natural forces (such as climatic change), evolution of species, brinks of extinction, and mammalian inclinations such as foraging, cleaning, mating, nursing, *etc.*[19] The speciation events that finally favoured the anatomically modern *Homo sapiens sapiens* occurred gradually in human history, as modern humans left Africa ("out of Africa 2") and spread over Eurasia displacing *Homo ne-*

17 We shall reflect upon the practical interest of history in part 1, section 8.

18 This frozen irreversibility was a moral question for critical theory. See the debate between Horkheimer and Benjamin about "anamnetic solidarity" as presented in Peukert (1978, 300-310).

19 Here, concepts are used which are also used in studies of animal behaviour, for example, mating, group decision-making, parental care, vocal communication, kin recognition, *etc.* See contributions in Kappeler (2010).

*anderthalensis*.[20] In Palaeolithic times, natural and human history blend into each other. Here, Darwinian evolutionary archaeology is the most promising approach. In this study, I shall omit both the period of hominization and Palaeolithic times and focus on prehistoric (and ancient) history. Natural history, of course, continues after *Homo sapiens sapiens* evolved. *Homo sapiens* had to cope with changing and often destructive telluric forces.[21] As we shall see in part 3, human and natural history (geology) converge in the Anthropocene.

Palaeo-geo-sciences reconstruct the natural environments in prehistoric times at specific locations. Mires are important archives, dendrochronology and pollen analysis are widespread methods. "Telluric conditions" are environmental and climatic conditions that humans had to cope with. The important role of the natural and geographical sciences in PA has been recognised since its origins.[22] This necessitates a *specific set of biological and ecological concepts to be integrated in TPCL*.

History was never an isolated human drama playing before the eternal "*kosmos*". Humans had to adapt to changing environmental conditions, including infectious diseases. An example for the integration of environmental change and infectious diseases in history is Harper's (2017) book *The Fate of Rome* which sheds new light on the decline of the Roman Empire. According to Harper, neo-biota, such as *Rattus rattus*, which found favourable conditions in the grain dominated dietary system of the Roman Empire, played a fatal role in the catastrophic epidemic in the fifth century CE. In our age of human-induced climate change, we may learn from past adaptation strategies with respect to migration, conflict resolution, diets, neo-biota, diseases, urban life, forestry, *etc*. (see part 4).

The dialectics between the observational and the emic side can be studied with respect to diets and diseases. If diets and diseases are to be addressed, medical concepts are needed. Ancient medicine was highly advanced and is praised by Sophocles (part 3, section 3.3), but healing practices are far older. With the help of current medicine, palaeo-medicine must conceive nosographic entities (maladies and infectious diseases) and indicators for health status (size, weight, age, bone density, and teeth status). Even the most sophisticated scientific research on past maladies, however, does not tell us how prehistoric humans experienced pain and sickness, but also healing processes and recovery under the general condition that death was always close to them. Prehistoric healing practices precede ancient medical knowledge (e.g. that of Galen or Hippocrates). Health and medicine are correlates.

Diets are also experienced from the emic side by taste as dishes and cuisine. Research supposes high dietary flexibility of humans and it searches for palaeo-dietary evidence. Food stuff of households can be reconstructed (see Earle *et al.*

20 There are several theories about Neanderthal extinction. One of the most likely theories is the interbreeding theory, since European DNA contains a good amount of Neanderthal ancestry. This was proven by Svante Paabo, who recently won the Nobel prize for medicine in 2022. See also Flannery (2018), chap. 25.

21 Take as an instance the airburst which destroyed Tall el-Hamman in the Bronze Age. See Bunch *et al.* (2021). Another instance is the destruction of Helike by an earth/seaquake in 373/2 BCE. See Walter (2017). See Gao *et al.* (2021) on the hypothesis that volcanic eruptions may have caused the collapse of Chinese dynasties. See Gill et al. (2007) on drought and the Maya collapse.

22 Droysen (1882/1974, 38) sees archaeologists as "*historisierende Naturforscher*". "*Die Naturforschung hat hier darum ihren großen Anteil, weil die Reste von Knochen, Vegetabilien, Steinarten, die aus denselben sich ergebenden Schlüsse auf die tellurischen Bedingungen* [...] *nur aus der genauesten naturwissenschaftlichen Kenntnis zu erkennen und zu verwerten sind*" (*ibid.*, 39). [English translation Ott]: "*Natural science plays a major role here because the remains of bones, vegetation, and stone types, and the conclusions drawn from them about telluric conditions* [...] *can only be recognised and exploited from the most precise scientific knowledge.*"

2022 for Bronze Age food). The steps from food to dishes and cuisine are important to understand a "diet". Diets point to health status and embodied wealth. What was "tasty" for prehistoric humans? If we find bee keeping in ancient gardens, it is likely that honey was perceived as sweet and tasty. If we find rising genetic adaptation to digest alcohol from hunter-gatherers to early farmers, we may infer the tastiness of beer and wine (see contributions in Hockings and Dunbar 2020). If humans had to invest much energy (calories) in hunting, it seems likely that they appreciated the taste of meat. Diets can be based on raw or cooked dishes. Cooking food by fire may have prevented premature dental death. Diets and diseases show how interdisciplinary research may address important topics in PA since diets and diseases still play a major role in modern human life.

Scientific methods, concepts and theories have been incorporated into PA with great success. Sets of scientific concepts may correlate to historical concepts in many ways. Natural science, however, relies on epistemic ideas that any event can be explained causally. For natural science, the world of nature is determined by physical causal laws. If natural forces determine human actions, science may bring determinism into PA. The incorporation of scientific concepts into PA does, however, not imply any commitment to naturalistic determinism (Arponen *et al.* 2019b). If so, PA has to reflect upon concepts of causality that are used in explanations (part 1, section 1.7). History sees humans as intentional and communicative beings facing choices "from inside" (emic side) and having reasons for action. Reasons are not a subset of causal forces, but a category of its own (Habermas 1981). If so, humans are almost never completely determined by natural forces.[23] Humans react, respond, and cope with such forces by way of choice and reason.[24] Rejection of general determinism, however, allows for claims such as "A was (partly) determined by X". PA must allow for causal forces and natural boundary conditions that motivate humans to react and respond. Liberal models of causal forces, such as DPSIR (Driver-Pressure-State-Impact-Response), can refine Toynbee's simple challenge-response-scheme (Ribeiro *et al.* in press).[25]

From an anthropological and historical perspective, humans are not just "reactive", but "responsive" beings. Reasons determine responses to given pressures. Even if a response fails, it remains a response. Responsive social beings must become reasonable since they must coordinate action and make collective choices. This necessity points to concepts such as "collective intentionality".

Claims on responsive capabilities rely on *anthropological* assumptions. Why are humans responsive beings? The bipedal structure is key to most specific human capabilities (Herder 1784/1976; McCaffree 2022, 11-12). The upright position of the head liberates the organs of lingual articulation: full-fledged speech emerges from vocal gestures (Mead 1934; Leroi-Gourhan 1980).[26] The difference between feet and hands contributes to such liberation. The upright bipedal structure constitutes a specific interactive field between the face and hands. Humans are "handy" animals (Mumford 1944, 5). The human brain operates as an active memory by which agents face choices in situations (Neuweiler 2008). "Facing"

---

23 If a human falls down a cliff, she is completely determined by the powers of gravity. But there was a choice to climb the cliff.

24 I will not go into the distinctions between reason and rationality since Kant. I just assume "reasons for actions".

25 The DPSIR-model was conceived in environmental science in order to address environmental problems and has been adopted by many environmental agencies (Kristensen 2004). It relies on linear cause-effect-relations, but it can be refined by feed-back-mechanisms, thresholds, *etc.*

26 A classical model of biological foundations of human speech was conceived by Lenneberg (1967).

situations constitutes choice and acts. The sensory capacities are integrated into a mental structure with self-consciousness and choice between alternatives. If so, humans have intentions and purposes.[27] If so, much human behaviour *must* count as agency even if there is a multitude of external stimuli, triggers, drivers, *etc.* It must also be presupposed that humans perceive, experience and recognise their behaviour as agency "from within" their interactions ("emic side"). For example, the following propositions may be considered: "I decided to turn to the right." – "I did it myself" – "I failed in reaching X". If such agency-propositions make sense, we must apply the language game of actions ("*pragmata*") to PA.[28]

"Agency" is a transcendental-pragmatic category for history (Dobres and Robb 2005). If so, *a set of agency concepts, such as "intentionality"* (Ribeiro 2022), *"purposiveness", "choice", "reason" and "self"*, must be included in TPCL. This constitutes specific epistemological problems since PA mostly deals with actions on the aggregation of groups (for instance, LBK or "steppe invaders", "Northern foragers", or "sea people") and far less with individuals. Thus, PA needs a terminology of collectives: "people", "group", "community", "society", "clan", "tribe", "band", "big men", "elites", "warriors", *etc.* I propose to take "collectives" as an encompassing concept to be specified. I am reluctant to speak of "communities" and "societies", since the distinction between society and community is a modern affair (Tönnies 1887/1979). Analytic theory of action starts "bottom up" with single actions and single agents, moving forward to collective agency, while PA implicitly starts "top down" from collectives, such as "funnel beaker groups", and must suppose individuals which remain largely invisible in the records. Historians give names to collectives, for example, "LBK".

Anthropology has often pointed at the *tool-making* capabilities of humans (Sachsse 1978). Tool-making can be observed in apes, which hunt with spears (Byrne 2007; Pruetz and Bertolani 2007), but human capabilities constitute a sphere of integrated technologies ("techno-sphere"). Thus, Hawkes (1954) saw technologies as crucial steps on the ladder. A well, a boat, a net, an arrow, and a door are instances of complex compound archaic technologies. An arrow is composed as a compound artefact made of timber, iron, and feathers. The same holds for archaic crafts, especially metallurgy, which requires mining and managing high temperatures. Since there was always a time before a specific technology T was established, *inventiveness* of the human mind must be presupposed (Dessauer 1927). Perhaps, there is a specific human capability combining curiosity, playfulness and inventiveness.[29] Inventions become traditions by ways of learning and dispersal. There is transport of technological knowledge through space and time even if archaic technologies might have improved and were dispersed

---

27 As Engels (1989, 166-168) argues, intentionality may constitute knowledge about functional equivalencies. Moreover, intentionality constitutes knowledge that one can interact with the same object in different ways. One can kill and eat an animal or tame it.

28 Here, we can rely either on analytical theories of action or on philosophies of practices. Classical articles on analytical theory of actions have been published in Beckermann (1985). The most sophisticated article on free will in archaeology is given by Stanton (2004). As we know since Kant, a proof of free will is impossible. The "free-will" assumption is a pragmatical supposition of self-understanding. It does not require to say how people activate cortical processes to perform actions (Stanton 2004, 47).

29 Contemporary critique against single technologies, such as military technologies, nuclear energy, genetic engineering, solar radiation management, surveillance technologies, and manned space flight, is coherent with some basic affirmative recognition about human technological inventiveness. The pressing problems of sound moral evaluation of technologies and comprehensive technology assessment are abstracted away.

very slowly. PA and HM have always been interested in the history of technologies and crafts as productive forces (part 2). The origins of the Anthropocene are close to paradigmatic technological Neolithic achievements (part 3). The *technological perspective* is not outdated, as it mediates between economy, culture, daily life, and knowledge. Agency and technology converge at the emic side in concepts of instrumental rationality. Technical artefacts can be also used for manipulation, control, and oppression of other humans. Since contemporary life is shaped by technologies (Borgmann 1984), we should be interested in its origins. Perhaps, we shall combine archaic technologies with digital ones in decades to come (part 4). Sheep and goats may graze under photovoltaic panels.

Agents as tool-makers produce artefacts which remain over time. These are presumptive findings. Archaeological findings are to be presented as classified objects (knife, roof, figurine, wheel, ship, wall, pantry, sword, hoard, coin, flute, *etc.*). If so, a set of *classificatory concepts* must be integrated in TPCL. Interestingly, such a set connects the prehistoric and ancient past to our present daily life within which baskets, vessels, knifes, doors, roofs, combs, flutes, *etc.* still play a role. This gives support to the claim that pre- and (post)modern human life are connected within the lifeworld and its reasons.[30] According to Husserl (1936/2012) and Habermas (1981), the human lifeworld is a reservoir of daily life practices and correlating perceptions and beliefs. Our contemporary *lifeworld-knowledge* is full of beliefs about what things might have been "good for" in past times. Robb (2015, 176) proposes to conceive material culture theory from the "bottom-up" which makes sense of a particular object. By way of example: If we see ancient combs, we imagine humans combing their hair intentionally, performing hair-dressing, and, perhaps, having had an intention to look more handsome to others. A person A can comb the hair of person B in love, care, or serfdom. If so, there must have been a preference for combed hair which is still alive today in most cultures. There is much evidence for hair-dressing in the past (Strenz 2001). In ancient times, women had flowers in their hair (Draycott 2015). Such life-world knowledge is the storehouse for past-present-connectivities. We can have both: a deep theory about the lifeworld *with* precise descriptions how single artefacts were used within particular cultures. This reveals a triadic relation within the logic of history.

## 1.4 The universal, the particular, and the individual

As Herder (1784/1976) outlined, history is dialectical, as it is, on the one hand, devoted to individual humans (as in biographies) and particular cultures and epochs, while, on the other hand, it can also refer to the entire (general) history of mankind ("*Universalgeschichte*"). *The universal (=general), the particular, and the individual (= singular*[31]*) are three basic (logical) categories of social philosophy.*[32] If so, there must be (either at least or exactly) *three types of history*: a) idio-graphic[33], b) particularistic, and c) universal. Idiographic history focusses on individual agents (such as Caesar, Wallenstein, *etc.*) and on micro-entities (such as singular

30 The lifeworld cannot be directly observed as such, but it is discovered on reflection in specific aspects of human beings and doings, beliefs and capabilities.

31 Strictly speaking, the individual and the singular are not exactly the same. Singularity is just numerical, while individuality gives some axiological emphasis to uniqueness.

32 In Hegel's logic, the universal, the particular, and the singular are basic ways to conceptualise.

33 The term "idiographic" was coined by Windelband (1907) who contrasted idiographic humanities with "nomothetic" natural sciences. See the next section.

settlements, single routes, single graves, *etc.*), particularistic history focusses on collectives (cultures, peoples, epochs, styles, *etc.*), while universal history is united under an (ethical) idea of humankind. Universal history survives in evolutionism. Idiographic history is manifested in micro-history, while middle-range theories (MRT) mediate between particular and universal history.

This divide between three categories is implicitly present in PA. On the one hand, PA works "idio-graphically" at specific excavation sites, having proper names, while, on the other hand, prehistory points at large-scale and long-lasting transformations stretching over millennia, such as the Neolithic transformation and transformations toward state-centred collectives. Idiographic history becomes positivistic archaeology in PA. The findings at specific excavation sites are to be ordered like a unique diachronic "biography" of a settlement. Particularistic history opens a vast field between idiographic and universal history. Since all three types of history may perform diachronic and synchronic comparisons, "comparative" history is not a fourth type but a mode of (analogical) reasoning. Any epistemic logic of history must account for all three categories even if the category of universality remains the most contested one. Theoretical investments can be made within all three types of history, although general histories will be more theoretical (as in Marxism and evolutionism, see McCaffree 2022).

Since Burckhardt (1905), universal meta-narratives have a bad reputation among historians, who presume that history should be rather specific, devoted to particular and/or individual people being located at particular places at particular times which might be connected by particular circumstances.[34] In the "*Postmodern Condition*", Lyotard (1987) repeated such scepticism against "metanarratives". Lyotard defines modernity via metanarratives, including Hegelian and Marxian ones. The post-modern attitude to narrativity and micro-histories looks similar to 19th century historism with its emphasis on individuality (Ott 1991).

Many historians see the history of mankind as an inexhaustible horizon which, in itself, cannot become a proper object of historical research and narration. If so, human history falls apart in many single, heterogeneous stories about particulars and individuals. History, then, becomes a kaleidoscope of fragments. Universality, however, remains just because there is only one biological species and there is only one planet. Anthropology and universal history are two dimensions of the general.

Cultural anthropology and history show how profoundly human ways of life can differ. These differences, however, rest in *the* general human way of life: malleable, mobile, niching, coping, acting, technological, lingual, *etc.* If so, EH must ultimately rest on a dialectical logic, as to be found in Hegel. From a dialectical perspective, history splits apart *and* unites. With high likeliness, all humans have to organise their metabolism with nature. Perhaps, kinship is a universal feature of humanity, while particular cultures arrange modes of kinship differently. Perhaps, festivities are universal while there will be many particular celebrations. Perhaps, as Vico (1744) claimed, all humans worship higher powers,

34 Burckhardt (1905, 2) saw the philosophy of history as a "*contradictio in adjecto*" because history "co-ordinates" events diachronically (narrativity), while philosophy "sub-ordinates" concepts synchronically (logic). The logic of arguments is, indeed, different from the logic of narratives. To Burckhardt, history must be organised in diachronic narrative ways, while philosophical arguments are organised in synchronic and logical modes. To Burckhardt, a universal meta-narrative would confuse both methods. Burckhardt's aversion against philosophy, however, remains bounded to a specific "logical" (and deductive) concept of philosophy.

marry by ceremonies, and bury the dead – although cultures perform such rituals differently.[35] Music is present in all human cultures, but there are many different styles of making music (see Honing 2018).

Universal history presents theoretically inspired meta-narratives, as given by Hegel (1822-1832/1970), Marx (1859), Spengler (1923), Toynbee (1976), Horkheimer and Adorno (1944/1947) and Habermas (1976; 2019). To Hegel, universal history can be regarded as progress in the spirit of freedom.[36] To Hegel, degrees of freedom and liberty have been largely enhanced in European modernity despite a long endurance of slavery and serfdom (on the history of slavery see Flaig 2018). To Hegelians, the interrelated topics of freedom, power, and capabilities are theoretical perspectives within history. Graeber and Wengrow (2021, 25) have made freedom the main topic of their *Dawn of Everything,* as they wish to identify the "playful possibilities" within human history.

Marx (1859, 9) hoped for "real" human history after the end of class societies.

> *"Mit dieser Gesellschaftsform schließt daher die Vorgeschichte der menschlichen Gesellschaft ab".* [English translation]: *"The prehistory of human society accordingly closes with this social formation."* [Translation available at: https://www.marxists.org/archive/marx/works/1859/critique-pol-economy/preface.htm; last accessed: 6 December 2023].

Habermas (1976) wished to combine a theory of social evolution with history via models of rational problem solving within history. History of technology and history of science were paradigmatic examples. Habermas (2019) conceived long-term learning processes in practical thought, especially in morals, as he combined narratives with evolutionary perspectives on moral progress towards ethical universalism. The concept of progress supposes that a history of humankind is somewhat more than just the history of a species "*Homo sapiens*" that is fragmented in particular collectives and mortal individuals.

A large-scale transformation perspective on the Neolithic encompasses a time span ranging from 15,000 years BCE until 1000 BCE. *If so, a history of transformations continues the spirit of universal history and evolutionism more than micro-histories which tell about minor changes on small scales.* The origins of the Anthropocene (part 3) are clearly not a micro-narrative. Interestingly, Perreault (2019) argues that the archaeological record is well-suited for macro-history or MRT.

> *"By emphasizing microscale processes, archaeologists are not only misusing the archaeological record, but underusing it" (Perreault 2019, 161).*

Perreault proposes to recalibrate the archaeological agenda to "macroscale patterns and processes" (*ibid.*). The new outlook on macro-history stems from an interpretation of the empirical record, not from a philosopher's speculation about

35 Interestingly enough, these universal traits lose significance in present times.

36 *"Die Weltgeschichte ist der Fortschritt im Bewußtsein der Freiheit – ein Fortschritt, den wir in seiner Notwendigkeit zu erkennen haben"* (Hegel, 1822-1832/1970, 32). [English translation]: "*The History of the world is none other than the progress of the consciousness of Freedom; a progress whose development according to the necessity of its nature, it is our business to investigate*." [Translation available at: https://www.marxists.org/reference/archive/hegel/works/hi/history3.htm; last accessed: 6 December 2023]. Hegel claimed that Africa is not part of world history. The debate on presumptive racism in Hegel has a grain of truth as Hegel believed that Africa had not contributed to universal history. Shillington (2019) shows the opposite. A comprehensive analysis about race and racism in Hegel is given by Bonetto (2006). Here, I only adopt Hegel's idea that all humans are free. As we know from Scott (2017) and Graeber and Wengrow (2021), earlier humans were well aware of their freedom.

the final destiny of humankind. If we give credit to Perreault's argument, PA should become more courageous in doing macro-history. If so, the "big questions" within universal history about progress and evolution cannot be silenced.

## 1.5 The concept of transformation

Humans do not remain the same over time. Humans are the only species that is able to transform its own socio-environmental relations and societal structures within its history. Thus, the concept of transformation must be integrated in TPCL. Any definition must distinguish transformations from other kinds of change, such as economic recession, political protest, military operations, pandemic situations, *etc.*, that do not affect the basic structure of societal life. The term "transformation" is defined (qualified) as directed, substantial, long-lasting, and often irreversible societal change. Müller and Kirleis (2019, 5) define a transformation as "directed and condensed change leading to a substantial reorganisation of socio-environmental relations". In any case, transformations must be substantial and enduring. Directedness is defined by reinforcements. Conceptually, it requires causal drivers and pressures. "Substantial" can refer to normative orders, economic structures, and ideological doctrines (or all of these), while "endurance" points to end states and, perhaps, basins of attraction. A "transformation" is a profound change in ways of human life which are lasting and are hard or impossible to reverse. After a transformation, nothing is as it was before: many aspects of life are affected. Transformations open new path dependencies over long periods.

Old progressive and optimistic stage-models also pointed to transformations by which a "higher" stage of civilisation should finally be reached. The concept of transformation, however, should not imply general progress throughout history. If so, the concept also includes collapse and long-lasting decay. Another option would be progress in the very long run, but with interruptions lasting for generations and centuries. Horkheimer's (1937/1968, 176) definition of Critical Theory entailed a prediction that capitalism might terminate in barbary ("[...] *und die Menschheit einer neuen Barbarei zutreibt."* [English translation]: "[...] *and drives humanity into a new barbarism."* [Translation available at: https://criticaltheoryworkshop.com/wp-content/uploads/2018/03/horkheimer_traditional-and-critical-theory.pdf; last accessed: 6 December 2023]). Thus, the concept of transformation is either neutral against progress and collapses into barbary or it remains on the side of progress. As moral persons, we must take an interest in progressive transformations, while historians may favour neutral concepts.

It remains doubtful whether transformations have always been perceived as such from the emic side. Contemporaries may overrate superficial change by which they are directly affected and may overlook profound transformations. If a collapse-like transformation is as rapid as in the 6$^{th}$ (catastrophic) century CE in Western Europe or in the industrialisation of the 19$^{th}$ century, contemporaries may have realised that they participated in an actual transformation. Industrialisation was a transformation that was realised by contemporaries. If transformations stretch over millennia, however, the transformations may only be revealed to historians (Danto 1965).[37]

Perhaps, historical transformations have an analogy in scientific paradigm shifts, as conceived by Thomas Kuhn (1962). A paradigm shift affects all build-

37 Thomas Kuhn (1962) claims in his *Structures of Scientific Revolutions* that paradigm shifts are disclosed by historians of science in retrospect rather than by participants.

ing blocks of specific epistemic knowledge systems. Biology, in general, is different after Darwin. Contemporaries cannot identify paradigm shifts and distinguish them clearly from "normal" epistemic dispute. Historians of science are in a better position to detect real paradigm shifts. Kuhn himself used the term "achievement" in close connection to "paradigm shift". Achievements indicate progress in theory formation, as one cannot return to pre-Darwinian biology any more. Pseudo-sciences do not last. If an analogy is permitted, there was no way back from the Neolithic way of life to a hunter-gatherer way of life. The divide between progressive and neutral transformations might, however, apply as one might regard alchemy, vitalism, "Arian physics" and "Lyssenkoism" as epistemic transformations as well. They did not entail any achievement and, therefore, did not last. If regressive modes of thought do not stabilise under modern conditions, we may hope that despotic regimes do not last for long.

Working within the research programs of ROOTS and the CRC 1266 at Kiel University, I am interested in the (Neolithic) agricultural transformation in Europe (Robb 2013; Shennan 2018). Starting with complex foragers,[38] humans became horticulturalists at different locations (*e.g.* the Fertile Crescent, the Indus Valley, and in China), as well as agriculturalists, farmers,[39] herdsmen, craftsmen, and metallurgists, and they started to form pre-state normative orders and, later, early states. Over millennia, humans settled post-glacial European landscapes and gradually became farmers. This transformation deeply changed the ways of human life, even if many details of this transformation remain contested. In their chapter on "*Ecology of Freedom*", Graeber and Wengrow (2021) make a strong case that the 3000 years of transition should not be seen as a quick "switch" from one way of life to another one. PA must take these three millennia seriously, not just in duration per se, but in the many ways how the cultivation of plants and the domestication of animals coexisted with other ways of foraging in the food-rich bonanza of the Holocene which, according to Graeber and Wengrow (2021, 258), has been a "forager paradise". There were many, often seasonal ways "in and out" of farming, "play farming", horticulture, and fluid foraging arrangements in which farming played rather a minor role. Perhaps, in its origins, plant cultivation was more of a meditative hobby than alternative foraging. People may have farmed if "there was nothing else to be done" (*ibid.*, 274). For many collectives and individuals, it remained an option to farm without becoming committed to the "logistic rigors of agriculture" (*ibid.*, 260). As Graeber and Wengrow present the story of the transition, many collectives voluntarily remained separate from the threshold of farming as a way of life for a long time, but tried to maintain a balance between foraging and farming (*ibid.*, 268). At the end of the chapter, however, the authors concede that the farmer's way of life had "explosive growth potentials, especially after domestic livestock were added to cereal crops" (*ibid.*, 274). This "explosive growth potential" is of interest here to the perspective of parts 1 and 2.

The concept of an "ecology of freedom", which Graeber and Wengrow (2021, 260) adopt from anarchist Bookchin (1977), is used historically, but implies some normative suggestions.

> *"If peasants are people 'existentially involved in cultivation', then the ecology of freedom ('play farming' in short) is precisely the opposite condition."*

38 Complex hunter-gatherer societies can emerge if there is a functional equivalent to agriculture, such as abundant fisheries. This may explain the complex hunter-gatherer societies of the Pacific Northwest coast. Thus, an increase in societal complexity does not necessarily require farming (Arnold *et al.* 2016, 457).

39 I suppose horti- and agriculture before farming.

Here, "play farming" is a shorthand for such freedom. There is freedom as long as collectives are not existentially dependent on farming, and failure in cropping is not a matter of life and death. Perhaps, we can make a past-present-connectivity out of the concept of ecological freedom under the supposition of dietary flexibility: Are there options to reduce dependency on cereals, rice, and maize in different modes of farming, gardening, and foraging in the Anthropocene or is the dependency on cereals a predicament in a full world of 8-10 billion humans? We shall address this question in part 4.

Slowly, the Neolithic way of life dominated almost all over Europe (Robb 2013). Obviously, this transformation was not reversible. Here, Graeber and Wengrow (2021) and Robb (2013) present different approaches. While Graeber and Wengrow point to the many options "in and out of farming" on a global scale (*ibid.*, 260), Robb presents mechanisms why almost all Europeans became farmers in the longer run. Thus, the divergence is one between freedom and determinism. To Robb, the long duration of this transformation (3000 years) shows a distinctive wave-like *pattern*: complex foraging remains longer in the North, but finally all of Europe turned to agriculture (with some horticultural residuals), while state societies became familiar in the Near East and reached Central Europe from Aegean and Mediterranean countries. We will examine Robb's approach (2013; 2014) as a paradigm case of a working MRT. From a theoretical perspective, one may ask, whether one can identify "points of no return" beyond which a transformation cannot be reversed anymore and path dependencies constitute specific trajectories.[40]

It makes sense to see a second transformation around 3000-2800 BCE[41] by which the more peaceful Neolithic was transformed into the more violent and hierarchical ("martial") Bronze Age and Iron Age. Within this transformation, one sees economic intensification, more violence, professional warriors, aggrandisers, fortification, specialised weapons, steppe invaders, heterosexual gender roles, *etc.* (Kristiansen and Larsson 2005; Treherne 2017). Prehistory, which includes the Palaeolithic, the Neolithic, the Bronze Age and the Iron Age, ended at roughly 1000 BCE. The European Bronze Age ended in the first millennium BCE.

Instances of "great" transformations after the Iron Age are the decline of the Western Roman Empire (Maier 2019), the Italian Renaissance, the European expansion after 1500, and the economic transformation from feudalism into market-based societies (Polanyi 1944/2011 from a Marxist perspective, Rostow 1960 from a growth-economy perspective), which was based on Baconian attitudes. A profound environmental transformation occurred in Europe between 1815 and 1914 that deeply affected land-use systems (Blackbourn 2006) and settlement structures. The divide between countryside and urban regions, metropolitan areas, mobility patterns (railways), industrial fabrication, warehouses, sanitation systems, electricity, *etc.* constituted new industrialised ways of life as compared to pre-industrial agrarian life. The U.S. deeply transformed Northern America, the USSR transformed Russia into an industrialised country, while China transformed itself deeply under Maoism and thereafter. The change

---

40 Robb and Miracle (2007) claim that this theoretical model overcomes the split between "migration" and "acculturation" approaches. The model sheds new light on the LBK (*ibid.* 2007, 110-113) which I have no expertise to judge. Perhaps, Kristiansen *et al.* (2017) point in a similar direction as they reconstruct interactions between migrant herding collectives and indigenous crop cultivators around 3000 BCE.

41 All dating points to a time span which can stretch over centuries and was different at different localities.

into a totalitarian regime in Germany was, despite all its mass atrocities, not an actual transformation because the Nazi-regime did not last.[42] In any case, the last five hundred years show an unprecedented pattern of globalisation and economic integration under European hegemony that finally turned into modern times and into the "full blown" Anthropocene (part 3). In some sense, the Anthropocene is a European project.

## 1.6 A brief history of theory formation in prehistoric archaeology (PA)

The divide between the "two cultures" (Snow 1961) of the sciences and the humanities is still alive today (Sørensen 2017), although some scholars would also classify the social sciences as a field that is distinct from the humanities (Smith 2017). As both cultures have met in PA, this divide sometimes became a "clash" between methods, concepts, and theories culminating into "science wars" between processualism ("scientific positivism") and post-processualism ("culturalism") (Preucel 1991; Yoffee and Sherratt 1993; Robb 2014). We have to understand such epistemic and theoretical clashes from a historical perspective. This section does not work on a history of PA for its own sake, but wishes to identify systematic theoretical problems in the origins of the discipline.

History tells stories about contingent "*pragmata*". The ontology of contingencies has haunted history since its origins in ancient Greece. To Greek metaphysics, there could be no science that is devoted to contingencies, singularities, and individuals because science has to deal with universals, eternal ideas, and necessities. From a metaphysical point of view, history can never reach the status of "*episteme*". As Aristotelianism was replaced by empirical science, history was incorporated into the post-Aristotelian realm of scientific disciplines in the 18th and the 19th centuries. The origins of PA have to be contextualised in the history of science in the 19th century (Schnädelbach 1983).

Scholars realised that history is different from the natural sciences. If history is to be recognised as a scientific discipline, it must have an epistemology of its own. Science rests on quantified data, while history rests on qualified sources (Ribeiro 2019).[43] While science combined empirical observation and quantification programs with general laws, the humanities took an interest in particular societies, periods, singular events and even in individuals.

History became the flagship discipline of the humanities throughout the 19th century, while prehistory and prehistoric archaeology became special boats within the large fleet of historical disciplines. The epistemology of history was dubbed "*Historik*" in the German tradition since Droysen (1882/1974).[44] This epistemology has an impressive tradition (Schnädelbach 1983, chap. 2). Prominent figures are Ranke, Droysen, Dilthey, Windelband, Rickert, and Burckhardt. Historism was based on concepts of individuality, genealogy and understanding ("*Verstehen*"), and it rejected Hegelian and Marxian philosophies of history. To Windelband (1907), sciences are "nomothetic" as they are interested in general laws, while historical humanities are "idiographic" as they are interested in par-

42 National Socialism was intended to last for a millennium, but it collapsed after 12 years. Soviet communism pretended to overcome class societies and reach a new stage of civilisation, but it collapsed after 72 years.

43 I will not tackle the semantical field of "sources", "findings", "data", and "information".

44 An overview of Droysen's intellectual biography is given by Rüsen (1969).

ticulars and individuals. This dichotomic separation, however, teared apart the Hegelian dialectics between generality, particularity, and singularity *within* the humanities. Under this separation, an "understanding" of particulars and individuals became the genuine historical method. The main method of "classical" humanities was hermeneutics as theorised by Schleiermacher (1838/1977). According to Schleiermacher, hermeneutics refers to written documents ("text") which should be properly understood in grammatical (meaning) and psychological (author intention) terms. Therefore, prehistory had a peculiar position within the humanities: it clearly belongs to history but it remains outside the "classical" hermeneutical universe. Ranke expelled it from the realm of history. He recognised that there were human cultures before writing, but he claimed that history must rely on written sources.[45]

> *"Wie könnte sich der Geschichtsschreiber zutrauen, das Geheimnis der Urwelt, also das Verhältnis der Menschen zu Gott und der Natur, zu enthüllen?" (Ranke 1922, 1).* [English translation Ott]: *"How could the historian trust himself to reveal the secret of the primeval world, i.e. the relationship of mankind to God and nature?"*

Ranke obscures the topics of PA. The secrets of prehistory are not metaphysical ones.

Since the 19th century, history was divided into historical research and the art of historical writing. The "*terminus a quo*" were sources, while the "*terminus ad quem*" were credible narratives. Historical research never relied on written sources exclusively. Weapons, coins, flags, costumes, buildings, devices, *etc.* were regarded as sources as well. The epistemology of history also had to reflect the logic of historical narratives as distinct from literature. Narratives are a mode of discourse by which particular lives and agencies can be represented. Biographies are paradigm cases of narratives. If so, narratives in prehistory are "biographies with no names", since names did not remain. Thus, individuals, as such, are largely absent in PA. Thus, PA must be more theoretical, since individuals are nothing but anonymous variables within larger patterns and structures.

In 1830, the Danish historian Thomsen distinguished between the Stone Age, the Bronze Age and the Iron Age (Olszewski 2020, 24). This distinction was material-based. The Stone Age was later split into three "lithic" periods. The crucial achievements of the Neolithic period, however, should not be reduced to tools made of stone. Perhaps, "archaic" history, or rather prehistory itself, should replace this lithic-bronze-iron periodisation according to different modes of production and social organisation (part 2). After Darwin, humans took an interest in the natural origins of their own species. PA often adopted a Darwinian perspective of hominization. Humans are seen as a product of natural evolution sharing many traits with apes. One crucial problem was about societal evolution since the biological mechanism of mutation and selection differs from technical progress, traditions, and learning.[46]

---

45 *"Die Völker [...] besaßen Anfänge der Kultur, lange bevor die Schrift erfunden war: und auf diese allein ist doch die Geschichte angewiesen. [...] Die Geschichte beginnt erst, wo die Monumente verständlich werden und glaubwürdige schriftliche Aufzeichnungen vorliegen"* (Ranke 1922, 1). [English translation Ott]: *"The peoples [...] had the beginnings of culture long before writing was invented: and history depends on this alone. [...] History first begins when the monuments become understandable and credible written records exist."* Ranke's authority continues in the parlance of "prehistory".

46 Troeltsch (1922/1961) reflected upon concepts of development, preluding post-colonial arguments against Eurocentric hubris.

Since 1850, scholars speculated about early historical periods of mankind and its societal organisations (*e.g.* Condorcet, Morgan, Maine, Bachofen). Morgan distinguished between the periods of *wildness, barbarism,* and *civilization.*[47] According to Morgan, the wild period had three sub-periods, ending with the invention of the bow and arrow. Morgan compared this stage with contemporary aboriginal groups in Australia (middle stage) and with tribal groups at the Western Pacific (late stage). The "barbarian" period started with pottery and ended with metallurgy and the alphabet. To Morgan, Greece in the Homerian period marked the transformation from barbarism to civilisation. Ancient Greece and the Roman Empire are paradigms for early European civilisations. At least the upper strata were able to live "civilised" lives. Eurocentrism can be defined as a project by which civilised European ways of life should become dominant worldwide. Colonialism became one means of civilising others.

Historical periods were often seen as "upward stages". The concept of a stage corresponds to concepts, such as "development", "cultural evolution" or "progress", which were reflected in the theory of history. Stage-models entailed, however, words such as "wild", "primitive", "barbarian", and "civilised" having evaluative and hierarchical connotations (Morgan 1877; Sahlins and Service 1960; Service 1966). Here, historians and cultural anthropology face the problem on how to stipulate the differences between ways of life by means of attributions ("qualification") without implicitly ranking ways of life as superior or inferior. Can there be a neutral terminology in PA and cultural anthropology which has been purified from all connotations? It makes a difference to speak of a "simple" or of a "primitive" way of life. This problem occurs, *mutatis mutandis,* at many steps and plateaus on the ladder.

Marx (1859) proposed a universal and teleological stage model that is grounded in modes of production with an outlook on the return of an egalitarian collectivity which would increase the productive forces immensely. Marx is clearly a universalist who sees revolutions as "locomotives" of world history.

Henry Sumner Maine published his book *Village Communities* in 1876. Maine argued that there was not much competition in prehistoric life. To Maine, prehistoric life was a mixture of permanent micro-warfare between small social units and strong egalitarian brotherhoods within kin-communities. Transformation to modern life civilised some kinds of warfare[48] into economic competition and civilised morals by universal principles. Intense, expressive, and emotional modes of life were transformed into expectations of rational behaviour.[49] Even emotional life transformed in civilisation. It was tempered.

There was an underlying "humanitarian" interest to demonstrate that there is progress within history towards "civilisation".[50] Such interest often collapsed into colonial doctrines of either "civilising" others or driving them to extinction by genocidal means. To "bring civilisation" was an ideology of colonialism, infamously put into

47 The term "archaic history" hopefully has fewer connotations than "wildness" and "barbarism", or even "primitive". The term "barbarian" had negative connotations: a civilised way of life was superior over a barbarian one. The same holds for the term "primitive".

48 War became the monopoly of the state which, however, expanded warfare to macro-warfare with large armies and imperial ambitions. Violence enlarged from ambush to battles and to large-scale destruction by air force.

49 Such transformations have been studied by Norbert Elias (1980).

50 Mbembe (2016, 11) sees colonialism simply as a highly primitive kind of racism. That is a bit too simple. A balanced history of European colonialism in Africa is given by Shillington (2019, sections 7-10).

the wording of "the white man's burden" (Cecil Rhodes). Different ways of human life were often arranged under a stage-model as "superior" and "inferior". To some authors, non-civilised societies had no right to exist in a "civilised" world.[51] At the end of the 19th century, some proponents of nature conservation argued that it should include the conservation of "wild tribes" ("*Naturvölker*"). "Wild humans" were exhibited in German zoological gardens. The peculiar dialectics between a humanitarian impulse to "civilise", scientific interest in "wild" and "primitive" cultures, curiosity about exotic aliens, sober colonial realities, and proposals to keep some "wild tribes" in their original condition shaped cultural anthropology in the 19th century.

Franz Boas conceived an approach in U.S. archaeology which had roots in German historical thought. Boas, who studied in Kiel, was familiar with Wilhelm Dilthey's writings and it seems likely that he was also familiar with Herder's cultural philosophy and the Romantic tradition. Boas was clearly a culturalist and a particularist (Stocking 1966). To Boas, culture is an integrated system of symbols, ideas and values that should be studied as a working system and an organic whole. Boas also influenced Kluckhorn's (1951; 1961) theory of values. There are parallels between Boas's ideas and post-processual archaeology.

Since the turn of the 20th century, cultural anthropology (= ethnology) became highly important for prehistory. The high times of ethnography were the decades between 1880 and 1940 because scientific methods (such as participatory observation) were established and, moreover, there were still many ethnic collectives without intense contacts to Western people.[52] In this "classical" period, books such as *Die Seele der Primitiven* (Levy-Bruhl 1930/1956) were important (even if such titles would not be permitted today). PA and cultural anthropology started to draw speculative parallels between such still existing collectives and archaic collectives. Interdisciplinarity between ethnology and archaeology has a long tradition, fusing into "ethno-archaeology". This epistemic connectivity is still alive today. From an epistemological point of view, it is based on the fragile premise that inferences of analogy can be made between recent indigenous ethnic and archaic collectives. The idea is to compare collectives which are not historically connected but live at the same (or a similar) "evolutionary stage" and to infer from observable behaviour and communication to past collectives. If there are ethnic collectives in Naga-borderlands of India that erect megalithic artefacts and if one can research their motives and reasons and even come into dialogue with them, then one may assume ("speculate") that past humans might have had similar motives and reasons to erect megaliths. This, however, is a fragile supposition. Might it be a mistake to conceive complex foraging of hunters and gatherers in Mesolithic times as close to the foraging of the remaining foragers of marginal areas, for example, the Kalahari Desert? Does the supposition itself rest on a stage model which most ethno-archaeologists reject?

If one does not allow such analogical reasoning, epistemological doubts fall upon the entire discipline of ethnoarchaeology. Why should one believe that present non-state collectives have similar motives and reasons as archaic collectives did? This point has been highlighted by Galley:

> *"Either we admit that ethnological studies may be useful to archaeologists, which means that an observation made at point X in space and time is equally*

51 In Soviet communism and Maoism, nomads had no right to exist in a worker-and-peasant society.

52 50 years later, the methods were refined, but the "original tribes" were almost gone or had been entitled to no-contact policies (as in some remote primary forests in South America).

> *valuable for a point Y* [...] *and in such case this approach is transcultural* [...] *or we admit that such transfer cannot be made, due to the endless originality of cultures" (Gallay 1990 in Gosselain 2016, 220).*

Does originality preclude comparisons by analogies? The problem of past-present-analogies in ethno-archaeology will be analysed separately, reflecting on Wylie (1985) (see part 1, section 1.11).

In 1927, Martin Heidegger (*"Sein und Zeit"*, § 11) argued that cultural anthropology (ethnology) must suppose a comprehensive analysis of human existence as its philosophical guideline. The German word was *"Daseinshermeneutik"* (Engl.: the hermaneutics of existence). Ernst Cassirer (1923/1964) had a quite similar idea to provide a philosophy of symbolic forms for a grounding of cultural anthropology. To my knowledge, neither Heidegger nor Cassirer played a major role in the philosophy of archaeology in these times. Arnold Gehlen (1944), author of *Der Mensch*, who was influenced by zoology, might be seen as forefather of niche construction theory. As Gehlen argues, humans have to produce their niches by their own agencies if they are to survive. The famous concept *"Mängelwesen"* means that humans lack a specific niche of their own. This deficiency is the source of evolutionary success, because humans can learn how to occupy many environments. They have no niche, but are "niching". By nature, humans are artificial and inventive beings. Since Gehlen did make a steep career under National Socialism and had to re-write the final chapter of *Der Mensch* after 1945, he was a *"persona non grata"* to post-war intellectuals. As far as I know, his book *Urmensch und Spätkultur* (1986) has not played a major role in recent PA debates.

The theoretical origins of PA in Germany were given by a *"siedlungsarchäologische Methode"* (Kossinna, see Bernbeck 1997, 26-30). Because this approach was adopted by PA under National Socialism, it was discarded after 1945. Compared to international standards, PA under National Socialism was ideological and regressive.[53] After this period, theory in general appeared to be all too close to ideology. Therefore, archaeology became rather theory-abstinent after 1945, restricting itself to excavation, dating, and collecting (Bernbeck 1997, 31). There is a striking parallel to German nature conservation after 1945. After a period of "blood and soil", a scientific period emerged in which nature conservation was seen as "applied ecology". Ideological overdose eclipsed into prohibition. Eggert (2012) presents the best overview on concepts and methods in the German tradition. A comparison between theory formation in different countries is beyond the scope of this section.

With some "caveats", one can divide theoretical approaches in PA into pre-processual, processual, and post-processual archaeology. Processual archaeology was proud to be scientific. An overview of "New Archaeology" is given in Bernbeck (1997, chap. 2) and Trigger (2006). Zimmermann (2003, 7) presents a nice picture of the theoretical landscape in archaeology since 1800.

Ecological archaeology became prominent in the 1930s. Ecology was established in biology in these decades (Golley 1993). There was an upshot of scientific-naturalistic theories in archaeology that has shaped the discipline until today. One may distinguish between Darwinian archaeology, human behavioural ecology, niche construction theory and similar approaches. On a meta-theoreti-

53 A basic flaw was based on the doctrine that "high Arian culture" spread from some Nordic origins into the south, while historical truth gives evidence to the opposite: Cultural achievements were transported from the south to the north. The doctrine is to be found in Rosenberg's (1935) *Der Mythus des 20. Jahrhunderts.*

cal layer, biological and ecological theories transported scientific standards into archaeology. This approach was called "processual archaeology" (Olszewski 2020, 23). Its epistemology often combined the Vienna Circle (Carnap, Neurath, Schlick) approach of data production, induction, operationalisation of concepts, testing hypotheses, verification, *etc.* with a Popperian approach to falsification (Kelley and Hanen 1988). Fritz and Plog (1970) conceived a famous scheme for archaeological explanation based on the Hempel-Oppenheim general-law-model. Processual archaeology sets the bars for scientific standards and hypothesis formation in archaeology on a high level. Current archaeology should take this as one legacy among many. Post-processual archaeology should not be anti-processual with respect to scientific standards of concept formation, control of data, and checks of conjectural hypotheses. It should not invent the wheel anew.

The concern about processualism was that it might naturalise history. The definition of culture, as given by Binford (1962, 218), a prominent figure in processual archaeology, was quite naturalistic (and anti-Boasian): "*Culture is viewed as the extrasomatic means of adaptation for the human organism.*" This approach was close to determinism and modelled human behaviour in behaviouristic terms as driven by external stimuli. Humans react automatically on stimuli. According to behaviourism (Skinner 1971), the emic side cannot be addressed by scientific means. If so, "patterned behaviour" as determined and triggered by external conditions became the interest of knowledge in PA. Humans were seen as "re-active". Processual archaeology is a paradigm case that scientific progress may come at the price of naturalistic reductionism. If scientific approaches in PA must rely on scientific epistemologies, including concepts of causality, they may contradict historical epistemologies, based on agency and social structures (as in Giddens 1979; 1984). I see a peculiar dialectics at work: On the one hand, archaeological sciences are highly progressive and contribute to PA in many impressive ways (Pollard *et al.* 2023). On the other hand, they remain "*ancillae historiae*".

Marxism and evolutionism were combined by Gordon Childe (1951) and by theories of increasing social complexity and stratification. Talcott Parson's general sociology claimed the correlation of increasing complexities and the improved outcomes of functional separation (Parsons 1954). The evolutionism of Childe (1951) can be seen as a functionalistic turn in cultural theory. Childe remained close to Morgan in crucial respects. There is a Morgan-Marx-Childe-Parsons line of thought. The basic intuition is that modern societies have reached a level of complexity which is unknown to tribal societies. Evolutionism claims the emergence of complexities on the long route to modern societies. Barrientos and Sanjuán (2021, 159) provide an overview on the "classical" literature on complexity and evolution.

Here, a moral problem emerges which haunted PA and ethnoarchaeology since then. The recognition of an increase in societal complexity should be reconciled with the moral principle that no human way of life is generally superior or inferior in comparison to another one. It is a categorical mistake to see any humans as "superior" or "inferior" compared to others as they live different more or less complex modes of existence (= ways of life). Particularism seems to be safer against "superiority" claims than universalism. Even if we adopt some kind of evolutionism, we should discard all ideas and suggestions about "superiority" and "supremacy" if we characterise and qualify the figurations of an (average) life in a hunter-gatherer band, a Neolithic village, ancient urban life, medieval mining towns, and, finally, the (post)modern lives we live ourselves. Foragers of the north, nomadic herdsmen, Bronze Age villagers, and ancient sailors have been "superior" to modern urban people in many respects. Their lives have been at least as rich as the life of an average contemporary "digital couch potato". *Racism* is a naturalistic supremacy doctrine being wrong *a fortiori*. If "Eurocentrism" claims superiority of European ways of life, it should be overcome – period.

The problem is to recognise differences without ranking them. Yes, modern life differs from past life in many respects. Yes, *we* appreciate such differences (such as literacy, life expectancy, global mobility, security, medicine, political liberties, *etc.*) as advancements, but our evaluations are made from our emic point of view. Life might be "better" according to some indicators that we appreciate (for example life expectancy, health status, diet, liberties). *If* we have reasons to believe that past humans did appreciate these indicators, they would, counterfactually, have had reasons to believe that modern ways of life are, on the average, better than medieval, ancient or prehistoric ones. But could Neolithic persons even imagine a society with more students than farmers, with a food supply from all around the world, with modern medicine, and with an average life expectancy of more than 80 years?

It is an epistemological question whether evolutionary concepts have explanatory force in history, while it is a moral affair to deny superiority (= supremacy) among humans. The concept of transformation should work without suggestions that there was a superior way of life after the transformation. One should not rule out the possibility of "*evolutionism without superiority*" in PA. Personally, I see the reflections of Habermas (1976; 1981, part I, chap. 2 and 4) on macro-historical learning processes with reason and understanding as the preliminary outlines of such an approach. The evolution of scientific, technological, legal, and even ethical knowledge does not imply superiority of ways of life, but the denial of superiority does not imply the denial of societal evolution.[54] We are "more advanced" in some respects, but we are not superior.

A wave of *post-processual archaeology* emerged in the 1980s. Post-processual archaeology was inspired by Wittgensteinians, such as Dray (1957/1964), von Wright (1971), Geertz (1973), and Winch (1958/1965), who argued that history cannot operate according to the General-Law-Model as presented by Hempel and Oppenheim (1948). The logic of history is different. At a closer look, the explanatory schemes in history entailed many regularities but not causal laws. Regularities were used to explain, but they were more often taken from common sense or lifeworld knowledge than from natural sciences. This theoretical controversy has been extensively analysed by Apel (1979). Post-processual archaeology can be seen as a second "cultural turn" with some parallels to pre-processual archaeology, especially Boas.

The recent decades (1990-2020) saw many post-modern and post-structuralist philosophies, augmented by post-colonial and post-humanist approaches. Post-x-theories became (over)abundant and their theoretical merits were hard to survey and assess from "ordinary" field-working archaeologists being concerned with excavations, archives, dating, collections, and records (Mizoguchi 2015; Ribeiro 2016). There was and is concern that archaeology might fall prey to a playful and sloppy "anything goes" (Bintliff 1993; Peebles 1993). Feyerabend's famous slogan "anything goes" (1975/1993, xvii) might have had a liberating effect against hard-boiled scientism, but it also paved the way to disinterestedness in scientific ways of producing robust knowledge. According to Feyerabend, science should become an anarchic enterprise (*ibid.* 1975/1993, 1). Feyerabend's theoreti-

54 Attentiveness of mind that is reached by meditation skills, contact to higher powers within trance, and local knowledge of how to survive a drought is different from scientific observation, but doing science may result in bodies of knowledge that are closer to external truth.

cal anarchism was endorsed by Graeber (2015), the "*spiritual rector*" of anarchism in PA. Therefore, the concept of "anarchism" seems to have both political and theoretical meanings which should be separated (part 4).

The recent period in theory formation can be either affirmed as pluralistic or discarded as messy (Robb 2014: "wishy-washy"). A comprehensive analysis of post-processual and post-modern theoretical investments in PA and its outcome is beyond the scope of this section.

Scientific methods have made progress and still bring robust results to PA (Martinón-Torres and Killick 2014; Pollard *et al.* 2023).[55] Natural scientists contribute to PA in many important respects, including topics such as population density, birth rates, diets and diseases, plant invasions, precipitation, climatic and landscape change. Genetic analyses report on migration and marriage patterns in the 7th and the 3rd millennium BCE in Europe. Palaeoecology describes the ecological effects of the extinction of mega-fauna on the road to farming (Spengler *et al.* 2021), on the spread of Eurasian neo-biota (such as millet), climate change and its impacts,[56] foraging, *etc.* PA profits from the sciences, but it remains history, dealing with human affairs and ways of life. From a systematic angle, science remains an auxiliary discipline to human history, while, from a methodological perspective, science imports more rigor into history. If one would have to choose between slow, but steady progress and a series of postmodern "turns", one should choose the former to remain on the safe side of PA. Martinón-Torres and Killick (2014) are right that there should not be a wrongful idea that science delivers pure facts while the "true" archaeologists interpret and theorise. Scientists theorise as well, but they theorise scientifically. According to Martinón-Torres and Killick (2014, 10): *"The seeds of archaeological theories are planted in laboratories."*

Appreciating science in PA does not make PA a scientific enterprise. In any case, the two cultures (Snow 1961) of science and the humanities will both remain present in PA. If so, PA is *constituted* by interdisciplinarity. Moreover, one has to integrate economics and sociological theory. By performing interdisciplinary correlations, PA might become a paradigm case of a "third culture", which overcomes the divide between science and the humanities not just in epistemology, but on a daily basis of doing PA.[57] Here, I follow Smith (2017) who argues that at least three epistemic cultures meet in PA (natural sciences, social sciences, humanities). Economics is seen as a social science (here part 2).

Epistemology must also identify the points at which scientists and historians are at crossroads. Materials and scientific methods reveal knowledge but will not bring past lives back. Scientific PA, as such, cannot take the decisive step to social archaeology. Intentions, action, reasons, rules, speech, *etc.* cannot be directly observed. There is the old philosophical question "*ta legomena*": "*What can be said within a discipline?*" Processualism might argue that there are limits of knowledge in PA and it might be better to remain silent than to speculate. My TPCL approach allows for controlled speculation in the lingual modes of analogical inferences, conjectures and refutations, interpretations, guessing, retrospective predictions, abductive and counterfactual reasoning, thought experiments, *etc.* The repertoire of historians and archaeologists to argue in support of claims which address past

55 I completely agree with Martinón-Torres and Killick (2014, 3-4) in their opinion on Latour.

56 Gill *et al.* (2007) claim that the collapse of the Maya culture was caused by a long harsh drought due to a minimum of solar activity.

57 In this respect, archaeology has some epistemological parallels with interdisciplinary environmental studies.

ways of human life should be as large as the repertoire we use in our daily life to understand actions, intentions, and symbolic meanings.

Finally, I follow Robb's diagnosis that the state of the art in current PA rests upon

> *"a broadly shared general theoretical platform* [...] *including a science-based methodology largely developed by processualism and a post-structuralist focus on agency and meaning" (2014, 24).*

Agency and meaning have been topics since Herder, Humboldt, Ranke, and Dilthey. A new "third-culture" coalition between scientific processualism and "old schools" of pre-processual PA, including Boasian culturalism, seems possible, as we scaffold on the ladder.

## 1.7 Understanding, explaining, and the role of reasons

The method of history can be conceived as "*erklärendes Verstehen*" (Weber 1921/1972, 4). This wording was prudently chosen and has been adopted by archaeology (Heinz *et al.* 2003). On the one hand, history wishes to *understand* motives of agents (actions, intentions, purposes, reasons, strategies, choices, selection of means) and collective belief systems (and the relations between beliefs and motives), while, on the other hand, it wishes to *explain* change, boom, decay, transformations, collapse, *etc.* by bundles of causal efficacies (stimuli, nexus, drivers, triggers, forces, incentives, regularities, and "factors"). Interests in explanations have connected archaeology to the sciences and to a "covering-law" model (Hempel and Oppenheim 1948) for a while, but the covering-law model has lost credit in PA-theory (Smith 2017 with further references). Martinón-Torres and Killick (2014, 10) come close to this model as they write that archaeological scientists have an understanding

> *"of the natural laws and constraints that – like it or not – govern much of our behavior."*

An interest in understanding is specific to the humanities. The operation called "understanding" as applied to PA supposes the unobservable *emic dimension.*[58] "Understanding" supposes teleological causality being entailed in the concept of agency which entails intentionality and purposiveness (Gewirth 1978). Von Wright (1971) has conceived a model of how to understand and explain instrumental action: An agent A intends to reach objective O. A chooses (effective or efficient) means M accordingly. Bystanders and historians can understand this O-intention and the M-selection. Understanding refers to *reasons* R for intentional actions. Any teleological explanation presupposes reasons on the side of the agent: O-reasons and M-reasons. One may add foresight and prudence that constitute planning. To migrate into new areas for settlement supposes planning. One can make plans and tell them to others. There can be common planning. There are reasons to act according to a plan as long as the plan might work. Reasons constitute *top-down*-causality within history. Deliberative decision-making is a type of *top-down*-causality. This simple model can be refined with respect to risks and uncertainties being implied in O or M. Since nature is not reasonable, it cannot be understood, but only explained.

58 "Etic" means the observer perspective, while "emic" refers to the perspective of the (former) participants.

There is a conceptual nexus from "understanding" to "having reasons". A person understands intentions and motivations of others if she recognises the reasons (or emotions) of others. Emotions and passions can be powerful reasons. Reasons are "actual" (Hegel: "*wirklich*") in human life. Whether reasons are reasonable (according to some standards), is a question that transcends understanding.

If a historian presents narratives or models, she must implicitly presuppose that participants, in principle, could have had agreed to historical narratives from their emic side. "Yes, we produced X on a daily basis." – "Yes, there were waste pickers in our settlement" – "Yes, we ate millet if grain harvests were bad" – "Yes, rye improved our food security" – "Yes, we sold captives as slaves". The language games (= speech acts) being used by historical observers and emic participants will differ on a semantic and grammatical level, but cannot fall apart completely on a pragmatic level (Habermas 1981). Counterfactually, we may imagine an agent applauding a historian: "You understand my reasons well."

The emic side of prehistoric and ancient humans and the attempts to understand them are connected by a concept of "reasons to act". We understand an action A if we can identify the reasons R an agent P might have had to perform A in a situation S. This is similar to the idea that we understand a speech act if and only if we know the reasons that support it (Habermas 1981). Motives and reasons are not radically enigmatic ("alien") to "us". Reasons must be "intelligible" to us even if we do not share them. Understanding presupposes that no reason is completely unintelligible. If it is, we do not understand. Misunderstanding, then, is an error more about reasons than about words.

Scholtes (2007, 29) distinguishes between "*alterity*" and "*alienity*". While alterity, despite all differences, supposes some commonly shared lifeworld knowledge, alienity means complete divergence and idiosyncratic behaviour. Alterity means that the other remains an "(reasonable) alter ego", while alienation cuts off understanding. It makes a huge difference to PA whether alterity or alienity is taken as a rule. In their epistemic practices, archaeologists and historians suppose alterity while some theorists may emphasise alienity. Here, I adopt the primacy of alterity as an epistemic standard. If it remains possible to understand reasons which motivate other people to act, such people are not enigmatic domains of "alienity". Alterity allows for analogical reasoning, while alienity does not.

There are many kinds of human motives: hunger, sexual desire, anxiety, anger, fear, envy, aspirations, economic interests, resentments, reputation, distrust, shame, doctrines, belief systems, *etc*. PA needs a *set of motivational concepts*. A motivational hypothesis takes the form: *P intends and performs an action A as she is motivated by a motive M*. An urge to react on a causal event in the environment of A also can be a motive. Theories of motivation are conceived within psychology. If so, PA and archaeology face a dilemma: They either suppose some folk psychology about motivations or they face theoretical contest within different schools in theoretical psychology, such as behaviourism, cognitive sciences, or Freudian psychoanalysis. Maslow's (1943) famous hierarchy of human needs and motives is still inspiring, even if the needs do not follow a strict lexicographic order. Probably, Maslow was inspired by his research at a Blackfoot reservation in the summer of 1938. One might suppose physiological needs, safety needs, affective needs and esteem needs in PA, but might be sceptical whether Maslow's highest stage of self-actualisation may apply to PA. The field of scientific credible psychology has, however, borderlines. It might be contested whether a theory of archetypes

(Jung 1981) is scientifically credible. If Jung is not credible, however, what about post-modern psychologies (*i.e.* Lacan, Deleuze, Butler)?

Motives and reasons are embedded in and shaped by institutions and belief systems. Belief systems have performative forces and motivate humans to act. Motives are never purely individual, but are shared or rejected by contemporaries (friends, bystanders, opponents, foes). Motives sometimes must be suppressed or overcome. There might be a strong impetus to flee and escape, but a stronger moral force to stay and fight. The distinction between motives (understanding) and causalities (explanation) implies a distinction between internal states of mind and external forces (in a broad sense). These distinctions are clearly imperfect since there are also beliefs, doctrines, and institutions that constitute a broad category of "symbolic" causalities.

Motivations, reactions to causal forces, beliefs, and symbolic orders merge into *reasons to act*. It must be supposed that human agents act out of reasons they themselves hold *as* reasons. Generally, agents can convey their reasons to others. If some evidence points to the likeliness of a drought to come, people have reasons to store resources out of the understandable motive not to starve. If there are threats from hostile raiders, people have reasons to organise defence with the understandable motive not to be robbed, raped, or killed. There are reasons to escape, reasons to attack, reasons to beg for pardon. One can regret to have acted crazy out of impulse. This liberal approach to reasoning clearly does not imply that historians have to share reasons which are based on beliefs that they do not share (afterlife, demons, witchcraft, hell, power of sacrifices, *etc.*). Hypothetical reasoning remains an option: "*If* an agent A holds a belief B, then she has a reason R to act in a situation S". As we know, there can be reasons *pro* and *contra*. In processes of migration, there might be both reasons to leave and reasons to stay. In processes of conflict, there might be reasons to fight and reasons to surrender. Humans weigh reasons and give weight to some reasons over others. Can we infer from the records which reasons might have been the strongest reasons in the prehistoric past? Interpreting megalithic structures and graves, archaeologists implicitly make such inferences. Thus, historians must and will try to understand reasons that are performatively at work on the emic side of life. *Thus, PA must squeeze reasons out of materials.*

There are as many reasons as there are matters of belief.[59] History supposes that it is possible to *understand* motives and reasons across temporal and cultural distances. Hans Jonas (1970) gave the example of Priamos' mourning over the death of his beloved son Hector. If high-ranked men or women are entitled to be equipped well for an afterlife, there might be obligations for survivors to equip them with burial goods. If there is a belief that a "big chief" cannot show up in the afterlife without a servant or a horse, one may feel obliged to kill (sacrifice) them. Religious reasons have been (and still are) very powerful reasons. The sacred constitutes taboos. Rules also provide reasons to act if persons either fear punishment or believe in the rightness of a rule (Barrett 2021; Ribeiro 2022). Honour, friendship and love are connected to many reasons. Hegelians will sum up that past ethical life must be full of reasons. If reasons are held by agents and can be understood properly by others, including historians, then humans are united under a concept of (practical) reasons despite temporal and spatial distance.

59 The moral tragedy of human life might be that very "poor" reasons may have a very strong motivational force, as revealed in political and religious fanatics. ("Fanatism" is clearly an ethical term.)

But how can reasons be found in the archaeological materials? We must allow some leeway for hypothetical conjectures and even imagination about presumptive reasons. Historians must present conjectural reasons (guesses) about former reasons. Let "hoarding" be an example. As a matter of fact, around 2000 BCE, a sharp increase in hoarded metals occurs in parts of Europe. How can we understand and explain hoarding in PA? Historians cannot avoid considering and judging competing hypotheses.

Let us look at the side of *explanations*. Since ancient times, philosophy has looked for epistemic explanations.[60] Explanations have a general structure: An "*explanans*" should be explained by an "*explanandum*". The question remains what counts as a sufficient "*explanandum*". For example, the port of Hedeby might have been abandoned *because* large ships could not reach the harbour anymore, and *therefore* trade shifted to Schleswig. One may add a geophysical theory of sediment formation in rivers and lakes and an economic theory of transport costs in the Viking period. If such an "explanandum" counts as sufficient within an epistemic community, one should not require more.

For the sake of explanations, historians need a *set of causality concepts*. According to science, there is only one kind of causality: "*causa efficiens*". This restriction is too rigid for history. Following Aristotle, there is a network of different causal efficacies in history and societal life being constituted by *causa formalis, causa materialis, causa finalis,* and *causa efficiens*. To Aristotle, all kinds of causality must be present in explanations.[61] The dominant scientific mode of causality is "*causa efficiens*", but the humanities must rely on "*causa finalis*" as they suppose intentionality, agency, and reasons. Even "*causa materialis*" and "*causa formalis*" may play a role in PA, as specific materials enable or restrict practices. The differences between bronze and iron swords are material and causal ones which have made a difference in warfare. *Historians must operate within an Aristotelian realm of different causal efficacies and not within a physical universe governed by general laws, efficient cause, and boundary conditions.*

*Explanations* in the social sciences (as distinct to the humanities) refer to causal forces (triggers, pressures, drivers, stimuli) which agents are confronted with[62] but also to reasons of how to cope with such forces. A common distinction holds between proximate and ultimate causes. At its surface, this set of causality concepts looks chaotic, but it may stimulate explanatory debates within PA. In the longer run, historians might agree upon the "best" explanation which rarely will be monocausal. There are different "depths" of pluri-causal explanation. The principle of parsimony does not apply to social science explanations. If a relation would hold: "the more parsimonious an explanation, the better", we might be biased by our tacit criteria of parsimony. Perhaps, we believe that economic explanations are always more parsimonious than explanations which rely on spiritual or moral beliefs. The criterion of parsimony works best as a tie-breaker: *Ceteris paribus,* the more parsimonious explanation should be preferred. But in many cases, all other things are not equal. Therefore, pluri-causal explanations can be better than parsimonious mono-causal ones.

60 Democritus was said to prefer the discovery of causalities over the status of a Persian king. See Henrich (2003, 32).

61 A fine analysis of Aristotle's concept of causality is given in Henrich (2003, 30-50). Henrich also provides a fine-grained analysis of recent theories of causality that is adopted here.

62 Climate change, infectious diseases, invasive enemies, scarcity of essential resources (food, water) may count as prominent examples of such forces.

Some approaches, such as historical materialism (see part 2), prefer to explain human behaviour via economic concepts, patterns, and models. Other approaches suppose emergent causation or top-down-causalities allowing intellects to modify material realities. Incentives are "weak" causalities. "Nudging" is a type of weak causal influence upon others. Persuasion is lingual nudging. PA operates within a complex "Aristotelian" field of pluri-causal efficacies ("*Ursachengefüge*").

Given this, the Hempel-Oppenheim model should be replaced in PA by the more flexible "driver-pressure-state-impact-response" model – the DPSIR model – that leaves room for different kinds of causality and entails the emic dimension at the stage of response (Ribeiro *et al.* in press). The DPSIR model is a refinement of the binary "challenge-response" model (Toynbee 1934-1961) which might represent a basic generic situation within human life: being forced to act. DPSIR is liberal and flexible. On the driver and pressure side, it remains possible that a) single drivers have single effects (pressure, impact) (which might be the exception), b) that single drivers have multiple effects, c) multiple drivers have few decisive effects, and d) multiple drivers cause multiple effects. Drivers can be single catastrophic events (such as tsunamis, earthquakes, volcano eruptions, and pests) or slow-onset encroaching effects (such as climatic change or soil erosion). Often, population growth and decline, environmental and climatic change, hostile invasions, and migrations are seen as drivers (= forces).

As we have argued, humans are responsive beings. Something X occurs in the environment of a collective of humans that cannot be ignored by them. X matters and humans have to respond to X. A challenge is not a neutral event but some type of forcing that one is confronted with. Challenges trigger and motivate agential response. Motives are not just immediate preferences, but are often mediated (shaped) by external triggers. Humans struggle to cope with a challenge. Now, concepts such as response, reaction, coping, adaptation, loss aversion, risk, uncertainty, choice, decision, perhaps even deliberation become meaningful.

## 1.8 The practical interest in history

Historical research is often motivated by present challenges. Such motivation might stimulate sound historical research, but it may also confuse historical facts and explanations with present concerns, anxieties, morals, and politics. History always competes with its nasty cousins such as folk history, biased memory, and political-historical doctrines. For instance, in German archaeology under National Socialism, "German" and "Arian" traditions were construed in order to make connectivities between the past and the present. By way of example: Carl Engel[63] delivered a speech at Greifswald University in 1942 connecting the past with the present, emphasising the importance of archaeology for national-socialist world-views (Engel 1942).

This and many other examples of the misuse of history for political interests may count as knock-down arguments against any "*historia magistra vitae*" approach. There always will be history that wishes to let the past simply be the past. "Pure" history for the sake of history always remains an epistemological

63 His diaries show Engel as a devoted National-Socialist who realised in 1943/4 that the war was lost. Engel adopted the attitude of heroic nihilism. One should not forget, however, that Engel took a leading role in saving the city of Greifswald from destruction by offering unconditional surrender to the Soviet Army. Engel noted the dramatic and extremely risky drive at night (28.-29. April 1945) from Greifswald to Anklam in his diaries (Engel 2007, 317-329). Engel's meritorious role was erased in GDR times.

option that is hard to refute. There is a large grain of truth in this approach: History should not become an orientation delivery agency that serves any political agenda.[64] According to Max Weber, history should be based upon an ethos of epistemic honesty (Ott 1997, chap. 3). Historians should be *respectful* of the past. Respectfulness of such "fact-fullness" of history is mandatory to PA. *If* radical constructivism denies historical facts and truth, it might become an ally of all kinds of historical ideologies.

History, as such, does not teach how one should act. If a person had perfect knowledge about the entire past in each and any detail, she could not logically derive a practical judgement of how to act now from such perfect knowledge. Such inferential derivation would fall prey to a "*historistic fallacy*". If derivation is unsound, there might be, nevertheless, some *relevance* of history for the present (Ott 1991). The logical relation "*X is of relevance for Y*" allows for many critical deliberations on past-present-connectivities. Part 3 presents a paradigm case: the presumptive origins of the Anthropocene are of relevance for an understanding of the full-blown Anthropocene. The relation of relevance[65] is indispensable for practical arguments from history.

Several epistemologists of history have been critical against pure history. Nietzsche (1874, 122) distinguished three modes of history as it serves specific ways of life: *monumental, critical* and *antique*. History should be done *for the sake of life* – but which lives? Should one ask: What in our (post)modern lives is PA "good for"? Nietzsche:

> *"Wenn wir nur dies gerade immer besser lernen, Historie zum Zwecke des Lebens zu treiben!"* [English translation]: "[...] *if only we always just learn better to carry on history for the purposes of living!"* [Translation available at: https://la.utexas.edu/users/hcleaver/330T/350kPEENietzscheAbuseTableAll.pdf; last accessed: 6 December 2023].

Nietzsche opposed Ranke's objectivism "just to tell how it really was", but remained trapped in an abstract antagonism to truth-orientation in history: relativism.

Heidegger (1927/1979, § 74-77) argued that the interest in history is grounded by the existential knowledge of oneself being a finite and mortal self within history ("*Geschichtlichkeit des Daseins*"). To Heidegger, history is rooted in historicity (Heidegger (1927/1979, 392-393): "*existentialer Ursprung der Historie aus der Geschichtlichkeit des Daseins*". Pure history obscures the existential dimension of "timely" being. It becomes more scientific but it reduces historical sense to "once upon a time there was...".

Walter Benjamin (1940/1974) argued that historical materialists should not creep back in time but should "jump" into specific periods of the past as tigers jump upon prey (Benjamin 1940/1974, no. XIV: "*Tigersprung ins Vergangene*"). To Benjamin, history does not operate within homogeneous chronological time, but specific historical times are full of presence. Materialists blow such specific

64 In 2022, we had to realise how Russian history was (mis)used in order to justify the military aggression against Ukraine. This disseminated history maintains that there never was a Ukrainian nation apart from Russia.

65 An analysis of this relation from the perspective of social phenomenology is given by Schütz (1971). Schütz distinguishes three fields of relevance which form an interdependent system. Something might be of relevance for a thematic problem description, for an interpretation or for motives. The negation of relevance is "irrelevance". Therefore, strategic moves within discourse are statements like "X might be true, but it is irrelevant".

periods out of the abstract continuum of time. History is not conspicuous consumption of luxury knowledge.[66] To Benjamin (1940/1974, no. XVI), the past and the present must be coiled into dialectical figures.

> *"Der Historismus stellt das 'ewige' Bild der Vergangenheit, der historische Materialist eine Erfahrung mit ihr da, die einzig dasteht".* [English translation]: *"Historicism gives the 'eternal' image of the past; historical materialism supplies a unique experience with the past."* [Translation available at: https://www.sfu.ca/~andrewf/CONCEPT2.html; last accessed: 6 December 2023].

According to Benjamin, historical materialism wishes to articulate a critical memory of the past as it is revealed in a moment of immediate danger (*ibid.*, no. XI). Benjamin's final note compares planetary time of evolution with human history since several ten thousand years. Under this timeline, a history of modernity is nothing but a tiny fraction of time. Benjamin's final note sounds like an upshot of the recent Anthropocene debate (see Chakrabarty 2015). I am deeply indebted to Benjamin's idea of jumping back into prehistoric times and to make past-present-connectivities as "saturated dialectical constellations". Benjamin's ideas on history are actualised here in part 3 and part 4.

To Habermas, history as a scientific enterprise is ultimately based upon a specific practical *interest of knowledge* (Habermas 1965). To Habermas, there are three basic interests of knowledge: a) *manipulation and mastery* of nature (science, technology), b) *practical self-orientation* within a historical universe (history and hermeneutics), and c) *emancipation* from repressive forces and doctrines (critical theory, psychoanalysis, ethics). According to Habermas, history serves the purpose to provide practical *orientation*. The term "orientation" implicitly refers to present challenges. Habermas makes a strong claim against historical positivism:

> *"Die Welt des tradierten Sinns erschließt sich dem Interpreten nur in dem Maße, als sich dabei zugleich dessen eigene Welt aufklärt" (ibid., 343).* [English translation Ott]: *"The world of traditional meaning is only revealed to the interpreter to the extent that his own world is simultaneously clarified."*

It is claimed that historical understanding is *ipso facto* closely linked to revealing the present. May this claim hold for prehistory as well? In part 4, I will give an affirmative answer.

Habermas' claim might be restated in terms of traditions that we wish to be continued. Any outlook for historical orientation requires a distinction between history and *tradition*. Traditions shape practical self-understanding (MacIntyre 1984). History refers to truth claims and facts, traditions refers to values and commitments (orientation). The past and the present are connected by traditions, not by historical facts (Hobsbawn and Ranger 1992). Facts are stylised for the making of traditions, but should be compatible with history. A tradition continues something X stemming from the past as being of arguable worth to be continued even if most traditions must undergo profound changes. Traditions require critical loyalty as they are full of ambivalences (as, for instance, German nature conser-

66 In no. XII, Benjamin (1940, 700) quotes Nietzsche: *"Wir brauchen Historie, aber wir brauchen sie anders, als sie der verwöhnte Müßiggänger im Garten des Wissens braucht."* [English translation]: *"We need history, but not the way a spoiled loafer in the garden of knowledge needs it."* [Translation available at: https://www.marxists.org/reference/archive/benjamin/1940/history.htm; last accessed: 6 December 2023].

vation).[67] The concept of traditions was often focused on intellectual and artistic traditions (Gadamer 1965). We should broaden the concept in order to make room for practical, technological, economic, and political traditions as well.

How far can a tradition reach back in time? If one recognises the legacy of the axial age (Jaspers 1955) ranging from 800-200 BCE as a decisive moral tradition of contemporary universalism (Habermas 2019), then there can be, in principle, traditions reaching back millennia. Traditions do not only refer to morals but, basically, to any other aspect of life, such as sedentism, gardening, storing food, playing the flute, hunting, *etc*. Are there matters such as, say, "prehistoric traditions"? I wish to defend an affirmative answer. Orientation and traditions do not necessarily diminish with remoteness in time. At first sight, orientation appears to be more evident the closer the past is to the present. The ties that bind the 21st century to previous centuries are stronger than the ties to 2000 BCE. The same holds *prima facie* for historical space, as ancient China, pre-colonial Africa, ancient Siberia, *etc.* appear to be far away. This prejudice has been challenged by Nietzsche, by Horkheimer and Adorno, and by Foucault. These authors conceived *genealogical* history as the presumed Christian genealogy of modern so-called "slave morals" (Nietzsche), the dialectical genealogy of self-destructive forces within enlightenment (Horkheimer and Adorno 1944/1947) and the origins of discourses, institutions, and practices in Foucault's major books. *Origins matter irrespective of temporal distance if the present has been shaped by such origins.* The fatal combination of climatic change and epidemic diseases as described in Harper (2017) came suddenly close to us during the Covid pandemic. A constellation of civic "Roman" tolerance and a multitude of religious doctrines (200 CE) appears to be quite close to our post-modern multi-cultural epoch. *History is shifting closeness.* This might hold for the search of the origins of the Anthropocene and its early material and intellectual markers. If the early Anthropocene hypothesis (Ruddiman 2003; 2007; 2014; Ruddiman *et al.* 2015; Scott 2017; ArchaeoGLOBE Project 2019; Horn and Bergthaller 2019) would hold, then one might closely connect the Neolithic to present times (see part 3). New questions emerge: How might the noble moral legacies of the axial age (Jaspers 1955) be reconciled with prehistoric traditions of struggling for life in changing and often hostile environments? What, if there are strong traditions of surplus, expansion, upscaling,[68] and growth in specific cultures that one wishes to overcome in the presence of sustainability reasons (part 4)? If there might be an "urge for more" alive in many humans (not just in white European males!), it might be hardly possible to be satisfied with "enough" (sufficient, sustainable, sharing, in solidarity). Given the tradition of consumerism (Trentmann 2016) not just in Europe, but also in China and India over the last 500 years, it might be wishful thinking to replace this growth-tradition by mere demands for sufficiency. Does a "more-than-enough" growth orientation, perhaps, belong to lifeworld knowledge? How might the moral legacies of the axial age be reconciled with the matter of fact that both economic life and the Anthropocene emerged in the Neolithic (part 2)? If so,

67 Current social movements wish to unravel how deep-rooted negative traditions, such as colonial, racist, and male-centred mindsets, still exist. Counter cultures search for "better" traditions (Hobsbawn and Ranger 1992). A denial of traditions is not an option for historical thought.

68 A theory of how political units upscale and how such upscaling requires adequate information processes is given by Shin *et al.* (2021). Shin *et al.* suggest "an explanation for the evolutionary divergence between Old and New World polities" (*ibid.*, 2021, 1).

how might a "second axial age" for a "good" Anthropocene be conceived which has to include the global ecological crisis (part 4)?

## 1.9 Antinomies and resolutions

Two *epistemological antinomies* seem to emerge within PA. Epistemological antinomies are situations in which two competing approaches ("positions") hold reasonable claims that contradict each other. Under unresolved antinomies, epistemic splits are likely.

The first antinomy has been outlined in the previous section: *History should provide practical orientation, but it should be scientifically credible (as neutral as possible)*. As we shall see, this first antinomy might be rather easily resolved within TPCL. It is possible to construe "practical arguments from history" if at least one present moral principle is connected to a narrative under the criterion of relevance. One crucial step on the ladder/scaffold constitutes a platform full of fragile *hypotheses of relevance* by which the past and the present are connected. I affirm practical interest in PA which is performed by such hypotheses of relevance. Such hypotheses are claims open for discourse at the interfaces of history, ethics, and politics. Part 4 will point out how past practices might be of relevance for navigating into a good Anthropocene.

The second antinomy is formulated as follows: *PA and archaeology must speculate, but they must not speculate*. On the one hand, archaeology as prehistory has a (transcendental) interest to understand former human ways of life (= culture), while, on the other hand, positive scientific archaeology has reasons to restrict itself to positivism with restricted sets of legitimate hypotheses. The antinomy can be resolved by a reflection upon the concept of speculation.

Some archaeologists may prefer to remain agnostic about theories. They have reasons to fear that theory "detracts from the 'real' business of doing archaeology" (Barrett 2016, 133). Moreover, a positivist may deny the premise on which theoretical ambitions within PA rest. She might say: "Scientific archaeology cannot reach former practical life as such. We can never (fully) understand it. *Ignoramus, ignorabimus*. The best we can do is to organise the materials that stem from a distant human past and add some moderate questions to be answered via credible methods. If we cannot speak scientifically on aspects of a remote human life, it might be better to remain silent than to speculate." There is no "available method to translate material remnants into the original meanings and practices of the agents" (Barrett 2016, 133-137). A positivistic epistemology becomes prescriptive if it demands that archaeologists *should* avoid all kind of speculation. Such prescriptiveness should rely on an analysis of all logical operations within the (broad) concept of speculation before it curtails and prohibits them. What counts as "speculation"?

A resolution of the second antinomy may start with *concessions*[69] which theorists may make in favour of prudent positivism and processual archaeology. Theorists might say: "We concede that the internal struggles within the theoretical camp are worrisome to scientific archaeologists. We concede scientifically based, positivistic archaeology being the empirical core of the discipline. Positivist archaeology can do better without theory as theory formation can do without

69 Concessions to opponents are intended to overcome either-or-controversies, mere standpoint-debates, and false exclusiveness.

empirical research. This constitutes an asymmetry in favour of positivism. Yes, theories often fly too high and sometimes fall hard. Yes, post-modern humanities often lack scientific rigor. Yes, there is much undeclared normativity being smuggled into archaeology via theories. Yes, theory is like perfume. Too much of it smells as if it should cover the stinky smell of bad data.[70] Yes, there is no comprehensive theoretical paradigm in the social sciences. There are competing schools of thought, instead. Moreover, it is doubtful whether there is much progress in theory formation. A sober look onto schools of thought and intellectual fashions casts doubts on the assumption that new theories are always improvements over old ones (as in science). Yes, theoretical investments often look arbitrary. If a sober positivist asks sceptical questions, the answers from the theory-camp will be Babylonian. From the side of archaeological research, the theoretical side looks arbitrary, slobby, murky, messy, lofty, even chaotic. All approaches are essentially contested, but the intellectual climate at the theoretical campsites (conferences) is highly liberal. Despite mutual criticism, almost all approaches can flourish within this mild and playful postmodern climate – at least for some time. How can historians and archaeologists decide between substantial theories and intellectual fashions in the humanities? What should be done with the series of "turns" to be replaced within a few years? How does the operation called "deconstruction" really work? Do theoretical investments entail commitments to specific moral or political beliefs (such as egalitarianism or anarchism)? Quite often, it is argued that theory T "bears the danger" of neo-liberalism, Euro-centrism, neo-colonialism, evolutionism, determinism, *etc*. Such pejorative "-isms" are never transparent, but shape the theoretical discourse.[71] Another problem is theoretical syncretism. There is the impression that there is *too large a distance* between the archaeological record and some "satellite" altitude of theories. Another aspect of this impression states that there are unwarranted "jumps" from empirical data to general theories – and *vice versa* from "*stratospheric philosophical models to cherry-picked examples*" (Robb 2015, 166). Moreover, too many theoretical loop-holes and theoretical investments, but less return of investment are assumed.

> *"By flooding the approved journals and publishers with new 'revolutionary' theories and approaches we trivialized the capacity to truly improve the state of the art" (Ribeiro 2016, 147).*

I fully agree with this verdict.

Things get even worse in theoretical archaeology, if social theory is conceived as "largely a game of make-believe" (Graeber and Wengrow 2021, 21). Graeber and Wengrow confuse the necessity to reduce historical complexity by way of simplifications with the approach of social theory as a "game of make-believe". This approach, as proposed by Walton (1990) in aesthetic and psychological contexts,

---

70 The perfume-metaphor is provided by McNeish, and quoted by Flannery and Marcus (2012, XIII).

71 To make things even worse, the pool of theories is surrounded by muddy waters of folk memory, pseudo-archaeology and ideologies. History is distinct from individual or collective memories. Collective memories have deep roots, but they are mostly partial to particular collectives and their glorious and tragic history, their heroes and villains. Collective memory is distinct from history in several respects (Halbwachs 1985). The former is particular, it is traditional, it is centred, and it is forgetful. It can be both friend and foe of history. It shall be a friend if and only if it is willing to correct itself according to historical standards. The rejection of the pitfalls of folk knowledge in archaeology also presupposes the "state of the art" of an epistemic discipline. "Folk novels" of Vikings, Celts, Goths, early Brahmin culture, *etc.* circulate freely in "esoteric" circles. Historical novels shape ideas about early Christianity, medieval monasteries, revolutionary movements, *etc.*

allows all sophisticated manipulations to make readers, audiences, students, journalists, *etc.* believe that X because the theorist T wants people to believe X for whatever reason. This is clearly a persuasive approach to social theory. Theories, then, are vessels of all kinds of moral and political suggestions about, say, debts (Graeber 2011), inequalities, war and peace, gender, *etc.* If scientifically trained archaeologists become aware that prominent figures in archaeological theory, such as Graeber and Wengrow, see social theory as a "game to make-believe", they are entitled to distrust theoretical suggestions. If they recognise that such figures see themselves as "anarchists", distrust will (and should) increase.

Such states of theoretical affairs are not completely fatal to theory formation in PA, but they may be helpful to resolve the antinomy about speculation. Positivistic archaeologists may and should make concessions as well, saying that scientific-positivistic archaeology endorses interpretation and classification of data, it conceives concepts, and it generates hypotheses, models, and explanatory schemes. Modelling is clearly a theoretical enterprise since there are different kind of models which often have to be integrated.[72] Archaeological records do not just contain artefacts, but are informative about ways of human life and its practices (Overmann and Coolidge 2019, 2). An argument against positivism is about "reification". Reification occurs if social relations are perceived as if they were relations between things. Archaeological positivism may spur (unintentionally) a tendency to reduce past ways of life to collections of things. In archaeology, however, things are not to be seen as passive items. As Wynn (2019, 501) argues, there are "embodied" and "enacted" approaches in archaeology which

> *"emphasize the active, and indissociable, roles that bodies and material objects play in mental life.* [...] *Archaeologists find things. And if prehistoric things played roles in prehistorical thought, then archaeologists are finding actual components of thinking."*

Wynn mentions Malafouris (2013) and his "material engagement theory" in this respect. Things in themselves point to functions and roles that they (might have) had in former minds and practices. Lombard (2019) notes the case of hunting with arrow and bows, while Wadley (2019) analyses the hypothesis that traps and snares were widespread in Palaeolithic times. *Material engagement theory overcomes mere positivism from inside.* Artefacts played roles in practical life.[73] Material engagement theory can be conceived in terms of cognitive psychology (mentalism) or in terms of practice theory which is closer to HM (part 2). Things are not just objects, but must have been practically used. Things refer to reasons why and how they should be used in practical life. A scientific mind *should* concede that archaeology should be more than a vast collection of polished and dated artefacts. This "more" is what makes archaeology history. Positivism can hardly deny this. This "foot into the door" will open the door more widely, since PA lives by guesses, conjectures, analogies, narratives, and abductions. "Death of theory" is not an option. The medical maxim "*dosis facit venenum*" might apply as well as the "perfume" metaphor. To Aristotle, virtues are middle grounds between opposing vices. Theories should be middle ground between an "overdose" of

---

72 A Peircean ontology of models, such as "icons", is given by Kralemann and Lattmann (2013). I would emphasise the relation of the model to an (overcomplex) "original" which the model "represents". Kralemann and Lattmann are right in arguing that models are embedded in a theoretical context.

73 If the houses of Catalhöyük had no doors, but daily life was constituted on the flat rooftops, such life on terraces is of historical interest.

theory and a mere lack of it. They should have explanatory strength, but should not "make believe".

Both camps may agree on the following post-metaphysical concept of speculation. The term "speculation" refers to phenomena being underdetermined by empirical evidence. Speculation means that some phenomenon X seems important and puzzling but remains, for contingent or principled reasons, under-researched or unobservable. The archaeological record is essentially underdetermined (Perreault 2019, chap. 2). Therefore, claims about X cannot be verified empirically. The impossibility of verification is, however, not a sufficient reason to ban all speculative claims from PA. "Speculations" are "surplus" assumptions which are neither strictly presupposed (implied) in basic concepts nor can be derived logically from the empirical findings and data. They are neither conceptual nor empirical truths. *The second antinomy can be resolved, if the logical operations within the concept of speculation are made explicit.* Such operations are different from induction and deduction but might be indispensable for PA. Speculation might be critical guessing, hypothesis formation, interpretation, analogical reasoning, and abductive inferences. A reflective turn (RT) shall not abandon but control speculation. What can be critically controlled, must not be prohibited even if it might sometimes come "out of control". One critical function of a RT is to prevent speculation within PA from getting out of control.

Archaeologists conceding the previous statements cannot oppose the general idea of TPCL. Taking the concessions from both camps together, a meta-epistemological postulate results that resolves the second antinomy about speculation in PA: *We have to outline an epistemology of theoretical investments in PA.* The ladder/scaffold approach is designed as such an epistemology. Both antinomies have been resolved. They do not haunt us any longer. We can start climbing the ladder, scaffolding on each step we take.

## 1.10 Theoretical investments

The concept of theoretical investment (TI) in PA operates as meta-theory. It is silent on the merits and substance of single theories, but it explains the operation of adopting, consuming, and investing specific theories for specific PA purposes.[74] It does not wish to enrich the number of theoretical approaches by adding one more approach. It rather presumes a *meta*-theoretical epistemological capacity to organise and clarify the theoretical side of PA via an analysis of TI. Following Evans (1998), I see Hawkes (1954) as a seminal outline of a meta-theory in PA preluding the TPCL approach. If so, the "ladder" approach is not outdated because specific theoretical approaches (Childe, Giddens, Bourdieu, Foucault, *etc.*) are not located at the meta-theoretical layer, but are substantial theories from which specific TI might be generated. To adopt this ladder model does not ignore the many theoretical moves in PA since the 1950s. If a multitude of social science theories will remain, such a multitude should not repeat itself on the meta-theoretical layer. *Ideally, there should be exactly one meta-theory in PA.* The meta-theory refers to the epistemic practice of making validity claims by theoretical investments in PA.

74 An example of a TI is Furholt *et al.* (2018) as they invest C. S. Peirce's theory of semiotic pragmatism in order to explain the social interactions, practices, and megalithic structures at a specific site. Another example is Arponen *et al.* (2016), who invest Sen's capability approach in order to understand and explain societal life in large Neolithic settlements. One can take practices and capabilities as correlates.

A moderate initial burden falls on the side of the person who makes a TI, since she has to explain why a TI may be helpful to resolve a puzzle in PA. TI cover a broad range from quite trivial assumptions about human dispositions to act to middle-range theories (MRT) and innovative hypotheses that explain specific transformations. TI can be made with respect to singularities, particulars, and universals. A TI will usually be stated in ordinary language and may find different locations within narratives, but it always can be made explicit according to its commitments and entitlements (*sensu* Brandom 1998). In principle, it must be possible to formalise TI by means of logic.

Science is puzzle solving. TI in PA can and should rely on puzzles, questions, hypotheses and interpretations *that originate at the side of positive archaeology*. TI should give answers to real questions. Theorists should listen carefully to field-workers who entertain hypotheses. Theory formation can take a receptive role waiting for questions, puzzles, interpretations and hypotheses to come from the empirical side. What puzzles the positivists should attract theoretical reflection: Which TI might resolve a puzzle? According to Popper, scientists *should* perform risky hypotheses. This prescription holds for PA as well. A hypothesis is not a claim yet. Such a receptive and responsive role of theoretical archaeology may serve well for selection processes among competing theories. Theorists should be able to overlook the spectrum of social theories and to select offers for TI which might resolve puzzles. This is clearly the logic of abduction.

Any TI consumes a specific theory from the natural or social sciences in order to resolve a puzzle. The theory T is applied to the puzzle in order to understand and explain it. Under a generic DPSIR scheme (Ribeiro *et al.* in press), there is much room for TI. TI can occur at any part of the DPSIR scheme. TI in PA presume explanatory power according to standards of scientific rationality. TI are devices to detect the (unverifiable) reasons past humans might have had. TI also allow for hypothetical and conjectural past-past- and past-present-connectivities.

*Theories and TI can fly at different altitudes.* Flying high or low is, as such, neither better nor worse, but different. In biology, a theory within population ecology (such as Volterra curves) flies at a different altitude than the general theory of evolution. The general model of theoretical physics is different from specific theories of magnetism and nuclear energy. Such differences hold true also for PA. Building on the metaphor of altitude, we see a *continuum of theoretical investments and theory formation in archaeology* (Bernbeck 1997; Smith 2011). This array can be organised as different layers (= levels) of theoretical investments (= steps on the ladder). A layer model gives a static picture of theoretical altitudes, while a dynamic perspective would explain, why and how theories can "reach" specific altitudes and how layers can come into contact. The metaphor of altitude is close to the metaphor of a ladder.

The discursive practice of performing TI in PA follows the epistemology and logic of Peircean abduction which is close to the logic of detective investigation, as to be found in the stories of Sherlock Holmes (see Seeboek and Umiker-Seboek 1980 on the Peirce-Holmes relation).[75] Peirce himself initially spoke of "hypothesis", later of "abduction". Abductive reasoning is about guessing. Interferences of *abduction* can result in new insights: If a phenomenon con-

75 From a philosophical perspective, a good volume on semiotic pragmatism is Wirth (2000). The concept of abductive inferences in history is addressed in the contribution by Bonfantini (2000). See Rohr (1993) on abduction and scientific creativity. See also contributions in Pape (1994) on Peircean inferential logic, especially Kapitan.

stitutes a puzzle P, and if TI-x might resolve the puzzling P, there is a reason to entertain TI-x. Perhaps, TI can be expanded to similar P. One can reconcile the Peircean logic of abduction with Popper's epistemology of falsification and corroboration. Any abductive TI counts as (a courageous) hypothesis that is open for rejection and confirmation. In general, science is fair, but merciless: If hypotheses and theories have to be rejected, books, careers and entire schools of thought become outdated. An epistemology of TI is both liberal and rigorous. It gives any credible theory a fair chance to be helpful in understanding and explaining past human behaviour. TI must serve an epistemic purpose. Investments are undertaken in order to receive some "returns of investment". This economic rule also holds, *mutatis mutandis,* for TI. Returns of investments must be paid in the currency of understanding and explanation. If a historian or archaeologist undertakes some TI, she should be ready to present some expectations on presumptive returns. Expectations are reasons why a specific theory should be consumed.

The scope of theories in the social sciences and humanities is dubbed "*pool of theories*". Single theories are assets within this large pool that are candidates for TI. Within this pool, we list the capability approach, discourse-power theory, semiotics,[76] phenomenology of lifeworld structures, historical materialism, evolutionism, habitus formation, cultural phenomenology, behavioural economy, sociobiology, postcolonial studies, theories of mechanic and organic solidarity, consumption theory, structuralism, social constructivism, postmodernism, gender theories, theories of "the" political, theories of functional differentiation, game theory, *etc. This large pool of theories is a portfolio of explanatory assets.* Most theories have been originally construed for present social science purposes and have been later applied to PA. Such application needs some additional premises why such TI are helpful to understand and explain some historical phenomena.

To repeat the ambition of the TPCL approach: It presumes not just to be one theory in the pool, but it presumes to teach how to move within the pool. Facing the pool of theories, the danger of epistemological anarchism looms with the motto: "Anything goes!" (Feyerabend 1975/1993, 1). While Popper argued how good scientists *should* behave, Feyerabend pointed at how many scientists *really* behave within specific epistemic communities: opportunistic, tricky, politically engaged, strategic, persuasive, *etc.* Popper was an idealist about science, Feyerabend was an ironical realist about it. From a realistic point of view, the pool of presumptive TI will further expand and we will have to live within this messy world of TI in PA. From a critical epistemological point, however, I do not wish to see an ever-expanding pool of theories. In philosophy, there was the idea to eliminate pseudo-problems to save the scarce resource of intellectual attention for "real" problems. Within the social sciences, theories are not just to be multiplied, but also to be selected. Let us be more selective within PA and exclude "bad" theories from the pool!

The TI approach adopts a functional (Hegel: "holistic") approach toward single concepts. On the one hand, concepts (terms) are embedded in theories and they fulfil specific functions within theories. One can isolate concepts by way of definition, but must keep their theoretical functions in mind. In contrast, many concepts remain part of ordinary language as well. Historical narratives cannot do without ordinary language. The ideal of a perfect scientific language within PA

76 A Peircean approach would hold that archaic humans lived in a meaningful universe of signs, divided in icons, indexes, and symbols. Icons can be distinguished in images, diagrams and metaphors.

is an indispensable illusion. It is alive in any definition, but vaporises in the multitude of stipulations, associations, suggestions, metaphorical use, *etc*.

The following sections intend to conceive an epistemological stage-model of TI in PA. Let us remain in the logic of this "ladder" metaphor, at least for a while. There is a leeway of choice how high archaeologists may climb the ladder. Any archaeologist and any historian in PA is free to take another step forward or to step back. One can make new TI or withdraw older ones. All the conceptual reflections about presuppositions and types of PA must find re-entry points in steps on the ladder. Such re-entry points are open for further refinement. The more sets of concepts and presumptive TI are addressed, the more the ladder turns into a huge theoretical *scaffold* being worked on at different altitudes.

## 1.11 Scaffolding on a ladder, stepwise

We are now in a position to suppose the epistemological ladder (*sensu* Hawkes 1954) which gradually becomes a theoretical scaffold (*sensu* Chapmann and Wylie 2016). Taking a next step on the ladder suggests "climbing upwards". There are remarks on theoretical investments (TI) of a specific set of concepts (SC) on each step that one takes. These remarks are incomplete and serve the purpose to explain what is conceptually at stake on each step. Of course, it often makes good epistemic sense to climb downwards in order to reflect upon more basis presuppositions. Thus, one can move on the ladder in both directions. The ladder is, metaphorically speaking, the backbone, while scaffolding fleshes out conceptual details. In a "big picture", the ladder is dominant, scaffolding is more important for detailed conceptual analysis.

I wish to stabilise the ladder in solid empirical "positive" ground. We assume a hard kernel of positivist archaeology being performed at excavation sites, in laboratories, archives, exhibitions, *etc*. The term "positive" refers to what is given empirically as the archaeological record. The "givens" stem from the past and have been produced by archaeological practices. The epistemic state of the art can be taken as the ground base of the ladder: training in the field, practices at excavation sites, familiarity with timelines and PA in world regions (Olszewski 2020; Jockenhövel 2009). Evidential reasoning starts from the records (Chapmann and Wylie 2016) by collecting and construing findings as evidence. Chapman and Wylie (2016) show how old evidence can find its way into new interpretations. In PA, there must be validity claims as "X counts as evidence for hypothesis H" which can be refined and rejected. The term "evidence" is a concept that bridges the gaps between material findings and hypotheses. Evidence means "giving some empirical support for H without confirming H". If some evidence supports the denial of H, it is counter-evidence.

### 1.11.1 Basic anthropology

PA studies human beings. Therefore, it is full of implicit anthropological assumptions. Very roughly, one can distinguish biological and philosophical approaches in anthropology. Both approaches differ from so-called "*Menschenbilder*" which are at the core of religious and political doctrines (socialist, liberal, Christian, Islamic, *etc*.). An epistemic strategy to reconcile biological and philosophical approaches in anthropology is to start at the biological side and move forward stepwise to the symbolic and ethical sides of life. Cognitive archaeology deals with the origins of mind and culture (see contributions in Overmann and Coolidge 2019). Human beings have been mindful and lingual beings since Palaeolithic times.

Presumptive generic dispositions of human behaviour are debated in a bulk of sociobiological literature: fear of pain and death, search for pleasure, basic needs, sexual desire, tool making, speech, cooperation, limited altruism, moral sentiments, loss aversion, aspiration to comfort and convenience, aggressive and destructive potentials, dominance, competition and the like. Such dispositions are inclinations of beings that have to struggle to stay alive and to proliferate. *Struggling* is what human beings, as all allotrophic animals, have to do. "Struggling for survival" (Charles Darwin) can be, indeed, regarded as part of the human predicament. Struggling in prehistoric times is mostly foraging. Successful struggling is adaptive on the individual and collective level. Adaptiveness opposes extinction since it implies proliferation of fertile descendants. Such embodied struggling for survival is not mere combat and fight, but it includes cooperation, sharing, caring, joy of life, play, breaks, festivities, *etc*. To Darwin, struggling means to be alert, active, busy, attentive, inventive, *etc*.[77] Struggling does not imply many working hours per day (Sahlins 1972/2004).

The original social unit is the "horde" (= "band") as an extended family and home-base unit (McCaffree 2022). The highly active role of women in mating, foraging, caring, *etc.* is without doubt (Tanner 1981). Nursing is just one female activity amongst many. Food supply of early humans largely stemmed from plants being gathered by women. Females were probably active in choosing males according to expectations of how individual males might behave in the longer run. With some likeliness, trustworthiness and reliability have been more important for females than physical strength. Nursing is a kind of struggling for the sake of descendants. In part 2, I hypothesise an active role of women in the process of sedentism. Human traits are alloparenting, allohunting, alloforaging and allodefense (McCaffree 2022, 4). Thus, humans are highly social beings who interact with each other. If they are not philosophical solipsists, humans usually suppose that there are other humans around.

Struggling is performed within an embodied "*Gestalt*". Since Herder,[78] the *upright bipedal structure* has been recognised as a decisive anthropological constitution. This generic structure is unique among mammalians. It liberates the hands, making agency possible. It opens the mouth for fine-grained articulation.[79] Humans are neither grazing beings nor do they catch prey by teeth, but they rather put food by hand into the mouth. The functional differentiation between feet and hands (with fingers and two thumbs) is a basic requirement for a combination of gesture and voice. Moreover, this differentiation allows humans to point with fingers to objects (and other people), showing something to someone (Tallis 2003). The important role of this bodily shaped "deixis" in order to identify objects in a commonly shared world is hard to deny. The different roles of thumbs and pointing fingers contribute to becoming human. Hands can

---

77 Inventiveness occurs in animals and is rewarded by evolution. See contributions in Weber and Depew (2003).

78 The "classical" book is *Ideen zu einer Philosophie der Geschichte der Menschheit* (Herder 1784/1976). It has been reprinted in different editions.

79 An anthropology based on hand and word has been outlined by Leroi-Gurhan (1980). A recent approach is Neuweiler (2008). An outline of Habermasian lingual anthropology is found in Hendlin and Ott (2016).

be used for clapping and generating rhythms. Humans can feel the beat. Humans can also shake hands.

The bipedal figure is responsible for the fact that infants must be born at a highly unusual early state, needing nursing for years. This fact provides infants with many stimuli and requires specific breeding structures which, as a side-effect, might make old age (beyond 40 years) adaptive for humans. When elders care for the young, adults can perform foraging. Thus, groups of relatives ("kin") take on different roles in material and symbolic reproduction. Herder also mentions kissing, suggesting that humans can mate "eye to eye". In the Hebrew Bible, heterosexual sexual intercourse is said to be "recognising each other" (as in Genesis 4:1).

Humans are not fixed into a specific environmental niche. Gehlen's concept of "*Mängelwesen*" points to a theory of niche-construction.[80] This concept does not point to a deficit, but to the capability to occupy many environments. This striking capability makes archaeology a global affair. Even if there have been strong national and colonial traditions in PA, the constitution of archaeological projects can be done by any archaeologist at any interesting site. The upright position of the head is essential for lingual articulation, i.e. speech (Lenneberg 1967).

### 1.11.2 Constitution of empirical research and data mining

PA must select topics, time scales, and sites. Reasons to select and prospect sites for fieldwork might be improved by new technologies such as remote sensing. A must outline an explorative research design, define research objectives, and make preliminary hypotheses.

Fieldwork is performed according to technical and ethical standards. Archaeology looks and digs for "findings". Findings are material human-made remnants from the past, such as settlements, piles, burial mounds, ports, cave paintings, figurines, hoards, bones, *etc*.

The supposition of "findings" is a *selection* of human-made items from mere natural stuff (soil, dirt, stone, and peat). This implies a distinction between mere natural objects and artefacts which are constitutive for archaeology. Without this distinction, archaeology is a pointless non-starter. A paradigm statement is: "I claim to detect human activity in X." It is not just a stone, but a lithic tool. "Traces" of human hands and minds are "human fingerprints". This supposition is reminiscent of Kant's argument that a person who walks on the beach and suddenly detects a regular triangle in the sand, *must* assume that the triangle has been made by a human being since geometric structures do not originate randomly. A megalithic structure is different from an assemblage of stones being placed here and there by natural forces. Probably, there is more anthropology in the supposition of "detecting human fingerprints" than one may believe.

There was a span of time between the practical use of artefacts and their discovery by archaeologists. Within this timespan, these objects were modified by surroundings and by natural forces, for example, pressure, weathering, or corrosion. Thus, there must be some "formation theory" (Schiffer 1987; Shott 1998). Formation theory explains what might have happened to artefact A between the period of its use and the moment of becoming an archaeological artefact. Formation theory makes some past-present-connectivity. As we shall see, there are

80 See Gehlen (1944): *Der Mensch. Seine Natur und seine Stellung in der Welt.* 3rd ed. I abstract away the repugnant political role of Gehlen under National Socialism.

reasons to distinguish formation theory from middle-range theory (see below). Taphonomy is formation theory as applied to organisms.

Positivistic archaeology has some presuppositions: a) time, b) space, c) matter and materials, d) use. If there is dating, there must be time. If there are sites, there must be space. If there are pots made of clay, there must be matter. If things are found that are broken or shaped by a formation process, it makes sense to fix them to a presumed former "original" state. Restoration and making copies presuppose ideas about "originals". This supposition remains true even if one assumes fragmentation practices according to Chapman (2000).

Excavations are performed at locations, called "sites". A site is a specific location for archaeological fieldwork. The performance of excavations reveals the practical side of archaeological positivism, including dealing with instruments and rules of precaution and care. I take settlements and burial grounds as paradigm cases for sites. Sites are locations for findings. Findings can be disappointing ("not worth the efforts") or spectacular.

Findings are measured by different techniques. Observed and measured findings become data. Strictly speaking, data represents results from measurements. The methods and techniques of producing data are part of archaeological training. Material remnants of past human lives are mined, dated, physically analysed, polished, sometimes fixed, and stored. Remnants are made from specific materials. Here, archaeology works close to material sciences. Positivism supposes that materials played a functional role in human life, but it focusses on the materials themselves: size, weight, age, *etc*. This is the realm of "*causa materialis*". If one finds timber in houses which can be dated, tree-ring analysis can imply some hypotheses about forest cover and forestry at different times and locations. Where did the timber come from? Timber supposes logging and one can perform experimental archaeology by measuring how long it might have taken to cut a tree with a stone axe. But even in the study of materials, theoretical ideas stemming from the humanities enter PA. Martinón-Torres and Killick (2014, 5) recollect Cyril Stanley Smith who associated the use of materials with an "extending sensuous engagement" which included colours and sounds. Thus, positivism can become speculative.

On the scientific-positivistic-empirical-material side of archaeology, we find research and data mining at different sites, we find refined dating methods, restitution of fragmentary remnants, inventories, collections, and archives. Findings can be arranged as exhibitions that disseminate PA and archaeology to the broader public. This positive side represents the actual and solid disciplinary work according to established and innovative scientific methods. It constitutes a growing database. Advances in computing result in "big data" and new ways to connect vast amounts of data by algorithms (Bevan 2015; Kristiansen 2014).

On this positivistic side, we see firm and impressive results and we register slow but steady progress over decades. One can regard this material dimension as the hard and successful core of archaeology (Kristiansen 2014; 2022). The history of positivistic archaeology, then, can be written as the development "of techniques of recovery and material analysis" (Barrett 2016, 133). Sequencing of ancient DNA, pollen analysis, and isotope analysis would be paradigm examples of scientific progress. Research on diets, diseases, plants, and bones explores the many ways of excavating, identifying ("Is this a grain of millet or an ant-head?"), preparing and dating materials. The "*Handbook of Archaeological Sciences*" (Pollard *et al.*, 2023) presents the state of the art in scientific archaeology. This highly impressive collection on the states of the art in various scientific disciplines (dating, bioarchaeology, archaeogenetics, materials analysis, remote sensing, and computational approaches) supposes that scientific approaches are essentially needed to pursue historical questions (Gosden 2023, xvii). Thus, scientific approaches are, ultimately, embedded in a historical enterprise, but they provide solid empirical ground for this conjectural enterprise. The epistemological dialectic reveals that ancillary disciplines can take the lead.

### 1.11.3 Set of classificatory concepts

Findings must be identified and classified. One identifies the *location*: X that is found at site S. *Quantities* are also identified: N numbers of some artefacts at S over time t. Findings are measured according to properties. *Dating* is a decisive measurement in PA: X being y years old. There are many suppositions in dating with reference to time. PA supposes a chronology as an implicit logic of time-related concepts. Time-scales are separated into periods, epochs, or ages. There is importance in dating because it allows us to constitute relations of "before and after". If X occurred after Y, X cannot have caused Y. I see chronology as part of the set of classifications, but one may give it a separate status. Relations are: X found "in", "together with", "outside of" Y (such as houses, graves, temples, enclosures, hoards). Such relations imply the need for formation theory. Classification supposes "classes" of artefacts. A bed is not a boat, and a spade is not a spoon.

If similar iconic patterns in potteries and figurines are discovered at different sites, archaeologists infer cultural networks within larger areas. Tokens represent cultural types. If so, a set of *typological* concepts is needed: "funnel beakers", LBK, *etc*. Classifying and typing are different epistemic practices. I focus on classifications because "classes" of artefacts refer to practices. Hawkes' layer of technologies can be distinguished into material artefacts and practices. If materials are classified as tokens of specific types of tools and devices (axe, dagger), the door to human agency and practices opens. What have things been good for in a daily practical prehistoric life?

### 1.11.4 Analysis of presuppositions

The analysis of *presuppositions* of empirical findings is called "*inferential pragmatism*". Brandom's (1998) inferentialism can serve as the reconstructive logic of the many presuppositions that are present in positivistic, material-based, field-work archaeology. Inferentialism is at the methodical core of TPCL. Positivism presents artefacts, *while inferential pragmatism makes inferences from artefacts to human practices and, further, even to symbolic spheres of life*. We can often add to such inferences: "since otherwise p would have been impossible". These are arguments "*per impossibilia*". If x is a necessary condition for p and if there is p, then there must have been x. A related topic is about "requirements". The existence of X requires Y. If X, an inference to Y is valid. The same holds if Y requires Z. Experimental archaeology also enables inferential reasoning.

There might be many other quite trivial suppositions: If there are pots, there must have been pottery. If there are arrowheads, there must have been bows. If there were children, there was sexual life. If there are animal bones, there was meat eating. Trivial suppositions are lifeworld convictions which can be taken for certain. Even scientists would not believe that they can be falsified. This makes trivial suppositions philosophically interesting, as they claim the status of certainty[81] and lifeworld knowledge.

Settlements presuppose sedentism. Population grew and declined at sites. There was migration and mobility. Settlements are internally structured. There are enclosures, ways, houses, yards, perhaps gardens, and townhalls. There must have been supply systems, especially for food and freshwater. There might be specific quarters for specific professional craftmanship. A special interest can be devoted to waste, since one can learn much about economic and cultural life (Thompson 1979/2017) and social inequality if one knows what counted as waste for specific agents (part 4). Some settlements display a more hierarchical order (with palaces, temples, *etc.*), while others look as if there was a more egalitarian way of life, as in some Eastern European mega-sites. Settlements were often attacked, occupied, plundered, left, abandoned, or re-founded at different locations. There must have been social arrangements in terms of "neighbourhood" (as we dub it) and collective decision-making that we dub as "politics". PA might also be interested in the possibility of prisons which refer to ways a collective might have punished forbidden actions. Settlements refer to daily life and taskscapes.

Settlements consist of houses. Houses imply dwelling. If one wishes to make an inference from the number of houses to the number of people living in a village, one has to assume the average number of people living in a house of a given size. Such assumptions are speculative, because no material analysis of housing can derive the precise number of inhabitants. If one could count "beds", one has to assume how many persons shared one bed. Can the arrangement of houses tell us whether there was a class of unfree persons ("slaves") in Bronze Age Scandinavia (Mikkelsen 2020)? Such questions take the inferential steps from materials to daily human life, to human agency, to capabilities, and to institutions. Beds are interesting since beds presuppose that human beings have to sleep on a regular basis, but beds also refer to sexual life, care for sick persons, kinship, dreams, symbols, and archetypes.

Some presuppositions are trivial: If there are burial sites, past humans were as mortal as we are. This trivial supposition, however, opens the door on how past humans coped with the predicament of mortality.[82] This points to the most speculative step on the ladder: religion. If there are megalithic structures or large city walls, there must have been institutions of control over labour. Some evidence in skeletons indicates violence. If there was violence, past humans were not perfectly peaceful. Burial goods and burials strongly indicate belief in an afterlife. Such an ongoing chain of presuppositions that are coiled by lifeworld *and* historical knowledge terminates in hypothetical assumptions about how past *daily life* was performed. How were the "*taskscapes*" determined for different people (children,[83] women, elderly persons)? It is interesting to know whether there were toys in a given archaic culture. *"Daily life" is itself a theoretical investment.* We may assume that daily life was mainly practical life with a focus on material reproduction,

81 See Wittgenstein's *On Certainty* (1969). Certainties mean that we cannot even imagine reasons why it could be otherwise.

82 Perhaps, vulnerability and mortality are traits in our lifeworld which may have ethical implications even for our present age. In any case, we are united with previous humans under the knowledge of mortality and finitude.

83 Smith (2006) shows that in Huron societies of the northeast woodlands of North America, children participated in intergenerational networks of teaching and learning interaction. Our moral aversion against child labour should be reconciled with the many teaching practices which made children "helpers" within households.

foraging, and face-to-face interaction. Daily life is full of routines and customs. It makes sense to draw a distinction between ordinary daily life and extraordinary events we dub as "festivities" or "celebrations". If we draw such distinctions, we may speculate about reasons for feasting: *rites de passage,* demonstration of wealth, redistribution of surplus, worshipping. We assume that the ordinary-extraordinary divide was perceived on the emic side. By way of analogy: We assume that people recognise that carnivals are not the usual state of affairs. It is, then, an inferential conceptual truth that in daily life there is no feasting in permanence.

Some inferences might be misleading. If there was snuffling and smoking of psychoactive plants in past cultures, we may speculate about motives and occasions of such consumption. If there was cannabis in 1800 BCE in the Baltic region, then, as some say, there must have been rituals and ceremonies. This claim entails the supposition that earlier humans consumed psychoactive drugs only at rituals. This supposition might be false since there is the possibility that humans consumed drugs at many different occasions or "just for fun". (Nobody would infer today from the existence of drugs to a spiritual renaissance of Europe). Thus, inferential reasoning is not self-evident, but might be biased. In logic, we try to identify "*non sequiturs*". Inferential reasoning is sound as a method, but not immune against fallacious reasoning.

### 1.11.5 Artefacts

Artefacts that are classified as types of artefacts are present remnants from the human past, some "*Zeug*" (Heidegger 1927/1979). Artefacts have been "used" (in a broad sense). Typing and classification identify something as something for human purposes. Finding X is classified as A (token of a type), for instance as a door, wheel, vessel, sword, plough, pot, figurine, boat, comb, *etc.* PA must suppose the usefulness of artefacts to humans (Overman and Coolidge 2019). Artefacts require agency while agency produces artefacts.

An understanding of remnants with respect to human practices can be performed according to the method of "*Daseinshermeneutik*" (Heidegger 1927/1979). The word is hard to translate, but the concept means to hypothesise daily practices, work, customs, taskscapes, lingual speech acts, technologies and other aspects of specific "ways of human life". The concept "ways of human life" may emphasise the particularities of collectives, but it does not exclude commonalities and similarities among different ways of life. *Artefacts are indicators for ways of life.* If archaeologists agree, they can climb the ladder further, interpreting artefacts as indicators of ways of life. If they *must* agree, they *should* climb further.

To interpret (Latin: "*interpretari*") means to add some hypothetical assumptions not being entailed in the findings. Hypotheses can be more or less trivial or far-reaching. Far-reaching hypotheses come at the price of speculation. If so, even positivists must reflect on the degree of speculation they might accept in hypotheses. Examples for interpretation are many: If X (pottery, textiles), then y (skills to make them)", "X indicates y (prestige, wealth)", "X must have counted as y (precious)", "X must have served as y (within a ritual)", "X was meaningful/important (in festivities)", or "Fortifications are likely at strategic places", "Fire pit rows may have delineated borders", *etc.* Some steps from artefacts to practices look trivial, while other remain puzzling and doubtful, for example, hoarding.

To wrap up: Findings must be classified as specific artefacts which allow for inferential reasoning and should be interpreted as indicators of ways of life.

These epistemic practices of classification, inferential reasoning, and interpreting indicators bridge the gap from artefacts to past ways of live. They constitute PA as history.

### 1.11.6 Agencies and practices

PA must presuppose human *agency*. We claim that *categories of agency are epistemically necessary* to PA. The concept of agency is not isolated, but part of a cluster of concepts. Agency, intentionality, purposiveness, and responsibility are conceptual correlates needed to understand practical life (Ribeiro 2022). Agency supposes intentionality and purposiveness (Gewirth 1978). It also supposes evaluations (Graeber 2001). Actions are at the same time individual and social (Ribeiro 2021). It does not make much sense to ask whether an action was an individual or a social one. If action and practices refer to values, the difference between "good" and "bad" emerges. Humans as agents are valuable beings that are able to admire, to appreciate, to refuse, *etc*. The ways humans act reveals the values they hold. Purposiveness means that agents can choose means to reach their goals (= objectives). They can consider whether means are effective or not and they can reflect upon chosen goals if they are hard to reach (or too costly). Agency points to mean-end-rationality as one kind of agency beside others. A theory of instrumental action is implied in purposiveness: A person P has an intention I to reach an objective O. If so, P must consider means M. Formula: $P(i): M \rightarrow O$. Instrumental action supposes some kind of cleverness and prudence on the emic side. However, theories of action should not be restricted to mean-end-rationality or to economic conceptions of rational choice. Weber (1921/1972, 12-13) distinguished the ideal types of instrumental, emotional, traditional, and value-based action, adding that actions are always social ones. Combinations of types of action will be likely in real life.

A well-known philosophy of agency is *pragmatism* (historical overview in Schneider 1963, chap. VIII and IX; James 1907/1975; see also Preucel 2006). Within pragmatism, one can distinguish between *single actions* (agency) and *collective practices*. Theories of collective practices are close to theories of society which emphasise the routines of daily life, customs, rituals, institutions, and the importance of social cohesion.

Pragmatism claims the primacy of common practical life among human beings. In the first instance, humans do not create religious world-views, but have to cope with mundane challenges on a daily basis.[84] Agency is realised, first, in daily life, and, second, in exceptional situations. Agency constitutes not just single isolated actions, but also common customs and practices.[85] Customs can be seen as proto-institutions.

Agency should not be confused with absolute freedom which is not a historical concept. Agency, however, supposes alternative courses of action and the possibility to choose between them. To humans, there is always choice ahead due to the structure and functions of the human brain, being a forward-looking

84 As burial goods indicate, assumptions about an afterlife are shaped by the mundane way of life. Burial goods point in two directions: a) to religious beliefs and b) to mundane practices in as far as religious beliefs about the afterlife mirror the real life. See contributions in Guratzsch and Carnap-Bornheim (2005). Literature is abundant.

85 The differences between single actions and practices has been analysed by Friedrich Kaulbach (1982) in his *Einführung in die Philosophie des Handelns*. Philosophies of "Praxis" are to be found in Hegel, Marx, Gadamer, Castoriadis, and other philosophers. See also Ott (2017b).

memory (Neuweiler 2008). Struggling for life supposes *agency* and *choice*. *Choice* can be spontaneous or considered. Considered choice can be defined as decision. Choice can be individual or common. "Shall we open the pit? Shall we embark in bad weather? Shall we fight? Shall we build a palisade? Shall we work another hour?" Conceptually, choice implies decision-making. "Who decides" is an empirical question for PA and a societal question on the emic side.

Choice is never completely free nor completely determined. A choice is something one is faced with. Choice comes *a fronte*. One has to make a choice in a situation which might be dangerous, uncertain, wicked, *etc*. Even if there are reasons to dislike the situation, choice is often inescapable, as in "*fight or flight*" situations. "*Duck-and-cover*" and "*wait-and-see*" strategies also count as choice. Agents will, for instance, opt for a "lesser evil". If concepts, such as "risk", "evil", "change", "gain", and "uncertainty" belong to human mind-maps, then humans can assess courses of actions according to consequences. Choice is conceptually tied to decision-making.

Humans interpret situations as if choice matters. Some neuro-biologists may see this as a transcendental illusion by which the brain deceives the mind (Ramachandran 2003). Recent neuronal determinism rests upon the premise that the human brain must be seen purely as a usual object of science: a natural entity processing via neurons under causal laws. This perspective is misleading (Tallis 2011). *To us*, the brain is a processing memory that continually checks and weighs, assesses and balances, and compares and judges options of how to make a choice. Even from a scientific perspective, analyses of how human brains operate do not support causal determinism (Neuweiler 2008). It is simplistic to argue that brains, as all physical entities, underly causal laws. I leave aside neuro-biological speculation about a self-deceptive brain and simply suppose that humans (must) experience their "being-in-the-world" (Heidegger) under the concept of choice. Choice and agency are correlative concepts, interpreting each other. Most often, choice occurs under specific conditions, constraints, risks, uncertainty of outcome, and divergent incentives. The more constraints, the less choice. Suicide is the choice of last resort. Agency is never to be understood in isolation and privacy.

Humans are neither completely free nor completely determined. There are always constraints as well as enabling conditions, barriers as well as leeway. Humans act under multiple constraints, but they also face options, alternatives, and choice. Agents know that there are other agents and non-agents (materials) around. This remains true if an emic ontology includes non-human agents, for example, demons, witchcraft, goddesses, and wise animals. Coordination of actions is a primary function of speech. Such coordination becomes more complex as communities enlarge and a division of labour increases (part 2). Another assumption states that it must have been possible to communicate reasons for choice and action to other humans, whatever the social relation. Agency is connected to reasons, and reasons are present in speech acts. Among humans, there is possibility of reasonable (collective) decision-making. The concept of agency implies that agents could have acted otherwise.

An important conceptual corollary to agency is "*capability*". Agents have some capabilities to perform specific actions and practices. An agent P is able to perform an action A according to her capabilities C at time t. Formula: C-P-A-(t). This formula opens option to negations: P is not capable of doing A in t. Not all people were capable of doing A. All people were not capable of doing A. C is a requirement for doing A. Thus, archaeologists have reasons to speculate about capabilities. Capabilities also refer to collective agency. It makes good sense to regard "collective capabilities" (for example the capability to erect megalithic structures). Arponen and colleagues applied Sen's capability approach to archaeology (Arponen *et al.* 2016). Such application is important for debates about elites, inequalities, ranks, status, conquest and defence, hierarchy versus heterarchy, *etc.*

Note, that some human capabilities are missing in Nussbaum's (2000; 2014, 205-206) famous 10-point list because the capabilities on the list have been preselected from a contemporary moral point of view. Only morally decent capabilities count in Nussbaum's theory of justice. Capabilities without moral value (such as capabilities to fight, to hunt, to tolerate pain, to ambush, to organise an army, to drink much alcohol, to give birth to many children, *etc.*) do not find a place on the list even if they might have played important roles in prehistoric and ancient times. If so, PA needs a set of capability concepts which are not restricted to capabilities that "we" appreciate morally today.

Capabilities are complex compounds of "*knowing that*" and "*knowing how*". Know-how refers to learning and training. If a person teaches knowledge, the social roles of teacher and pupil emerge. Know-how is apparent, when we know: "how to find eatables", "how to prepare or store food", "how to throw a spear", "how to make a basket", "how to keep a fire burning", "how to repair something broken", "how to trap an animal", *etc.* Practical knowledge is richly textured, as gardening, breeding, tilling, counting, hunting, shipping, *etc.* One can learn how to use an arrow as a one-string-guitar, as the !Kung do. Pathfinders have capabilities to move to distant and remote, even secret places. Archaeologists cannot observe capabilities directly but they can interpret artefacts as indicators for capabilities: If there are large megalithic structures, some humans ("chiefs") must have been capable to organise and control labour forces. If there are remnants from mammoth and deer, humans were capable of hunting such game. If there was shipping trade, some humans must have been capable of navigation. If there was beer, some humans must have been capable to brew it. If there are pantries, some humans must be capable to store food. And if there are no scriptures, no one was capable of writing them. Abductive interferences pave the way to past capabilities. Such abduction, however, may face limits. How refined were the capabilities for meal preparation? Was there a difference between food and dishes? In any case, we should see the capability set of archaic humans as richly textured. But differences in capabilities may have also played a role in the division of labour, since capabilities are not usually equally dispersed among humans. We may assume different talents and individuals who are more gifted than others in some respects.

Some capabilities refer to other people. There are capabilities to rule over other people by persuasion or authority. *Power* (in a strict and narrow sense) means that the choice of A binds the will of B (Max Weber). If power continues over time, there is *domination*. *Violence* is immediate embodied power. Power and domination constitute another set of concepts that emerges out of the agency-choice-capability-set. We will take a closer look at this "power" set below. If one expands the concept of power, there is power everywhere in societal life. If so, the expanded concept of power loses moral significance. Power always – so what?

Theories of agency imply interaction with other persons. PA also supposes that humans live a social life among other humans whatever the conceptual units (families, hordes, bands, clans, villages, tribes, neighbourhoods, "oikos"). Presuppositions of *inter*action are essential for PA. *Practices* are recurrent actions in a daily life that are "meaningful" to the agents (Kaulbach 1982). Values within practices indicate "goodness" of practices from the perspective of participants. People can succeed or fail in maintaining practices. The concept of "praxis" is important to all Aristotelian-Hegelian philosophies of social practices. It is also crucial to HM (part 2). We take practices to be an important concept which is implied in the concepts of agency and capability. Practices and capabilities are correlates. If agency is performed under conditions of an ordinary daily life, then there must be customs and routines. Ordinary daily life is full of practices. In prehistoric times, "food related activities dominated everyday life" (Earle *et al.* 2022, 16). We assume that this holds not just for Bronze Age Denmark but also generally. Practices are "taskscapes" (Ingold 2017) that must be organised (Rajalla and Mills 2017). Cooking and cleaning (Hannah Arendt: "work" as opposed to production) are daily tasks.

The set of agency concepts implies that humans have *reasons to act*. It is in line with Graeber's and Wengrow's (2021, 24) objective to restore "our ancestors to their full humanity" to see past humans as reasonable agents. Beliefs count as reasons to people who hold them. Reasons are embedded in complex belief systems and ontologies ("world views"). There are reasons for "belief-embedded prudence" (Evans-Pritchard 1937/1976). If so, past humans must have had some ontologies. Ontologies denote what entities exist and what events may happen. All humans must make assumptions on what there is (Quine 1948).[86] Ontologies can widely differ among human collectives in a way that causes epistemological and even ethical problems. Can we step out of our modern, scientifically shaped ontology? Are we committed to respect non-Western ontologies as such ("recognitional justice")? Are there reasons for us to believe in spirits, as Sahlins (2022) seems to suggest? Can we moderns deliberately choose to re-enchant the universe and become neo-pagans and shamans? I shall address some of these topics in part 4 because they are located at the intersection of epistemology and ethics.

### 1.11.7 Synthetic correlations

Agency is always specific and should be specified *as* production, labour, leisure, feasting, hunting, worshipping, fighting, enslaving, hoarding, sacrificing, *etc.* Artefacts as such are "abstract", whereas they become "concrete" if they are classified and taken as representatives (material correlates) of practices such as cutting, baking, storing, sleeping, fighting, worshipping, *etc.* A hammer implies a human hammering upon something. An arrow implies targeting at something. An arrow can become the starting point of a psychological investigation on the mindsets of bow-hunters (Lombard 2019). There are artefacts that are used in rituals and worshipping. There is no such thing as a single isolated device. Rather, any single device exists as such within an ensemble of intertwined devices, such as in the devices within a domestic mode of production.

"Synthetic" correlations between artefacts and agencies are a robust conceptual core of PA. The logical concept of correlation means that one cannot conceive A without having B close in one's mind – and *vice versa*.[87] Artefacts can be classified and humans are full-fledged agents. If so, artefacts and agencies can be correlated. By doing so, one can suppose specific kinds of actions and capa-

86 If one really believes in the possibility of hell, one has very strong reasons to avoid ending up in hell eternally, as the logic of Pascal's bet tells us.

87 Correlations are an instance of intrinsic relations. The philosophical debate about such relations is reconstructed in Horstmann (1984).

bilities being performed and displayed by archaic humans. If, for example, there are knifes in hunter societies, there must have been the practice of butchering animals (mammals, birds, fish). The bloody practice of butchering implies the discoveries of inner organs such as kidney, liver, and gut. Handling inner organs, butchers may have speculated about their "functions". Another bloody practice, warfare, may have detected similarities between animal and human organs.

The following list that correlates artefacts with kinds of actions and capabilities might look boring to archaeologists, but shall illustrate how richly textured practical prehistoric life was:

- Knife → cutting something apart, making pieces, butchering a killed animal
- Spear → throwing at prey or foes, hunting and fighting, perhaps competitive games
- Pottery → cooking, storing
- Baskets → picking, transporting
- Alcoholic beverages → drinking, getting drunk, social bonding, "buddies"
- Figurines → worshipping, ornaments, decoration, "symbols", aesthetics
- Nets → fishing, bird catching, aquacultures
- Traps, snares → trapping, deceptive ambush ("cheating")
- Combs → combing hairs, hairdressing
- Flutes, drums → making music, dancing, clapping hands, singing
- Pathways → travelling, migration, transport
- Textiles → dressing, undressing
- Paintings → painting, symbolising, imagination
- Houses → dwelling, "being at home", neighbourhood
- Beds → sleeping, loving, dreaming
- Settlements → dwelling, living in neighbourhoods, communal life (suppositions of communal life: facing each other, endo- versus exosphere of life belonging to a community; see Müller (1987)).

Artefacts indicate a repertoire {R} of agencies a in society S at time t. {R} refers to a set of capabilities {C}. {R} is essentially underdetermined by the record, since many agencies are not directly represented by artefacts (such as speech acts, sexual practices, education, and rituals). There is a direct correlation between artefacts and agencies and another relation to speech acts (see below).

### 1.11.8 Hypothetical speculation

The logic of pragmatic inference and correlation gradually turns into hypothetical speculation, as some examples may indicate. Hypotheses imply "perhaps (not)". Assumptions become "plausible" and "more or less likely" according to underlying beliefs on the side of historians.

If there are burial sites, people must have held beliefs about an afterlife. Perhaps, personal belongings, such as swords, jewellery and even playing toys, must be given to the dead because they will need them in an afterlife. Perhaps, some dead should not show up as being poor in the afterworld. Burial goods may, perhaps, decline or perish in a more affluent society if assumptions on the afterlife change.[88] There are many "perhaps" statements in PA. "Perhaps" statements refer to degrees of likeliness. PA should try to become more specific on likeliness and may introduce so-called confidence-intervals.

If there are ashes, there must have been fire. If there are ashes from burnt houses, one may speculate whether such burning resulted from incidents of open fires (accident), from revolutionary class struggles against local elites, or from voluntary burning of houses due to a doctrine that a house must perish with the death of its owner. Perhaps, with the death of a big chief, a house has "fallen" if the chief left no descendants. A material analysis of ashes alone cannot decide which hypothesis is the most plausible one. Lifeworld knowledge tells us that humans may burn something deliberately or that fires occur as involuntary accidents. If one knows about involuntary fires in ancient and medieval towns (as written sources on preventive measures tell), the hypothesis seems *more* likely that most fires occurred accidentally in such settlements or occurred by warfare and raiding.

If there is weaponry, there must be violent fighting or even warfare. If we find much weaponry and bones at one site, there might have been a battle. If so, there was violence and killing. There are reasons for fighting even if fighting always comes at some risk. Perhaps, weaponry indicates the emergence of professionals: warriors. If one assumes warriors, then one may or must ask whether warriors had a special self-understanding, say, a doctrine. Did warriors worship a special "martial" deity? Perhaps, some meanings are enshrined in the weapons themselves, as in some swords (with symbols or ornamentation). By way of doctrines, one may explain why swords of killed warriors are not overtaken by other warriors but remained on the battlefields and burial grounds. What looks like wastefulness, is perfectly meaningful under the assumption that warriors and swords belong together intrinsically. A sword might not have been tradable as a commodity but, perhaps, was an "essential belonging" that must perish as the warrior dies. As long he lives, he must not lose possession of his weapons.[89] Does this presumed doctrine change when mass production of weaponry started around ca. 1500 BCE? The more fundamental questions about weaponry ask why and how more peaceful times transformed into more violent ones.[90]

If an archaeologist believes that a building may have served as an assembly hall, she cannot avoid asking what kind of assemblies took place in such settle-

---

88 It is possible that a poor society holds strong beliefs about an afterlife. Moreover, its members accepted an obligation to provide the dead with many precious things that were needed in such an afterlife, even horses and servants. In such societies, *ceteris paribus*, mundane opportunity costs of burials are high. Additional premises may allow one to conceive burial goods as investments, e.g.: a dead chief will show up as a rich person in the afterworld, will have high rank, will be able to counsel the Gods, will counsel the Gods on our behalf, and the Gods will thus protect our community. Imagine now that a society gets richer and, in parallel, loses faith in such beliefs. If one believes in a "final judgement", precious goods will not help in such a situation.

89 Did the Romans see the soldier-weapon-relation in a more instrumental way, while the Goths saw it symbolically? This might explain, while the Goths were so reluctant to get rid of their weapons as they were allowed to enter Roman territory. See Gibbon (1776-1788/1952), chap. 14 and 15.

90 There can be lasting transformation into belligerent epochs. This question is clearly connected to the speculation about the root causes of warfare, as to be found in Kant's *Perpetual Peace* for early modern times of territorial states. A profound answer of the root cause of warfare for periods without states may indicate peace and violence in periods and regions when states lose political significance and tend to "fail". The hypothesis points to population events. In an empty world with no competition for territories, there are prudential reasons to avoid fighting. If there are good life prospects in a region, why take the risks of fighting? Another cause of war can be collectives that specialise in robberies and plundering. Some reasons for fighting might have been trivially materialistic: conquest, plundering, and tributes. Raiding seems to have also been a "way of life" (Scott 2017, 222-256), including naval raiding of sea nomads.

ments. In any case, we suppose lingual interaction in assemblies. An assembly hall might indicate some assumptions about common affairs which must be regulated. This supposes that there must have been common matters. But is there any evidence for past local democracy? Can we ever know who had a voice about what matters in such assemblies? Should we assume that there are modes of direct local democracy over millennia in Africa and Amazonia (Graeber and Wengrow 2021, 530) which have analogies in the remote past? Here, inferential reasoning clearly reaches its limits.

These examples point at the interfaces between inferential reasoning and abductive hypothesis, between the "must" and the "may". The higher we climb the ladder, the more we operate hypothetically.

### 1.11.9 Agency *within* natural environments

PA must suppose that human systems have been embedded in natural environments full of non-human beings. It supposes radiation of *Homo sapiens sapiens* on Planet Earth ("Out of Africa 2") and the capability for niche construction as enculturation. Humans take the earth under their feet as settlers on a planetary scale. Global radiation is a precondition for the Anthropocene. If human life was restricted to Savannah-type environments, there would be no Anthropocene (part 3).

The radiation of humans onto all continents except Antarctica established cultural niches within different natural environments.[91] Palaeoecology presupposes that there "were" environments that were suited for human life. Humans can adopt many foraging strategies with different environments providing different resources. To understand foraging and coping strategies, we must reconstruct past landscapes, as is done by palaeobiology, palaeolimnology (Bell and Blais 2021) and palaeoecology. Here, we have research on sediments (marine, lakes, peatlands), soils, plant remains, and pollen. History asks, how such past landscapes may have been experienced by humans? Was there a sense for natural beauty?

There are marginal habitats for humans, for example, high latitudes around the arctic, deserts, high mountain ranges, tropical forests, mires, and water-dominated zones. Humans can go to the extremes, but most humans have stayed in the natural comfort zones that are located in sub-tropical and temperate zones. The comfort zones are not the African locations of human origins. In the post-glacial ages, Europe was not a comfort zone at all. Habitable Europe originated at the end of several glacial ages in the mild Holocene 12,000 years ago (Weniger 2009). Before the Holocene, there must have often been many collapses of human populations in Central Europe. Since the Holocene, Central Europe is a habitable comfort zone for humans up to Scandinavia (and it will remain so under conditions of moderate climate change (part 4)). Farming became dominant across Central Europe between 6000 and 3000 BCE (Robb 2013). Greenland is interesting as a marginal habitable zone in medieval times whose settlements were abandoned later in the Little Ice Age (15th century CE) (Müller 2016). At very high latitudes, as in Svalbard, human life requires imports and artificial shelter (Kruse *et al.* 2021).

91 Niche construction theory can be applied to understand and explain specific hunter-gatherer societies. See Groß *et al.* (2019).

Complex hunter-gatherer practices might have been an alternative to European Neolithic farming in some parts of the Pacific West.[92] Farming, however, became a dominant mode of metabolism in Eurasia. Scott (2017) focusses on the laboratory of Mesopotamia which was a large wetland before agriculture. Palaeobotany explains how new crops, such as millet, reached Europe and contributed to food security in many regions. The case of millet shows how palaeobotany and a history of agriculture can work together in order to reconstruct material living conditions in the Late Neolithic and the Bronze Age. PA can research the spread of exotic animals, such as camels, in ancient and medieval Ukraine.[93]

A conceptual investment in terminology is called for here. The concept of *environment* denotes a surrounding of human activities. Via niche construction, specific cultural-natural environments emerge. Environments are fields of relevance and significance. In the beginnings, environmental conditions are mainly natural ones. In the course of history, environmental conditions become more artificial, for example, in agricultural landscapes, gardens, villages, and towns. The concept of *nature* denotes all entities that are not completely produced by humans (such as artefacts, writing, works of art, normative orders). Thus, the concept of nature itself becomes gradual as humans start to modify nature and transform wild areas into cultural landscapes. The concept of *landscape* mediates between geography, ecology, and cultural history (Haber 2016). Even in cultural landscapes, however, there exist many "wild" living beings, including bacteria, fungi, plants, and animals. The concept of *wilderness* is one extreme part of nature being defined as "devoid of human impact". The term "wild" denotes natural forces that also may be displayed in cultural landscapes. There was a rather overabundance of wild areas in PA, but there was *formation* of nature as humans became horticulturalists, peasant farmers, and pastoralists. Formation is intentional and mostly coordinated conversion of nature, while interference might be sporadic and random. Formation of nature is never purely instrumental, but might have been interactive, symbolic, and ritual.

An overview of the dynamics of interaction between landscapes and cultures is to be found in Haug *et al.* (2018). This volume entails a post-modern approach to landscapes (Davidovic 2018). It seems misleading to conceive landscapes as analogies of texts, as Davidovic (2018) does. This analogy is not helpful in understanding human-nature-interactions in prehistoric times. Earlier humans could not "read" landscapes as if they were texts, since there was no writing. The analogy of landscapes with stages in theatres is misleading as well, since struggling for life is not a game. At the end of her essay, Davidovic (2018, 67) deconstructs the concept of landscape:

> *"As a theoretical concept landscape stands on melting grounds, is a liquid term, constantly changing its context intention, meaning and form, and therefore does not appear to be very useful."*

The search in the final sentences for more precise concepts is fine, but it ends with the proposal to use "-scape as a suffix", as in "ethnoscapes, mediascapes, technoscapes, finanscapes, and ideoscapes" (*ibid.*), which seems even more

92 See Arnold *et al.* (2016). Political complexity without farming occurred if there were productive coastal places that allowed for mammal hunting on sea (seals, whales) and land and provided shellfish, plants, roots, *etc.* See also Graeber and Wengrow (2021) on complex foraging.

93 There are camel finds from more than 50 sites in Europe. Most of the finds are from Ukraine. They often date to the age of the Roman Empire, in Ukraine also to medieval times. I am grateful to Ulrich Schmölcke for information.

obscure than the landscape terminology itself. (As often, deconstructivism increases conceptual messiness.)

A richly textured set of ecological and dietary concepts is supposed in conceiving "niching", "struggling", "foraging", "hunting", and "farming":

- Latitude: tropical, sub-tropical, temperate, boreal
- Climatic conditions: arid, humid, seasons, solar influx, temperatures, day-night-temperatures
- Territory: plains, mountains, hills, coastlines, lakes, rivers
- Natural hazards: forest fires, storms, extreme events, pests, predators
- Freshwater: precipitation, creeks, rivers, lakes, digging wells, catchments
- Plant species: wild (eatable, poisonous), domesticated, "cultivated" (see Kirleis 2018)
- Animal species: animal predators, wild (game), hunt-mutualism with grey wolves, tame, domesticated (for domestication see Cassidy and Mullin (2007))
- Woodlands: timber, non-timber products (nuts, honey, mushrooms)
- Optimal foraging and the radius of a meal: as conceptual mediation between natural environments and dietary reproduction
- Diets: "humans being omnivore", dietary styles, eating taboos, poisonous stuff
- Alcohol and other drugs: stimulation, festivities, rituals (for alcohol see Hockings and Dunbar 2020), alcoholic beverages as mediation between intake of calories, good humour and social cohesion among buddies
- Infectious disease: medical plants, healing strategies, the symbolic dimension of healing in shamanism
- Special places and sacred sites: locations of sacrifice and worshipping, step from ecology to religion, rites de passage in wild nature, ecstatic mental states and auratic experiences.

Past humans lived in an "empty world" with an overabundance of wild areas. Human population was low or very low. Nature was hostile and humans could have become prey. Starving to death was a risk to almost all foragers at higher latitudes. Extinction of entire groups might have been common. Staying alive must have been the primordial objective of struggling. The implicit question was: How can one have a daily life as far away from death as possible? How can death be kept at a distance? From our interest in safety and security in our daily life, we may try to understand prehistoric lives under common human values of safety and security. In PA, foraging and nursing were focal practices for almost all humans.

In such an empty world, there was not much competition over land, but much space to escape to and to divide up. Prehistoric and ancient humans were highly mobile, but a difference emerged between nomadism and sedentism as two distinct ways of human life. Sedentism has many pragmatic implications for senses, emotions, sleep, privacy, *etc.* (Wilson 1988, see part 2). In the very long run, sedentism became the dominant way of life, manifesting itself in settlements. Mobility patterns remain in sedentary ways of life (migration), but there is a difference between a) moving and settling down and b) living as a foraging nomad. Very often, the difference was turned into a hierarchy, in which sedentism was judged superior to nomadism. To humans, the more artificial sedentary way of life has been more adaptive in biological terms: reproduction.

### 1.11.10 Basic societal problems and the origins of symbolic orders

I suppose that all human collectives (hordes, bands, tribes, communities, later: societies[94]) have to organise material *and* symbolic reproduction via material metabolism and by lingual (Cassirer 1923/1964: "symbolic") activities. Symbolic activities presuppose both lingual and visual-imaginative capabilities. The distinction between metabolism ("labour") and lingual articulation ("speech") allows for many historical mediations such as rituals of fertility. Symbolic reproduction is another step on the ladder.

Individual and societal metabolism with nature is the eternal human predicament. Early human history is, basically, a long and monotonous history of foraging in different natural environments. *Material* reproduction includes foraging, freshwater provision, shelter, cooking with fire, removing waste, cleaning camps and houses, washing, laundry, sanitation, *etc.*

*Sexual* reproduction is a requirement of all human collectives, which involves heterosexual intercourse, pregnancies, giving birth, birth rates, time-span between births, caring for offspring as a K-strategy, nursing, child mortality, adaptive function of grandparents, healing practices, taboos against incest, periods of abstention, separation of menstruating women, *etc.* All humans are born by mothers: motherhood is biologically unavoidable whatever the societal gender roles are. On the symbolic side of sexual reproduction, there are weddings and the status of female virginity. Cultural options are monogamy, polygyny, and polyandry. Here, the correlation of biological sex and cultural gender roles matters. Any cultural gender configuration presupposes biological sexes. Ultimately, there are only two biological sexes: male and female (Ponseti and Stirn 2019),[95] but many cultural gender roles. Symbolic expression of genitals: "*priapos*", "*lingam*", "*baubo*" are to be found in many cultures (for female genitals see Devereux 1985). Human genitals have been painted in caves (Flannery 2018, chap. 31). Erected penises are painted and sculptured from Cyprus to Sweden in the Neolithic and the Bronze Age.

Sexual practices among humans can take different forms. By inferential abduction, prohibitions (taboos) to perform a sexual practice S presuppose the knowledge that it is possible to derive sexual pleasure from S. The strict prohibitions against homosexuality, sodomy, and bestiality that are found in the Hebrew Tora (Leviticus 18:22; Exodus 22:18; Leviticus 20:16) indicate how sexual life might have been among Canaanites. All human collectives regulate sexual agency and it was a myth that the coming of age in Samoa was highly permissive in sexual affairs, as Mead (1928) claimed. As Freeman (1983) has shown, Mead was hoaxed by young Samoan women and she uncritically believed that their tales on sexual liberty were true. We should not generally assume that sexual liberties were larger in prehistoric and ancient times than in modern societies, even if homosexual activities were common in ancient Greece.

The sex-gender-relation might (or might not) have changed between the Neolithic and the Bronze Age (Robb and Harris 2018). Bronze Age gender is binary male-female-patterned. As Robb and Harris point out, the Neolithic evidence (mostly figurines) "*does not behave as we expect or want it*" (2018, 140). The Neolithic

94 The modes of living in communities differ from societal modes. See Tönnies (1887/1979) for the basic difference between community and society. Pre-state collectives are seen as communities.

95 I leave aside the problem of transsexual individuals, which is hotly debated in academia, hoping that this abstraction will not be taken as evidence for "trans-phobia".

evidence on gender roles remains rather obscure. Neolithic people "everywhere acknowledged, referenced, made use of and, sometimes created biological differences between males and females" (*ibid.*, 141). Thus, sex in terms of males and females is undeniable. In prehistoric times, people actually did what our current feminist-constructivist doctrine penalises: essentialising "their own gender and imposed normative binarism on themselves" (*ibid.*, 132). Was there any "normative binarism" in the Neolithic belief system? Was this binarism wrong in the Neolithic? Did humans "impose" the binary scheme (who might have invented it in prehistoric times?) upon themselves, did they take it as naturally given or did they perceive themselves as females or males? Did they impose and essentialise or did they realise and symbolise their actual sexual life? From an epistemological point of view, one should not impose our current LBGTIQA values onto prehistoric people, which may happen if we "broaden our theoretical imagination (perhaps drawing on queer theories and other areas [...]" (*ibid.*, 15). Robb and Harris plea for "theoretical imagination". Since "gender trouble" (Butler 1991) is so hotly debated in current academia, we should carefully ask what really can be known about prehistoric sexual life and gender roles. For the time being, I do not wish to pay intellectual tribute to constructivist gender theory. Contrary to Kristeva's famous slogan, that, strictly speaking, women do not exist, I believe that there have been real women in prehistoric and ancient times.[96] In the Hebrew Bible, divine blessing is about a great or even "countless" number of descendants (Genesis 15:5).

Gender is one aspect in human life which mediates between biological-reproductive and symbolic order. Childhood is another aspect: How was the coming of age realised in archaic societies and which "*rites de passage*" can we identify as symbolic practices. At this point, analogical reasoning which looks at childhood in present non-state communities may provide an understanding of how it might have been to be a child in the archaic past. Metabolism, foraging, gender, and childhood point to the concept of "embodied wealth".

### 1.11.11 Agency and symbolic orders

Worshipping, weddings, and burials belong to the symbolic dimension of human life. Death is a natural event, funerals are ceremonies. *Symbolic* reproduction includes feasting, gifting, rituals of cohesion, normative orders, penalties (ostracism, executions), the differences between friends and foes, exchange of women, sacrifice, *etc*. These symbolic activities reveal symbols and archetypes (Jung 1981), for example, in special meat, fireplaces, swords, ritual washing, "*hieros gamos*", sacred sites, sacrifices, and magic. Archaic symbolic orders and their renewal should not be imagined as fancy festivals. They were often painful and cruel. Sacrificing humans was widespread. Graeber and Wengrow (2021, 511) point to the option among the Wendat that captives were slowly tortured to death over days in a theatrical spectacle. We should not forget that executions were public festivities until the 18th century CE (Foucault 1975).

*Feasting* is a trait in human collectives which can be traced far back into prehistoric times (Hayden 2009; 2014; Nahum-Claudel 2016). It implies special meals and a difference between ordinary and extra-ordinary times. Feasting interrupts daily routines. Feasting (special meals) requires organisation: food, drinks, music, dance, celebration. There are many reasons for feasting that we can un-

96 The slogan is quoted by Butler (1991) at the beginning of chapter one.

derstand or even share. It remains unclear who was entitled to join a feasting and whether there have been customs such as invitations. Feasting is organised by wealthy persons, and even if special meals are expensive, and even if feasting has some positive distributional effect on the poorer participants (if they were allowed to join), these effects cannot outweigh structural economic patterns by which inequality is (re)produced.

Making music and dancing are also to be supposed in the symbolic dimension of human life.[97] Singing humans are accompanied by clapping hands, rhythms, flutes, drums, and lyres. A painting from Mesopotamia (3rd millennium BCE) shows six males singing together. This comes close to a chorus. The human voice can scream, sing and speak and can mix screaming, singing and speaking. A mixture of screaming and singing occurs if warriors attack. A mixture of singing and speaking occurs in ancient tragedies. A similar kind of mixture occurs at political demonstrations today or at soccer matches. The capabilities of the voice belong to symbolic life. Since music is present in all human collectives, there might be an underlying human capability, named "musicality". As Honing (2018, 4) points out, "the study of the origins of music is conditional on the study of musicality." The basic components of musicality might be "regularity and beat perception [...], tonal encoding of pitch [...] and metrical encoding of rhythm" (*ibid,* 6).

Humans also seem to like some kind of embodied decoration. Body painting (tattoos) is a type of self-decoration until present times. It belongs to a symbolic order. There is a way from embodied decoration to ornaments and jewellery, being beautiful wealth. Ornamental arrangements of beautiful wealth are part of symbolic life since prehistoric times.

*Normative orders are also to be presupposed.* Institutions are a crucial step on Hawkes' ladder. Scaffolding on the ladder should try to reconstruct specific normative orders with the help of general concepts. In deontic logic, there are few basic deontic operators that apply to types of action: *obligations, prohibitions, permissions.* Types of actions are stealing, killing, betraying, helping, *etc.* If there are normative orders, humans are able to subsume single actions under types of action which can be permitted, obliged, or forbidden. This categorical frame might be universal. It may be assumed that in all past collectives there have been commitments, entitlements and prerogatives, but it is unclear whether the operator "*P has a right to do x*" already existed in the prehistoric past. The institution of human rights comes very late in history. Taboos are strict prohibitions. Prohibitions usually entail sanctions. Ostracism, executions, and blood money seem to have been widespread. Rules provide strong reasons to act. Normative orders refer to standards of honour, practices of blaming and shaming, and executions of punishment. Humans know on the emic side what it means to follow a rule, even if the differences between customs, religious taboos, legal norms, and moral obligations are not as clear as they are (or should be) today (to enlightened people).

*Institutions* are seen as systems of rules and social roles that are enforced by authorities. Authorities exist throughout history. Authorities presume legitimacy, they execute control over labour, they command others (speech acts of imperatives), they make decisions, and they claim a specific unequal status. Whatever they are named ("Big Men", chiefs, aggrandisers, knights), they have power over women, servants, captives, slaves, outcasts, aliens, *etc.*

97 See the contributions in Honing (2018) on the origins of music, especially Patel (2018), who sees music as a transformative technology of the human mind. Patel argues that music is "both a human invention and biological powerful". See also Huron (2018) on affect induction by music.

Sedentism as such requires some normative orders (codes of conduct) which cannot be negotiated on a daily basis. Normative orders release humans from transaction costs of permanent re-negotiation. They stabilise expectations (Gehlen 1944). Revolt against normative orders and authorities always remains an option which may take the specific forms of escapism, seeking refuge, subversive actions, rebellion, riot, resurrection, disobedience, revolution, and civil war. Perhaps, normative anarchism claims that revolts against normative orders, states, and authorities are always "on the right side of history". Such claims, however, would need some ethical grounding (part 4).

## 1.11.12 Agency coordinated by means of language

Language is missing on Hawkes' ladder. As the term "oral culture" implies, PA must suppose that there was human speech in archaic collectives.[98] In his *Philosophical Investigations,* philosopher Ludwig Wittgenstein (1958, no. 415) states: "What we are supplying are really remarks on the natural history of human beings." Wittgenstein proposes a theory about human language games which can be applied to oral cultures (Bezzel 1996, 97-116). The term "game" is, however, misleading since the pragmatic use of language is not a game (such as chess, poker, soccer, *etc.*). By the term "language game", Wittgenstein wished to emphasise that he refers to speech as a practical enterprise being an essential part of the human way of life.[99] The term "form of life" does not refer to particular cultures, but to *the* human way of life as such. Sometimes, Wittgenstein speaks about the "grammar" of the human way of life. To Wittgenstein, commanding, asking, accusing, warning, telling stories, demanding, praying, *etc.* belong to our natural history just as walking, eating, drinking and playing (*ibid.*, 30, no. 25). Wittgenstein points to lingual performatives by which humans do something and interact. He points to exclamations which are sometimes seen as one-word sentences, for example, "Away!", "Ow!", "Help!", "Fire!", *etc.* (*ibid.*, 30-31 no. 27). Wittgenstein also asks how many kinds of sentences there are (questions, imperatives, propositions) and in no. 23 (*ibid.*, 28), he presents a long list of speech acts (= language games). To TPCL, the pragmatic side of language is decisive. Giving advice, praying, commanding, bargaining, judging, giving thanks, ordering, warning, promising, teaching, asking questions, cursing, joking, greeting, cheating, defining situations, presenting narratives, gossip, *etc.* are examples for speech acts. The long list indicates the richness of human speech which makes human life different from animal life.[100] In ethnoarchaeology, we can devote special interest to "we designations" of ethnic groups and ask whether they, from the emic side, are seen as proper names or as revealing modes of "being many" (Bird-David 2017).

Humans are essential lingual beings. Oral speech, however, does not fossilise and did not remain in the archaeological records. This seems to be a trivial matter of fact, but it is of importance to a theory of PA. In PA, past speech acts must be supposed and speculated. I make the theoretical investment that speech acts, not words or propositions, are the decisive units of speech. We have to assume full-fledged oral communication performed by speech acts. We should assume that all

98 As G. H. Mead (1910/1987) has argued, human speech may have originated out of vocal gestures. The vocal-gesture theory is taken as a theoretical investment.

99 "Here the term "language-game" is meant to bring into prominence the fact that the speaking of language is part of an activity, or of a form of life" (Wittgenstein 1958, no. 23).

100 The importance of speech for the human way of life has been emphasised in Gadamer and Vogler (1974). There is broad agreement in philosophical anthropology.

the main kinds of speech acts were present in prehistory. For analytical and typological purposes, we can rely on Austin's classification (Austin 1955/1962, 150-163): 1. verdictives, 2. exercitives, 3. commissives, 4. behabitives, 5. expositives. Speech acts entail validity claims and implicit reasons which are stored in the lifeworld.[101]

Communication occurs within domestic households, in neighbourhoods, across bands, clans, and tribes, on journeys and markets. Common hunting is a paradigmatic example. If there was group hunting, there must have been coordination by lingual means: "You turn to the right!" Economic communication occurs within domestic households, in neighbourhoods, across bands, clans, and tribes. "Pass the instrument over." – "Sharpen the knife" – "You are far too lazy!" – "Well done!" – "You owe me a favour", *etc.* At markets, there must have been lingual bargaining. Offers and bets are essential to trade. Organising great megalithic projects supposes coordination via speech. Leisure may stimulate people to sing and to tell stories, proverbs, riddles, and jokes. Written sagas are late outcomes of oral cultures. The main epistemological point to be made here is that archaeologists should not implicitly silence the prehistoric past. Even if archaeologists would not deny speech explicitly, they rarely take the invisible lingual performances in daily prehistoric life into theoretical account. We must speculate and imagine oral communications and may infer social conventions from speech acts.

### 1.11.13 Economics

If we suppose material reproduction, we implicitly refer to economic life. I see hunting and gathering as proto-economic activity. A search for hunting and picking grounds implies assessments about distance, abundance, transport costs, and risks. Such assessments can be conceived as reasonable preferences of "optimal" foraging (Smith 1983). If, however, some food is seen as superior or if there are special rewards for special food (prestige, rank), it might also be reasonable to search or hunt even under conditions of risk and uncertainty. Optimal foraging theory supposes rational behaviour, but it can be accused of being overly deterministic and naturalistic.

The set of economic concepts will be refined and theorised in part 2. Here, I present one crucial theoretical investment: the *economic inequality frontier* (Milanovic 2016) is the dynamic locomotion in history (for better or worse). The studies of how to identify and measure inequalities in PA do not give strong reasons to mourn economic inequalities in wealthy welfare states. At present, we rather see instances of the Tocqueville-paradox: The greater that equality among humans in law, culture, education, politics, dress codes, and patterns of recognition becomes, the more sensitive young intellectuals become against inequalities in income and wealth. We might invest the distinction between cultural diversity and economic inequality. We have to ask whether one can have both: high cultural diversity, but low economic inequality (see part 4).

### 1.11.14 Analogical reasoning

In PA, we see many similarities, for example, between tools, graves, ornaments, settlements, and institutions. As a result of clustering similar entities together, there can be taxonomy and pattern recognition. Analogical inferences rest on

101 The implicit knowledge about social conventions that are stored in speech acts has been addressed by Vossenkuhl (1982).

similarities and comparisons. Analogical reasoning is indispensable for (ethno) archaeology. Let us call this the "indispensability" thesis. If a pattern of inferential reasoning would be "indispensable *and* radically faulty", this would imply an epistemic catastrophe to PA, shifting at least ethnoarchaeology into the realm of the pseudo-sciences which epistemology has to combat. Thus, we shall invest theoretically that analogical reasoning is both indispensable and legitimate.

The problem of (dis)similarities was discussed in Plato's *Parmenides*. Medieval philosophy distinguished between "*analogia proportionis*" and "*analogia attributionis*" (Thomas Aquinas). This distinction makes good sense because analogies between relations are different from analogies between attributes.[102] A proportional analogy has the logical structure: (A & B) analogous to (C & D). Kant refers to "*analogia proportionis*".[103] Any analogy, be it proportional or attributive, is a special case of similarity.

Analogies, however, have no good reputation in logic (and in general epistemology) because they cannot make the validity of conclusions safe. They are seen, at best, as heuristic tools. Analogies amplify our intellectual horizon, but they are always liable to error (Wylie 1985). An instance of fallacies of similarity is, for example: An entity E-1 is similar to an entity E-2 with respect to R, *therefore* E-1 and E-2 must be similar in other respects. This is a "*non sequitur*". We find many suggestive verbal analogies in politics, if, for instance, Mao Zedong is said to be the "great navigator". Analogies between biology and sociology have been often criticised as ideological: for example, if biological concepts, such as "struggling for life", were seen similar to "economic competition". States are not analogous to colonies of ants or beehives, since insects are not "social". Analogies between macro- and micro-cosmos are often flawed. All in all, warnings against analogical reasoning are appropriate.

Bernbeck (1997) distinguishes between similarity configurations (ontology) and analogical reasoning (epistemology). Analogical reasoning relies on some ontological commitments: If entities and relations are not similar, analogical reasoning would be impossible. Similarities between entities, structures, processes, *etc.* are ontological commitments of analogical reasoning. Similarities, however, come and go in degrees. They are fluid in a zone between identity and diversity.

Analogies are needed to detect similarities in between or between different human systems (societies, groups, tribes, *etc.*) at different locations and times. Without similarity detection and analogical reasoning, the entire discipline called ethnoarchaeology would be pointless. A sharp attack was performed by Olivier Gosselain (2016). I leave aside all accusations made by Gosselain against "racism", "colonialism", "evolutionism", "ideology" and focus solely on the epistemological point. Gosselain relies on Gallay's either-or-claim:

---

102 The distinction between relational and attributional analogy survives in the distinction between structural and functional analogy. If some internal relations between the elements of a system A are similar/comparable to relations between the elements of another system B, there "is" *structural* analogy between both systems A and B. If two entities can substitute each other in terms of function, there "is" functional analogy (adequacy) between them.

103 *"Eine Erkenntnis nach der Analogie, welche nicht* [...] *eine unvollkommene Ähnlichkeit zweier Dinge, sondern eine vollkommene Ähnlichkeit zweier Verhältnisse zwischen ganz unähnlichen Dingen bedeutet"* (Kant 1783, *Prolegomena*, 124, § 58). [English translation]: *"Such knowledge is knowledge by analogy. This doesn't involve* [...] *an imperfect similarity of two things, but rather a perfect similarity of relations between the members of two quite dissimilar pairs of things."* [Translation available at: https://www.earlymoderntexts.com/assets/pdfs/kant1783_3.pdf; last accessed: 6 December 2023].

> *"Either we admit that ethnological studies may be useful to archaeologists, which means that an observation made at point X in space and time is equally valuable for a point Y* [...] *and in such case this approach is transcultural* [...] *or we admit that such transfer cannot be made, due to the endless originality of cultures" (Gallay 1990 in Gosselain 2016, 220).*

If analogical transfers cannot be made, the ethnoarchaeological approach must be abandoned. Should we presuppose "originality of cultures" (singularity, individuality) in such a radical sense ("alienity") that comparisons, similarity detection, transfers, connectivities, common structural features, patterns, *etc.* should be discarded in general? Gallay (1990) is aware of the implication: "*We must then confine ourselves to case studies*". Such restrictions would be fatal to theoretical ambitions in PA. Gallay, however, shies away from such radical implications. He concedes "*direct historical analogy*" where the "transfer is limited to specific archaeological contexts". "*Direct historical analogy*" means that modern traditions are used to interpret historically related archaeological sources (Gosselain 2016, 224). Gosselain calls this operation "back-pedalling". This means that direct analogies are valid claims, while indirect ones ("crossovers") are not. Even if one accepts the fuzzy distinction between direct and indirect analogies, there is no argument against indirect analogies being made. Many analogies in ethnoarchaeology are indirect ones. Can we understand patterns of, for instance, nomadic ways of life if we have to discard all indirect analogies? Why not make some analogies between, say, Japanese and West Pacific fishery culture in order to ask whether rich fishing grounds may be functional equivalents for agriculture and, by doing so, explain why there can be highly complex hunter-fisher-gatherer collectives (Arnold *et al.* 2016).

In contrast, analogical reasoning is an inferential device in (ethno)archaeology which is hard to avoid completely. Thus, one cannot simply ban analogical reasoning (Wylie 1985). Thus, we face a new antinomy: There are good reasons to perform analogical reasoning, but there are good reasons to abstain from it. Analogical reasoning is unavoidable, but it will remain a source of messy reasoning, flaws, rhetorical suggestions, and confusions. According to Wylie (1985, 64):

> *"Most archaeological inference remains analogical.* [...]. *My thesis is that though a candid appreciation of its limitations is appropriate where analogical inference is concerned, its use in archaeological contexts is neither dispensable nor radically faulty."*

Criticism against some flawed analogies should not be generalised to criticism against the whole class of analogical interference since this would be a *pars-pro-toto*-fallacy. A RT demands critical reflection on any kind of specific analogical reasoning in PA. Analogical reasoning is to be seen as a paradigmatic instance of "controlled speculation". We must be self-critical against each and any single analogical inference, but cannot do away with this form of inferential reasoning. Wylie (1985, 107):

> "[...] *raising the credibility of those necessary ampliative* [...] *analogical inferences on which archaeology must rely if it is to bring unfamiliar and otherwise inaccessible aspects of the past into view."*

Wylie rightly points to the *ampliative* function of this kind of reasoning. To abstain from analogical reasoning out of logical rigour comes at a high price to PA. Without analogical inferences, we can move forward to other intellectual operations in PA, such as a) comparisons, b) pattern recognition, and c) modelling. Analogies are essential requirements for both comparisons and pattern recognition. If A is a (necessary) requirement for B, and if B is essential for an epistemological practice P, then A cannot be discarded completely if P shall be continued. McGranaghan (2017) gives a balanced analysis how ethnographic analogies may and may not work in archaeology. It seems unlikely that analogical reasoning can be completely replaced by theoretical explanation. At the end of her brilliant article, Wylie (1985, 107) concludes that PA should not shy away from analogical reasoning, but rather explore it since otherwise PA might not bring about "*unfamiliar and otherwise inaccessible aspects of the past into view*".

*Pattern recognition* relies ontologically on recurrent similarities between entities that are associated under specific criteria and indicators (South 1978). Pattern recognition in PA is different from pattern recognition in cognitive psychology. Explanations point to presumptive *patterns* of human behaviour. If a specific explanation works well at different instances we can try to identify patterns. "Humans are disposed (inclined, susceptible) to response with X in situations of type S." Patterning, however, is an epistemic activity being performed at present. Generally, historical patterns are recurrent similarities being associated with the help of analogical reasoning and modelling. Patterns are rather static and are often visualised in schemes. Models may bring more dynamics into pattern recognition. Static patterns are *schemes*, while dynamic patterns are *models*. Patterns and models reduce complexity, but they refer to reality. DPSIR is a general scheme that can be used for modelling. DPSIR may be an instance why the "ladder" turns into a scaffold. Pattern recognition is a crucial step in order to explain recurrent human behaviour (South 1978).

### 1.11.15 Middle-range theories

The ladder model wishes to reduce the abstract distance between fieldwork and general theories stepwise. Generally, theories must be presumed to have explanatory force. Arponen *et al.* (2019a) argue that theories can fly at different altitudes. Within a pragmatist approach, it is fair to ask: "How is a theory T helpful to problem solving in PA? What exactly is the specific TI? What is a theory T about to explain?"

*Middle-range theories* (MRT) are paradigmatic cases of how TI may work in PA. The concept of MRT was originally part of a refined search for levels of theory formation in archaeology (Willey and Sabloff 1980). Thus, it fits into the TPCL approach. Important contributions to the MRT debate are found in Trigger (1995), Raab and Goodyear (1984), and Kosso (1991).[104] The ladder approach allows us to resolve some confusions and ambiguities about MRT. One can distinguish two distinct approaches to MRT, one approach is Mertonian, the other is Binfordian (Raab and Goodyear 1984). Binfordians and Mertonians take different steps on the epistemological ladder. Merton's approach (1949; 1968) was a critical departure from Talcott Parson's general sociology.

According to Smith (2011, 169), the term "middle-range theory" was "hijacked by Lewis Binford [...] to refer to an idiosyncratic body of theory on formation processes." According to Binford, artefacts (products, records, residuals, traces) that can be observed in the present must have been produced and used

104 An application of MRT to theories about urban life is given by Smith (2011).

by humans in the now unobservable (vanished) past. Formation theories denote "our understanding of how the archaeological record formed" (Shott 1998, 311). The record is the present product of past formation processes (Schiffer 1987). PA is right to point to formation processes, but one should hold the problem of "filtering" distinct from MRT (Bernbeck 1997, 67; Shott 1998).

According to Shott (1998, 307), "Merton's middle range theory begins where Binford's ends". If so, both approaches fly at different altitudes. MRT in a Binfordian sense should be better labelled as "formation theories" (Shott 1998). I do not include theories about formation processes into the concept of MRT, but see it more on the empirical and positivistic steps of the later. If one wishes to place "formation theory" and MRT on the same step of the ladder, confusion results. Thus, I restrict the concept of MRT to the Mertonian type.

Merton originally wished to escape the divide between empiricism and abstract theorising and he wished to make the methodological divide between induction and deduction pointless. MRT should guide empirical inquiry and they should be substantive and testable.

> *"Middle range theory involves abstraction, of course, but they are close enough to observed data to be incorporated in propositions that permit empirical testing" (Merton 1968, 38).*

Such testable propositions can be defined as "hypotheses". Thus, MRT lie between working hypotheses that "evolve in abundance during day-to-day research" (Merton 1968, 39) and comprehensive and unified (scientific) theories. MRT are substantive and explanatory, not merely methodological. Optimal foraging and niche construction theories are an instance of substantive, explanatory Mertonian MRT.

MRT may overcome the split between processual and post-processual archaeology. MRT can be founded in scientific theories, for example, biological ones such as "carrying capacity", "optimal foraging", "niche construction", and "adaptation", but they may also be rooted in economic approaches, such as Historical Materialism (see part 2) or behavioural economy. They can also be based on some structural mechanism by which transformations can be explained.

If the distinction between actual (Mertonian) middle-range theories and (Binfordian) formation theories holds, there would be at least four layers ("altitudes") of theory formation: a) formation theories, b) hypothesis formation and testing, c) Mertonian middle-range theories, d) general theories.[105] Analogical reasoning would belong to b).

In PA, there are instances of MRT to be reflected upon. In his *"Material Culture, Landscapes of Action, and Emergent Causation"* (2013), John Robb conceived a paradigmatic Mertonian MRT by which the origins of the European Neolithic might be explained. A similar model was given by Zimmermann (2007). Both models, taken together, can serve as the standard model of Neolithisation in Europe since 7000 BCE.[106] Europe was a continent of foragers, while at ca. 4000 BCE, it was "mostly a continent of farmers" (Robb 2013, 658).[107] One should take the time-

105 Seen from this angle, Hodder's hermeneutic approach would then fall somewhere between a) and b), because hermeneutic interpretation goes beyond causal inference (Kosso 1991) and paves the way for testable hypotheses. Hodder's theoretical approach, then, would find its place within a meta-theoretical layer-scheme that Hodder himself denies.

106 See also Strahm (2006); Scharl (2003); McCaffree (2022), 25-92; and Shillington (2019), 23-34 for Africa.

107 See also Terberger *et al.* (2018). Aquatic resources played an important role in foraging in Europe within the transition to farming. This supports the wetland hypothesis.

scale of three millennia seriously. Neolithisation was a very long transformation. There was steady directedness, but there were also periods of stagnation. The Neolithic package of

> *"sedentism in villages, domesticated animals and grains, pottery, axes and grinding technologies* [...] *seem to be a result, not a cause of the transition" (ibid., 659).*

Agriculture was first introduced and later fully established. We adopt the claim which Robb (*ibid.*, 663) draws from Woodburn (1982):

> *"Economies where food is produced in long-term projects and can be stored are inherently susceptible to accumulating surplus and developing inequality."*

We also adopt the materialist perspective upon things which is present in many of Robb's publications (Robb 2015). In comparison, the Neolithic is a "thing-heavy" world (Robb 2013, 665). Since things often have a symbolic dimension, the Neolithic is a more complex symbolic order, although farmers may have seen domesticated animals with more sober eyes than foraging hunters perceived game. Robb's MRT explains why the Neolithic transformation took so much time, but was one-directional and irreversible. It took many generations to invent pottery, weave textiles, practice metallurgy, domestication, and agriculture (see Levi-Strauss 1962/1981, 26-28). Such techniques suppose centuries of observation, "trial-and-error" experiments, curiosity, insight and memory. To Levi-Strauss, Neolithic knowledge is practical knowledge based on experience and tested in daily life. To Robb, Neolithic farming occupied Europe via many small one-way doors. The advantages of the farming way of performing metabolism in terms of survival, life expectancy, and reproduction are hard to deny

> *"even if farming is not a healthier way of life than foraging, birth spacing tends to become shorter and fertility tends to rise" (Robb 2013, 662).*

Armelagos *et al.* (1991) present the big picture of long-term population growth and declining individual health. The theoretical question remains: Why did the agricultural way of life become dominant despite its disadvantages (hard work, declining health status, monotonous food, social hierarchies, tributes, *etc.*)? Many PA scholars tend to believe that humans must have been forced into this way of life.

My abduction speculates about the active role of females in the long process of sedentism.[108] Life in pre-state Neolithic settlements was safer for females and children than foraging in open landscapes and dwelling in camps. Recent findings indicate that population dynamics in the Neolithic and the Bronze Age is not characterised by constant growth. Periods of boom-and-bust interchange (Feeser *et al.* 2019; Kneisel *et al.* 2019).[109] In the very long run, however, the Neolithic way of life increased the number of humans. Scott (2017, 6) presents the following numbers: the human population equalled roughly 2-4 million people in 10,000 BCE and roughly 50 million in 1000 BCE. In Europe, 1 million people lived in 7000 BCE, while up to 20-30 million lived in Europe in 1500 BCE. Farming is not an easy way

108 One can read the Biblical story of Jacob, Esau, and Rebecca in this respect (Genesis 25-27). Esau is a wild hunter, while Jacob is a decent pastoralist and horticulturalist, cooking lentils. As I suppose, Rebecca strongly prefers Jacob's pastoralist-horticulturalist policies over Esau's presumable hunter policies.

109 For methodological aspects of population density measures, see Müller and Diachenko (2019).

of life, but it looks more adaptive (in sociobiological terms of proliferation). Fertile descendants are the currency of evolution. Humans had to domesticate *themselves* in order to become biologically more adaptive (McCaffree 2022, 30). *Humans are biologically fitter if they live as settled cultural beings.* A sedentary farming life is rewarding in the currency of evolution: fertile descendants

The dispersal of humans was highly uneven, concentrated within some regions, but an agricultural life may have brought about emergent societal institutions and a division of labour. The Neolithic way of life was a life in villages and in domestic modes of production which did not abolish the older ways of gathering and hunting. Slowly, human collectives became more complex, more dynamic, but also more stratified. Population growth increases the number of "hands" that can be put to work. Control over labour implies the capability to undertake great projects. Professionals specialise in crafts, warfare, and access to the divine. I see no strong epistemic reasons to discard this conventional "big picture" for Eurasia.

MRT can be further generalised to theoretical models that can, in principle, be applied to any human collective. Arnold *et al.* (2016) propose such a theoretical model that is composed of seven overlapping *platforms of societal dynamics*:

1. Agency and authority (rules), normative orders
2. Social differentiation (stratification)
3. Participation in communal events (decision-making)
4. Organisation of production and exchange (economy)
5. Labour obligations (economy)
6. Articulation of ecology and subsistence (metabolism)
7. Territoriality and ownership (property rights).

To Arnold *et al.* (2016, 466), the order of platforms is unimportant. Platforms are just epistemic lenses to look upon communities, collectives, and, later, societies. Two platforms refer to environments, two to economy, three to institutions. The specific constellation of the platforms shapes the character of a particular culture. Thus, Arnold *et al.* (2016) present a general model designed for particularistic cultural PA. They seem to rely upon a pragmatic and materialistic framework without a Marxian stage-model. They point to niche construction theory and emphasise control over territories, as to be found in complex hunter-gatherer societies of the Pacific West. Parallels to Arnold *et al.* (2016) are found in part 2. The platforms can be seen as steps on the ladder and specific scaffoldings. But why is the platform approach superior to ladder and scaffolding? To Arnold *et al.* (2016, 466), platforms could serve as "chapters in grand narratives", but they are not "steps, stages, or foundations" (*ibid.*). I see no distinctive methodological progress of the platform approach over the ladder approach.

## 1.11.16 Explanatory narratives

The definition of the term "narrative" should include temporal scale, location, beginning, plot ("drama"), agents, motives, circumstances, symbolic and political structures, causalities, environments, results, and end (Meuter 2014). Quite often, a literary story entails some moral or political messages about honesty, decency, hubris, deceptiveness, envy, *etc.* Virtue ethics were always close to narrative ethics. Suppositions of historical narratives are its discursive credibility, degree of uniqueness, named people (individuals, collectives), agencies ("*pragmata*"), "understanding" and some explaining. Internal explanatory and inferential elements occur within narratives ("therefore", "because", "since", "thus"). Such inferential elements constitute storylines. Ribeiro (2023, 102-104) argues that narratives are essential to PA, but archaeologists are often reluctant to produce narratives.

All narratives are hypothetical and are open for revision and the addition of details, but they must presume *credibility* (= narrative intelligibility", see Descombes 2001) according to archaeological and historical standards. The transcendental supposition of historical narrativity is that there can be truth in history despite different theories of truth such as correspondence, coherence, and consensus theories. The presumption of scientific credibility is a decisive epistemological feature of historical narratives which is to be distinguished from literary and fictitious ones. All narratives are about change because at the end of the story things and persons have changed. Narratives of transformations must meet specific additional conditions: explanation of substantive and profound change, its endurance, emergence of new orders and structures, *etc*.

As a result of long-lasting debates in the epistemology of history, one can assume that historical narratives should not be grounded in common sense, folk psychology, prudence or even wisdom of the historian, but are full of TI on all layers (singulars, particulars, universals). There are TI as well within micro-narratives just as in MRT and in macro-narratives. Narratives play at different spatial and temporal scales. Take Braudel *et al.* (1986) as an example for a history of "long duration". In principle, micro-narratives must be able to be upscaled, while macro-narratives must keep credibility if downscaled. A cluster of micro-narratives may contribute to MRT. Perreault (2019) argues that the archaeological record is well-suited for macro-narratives. A fine-grained detailed analysis of intentional and structural explanations within historical narratives has been provided by Gerber (2012). Explanatory narratives of transformations are not simple storytelling, but can consume both scientific results, interpretations, models, and social science theories. A recent volume addresses the role and function of narratives in PA (Miera 2023). Contributions im Miera (2023) emphasise a reflective approach to narrativity in PA. Here, I see good prospects for ambitious and reflective narratives in PA. Philosophers do not write history, but may encourage historians to do so. PA should take the step to collective authorship of "grand" narratives of transformations.

### 1.11.17 Connectivities between the past and the present

History has always been a discipline open for political misuse. In a digital world full of fake news, conspiracy theories, propaganda, "phony wars", *etc.*, historians assume some ethical responsibility if they offer past-present-connectivities. There are reasons to be reluctant. Here, we have to return to the antinomies (section 1.9): There are good reasons to make past-present-connectivities and there are good reasons to abstain from doing so. The antinomies have been resolved in a discourse on ethical spirit: Make explicit, transparent, and discursively open what can hardly be avoided completely or would unduly impoverish PA. This principle holds for past-present-connectivities as well. If prohibition only creates a "black market" of implicit past-present-connectivities, it seems better to give permission under strict rules. The supreme rules are: a) Make your connectivity explicit, b) declare your hypothesis of relevance and your analogies,

c) separate facts, evidence, and theories from value-judgement, d) be transparent with your own contemporary values, morals, and politics, e) do not stylise the past according to your own values, f) make the weak part of your argument transparent.

This rule-based strategy will not ban the dangers of politicising and moralising history, as done in despotic regimes. It will also not help against historico-political narratives circulating around in digital media without control. By following this strategy, scientific credible PA will give more credible support to public debates than by mere abstention. Rule-based past-present-connectivities are presumed to play a role in public debates about real-world problems. They require *trust* from the side of the citizenry and *caution* from the side of historians and archaeologists. Part 4 shows how this strategy may work.

Diagnoses of present challenges are implicit in such connectivities, for example, about adaptation to climate change, inequalities, migration, social cohesion, legitimacy of normative orders, sustainability, warfare, food security, neo-biota, *etc.* (part 3). They require well-considered value judgements on what is going wrong today (moral, politics, justice, ethics) and some assumptions of relevance of the (remote) past to the present. Take the following value-judgement as an example:

> *"There is no doubt that something has been terribly wrong with the world. A very small percentage of its population do control the fates of almost everything else, and they are doing it in an increasingly disastrous fashion" (Graeber and Wengrow 2021, 76).*

How many assumptions are supposed in this statement? Are they plausible? Who is meant by the tiny fraction of mankind controlling the vast majority of eight billion people: Putin, Xi Jingping, Biden, "deep state" agents, CIA, the Pope, multi-national companies, wall street brokers, CEOs, multi-billionaires? Is the disaster that humanity might be in a direct result of this presumed control? Which tacit assumptions are made about the relation between control and disaster? Is such control responsible for 37 Gt of annual $CO_2$-emissions or microplastics in the ocean? The quoted statement has a smell of conspiracy theory and it is not transparent. Perhaps, Graeber and Wengrow share the opinion of Jean Ziegler who claims (without argument) that the financial capitalists are the actual rulers of the world (Ziegler 2021, 76), and are more powerful than any powerful state. If Graber and Wengrow share this doctrine, they should say so. The rhetoric of "there is no doubt" should motivate doubtfulness. Such highly generic statements are clearly beyond scientific PA.

Past-present-connectivities are mostly made between the not too remote past. If the distance in time becomes longer, one has reasons to lose confidence in connectivities. At first look, our (post)modern Western (and Westernised) societies are completely different from archaic collectives, which had no writings, no money, no state, no insurance, no universities, no modern health care, no communication technologies, no bank accounts, no cars, *etc.* They had to cope with life without the many devices and comforts we take for granted. The life of prehistoric people was not "primitive". In daily life, there was agency, speech, technologies, knowledge, healing practices, economy, art, music, work, domestic modes of production, neighbourhoods, festivities, *etc.* As we have argued, prehistoric humans had many capabilities, some of which we might have lost. Despite distance in time, we are united with past humans within the horizon of our common lifeworld. I do not believe that prehistoric people playfully experimented with options, but they faced choices and had some leeway to respond to pressures. To us, the prehistoric past and the many non-Western ways of life which still exist in the peripheries of the globalised Western world, may look *as if* they were a carnival of experiments (Graeber and Wengrow 2021). On reflection, however, we should be aware that this is *our* curious way to recognise unfamiliar ways of life. To us, the past may *appear* as experimental playfulness, but to them it was struggling against death, famine, collapse, being victimised, being enslaved, *etc.* In history, dignified lives of human beings may not have been "happy" and "easy" ways of life, as we understand it.

In any case, past-present-connectivities have to connect different ways of human life and should do so without any prejudice of superiority (which are also alive in the immortal figure of the noble savage). Even if we reject all superiority claims, there might be a transcendental idea over all past-present-connectivities such as *humanity*. There is, however, a deep ambiguity in the term "human". On the one hand, it points descriptively to members of a specific species. On the other hand, it transports ethical meanings. This ambiguity can be resolved in distinguishing "human" and "humankind" from "humane" and "humanity". Humans should represent an ethical idea of humanity. This idea is alive in the religious doctrines of the axial age, in the Hebrew doctrine that humans are created in the image of God, in ancient Greek and Roman ethics, the Renaissance, and in the ethics of the Enlightenment. In his *Briefe zur Beförderung der Humanität* (1793-1797/2022), Herder implies that Kant's categorical imperative stands in need of historical amendments. Kant's categorical imperative is a synthetic judgement *a priori* whose validity is independent from all history and psychology. It is safely located in the transcendental realm of pure practical reason. Even if one adopts such a categorical imperative, humans live at particular historical and geographical locations. Real humans make moral experiences within their specifically situated lives. If they share such moral experience with each other, a historical concept of humanity ("*Humanität*") enriches the monolithic majesty of the categorical imperative. Herder pointed to the idea of a covenant of free republican states, a deep aversion against warfare and atrocities, fairness in negotiation, a liberal mind, compassion for the disadvantaged, *etc.* We shall adopt these two-fold ethics (transcendental Kantian core and historical Herderian amendments) and will apply it to the situation of the Anthropocene (part 4).

### 1.11.18 Anthropology on top?

We have supposed anthropology right from the scratch (basic anthropology) and at all steps on the ladder, because our conceptual scaffolding pointed to human capabilities, agency, intentionality, material and symbolic reproduction, reasons, speech acts, *etc.* The different sets of concepts, as such, point to the option (or: temptation) toward an anthropological synthesis. The supreme point (metaphorically: "crown") of our scaffolding might be a theoretical answer to Kant's question: "*Was ist der Mensch?*" For more than 100 years, there have been different theoretical candidates at hand upon which a synthesis may be built:

- Sociobiology: humans are clever, adaptive, opportunistic, tool making animals
- Cognitive archaeology: mindfulness is key
- Gehlen (1944): niche construction, agency, "*Mängelwesen*"

- Cassirer (1923/1964): symbolic life
- Plessner (1928/2011): "eccentric positionality", a reflective mode of being, three anthropological laws
- Heidegger (1927/1979): *Dasein* as *"In-der-Welt-Sein"*, *"Zuhandenheit"*, *"Sorge"*, *"Mit-Sein"*, *"Geschichtlichkeit"* and other existential categories.

The ultimate Kantian question, however, is not an isolated one, since it has been, at least in part, already answered by Kant's three previous answers about knowledge (and its limits), morals, and religion. It has been also answered by Kant's anthropology, which was given *in a pragmatic respect*. The human being is free to constitute him/herself via agency and speech. He/she must make his/her life him/herself. The "self" is not a substance (*"das Selbst"*), but the term "self" indicates that human beings are free to perform a life on their own. There is no freestanding, final and essential "what-is" question left. This is precisely the epistemological situation at the end of scaffolding. The different sets of concepts that we now must presuppose point to the many doings and beings of humans. Being human results from specific human doings. On reflection, we should *resist* the temptation to "top" these conceptual aspects of the human way of life with an anthropological synthesis. Within the TPCL approach, such a synthesis can be nothing else than an abstractive generic result on top of many sets of concepts. Such a result, however, must face the critique against positive anthropology as found in Critical Theory. Critical theorists argued that anthropology might reify human beings and defines an "essence" of the human being, which might mirror specific cultural standards stemming from specific economic affairs, such as competitiveness. The answer to a "what-is-X" question requires concepts of substance and essence which might be inadequate to the human way of life.

Since Hegel, there was the alternative to conceive a so-called negative anthropology.[110] To Hegel there is, indeed, an essence of humans: *"Geist"* (conceptual intelligence). The essence of *"Geist"*, however, is freedom (Hegel 1845/1958). Thus, freedom is the essence of human beings which comes to mind within history (Schüz 2021). Such essence is a paradox since it is realised in an almost infinite variety (= multitude) of ways of life. To Feuerbach, who studied the embodied, sensual side of the human being, anthropology was not a science of humans, but a project for the sake of humans (Loos 2021). To Feuerbach, the human being is a "living university" which creates itself anew. As Marx states in his claims on Feuerbach, the human being is an "ensemble" of societal relations, especially economic ones. Marx's negative anthropology is, however, more deterministic than Hegel's and Feuerbach's, since humans almost never choose freely under which economic institutions they wished to live. We shall say more about Marx in part 2. To Nietzsche, the human being is not *"feststellbar"* (= not to be theoretically fixed). In some sense, Gehlen also presents a negative anthropology as he starts with a negative category: *"Mängelwesen"*. To Sartre (1977), human beings "exist" without a prefigured essence. Humans must live the paradox of essential freedom. To Sonnemann (1969), humans are paradigmatic instances for Adorno's concept of non-identity. Thus, there is a philosophical background of Graeber and Wengrow (2021) who also emphasise freedom.

The multitude of human ways of life are recognised by the entire set of concepts, but I do not give up the minimalistic anthropology that these ways of life are

110 See contributions in Bajohr and Edinger (2021). This approach was made explicit by Sonnemann (1969) who relied on Adorno (1966/1980).

ways of *human* life. Graeber and Wengrow (2021, 9) remind us of Gordon Childe's book *Man makes Himself* (1936). The spirit of *The Dawn of Everything* (Graeber and Wengrow 2021) is "Childe-ish", as Graeber and Wengrow say: "*This is the spirit we wish to invoke. We are projects of collective self-creation*" (*ibid.*, 9). Additionally, they wish to see people, "*from the beginning, as imaginative, intelligent, playful creatures*". These are clearly generic human attributes whatever humans make of them.[111] Graeber and Wengrow want to make believe that we are trapped in modern cages and should look upon the carnival of lifestyles with grief from our cells. Are we really trapped? We shall return to this point in part 4.

## 1.12 Results of the analysis: Sets of concepts

As we have seen, there "are" (at least) 12 sets of concepts (SC) to be used for theoretical investments in PA, which constitute different stages of the ladder/scaffold working at different altitudes:

1. SC-basic-anthropology
2. SC-data-chronology-classification, typing
3. SC-intentionality-purposiveness-agency-practices
4. SC-ecology-environmental
5. SC-reproduction (material, symbolic)
6. SC-speech-acts
7. SC-economic
8. SC-analogy-comparison-patterns
9. SC-MRT-theoretical-explanations
10. SC-narrativity
11. SC-connectivity (past-past, past-present)
12. SC-lifeworld (reasons).

Any concept is a small TI. These sets of concepts are correlated to a pool of theories. Theories are large TI. These sets of concepts are open for refinement and additional conceptual and theoretical investments. Members of the PA-community are now enabled to debate any proposed TI be it small or large. By doing so, they are *ipso facto* engaged in the epistemic practice of scaffolding. A RT does not present a perfect scaffold, but makes the common practice of scaffolding on the ladder explicit. The image of the "ladder" remains useful in as far as scaffolding moves stepwise from more positive to more conjectural ("speculative") domains.

The scaffolded ladder is *meta*-theoretical in structure, and it can be filled (= determined) with different concepts and theories. The TPCL approach is liberal, but anti-chaotic. Since it is reflective upon all theoretical investments (TI), it forces us to argue in favour and against specific ones. It includes inferentialism, but also points to its limits. Inferences gradually transform into conjectures and educated guesses. The many "perhaps" statements refer to degrees of likeliness. The approach allows theories to fly at different altitudes. It enables us to identify

111 With reference to playfulness, I wish to remind of Huizinga's *Homo Ludens* (1938/1949). To Huizinga, there are words for "play" in many ancient languages and in languages of First Nations. Interestingly, in most languages it is said that humans "play" musical instruments.

disagreement at specific points. It defines rules under which past-present-connectivities are permitted. TPCL belongs to the camp of revised and refined modernity. And it may harbour the legacy of the historical school of the 19th century when PA dawned.

# Part 2: Historical materialism reloaded: The transformative emergence of economic life[112]

## 2.1 Historical materialism reloaded

The TPCL approach (part 1) allows for specific TI. I see the tradition of Historical Materialism (HM) as one comprehensive TI. In this second part, I wish to elaborate on the intuition that "classical" historical materialism stands in need of refinements and adjustments but can serve as a robust macro-historical framework (= paradigm) for PA. In a nutshell: *HM is a specific theoretical investment of the overall TPCL-method within PA under the idea of a RT.* In the first instance, I abstract away all Marxian ethical and political ideas on distributive justice, exploitation, alienation, revolution[113] and emancipation, and take only the theoretical approach of HM in order to *explain* the "great" transformation to a full-fledged (= actual) economic life within prehistoric pre-state collectives in Neolithic Europe after the end of the last Ice Age (8000 BCE). As Marx himself argued, HM does not moralise about the past. Given this premise, I built on Trigger (1993), McGuire (1992; 1993) and Spriggs (2009), wishing to separate HM from political Marxism.

HM presents macro-history. It presumes to have explanatory force with respect to societal transformations according to productive forces and economic relations. To HM, the set of economic concepts is not just a set of concepts among

112 This part is dedicated to the memory of Johannes Bröcker who, as an economist, took a deep interest in the economies of past societies at the beginning of the ROOTS Cluster before he died unexpectedly.

113 I have addressed the problem of revolutions elsewhere (Ott 2017a).

many. Technologies and economic activities and relations are (ultimate) drivers of societal life ("*Unterbau*"). HM can research many *past-past*-transformations, for example, from the Mesolithic to Neolithic times and into the Bronze Age and the Iron Age, and from the transformation from ancient to medieval economic life. HM has its roots in climate theory and in the materialistic philosophies of the 19$^{th}$ century, especially but not exclusively in Marx and Engels. At its core, HM is a theory about past and present technological and economic life. As I argued at the end of part 1, any set of concepts meets an aspect of human life. This also concerns economic concepts. From the TPCL perspective, a set of economic concepts (SC-economic) will be introduced and refined here. Economic theories integrate economic concepts in order to model, to predict, and to explain.

I claim that economic life, *as such,* originated before the Neolithic (better: agricultural transformation (AT)) and came stepwise to mind from an emic perception. Foraging people realised that they were performing economic activities. The basic assumption is that since the Neolithic transformation most humans spent many, if not most hours of their waking life with economic activities. The Neolithic transformation placed humans at work.

> *"Man has been an 'economizing' animal, and during the millennia now past no other activity has claimed so many of his waking hours" (Lowe 1965, 3).*

Economic activities are pervasive for human life and they shape the superstructures of law, religion, art, *etc.* Performing economic activities is struggling for useful, valuable and precious goods. Many PA scholars will be ambivalent about this claim. On the one hand, they feel committed to the legacy of HM, while, on the other hand, they do not wish to see past agents primarily as economic agents. Thus, they should, in a critical spirit, consider the claim to be provoking and try to falsify it.

HM has four topics that are relevant to PA:

1. natural (or "climatic") boundary conditions of material reproduction,
2. pre-economic egalitarian modes of human life (Marx: "original communism"),
3. pre-state organisation of material and symbolic reproduction, and
4. the emergence of economic activities and its implications (stratification, inequalities, division of labour, increase of productive forces, and class formation).

I see 1) *climate theory* as a pre-Marxian variant of HM. A history of climate theory is provided by Falter (2006).[114] The legacy of pre-Marxian climate theory (Montesquieu, Herder, and Tetens[115]) within HM can be harboured by the set of ecological and environmental concepts within TPCL as they are applied to palaeoecology, palaeobotany, and palaeolandscape analysis, and climate change in the past (part 1, section 1.11). Climate theory belongs to the particular way of doing history, since landscapes, climates, and territories are always particular. Climate theory was not based on a dichotomy between humans and nature, but speculates on the many influences of specific natures (for

114 Falter is an extreme right-wing intellectual who writes with polemic rhetoric. Thus, the book does not meet scientific and moral standards. Nevertheless, it gives a broad collection of widely unknown sources to climate theory since ancient times, in the Enlightenment and in the 19$^{th}$ and 20$^{th}$ centuries.

115 Tetens' book *Gedanken von dem Einfluß des Climatis in die Denkungsart des Menschen* (1774/2014) has been interpreted by Ott (2014c).

example borealis, tropics, and temperate zones) upon human bodies, attitudes, and characters. It took an interest in geographic specified ways of human interference into nature for the sake of material reproduction. Water, soils, forests, husbandry, meadows, diets, settlements, *etc.* matter to climate theory. It was claimed that climatic conditions and modes of interference constitute cultural temperaments and characters via "fibers"[116]. Physico-theology of the 18th century was a theologian variant of climate theory trying to understand Planet Earth as a habitable planet (Glacken 1967, chap. 8). Hegel (1822-1832/1970) noted geographical grounds of human history. Climate theory was Eurocentric as it praised the post-glacial temperate zones as being best suited for "higher" culture. To Hegel (1822-1832/1970, 106), tropical heat and Northern freeze are mighty natural forces which allow human survival, but prevent humans from building higher cultures.[117] In Romanticism, climate theory was conceived as mutual influence between land and its inhabitants (Arndt 1820), motivating early calls for the preservation of "wild" and less civilised regions (Riehl 1850/1907). The political philosophy of Romanticised climate theory was conservative and remained sceptical about industrialisation because industrial civilisation would homogenise the land and weaken the population. Industrialism produced monocultures in agriculture, in forestry, in commodity production, and finally human characters. Climate theory became anti-Marxian after 1860. Some Marxists, such as Wittfogel (1931, 1-7) in his *Wirtschaft und Gesellschaft Chinas,* remained aware of the tradition of HM.

Marx and Engels argue in *Die deutsche Ideologie* (1846) that any mode of production has a natural side which should become the starting point of each and any economic and historical analysis.[118]

Given the tradition of climate theory and given the many ideas about human-nature-interactions since ancient times (Glacken 1967), there has never been a dichotomy between humans and nature in practical terms, even if modern philosophers draw a sharp distinction between "*res extensa*" and "*res cogitans*". Descartes, however, was the exception, not the rule. The dichotomy (dualism) between humans and nature, as presented by Descola (2005), is a straw man.

With respect to 2), the Marxian term "original communism" denotes an egalitarian, but "raw" mode of existence which has been often idealised as "paradise lost". The basic idea was stated by Engels (1884).[119] According to Engels, such original communism has been undermined by the encroaching division of labour.

---

116 The "fibres" of Northern people were said to be harder and stronger than those of humans living in the tropics.

117 Hegel (1822-1832/1970, 107): *"Der Mensch ist beständig darauf angewiesen, seine Aufmerksamkeit auf die Natur zu richten, auf die glühenden Strahlen der Sonne und den eisigen Frost. Der wahre Schauplatz für die Weltgeschichte ist daher die gemäßigte Zone".* [English translation]: *"In the extreme zones (...) men are constantly impelled to direct attention to nature, to the glowing rays of the sun, and the icy frost. The true theatre of History is therefore the temperate zone."* [Translation available at: https://asq.africa.ufl.edu/wp-content/uploads/sites/168/Vol-1-Issue-4-Taiwo.pdf; last accessed: 6 December 2023]. This belief was "*opinio communis*" within climate theory.

118 "Alle Geschichtsschreibung muß von diesen natürlichen Grundlagen und ihrer Modifikation im Lauf der Geschichte durch die Aktion der Menschen ausgehen" (Marx and Engels 1846, 21).

119 Engels (1884, 299-300) argued that small communist communities ("kommunistische Gemeinwesen") existed before civilization. *"Diese Gemeinsamkeit der Produktion fand statt innerhalb der engsten Schranken; aber sie führte mit sich die Herrschaft der Produzenten über ihren Produktionsprozeß und ihr Produkt. Sie wissen, was aus dem Produkt wird; sie verzehren es; es verläßt ihre Hände nicht".* [English translation]: *"This collective production was very limited; but inherent in it was the producers' control over their process of production and their product. They knew what became of their product: they consumed it; it did not leave their hands."* [Translation available at: https://www.marxists.org/archive/marx/works/1884/origin-family/ch09.htm; last accessed: 6 December 2023]. At this stage, production cannot generate alien powers (Engels: "gespenstige fremde Mächte"), as in civilization.

Even if we follow Graeber and Wengrow (2021) in abandoning the original Garden Eden, the Golden Age, the myth of the noble savage, the Rousseauian state of original innocence and all related utopian images, we have to take one final look at Marx's and Engels's concept of original communism as a background imaginary of PA. After such a consideration, we may be in a better position to discuss Graeber and Wengrow (2021), who shift the normative concepts from (communist) equality to (anarchic) freedom (see part 4). The real question of "original communism" is whether past humans actively worked to preserve original equality until elites became hereditary, as Flannery and Marcus (2012) argue.

At point 3) it is argued that economic life is far older than state-like authorities, although states are, at specific points of economic affairs, required by economic life. This is a Hobbesian perspective: In an anarchic (= anomic) way of life, economic prosperity is unlikely (Pinker 2018). Hobbes' anomic "state of nature" is a thought experiment, not a historical epoch (Oakeshott 1960). An anarchic state of affairs implies not sharing, but robbery, plunder and looting: "Take what one can take". To Hobbes, laws must be enforced by authorities. Within history, security is fragile. Economic agents profit from legal security of property rights, while states can tax economic gains (for example staple food) (Scott 2017). Economic and political elites often cooperate for mutual benefit. By doing so, they form ruling elites and "grand" families. A state-economy-correlation emerges. There was, however, economic life before there were states. In the following path of reasoning, point 4) is crucial: the emergence of economic life *as such*.

## 2.2 Claim

The basic claim of this part can be stated as follows: *The transformation from simple hunter-gatherer bands to complex foragers and to Neolithic ways of life pragmatically implied the emergence of economic life as such. The economic side of life came to the minds of people (emic). Past humans became conscious economic agents.* The core of economic mindsets is the idea that economic activities are not done for their own sake but should be rewarding for the agents (in a broad sense). The concept of surplus is key.

If this three-fold claim can be substantiated, then the trajectory to the full-fledged economic life of advanced ancient societies (as in Greece and Rome) can be outlined as a past-past-connectivity. The claim supposes basic ideas about what counts as economic life. In the following, I distinguish between "economy" as practice and "economics" as theory about economic practices. The third category is "pre-theoretical economic knowledge". "Buy low, sell high" might be a good pre-theoretical maxim for merchants, but it is not an economic theory yet. Economic life is about production, consumption and exchange. Reciprocity is one mode of exchange that is dominant in earlier societies (Karatani 2014; Graeber 2001). Reward and reciprocity might be conceived as correlative concepts.

## 2.3 Investing economic theories

Throughout part 2, an epistemological problem remains. Scholars are entitled to make TI about economic life and economic knowledge in prehistoric and ancient times. We may perform analogical reasoning with respect to contemporary modes of production and consumption in non-state ethnic groups since we have given permission for critical analogical reasoning in part 1. Given the claim that economic life as such emerged as a profound transformation in the Neolithic, we need to invest a *set of economic categories* to understand and explain such a transformation. On the one hand, the basic categories of modern economic theories (production, labour, commodity, exchange value, opportunity costs, trade, price, investment, wealth, *etc.*) cannot be abstracted away if one wishes to understand and explain economic affairs in prehistory via TI. This is to say that these categories apply to PA. On the other hand, such modern categories may distort our views as they might be full of modern biases, be they affirmative *or* critical against contemporary property rights regimes, such as capitalism, or against allocation schemes such as markets. I would not rule out the possibility of, say, "anti-capitalistic biases".

TI into PA stem from economic theories that have been conceived since ancient and modern times. The first economic theory was conceived by Aristotle, but the origins of modern economic theories stem from the 18th century up to the present (overview in Kruse 1997, see epistemological reflection in Hodgson 2001). Aristotle distinguished two kinds of economies: a) *household economies* that were close to a domestic mode of production (*oikonomia*) and b) *market economies* being performed in order to make a profit in terms of money (*chrematistike*). Aristotle was aware of the difference between use value and exchange value. Households are the realm of use value, while exchange values are traded on markets.[120] The merchant might be primarily interested in exchange value, while the consumer takes an interest in use value. To Aristotle, *oikonomia* is restricted by the boundaries of a household. Thus, it is a "natural" domestic mode of economic life (*sensu* Sahlins 1972/2004). The market-driven *chrematistike,* however, does not have intrinsic limits, as it is always good to earn another unit of money (gold, silver). Thus, to Aristotle, it has no "measure" ("*Maß*") and is therefore "unnatural".[121]

To Aristotle, trade and money are not productive and taking interest is morally repugnant (Kruse 1997, 10-11). To Aristotle, money cannot multiply itself. Interestingly, the Romans did not conceive economic theories although they organised mass production and industries. There are, however, special treatises on rural production, for example, in Columella's "*De re rustibus*" (see Keßler and Ott 2017). The collapse of the Western Roman Empire was, in economic terms, a return to natural based ("feudal") economies combined with a theologian superstructure that was critical against mundane commerce (LeGoff 1988). "*Fenus pecuniae, funus est animae*" (Pope Leo I, 5th century CE). In medieval times, there were theologian rules to restrict economic activities, but no economic theories. Commerce had the smell of sinful greed.

Modern economic theories have been conceived from John Locke and Adam Smith onwards (see Smith 1776/1976[122]). Hegel (1821/1970) was the first German philosopher who gave due respect to economic theory (Smith, Ricardo, Says) being able to decipher general patterns ("laws") out of the multitude of individual economic activities. Economic laws are not natural laws, but patterns of eco-

---

120 Economy modelling often starts with two persons ("producers") who own one specific good (grain, fish, oil, *etc.*). In the background, there is a Lockean assumption that they have acquired the good by their own labour. Because they prefer a bundle of multiple goods over a high amount of a single good, they start exchange. Far later, Adam Smith assumed a basic human inclination to barter, truck, and trade.

121 Marx (1863, 167) quotes Aristoteles at a crucial point in his pure commodity analysis which results in the statement: "*Die Bewegung des Kapitals is daher maßlos*". [English translation Ott]: *"The movement of capital is thus therefore beyond measure."* I prefer "beyond measure" over the official translation "excessive".

122 It is an open question whether Smith's social philosophy is compatible with reciprocity. We should not ignore that Smith was a moral philosopher as well. We have to see the parallels between the impartial spectator and the invisible hand. See contributions in Fricke and Schütt (2005).

nomic regularities which can be observed (and tested) in different societies.[123] Such regularities may find exceptions in specific cultures. It might also be the case that regularities are camouflaged (made invisible) by morals and religion, but might be detectable to economists. Regularities might be "underlying". If so, we need to integrate economists into PA. Here, HM cannot ignore the tradition of the Historical School in economics (Schmoller 1919).[124] The Historical School, however, belongs to particularistic history, while neo-classical mainstream economics is about (rational) individual behaviour and about general regularities. Individual economic agency, cultural specifications (environment, religion, *etc.*) and general patterns of economic activities resemble the three-fold structure of historical thought in the economics of PA.

On reflection, applying economic theories in PA is ambivalent. On the one hand, HM and many approaches in PA implicitly give a prominent role to economic life, while, on the other hand, many archaeologists are reluctant to make use of "Western" economic concepts (with the exception of Marxism and heterodox schools of thought) to explain the behaviour of non-Western people. Archaeologists may refuse to apply modern economic concepts onto past times either due to epistemological or moral and/or political reasons. Epistemological reasons are described as follows: Archaeologists may argue that, for past humans, labour, leisure, production, education, consumption, festivities, *etc.* are integrated into seamless webs of life that we should not split apart into distinct spheres, economy among them. The "seamless-web-of-life" approach should not be taken for granted. Why should we not assume that prehistoric human beings were capable of distinguishing between, say, different "spheres", "roles" and "domains" in how their way of life was organised? Another argument warns that historians should not conceive prehistoric modes of life as being determined by economic activities. Fair enough, but economic TIs do not imply determination. Economic TIs only stipulate that there was a domain of economic activities among other domains (= spheres). Cores of this domain are production, exchange, and consumption.

There are also moral and political motives against such TI. As I heard archaeologists often say, we should "impose capitalistic categories" neither on past collectives nor on present tribal collectives. Even if epistemic concerns might be settled, these anti-economic motives remain. Past humans *should* be different from modern economic agents as they shared, feasted, gifted, worshipped, loved, *etc.* They *should* not have been as greedy and selfish as we believe we are today. They *should* have been more disinterested in economic affairs, in profit, accumulation, wealth, luxury, *etc.* than "we" (or most of us) are. They *should* have done more in a reciprocal common mode and out of solidarity. Their lives *should* provoke us to think about non-commercial modes of production and exchange. Such moral motives are hard to falsify. As I believe, we are not disrespectful against past people if we take them seriously as self-conscious economic agents.

---

123 An additional unit of the same commodity has less marginal utility than the previous unit (Gossen 1888, 12). Supply and demand regulate prices. There is no such thing as a free lunch.

124 Schmoller (1919, 33-34) asked whether there is a basic drive of humans to acquire and accumulate personal or clandestine properties. To Schmoller, such drive can be observed since Neolithic times. Schmoller affirmed J. S. Mill's claim that humans desire to possess wealth, but added that accumulation supposes sedentism or nomadic herding.

Marx himself was not reluctant to apply modern economic concepts to past societies. He was rather demanding in this respect.[125] To Marx, the present full-fledged liberal capitalistic and commercialised economy was a key to understand past economies. To Marx, we are in a better position to understand feudal, oriental, ancient, and I add: prehistoric modes of economic life because we live in a commercialised order of production, labour, consumption, exchange, investments, credits, taxes, monetary policies, *etc.* Modern economic life since the 15th century BCE itself constituted, first, economically educated mindsets (as in merchants) and, second, "classical" economics as a theoretical enterprise (Smith, Ricardo, Marx, Mill, Jevons, Walras, among others). Thus, HM is not in line with approaches that refuse to apply modern economic concepts (models, theories) to past economies. Following Marx, I wish to be more courageous: Economic TI stemming from modern economics should not be omitted from moral anxieties, but should be checked according to their epistemic success or failure.

HM can and should take account of a plurality of economic theories that have been proposed in recent years, such as behaviour economics, welfare economics, ecological economics, household economics, institutional economics, cultural economics, neuro-economics, *etc.* HM should endorse this theoretical pluralism. *It seems likely that one needs the full scope of contemporary economic approaches, including heterodox ones, to understand the transformation towards economic life.* Given the plurality of contemporary economic theories, one *can consume different specific economic approaches for TI within the paradigm of HM in the spirit of the RT.* Given the plurality of economic theories, comparing them with respect to PA might become a playful intellectual enterprise.

If one, for instance, invests the concept of exchange, one may rely on a historical theory about different modes of exchange (Karatani 2014). Commercial trade is only one mode of exchange among others, such as gifting, plundering, pooling, taxing, sharing, *etc.* Human beings have, as Adam Smith noted, a "propensity to truck, barter, and exchange one thing for another" (Smith 1776/1976), which paved the way, first, to a division of labour and, later, to commercialised trade systems. Karatani (2014, 7) distinguishes between a) plunder and redistribution, b) reciprocity and gifting, c) commodity exchange, trade and d) some obscure X which would be a utopian mode of communist exchange. Leaving such a-historical X aside, one can argue that modes of exchange can vary throughout history and can find many combinations. One may ask, whether b) and c) imply that (free) exchange is performed for mutual benefit. If one invests "mutual benefit", one implies the Pareto-criterion. A project fulfils the criterion if one party profits while other parties do not lose. If all parties win, there is Pareto-superiority.

Economic TI may either stem from orthodox or from heterodox modern economic theories. I leave it open whether the political economy of Marx, as given in the "*Capital*", is orthodox or heterodox. It is perfectly reasonable to make TI based

125 "*Die bürgerliche Gesellschaft ist die entwickeltste und mannigfaltigste historische Organisation der Produktion. Die Kategorien, die ihre Verhältnisse ausdrücken, das Verständnis ihrer Gliederung, gewährt daher zugleich Einsicht in die Gliederung und die Produktionsverhältnisse aller* [! KO] *der untergegangenen Gesellschaftsformationen.* [...] *Die bürgerliche Ökonomie liefert so den Schlüssel zur antiken etc.*" (Marx 1859, MEW 13, 636). [English translation]: "*Bourgeois society is the most developed and the most complex historic oganization of production. The categories which express its relations, the comprehension of its structure, thereby also allows insights into the structure and the relations of production of all (! KO) the vanished social formations* [...]. *The bourgeois economy thus supplies the key to the ancient, etc.*" [Translation available at: https://www.marxists.org/subject/dialectics/marx-engels/grundisse.htm; last accessed: 6 December 2023]. I endorse this licence to invest economic concepts into PA.

on heterodox theories, but one should not dogmatically stipulate that heterodox theories in general better apply to earlier modes of life. Heterodox theories made us attentive to kinds of pre-modern economic activity which were not performed in order to maximise utility either on the side of production (profit) or on the side of consumption (pleasure). It is an open question: May we better understand and explain economic life in pre-modern societies if we invest current heterodox economics as, for instance, economics of gifting (Mauss 1925), economics of wastefulness (Bataille 1985), stationary state economics (Mill 1871/1909, book IV, ch. 6; Daly 1996), theories of conspicuous consumption (Veblen 1912), or economics of the commons (Ostrom 1990)? Should TI focus on modes of production or modes of exchange (Karatani 2014)? Such open questions must be answered in a HM approach to economic life in PA. It is true that heterodox theories had a deeper interest in cultural anthropology studies than orthodox ones, but this matter of fact does not indicate that explanatory potentials are superior. Even if heterodox modern economic theories are applied to pre-modern economies, they remain modern ones.

The problems of economic TI cannot be resolved once and for all, but they must be kept in mind constantly throughout part 2. The overall epistemic community of PA scholars will have to reflect critically on each economic category (concept, model, theory) as it is applied to PA. Facing this problem implies that the meta-theoretical idea of TI as outlined in part 1 makes good sense for PA.

## 2.4 On Marxian legacies in contemporary historical materialism

In 1846, Marx and Engels wished to presuppose nothing more than the "real" conditions under which humans had to reproduce their lives.[126] Marx's early version of historical materialism starts with the natural boundary conditions of economies, as climate theory did (see part 1, section 2.1). Marxian HM and climate theory share some assumptions: Humans have to struggle for life under specific natural conditions they face on specific territories. Staying alive is the foremost imperative of human life. Struggling for continuous metabolism (foraging) and reproduction (offspring, care, shelter) under different environmental conditions constitutes niches and cultures. Thus, Marxians must allow for such TI in PA.

> *"Alle Geschichtsschreibung muß von diesen natürlichen Grundlagen und ihrer Modifikation im Lauf der Geschichte durch die Aktion des Menschen ausgehen" (Marx and Engels 1846, 21).* [English translation]: *"All history-writing must set out from these natural foundations and their modification in the course of history by the action of human beings."* [Translation available at: https://www.marxists.org/archive/ruhle/1928/marx/ch03.htm; last accessed: 6 December 2023].

126 See Karl Marx and Friedrich Engels (1846, 20-21): *"Die Voraussetzungen, mit denen wir beginnen, sind keine willkürlichen, keine Dogmen, es sind wirkliche Voraussetzungen. [...] Es sind die wirklichen Lebensbedingungen, ihre Aktion und ihre materiellen Lebensbedingungen, sowohl die vorgefundenen wie die durch ihre eigene Aktion erzeugten. [...] Die vorgefundenen Naturbedingungen, die geologischen, oro-hydrographischen, klimatischen und andern Verhältnissen [...]".* [English translation]: *"The premises from which we begin are not arbitrary ones, not dogmas, but real premises [...]. They are the real individuals, their activity and the material conditions under which they live, both those which they find already existing and those produced by their activity. [...] the natural conditions in which man finds himself – geological, hydrographical, climatic and so on. [...]."* [Translation available at: https://www.marxists.org/archive/marx/works/1845/german-ideology/ch01a.htm; last accessed at: 6 December 2023].

Humans have no alternative: They must interfere in nature, but can do so in many ways. Human agency constitutes modes of production and exchange as well as culturally shaped landscapes. Marxian HM presupposes specific environments, nature, landscapes, and metabolism, but it does so under the perspective of universal history.

In 1859, Marx presented a progressive stage model of universal history as a general result of his studies in political economy.

> *"In groben Umrissen können asiatische, antike, feudale und modern bürgerliche Produktionsweisen als progressive Epochen der ökonomischen Gesellschaftsformation bezeichnet werden" (Marx 1859, 9).* [English translation]: *"In broad outline, the Asiatic, ancient, feudal and modern bourgeois modes of production may be designated as epochs marking progress in the economic development of society."* [Translation available at: https://www.marxists.org/archive/marx/works/1859/critique-pol-economy/preface.htm; last accessed: 6 December 2023].

The stages are seen as evolutionary ones ("*Entwicklungsstufen*", Marx 1859, 8). Thus, Marx is a representative of 19th century stage modellers. Universal stage models have come under sharp theoretical attack from cultural history as they press the multitude of culture into a few stages and suppose the idea of evolutionary progress. If one discards all progressive universal stage models, one must discard Marx's model as well. If one discards it, why should one believe that there will be a final step to take to a new "communist" stage from which all previous stages, including capitalism, look like pre-history (Marx 1859, 9)? It is a simple rhetorical trick to declare all class-societies "prehistory", because it suggests that "real" human history will really start after (or within) the revolution. The final revolution would be the first true act of "real" history.

In Marx's stage model, prehistory is either missing or subsumed under an "Asian mode of production", which would be clearly wrong. I assume that prehistory has been ignored because Marx dubbed an "Asian" mode of production as "oriental despotism" presupposing hierarchically organised states. In 1859, prehistory was simply a missing initial piece in Marx's stage model. The archaeological studies of late Marx in the 1870s motivated Engels to make a correction. Let us take a closer look.

The *Communist Manifesto* (1848) opens with the famous macro-historical claim: "*Die Geschichte aller bisherigen Gesellschaft** ist die Geschichte von Klassenkämpfen*" (Marx and Engels 1848, 462). [English translation]: "*The history of all hitherto existing society** is the history of class struggles.*" [Translation available at: https://www.marxists.org/archive/marx/works/1848/communist-manifesto/ch01.htm; last accessed: 6 December 2023]. I will not debate this claim, but point to a correction that was made by Engels in the 1888 English and 1890 German reprint of the manifesto. The correction is indicated via two marks **. Engels writes in his corrective footnote:

> *"Das heißt, genauer gesprochen, die schriftlich überlieferte Geschichte. 1847 war die Vorgeschichte der Gesellschaft* [...] *noch so gut wie unbekannt.* [...] *Schließlich wurde die innere Organisation dieser urwüchsigen kommunistischen Gesellschaft in ihrer typischen Form bloßgelegt durch Lewis Henry Morgan* [...]. *Mit der Auflösung dieser ursprünglichen Gemeinwesen beginnt die Spaltung der Gesellschaft in besondere und schließlich einander*

> *entgegengesetzte Klassen" (Marx and Engels 1848, 462).*[127] [English translation]: *"That is, all written history. In 1847, the pre-history of society, the social organisation existing previous to recorded history, all but unknown.* [...] *The inner organisation of this primitive communistic society was laid bare, in its typical form, by Lewis Henry Morgan* [...]. *With the dissolution of the primeval communities, society begins to be differentiated into separate and finally antagonistic classes."* [Translation available at: https://www.marxists.org/archive/marx/works/1848/communist-manifesto/ch01.htm; last accessed: 6 December 2023].

In this noteworthy footnote, Engels refers to studies that Marx conducted in the last years of his life.[128] Late Marx was highly interested in archaeological studies since he speculated that there must have been a societal way of life before the emergence of class societies. Marx dubbed this presumptive way of life "original communism". Marx relied on Lewis Henry Morgan's *Ancient Society* (1877). Morgan assumed that the internal organisation of archaic collectives has had a typical form: "*gentes*" (Morgan). Morgan exemplified this form with respect to Australian, American, Greek, and Roman "*gentilism*". Marx assumed that "Asian" modes of production (states) replaced this ancient "*gentilism*" in Eurasian zones. "Asian" modes of production were found in Mesopotamia, Egypt, Persia, among other ancient empires, that were based on slavery, tribute, state, and were hierarchically organised. Morgan conceived a triadic stage-model as well: savagery, barbarism, and civilisation.

Krader (1972) edited the ethnological notebooks of Marx (1972) and wrote a long introduction. Marx's speculation about original communism has roots in Morgan's and Main's ideas that the decisive criteria for progress to "higher" stages of human development are economic ones: production of food, accumulation of property, sedentism, exchange and trade, *etc.* Morgan was influenced by Rousseau's idea that private property has been overrated in modern societies. To Rousseau (1755/1984), landownership was a kind of original sin that caused the many ills and evils of civilised societies. Rousseau argued that equality among humans was lost as surplus emerged (Künzli 1986, 249-259). Rousseau imagined a scenery within which a person claimed private property over land by fencing it in. Rousseau adopts the accusation against private property as a "source of all evils" which can be traced back to ancient times.[129] Rousseau argued with his imaginary idea, how many crimes, wars, and misery could have been avoided, if a courageous person would have destroyed the first fence shouting to his fellow humans:

---

127 To Engels, the divide into classes can result in specific classes or in classes which contradict each other. Class struggles are the Marxian equivalent to the Darwinian struggle for life. To Engels, classes can be different or antagonistic. The mere existence of classes does not imply class struggle ("*Klassenkampf*"). To Marx, there have been centuries without intense class struggle (Flechtheim 1963, 31). In principle, there can be non-antagonistic class societies with high levels of welfare and coherence.

128 Marx's archaeological studies were done parallel to the work on *Capital* (Marx and Engels 1894, MEW 25) that Marx could not complete. Engels (1884) relied on Marx's studies.

129 The idea that private property is the source of all evil was proposed by Morelly (1755/1964). To Graeber and Wengrow (2021), the idea that money is the source of all evil originally stems from the Native American chief Kandiaronk. This claim is highly doubtful, since there was a common practice in the 17th and 18th centuries to give authorship for critique against European civilisation to non-Europeans. See Graeber and Wengrow (2021, 48-59) on the problem of "imagined outsiders".

> *"Beware of listening to this impostor. You are lost if you forget that the fruits of the earth belong to everyone, and that the earth itself belongs to no one" (1755/1984, 109).*

Rousseau implicitly denies Locke's theory of legitimate property by which agricultural labour constitutes legitimate property on land. The Rousseau-Morgan-connection was adopted by Marx, who shared Rousseau's aversion for private property since his early writings.[130] To Marx, private property de-humanises production and exchange completely. Graeber and Wengrow (2021, 65) interpret Rousseau as follows: To Rousseau, Europeans are, "by and large, atrocious creatures [...], and he agrees that property is the root of the problem". This tale has been told since ancient times. Rousseau's proposed property rights regime is, of course, highly simplistic. Are we still "lost" or "stuck" in private property, whose demonic force turns us into greedy and atrocious creatures?

Marx speculated that a communal and egalitarian disposition of modern man was "anchored" in archaic dispositions (Krader 1976, 23). Krader writes (*ibid.*, 14-15):

> *"Die aus Gleichen bestehende Urgemeinschaft ist die revolutionäre Form der Gesellschaft, welche nach der historischen Veränderung, die die Menschheit erfahren hat, und nachdem die Ausbeutung in Form von Sklaverei, Leibeigenschaft und Kapitalismus überwunden ist, einen neuen Inhalt haben wird."* [English translation Ott]: *"The original community of equals is the revolutionary form of society, which will have a new content after the historical change that humanity has undergone and after exploitation in form of slavery, serfdom and capitalism has been overcome."*

To Krader, pre-state egalitarian collectives are an archaic societal format with utopian content and prospects. If so, the origins of inequality look like the Biblical fall out of paradise into a sinful state being dominated by economic attitudes (such as greed). I am doubtful, whether the term "revolutionary" applies to original egalitarian collectives.

Marx's stage model, seen together with Engels' amendment on original communism, is clearly a progressive meta-narrative: Finally, original equality among humans will return in a socio-economic state of affluence. This is a crucial divide between Hegel and Marx: To Hegel, history is progress in the recognition of freedom, while to Marx history is loss and regain of equality.[131] To Marx, humankind must make a long journey from one class society to the next, developing productive forces, before the final antagonism is resolved and affluence can be enjoyed among equals.

Past equality connects the past and the present as original communism works as a political vision for the future. Marxian archaic history of original communism became prominent 100 years after Marx's studies, because intellectuals took an interest in past pre-class and pre-state societies. It seems fair to say that archaeological and ethnographic literature since the 1970s shows much sympathy

---

130 A utopian ideal of production is to be found in Marx (1844, 462). Marx: *"Unsere Produktionen wären ebenso viele Spiegel, woraus unser Wesen sich entgegenleuchtete."* [English translation]: *"Our productions would be just as many mirrors from which our natures would shine forth."* [Translation available at: https://philarchive.org/archive/BYREAA-2; last accessed: 6 December 2023].

131 The approach of Graeber and Wengrow (2021), which emphasises human liberty to experiment with social orders and is more sceptical about equality, is implicitly rather Hegelian than Marxian.

with modes of life which are not dominated by the modern powers of law, money, states, contracts, controls, *etc*.

Four points are noteworthy: *First*, a pre-class stage of human existence (= way of life) is supposed. This supposition has utopian content as original communism ("*urwüchsigkommunistisch*"). Morgan counts as an authority. *Second*, in his footnote, Engels distinguishes *specific* from *contradictory* classes. Proletarians and capitalists are seen as contradictory (= antagonistic) classes. Under this conceptual distinction, it remains doubtful, however, whether specific classes must have always combated each other. The idea that history is essentially a history of "class combat" ("*Klassenkampf*") is undermined by this conceptual distinction. The option of specific, but non-contradictory classes, which may coexist over time, remains open. Thus, HM remains interested in class *formation*, but it is not committed to the claim that class *struggle* between contradictory classes is the major combat which triggers transformations. *Third*, "class" is clearly a modern concept. If historians talk about "class" they apply a concept which was coined in the 19th century. Hegel (1821/1970, § 243) saw the poor strata, which had to sell their mere faculties as embodied labour, as "class". If we speak of "pre-class" societies, we implicitly invest our concept of "class societies". As Marx argues, peasant farmers might have had no idea that they belong to a specific class in a "feudal" formation, but they might have believed that peasantry is a predicament of an order of things given by God. Did a captive, who was sold at a slave market, realise that she now belongs to a class of slaves in a slave-owner mode of production, or did she just mourn about bad fortune in an order within which captives are usually sold as slaves? To Marx, proletarians are the *first* and the *final* class. They form the first actual class as they realise that their way of life is determined by economic forces of capitalistic modes of production, and they constitute the final class, as their destiny (Marx: "*weltgeschichtliche Mission*") is to make an (irreversible) end to all class-based regimes.

*Fourth*, Marx's communist utopia can be understood as a vision of a mode of human existence where ordinary economic life has been uplifted ("*aufgehoben*") to a radically different mode of production and consumption beyond scarcity. To Marx, all class societies are pre-history ("*Vorgeschichte*") and pre-history ends with communism. As soon as the forces of production are fully developed, collectives realise affluence for all by new modes of exchange. This speculative idea has often been seen as an eschatological vision that motivated many young intellectuals at the end of 19th century who became "Marxists" (Morina 2017).

As a *historical* approach, HM remains interested in the emergence of economic life in past societies. We can adopt this epistemic interest without Rousseauism and Marxism. Here, I cannot demonstrate why Marx's "cellular analysis" of the very form of commodities fails (see Schampel 1982) and why a decline in the rate of profit is not deadly for capitalism. It must suffice to reject a universal progressive stage model which terminates in utopian visions (Marx is a theologian of world history.)

This rejection may shed a different light on inequality as a historical force. Inequality, not revolutions, might be the actual "locomotion" within history. This idea has been inspired by the concept of an *inequality possibility frontier* (Milanovic 2016, 52-53), which has been applied to PA (Kerig *et al.* 2023). To Milanovic, this frontier must be small if income is slightly above subsistence level (and if it is assumed that nobody must starve to death). Even if the entire surplus is acquired by small ruling elites, inequality remains limited. The overall collective remains a collective of equals since almost all people are equally poor. It has been argued that members of such collectives have no concept of poverty yet (Rahnema 1991). Poverty comes to mind if there is more overall wealth being distributed unequally.

## 2.5 Explaining the thesis in detail

As it has been argued in part 1, all human collectives have to solve two problems: They have to organise material reproduction, including biological proliferation, and they have to institutionalise symbolic reproduction. HM adopts this claim. Biological reproduction is essentially sexual, while symbolic reproduction is essentially imaginative and lingual (Leroi-Gourhan 1980). Material reproduction starts with foraging. Symbolic reproduction starts (probably) with vocal gestures which are both visual and lingual and it continues with simple speech acts by which behaviour is coordinated ("Go there!", "Help!", "Take it away!"). We have pointed to a specific set of reproductive concepts in part 1, but shifted the determination of this set to part 2. *Hic Rhodus, hic salta.*

Marx sees *economic activities* as basic to human life. Conditions of material production matter (materials, technologies, societal relations, property rights, logistics, *etc.*). Materialism, taken literally, is interested in all materially shaped human enterprises, including modes of exchange (Karatani 2014). Material life, however, is not economic life yet. At this point, I wish to refine HM. To Marx and Engels, humans become distinct from animals as they start to *produce* food. Marx and Engels (1846, 21) state:

> *"Sie (die Menschen, KO) fangen an sich von den Tieren zu unterscheiden, sobald sie anfangen, ihre Lebensmittel zu produzieren [...]. Indem die Menschen ihre Lebensmittel produzieren, produzieren sie indirekt ihr materielles Leben selbst."* [English translation]: *"They (humans, KO) themselves begin to distinguish themselves from animals as soon as they begin to produce their means of subsistence [...]. By producing their means of subsistence men are indirectly producing their actual material life."* [Translation available at: https://www.marxists.org/archive/marx/works/1845/german-ideology/ch01a.htm; last accessed: 6 December 2023].

There is both truth and error in this. There is painful error since hunters and gatherers were fully human but did not *produce* food. But there is also a grain of truth in the statement that once humans started producing food, they also became productive in other economic respects.

> *"Die Weise der Produktion [...] ist vielmehr schon eine bestimmte Art der Tätigkeit dieser Individuen, eine bestimmte Art, ihr Leben zu äußern, eine bestimmte Lebensweise derselben. Wie die Individuen ihr Leben äußern, so sind sie" (Marx and Engels 1848, 21).* [English translation]: *"This mode of production [...] is a definite form of activity of these individuals, a definite form of expressing their life, a definite mode of life on their part. As individuals express their life, so they are."* [Translation available at: https://www.marxists.org/archive/marx/works/1845/german-ideology/ch01a.htm; last accessed: 6 December 2023].

To Marx, humans are nothing but their ways of life.

Thus, HM is interested in the transformation to a way of life being shaped by productive activities. Marx' painful anthropological mistake reveals the importance of the Neolithic transformation, but it also sharpens our views about complex foragers (Graeber and Wengrow 2021, chap. 4 and 5), often based on fisheries (Arnold *et al.* 2016). Once upon a time, humans started to *produce* food on a regular basis. Since humans are dietary flexible omnivores, food can come from animals, plants, and even mushrooms and algae. Regularities correspond to food production: transport, processing, cooking, cleaning, storing, and perhaps, removing waste. If there is regular food production, then there will be, with some practical necessity, the emergence of material economic life. The crucial question is at hand: *Why and how did practical material life become economic life?* This part wishes to explain and understand this transformative step. As we have argued in part 1, humans have reasons to act that can be understood by historians and anthropologists. We will have to ask for presumptive economic reasons which "fit" the material side of life as it is present in archaeological records. *If humans have reasons to act, and if economic activities were persistent with regard to practical material daily life, a set of economic reasons must have come to mind gradually.* At least some humans may have recognised that pooling, gifting and sharing are modes of exchange, among others, such as barter and trade. Since choice is a crucial concept in the set of agency concepts, it can be specified to choices in economic affairs.

If I pick some wild berries and eat them up immediately, this is not an economic activity yet. It is just intake of tasty calories. If I pick the berries, bring them home, dry and store them, I perform an economic activity. I perform foraging for delayed consumption. If I plant some berry shrubs in my garden and harvest berries on a regular basis, I have taken another step into horticultural economic life. If I exchange my surplus berries on a market against other goods, I have taken another step as an "economic human being". If I sell berries for money, another step has been taken. If I speculate demand for berries, I have a business idea. If I take a credit, invest in a large-scale production of berries and hire workers for salaries, I have become an entrepreneur. If I organise the logistics of berry distribution, I have become a merchant. If I dry berries to dried fruit, I make my business independent of seasons. If I criticise unsustainable berry production (e.g. blueberries harvested and delivered from Peru and Chile in January), I have become an ecological economist. If I boycott such berries, I have become a critical consumer. Stepwise, berries are commercialised. Commercialised berry production will supply many people with tasty berries who have no real opportunity to pick berries in the wild.

By thought experiment, historians might speculate whether they were able to describe an archaic collective properly without any use of economic concepts. If one denies such a possibility, one supposes economic life to be understood in its own terms. As matter of fact, archaeological studies are full of economic concepts. The set of economic concepts is linked to materials and technologies. Thus, it has some background in the material records.

*As I claim, economic life as such emerged in the agricultural transformation from its proto-types in complex forager collectives.* Zimmermann (2007, 104) argues that there was the great transformation from acquiring to producing economies. Although direct and immediate acquisition and consumption of food is not economy yet, foraging goes far beyond immediate consumption. Economic relations must go beyond immediacy to become actual relations. If one rejects Sahlins's (1972/2004) suggestion that prehistoric forager collectives lived similar to contemporary egalitarian societies, and if we realise the complex world of foraging without agriculture (or just with tobacco being grown), then we shall realise full-fledged economic life among complex foragers some of who already knew money (Graeber and Wengrow 2021).

I assume that the way of life that was lived by direct acquisition and immediate consumption was a proto-economic way of life to which economic concepts and attitudes do not apply well. The assumption implies that there was, indeed, a prehistoric egalitarian mode of human existence without "actual" economy. Perhaps, at some peripheries, such pre-economic egalitarian ways of life persist. Such ways of life have been idealised as "original affluence" by Sahlins (1972/2004, chap. 1)) (see below). In pre-economic life, social relations are not economic relations yet – and this looks attractive and promising. May humans, perhaps, "uplift" economic life to a post-economic state beyond scarcity, labour, contracts, property rights, and calculations, as Marcuse (1955) hoped for? If we take a closer look at the archaic origins of economic life, we may come in a better position to address this question. Perhaps, one will prefer the continuity of economic life over utopian outlooks of an Orphic culture (Marcuse 1955). To HM, there are many options *within* economic life, but there is no human way of life *beyond* economy. Rousseau put aside, there is no human way of life beyond property rights regimes. If so, humans are, in principle, free to select specific modes of production, exchange, consumptions, and regulations. Such freedom has increased in modern societies where there is much debate in the field of political economy (part 4). We must study economic life under the idea of freedom (Hegel 1821/1970).

Since prehistoric times, humans are economic agents and shall remain economic agents if they wish to replace liberal market capitalism by something else (for better or worse). *From a HM perspective, prehistory shall be studied as the emerging practical performance of economic life as a mode of existence.* The TI is based on the concept of emergence and basic categories of economic activities. The emergence of economic life itself (= as such) is one crucial transformation from the Neolithic Revolution to the ancient civilizations (and, finally, to the full-blown Anthropocene of the present era, see part 3 and part 4). A transformation is substantial if it endures and if it affects the mode of human existence. If a transformation is, by definition, profound, enduring, and, perhaps, irreversible, then economic life is here to stay. "Irreversibility" means that human life after X will never be like it was before X. If one tries to reverse a transformation to a previous state, you always have to deal with the legacy of the transformation. If so, the presumptive return will always reach a new state of affairs. The emergence of economic life is a key event in the transformation towards complex class-and-state-societies. In historical economic life, humans enter economic relations, sometimes deliberately (as in trade), far more often forced, as in slavery, serfdom and in proletarian modes of existence, which were in some sense inescapable in early stages of capitalism (Engels 1845).

In his *Material Culture, Landscapes of Action, and Emergent Causation,* John Robb (2013) conceived a highly convincing Mertonian MRT by which the origins of the European Neolithic might be explained. At 7000 BCE, Europe was a continent of foragers, at 4000 BCE, it was "mostly a continent of farmers" (*ibid.*, 658). The Neolithic package of

> *"sedentism in villages, domesticated animals and grains, pottery, axes and grinding technologies [...] seem to be a result, not a cause of the transition" (ibid., 659).*

Seen at large, the contributions in Jockenhövel (2009) and Olszewski (2020) support Robb's theory.

Husbandry seems to be older than agriculture. Nomadic pastoralism was a long-lasting way of life parallel to agriculture. To Smith (1776/1976), cattle economies are the first mode of an accumulation of wealth, since animals proliferate and herds grow as living funds. The origins of the word "capital" go back to "*caput*" and refer to cattle heads. Cattle breeding is, however, an economy of fortune. Agriculture was slowly introduced and later fully established. The difference between gardening and farming was established. Robb's model includes basic economic concepts: sedentism, food production, surplus, storage, inequality. We will give this model the epistemic status of a TI of a HM-theory. We have to integrate the following points: Sedentism fits better to plant-based food production than nomadism. Sessile plants correlate with sedentary humans. There is sedentism before agriculture. Even in peasant and pastoral societies, practices of gathering and hunting remain. Still today, children and young adults gather plants or small animals (such as shrimps and frogs from mangroves in Southeast Asia). Gathering enriches diets and wild plants are used as medicine. Off-farm foraging contributes to seasonal surplus of farmers. Thus, combinations of food production, gathering and hunting seem to have (evolutionary) advantages over modes of foraging solely being based on either gathering and hunting or cropping. A concentration of food production *and* a diversification of the food supply seems to be a prudent strategy: safe nourishing staples and many tasty additives. The concept of seasonality is important for the emergence of economic life. Seasonality mediates between ecology and economy, as a temporal abundance of a specific food is prolonged by storage (see below). The domestic mode of production (DMP) constitutes new economic relations. The DMP is "cellular" economics. It produces use values and livelihoods, not primarily commodities, but production that is devoted to exchange also becomes an option within a DMP.

We also adopt the materialist perspective upon "things" (artefacts) (Robb 2015). Compared to Palaeolithic life, the Neolithic way of life is a "thing-heavy" world (Robb 2013, 665). Since things, such as figurines, may have a symbolic dimension, the Neolithic has a more complex symbolic order, although farmers may see domesticated animals with more sober eyes than foraging hunters who perceived game in "magic" ways. Hunt paintings have indicated the symbolic dimension since more than 50,000 years, although only a fraction of cave paintings is about hunting scenes. Symbolism precedes economic life, but economic life produces a new "super-structural" symbolic order (status, conspicuous consumption, prestige, rank, luxury goods, works of art).

Let us take a look on the ancient *results* of economic activities since the agricultural transformation. In Europe, we see highly advanced city life in ancient Greece ("poleis"). In his *Ancient Greece at Work* (1926), Gustave Glotz outlined the economic history of ancient Greece, culminating in the Athenian and Hellenistic periods. Advanced economic life includes domestic modes of production, division of labour, enforced labour, a class of free labourers, craftmanship, transport, trade, markets, commodities, currencies, contracts, credits, and the formation of stocks of capital. We see colonialisation, industries, long-distance trade, including slave trade, organised ports, merchants, luxury goods, and, as superstructures, the emergence of Olympic games, democracy, philosophy and fine art (sculptures, theatre). The advanced ancient *poleis* did not fall from heaven, but rests on many requirements. I take such ancient economies as "*explananda*".

What must have happed in advance to make such advanced ancient economies real? There is a puzzle to be answered by abduction: There is X

(Athens 5th century BCE). X is striking as a flourishing ancient polis which differs widely from hunter-gatherer communities and from Neolithic villages which were still dominant in other parts of Europe. One wishes to explain X. What are necessary enabling conditions and requirements for the emergence of X?[132] Hypothesis 1 (H-1): Learning to perform economy. Hypothesis 2 (H-2): Economic activities are in themselves transformative. H-1 and H-2 can be conjoined: *There was a long transition toward X, pragmatically implied in performing activities and establishing social relations among humans which from the point of the participants themselves become gradually visible as being economic ones.* Humans had to learn to see themselves as performing economic life long before some humans regarded themselves as professional merchants or carpenters.

This establishes another implication of the thesis. Humans are mind-full and lingual beings (part 1). *If so, economic life gradually comes to mind and will be lingually (and symbolically) represented.* As we perform economic activities, we have to speak to each other. A paradigmatic lingual representation is, for example, dispute over prices such as that practiced today at bazars and flea-markets. A merchant requires price P-1, and a customer offers a price P-2, usually less than P-1. The difference between P-1 and P-2 becomes the topic of bargaining. If a customer realises that a merchant requires P-1, but one's willingness to pay is less than P-1, she will implicitly understand the concept of a "consumer's rent". If the consumer bargains over the difference between P-1 and P-2, she wishes to maximise her consumer's rent, while the merchant wishes to minimise it without exactly knowing where the customer may draw the line. At many non-Western markets, such bargaining is part of the game, but theoretical economics will make the point that different prices circulate (or float) around the real price even at bazars.

There is practical economic activity first, then states of mind represent such activities, language represents states of mind, economic reasoning emerges, and economic theory is a final result. If economic life comes to mind, the participants may either endorse it or become critical of it. If values are embedded in the significance of actions (Graeber 2001), it seems more likely that prehistoric humans took an affirmative attitude to their activities. It seems rather "good" than "bad" to produce food and other things. It was "good" to have some surplus. It was "good" to store food and hoard wealth in houses. Later, it was "good" to earn or save some money. Such hypothetically assumed original affirmation of economic life might, however, turn into criticism, if consequences of economic life, such as hard labour, serfdom, and inequalities, become manifest. Struggle over labour, resources, property, *etc.* might have been as old as economic life itself. Economic life comes at some price. Ethical criticism against economic life are an intrinsic part of the axial doctrines, as criticism against the vices of greed. The doctrines of the axial age (Platonism, Christianity, Buddhism) are anti-commercial. Thus, in many cultures, advanced economic life is accompanied by anti-commercial doctrines. Commerce will always be under moral attack: greed, egotism, exploitation, alienation, *etc.* This peculiar constellation is also part of the "project of modernity" (Habermas 1984).

132 In German philosophy, there is the concept of "*Erfüllungsbedingungen*" (Hönigswald 1937), which is close to abductive reasoning.

## 2.6 Household economics and the domestic mode of production

If prehistoric economic life was largely characterised by a DMP, modern *household economics* might be of special interest to PA. A household economy cannot be applied to hunter and gatherers since there are neither houses nor holdings. A household can be modelled as a single unit U(H) which cooperates with other households in order to maximise the overall utility of U(H), even if some members of the household (as the tale of Cinderella tells) have to shoulder more burdens of hard work than others. In current economic theory, households are units of consumption which have to divide a monetary budget among its members, while in PA, households are units of production as well which have to organise labour. Money is absent in prehistoric households. We should not simplify household economies according to our modern consumptive households. Past households were complex units. The single-person household is a modern phenomenon. It is a historical question who we consider to belong to a household (close friends, servants, guests, travellers, perhaps even animals).

In PA, a plurality of persons organises the economy of the household. There are many modes of inequality within households such as those related to age, sex, kinship, and status. Economists would consider servants and slaves as members of households. It remains an open question whether animals might have been regarded as members of households in PA, as some people do with their pets today. Guests become full or even privileged members of a household, but there can be ostracism also. A "*mensa*" originally means that a person was adopted as a member of a household. Any household economy must include gender roles and resilience strategies against hard times. In economic terms, resilience consists of resources and strategies to cope with pressures and external disturbances, *etc.* Bad harvests are paradigmatic. Resilience allows households to continue their material and symbolic reproduction. The internal ("organic") solidarity between household members may contribute to its resilience. Within the DPSIR model, resilience belongs to the response-side.[133] A good case study on Late Bronze Age farmstead households in Denmark and their daily routines is given in Earle *et al.* (2022). Such a DMP combined a high level of self-sufficiency with outward trade (as amber).

Today, subsistence farming still can be seen as a paradigm case of a household that is productive and consumptive. The economy of a single household must find some equilibrium between production and consumption over time, if there is no input from outside. Households can accumulate wealth over generations but can also sink into poverty. PA economics should ask which capabilities households may have had at different locations to stay resilient and to accumulate wealth. A disposition of earlier households to accumulate wealth over time would be an indicator for "growth" orientation of economic life (parts III and IV).

Any household has limited resources. Such limits make household decisions necessary. The power of decision-making might be concentrated or not. Households can be modelled a) as hierarchical command-systems governed by dominant persons ("*pater familias*"), b) as bargaining systems between members who wish to maximise individual utility but have different bargaining power, or c) as a genetic kinship community dominated by mutual help, care, protection,

133 Bradtmöller *et al.* (2017) propose a theoretical approach to resilience in archaeology based on the adaptive-cycle model in theoretical ecology. It remains doubtful whether this ecological model is helpful in operationalising resilience of human systems.

solidarity (Wilson: strong kin-altruism). One can also include a d) model with a benevolent household-dictator who wishes to maximise the overall wealth of an intergenerational family line by prudent long-term investments. If one models households as family lines (lineages), one may take a closer look at the emergence of inequality via legacies. With high likeliness, most real households are mixtures of a) to d), while some households might have come close to an ideal type. One may also speculate whether specific household institutions might have entailed ideas on distributive fairness with respect to women, children, servants and elderly individuals and, if so, how such ideas were realised. Adult males are not the majority of archaic households. Perhaps, the concept of "hard" or "rigid" household decisions also apply. A household decision is to be qualified as "hard" if it impairs essential needs of household members, as in cases of war, draught, famines, *etc*. Conflicts over scarce resources have to be settled within households if one cannot make a legal case out of them. It is of great interest for an understanding of normative orders in archaic times (part 1) to investigate whether household behaviour was regulated by codes of conduct.

If we analyse the DMP, and if we keep in mind the two different kinds of economy in Aristotelian economics, we can inquire about the present and future roles of *oikos*-economies in sustainable and resilient systems of production, consumption, and exchange. There might be reasons to integrate *oikos*-economies in post-modern ways of life (see part 4).

## 2.7 Anatomy of economic transformation

HM scaffolds a model with "classical" economical concepts, which are essential to understand and explain material reproduction in former times as well as the transformative emergence and advancement of economic activities as such. The scaffold shall provide an *anatomy of transformation* that is conceived in economic terms. The main TI of this presumed anatomy of transformation toward economic life are:

1. Original egalitarianism
2. Foraging among hunters and gatherers
3. Sedentism
4. Territories and "*Landnahme*"
5. Surplus
6. Storage
7. Division of Labour
8. Modes of Exchange
9. Property Rights
10. Inequality
11. Hierarchies and Heterarchies.

Such conceptual TI are open for refinement and hypothesis formation. The points 6-11 pragmatically imply the origins of law, social stratification, and economic and political power.

Before we enter the analysis, some preliminary conceptual remarks are appropriate. *First*, these economic concepts are not deductive in a linear-causal order. Often, they are correlative concepts which cannot be understood in isolation. One always must have an eye on the other "correlated" concepts. One should not ask for a "*causa prima*" but should see these concepts as parts of a scaffold that might explain why and how prehistoric collectives organised their economic practices. There are many feed-back mechanisms between practices. Practices are correlated with positive or negative incentives, but also with social roles and customs. Crucial concepts often refer to requirements. If we can identify some X, and if we can make an argument from requirement (X requires Y), we can abductively infer Y. We may also find "weak" causal correlations such as "stimulations", "incentives", "triggers", "drivers", "nudges", *etc*. The DPSIR model includes weak causalities leaving leeway for choice.

*Second,* HM is not committed to the claim that symbolic reproduction is always determined by imperatives of material reproduction. HM does not have to deny Weber's point against Marx that doctrines ("belief systems") can also influence material and economic life. If one believes that economic success indicates divine grace, one has an incentive to strive for prosperity. Religious, moral, and political beliefs can determine activities and artefacts. HM allows for "top-down" causality (from beliefs to materials, from speech to actions). Even to Engels, the priority of basis structure over superstructure holds in the "final instance" only. The directives to erect megalithic structures and burial mounds might count as an instance where doctrines (= belief systems) have impacts on materialities. The opposition "materialism versus idealism" is outdated from a HM perspective.

*Third*, much data from archaeological records counts as an indicator for economic activities. The method of abduction (see part 1) works well within HM: If we find X, we can infer P.[134] The gap between artefacts and agencies will be bridged by taking a closer look at the functions of tools as a means of production. Products require production, commodities require consumption.[135] "*Consumere*" originally means to "eat it up" ("*Verzehr*"). In short, I define consumption as a process of utilising a good to its end. The act of purchasing is not consumption yet. Wearing, not buying shoes is consumptive. Consumption is performative. Consumption presupposes use-value *and* exchange value because it could be also consumed by other persons. An agent can either consume a good herself or can exchange it against another good or immaterial service. One can exchange wine against songs and jewellery against kisses. Money is not needed for exchange. Some belongings, of course, may have a symbolic dimension and are "not for exchange".

Remnants from burial mounds are always to be taken with caution as economic indicators, because such remnants are not just items of mundane activities, but are entangled with beliefs ("worldviews") about an afterlife. Burial goods are dialectical as they point in *two* directions: to mundane life and to religious beliefs about the afterlife. On the one hand, burial goods require complex "spiritual" interpretations. On the other hand, burial goods also refer to daily practices and customs. The relation between monuments, burial goods, and long-term economic change remains unclear (Brozio *et al.* 2019). Perhaps, the emergence of

134 The idea has some roots in Brandom (1998). Brandom distinguishes between inferential semantics and normative pragmatics. Inferential pragmatics is about abductive inferences from materials to practices.

135 "*Ohne Produktion keine Konsumption; aber auch ohne Konsumption keine Produktion*" (Marx 1859, 623). [English translation]: *"There is no consumption without production, and no production without consumption."* [Translation available at: https://www.marxists.org/archive/marx/works/1859/critique-pol-economy/appx1.htm; last accessed: 6 December 2023]. See Marx's remarks on production, consumption, and circulation as identity and contradiction (*ibid.*, 622-631).

economic life can explain why richer societies deposit fewer goods in graves than poorer ones. If mindsets become more economically shaped, burial goods appear to be wastefulness. Then, the superstructure may change. The afterlife becomes spiritualised. For Christian doctrine, burial goods are pointless in the afterlife since they are not needed in heaven and are of no help in hell.

*Fourth*, economic activities may, in the long run and in effect, bring about results that go far beyond intentions of economic agents. No one intended to invent economic life. Humans are intentional beings, but large-scale historical achievements have not been directly intended and invented. Something comes about "behind the back" of the agents, bringing about unintended, emerging novelties.[136] Thus, we must adopt and clarify the concept of unintended economic *emergence*. The concept of emergence roughly means that some entities E have come into existence that necessarily suppose other beings B whose traits (properties, features) are not sufficient to derive or to describe the traits of E. Thus, emergence implies some kind of novelty (= innovation). The concept of emergence plays a prominent role in biology. Ecosystems are emerging orders, composed of activities of living organisms. Market systems are another instance of emergent properties. A division of labour constitutes an emergent order of mutual dependencies. Advanced societies become systems of cooperation which are far more productive than subsistence economies, but whose single units are far more dependent on each other than self-reliant households. Mutual dependency must be organised and regulated by emerging governance schemes.

Let us take the example of *cooking* as an emergent human practice. The species *Homo* is an omnivore who invented cooking by fire. Only humans can control fire. The importance of fireplaces for human evolution is beyond doubt. The broad spectrum of food digestion is a natural precondition for the emergence of diverse cultural styles of cooking food and the emergence of "*haute cuisine*". Originally, cooking was likely an adaptive strategy of humans to avoid dental death. By various ways of cooking, diverse possibilities were achieved for many human cultures to prepare and enjoy food. What is the difference between meals and dishes? When did a difference between ordinary food and "big" eating and drinking festivities emerge in prehistoric times? Was there a hidden French top restaurant present at a prehistoric fireplace? Clearly not. But once upon a time, professional cooks must have emerged as part of the division of labour: A cooks dishes for B. Other paradigm cases for the emergence of cultural achievements could be added (*e.g.* making music from drumming on wood and clapping one's hands to the emergence of symphonies and operas). The emergence of economic life might have occurred "behind the back" of agents, but economic life also became gradually visible to its participants.

*Fifth,* we should not conceive prehistoric and ancient people according to our recent "*Homo oeconomicus*" model. This maximising-personal-utility-model is either always true by definition or empirically false. As prudent economists will concede, "*Homo oeconomicus*" is helpful in modelling, but it is not based in anthropology. Humans often reveal *satisficing*, not maximising behaviour. Economic rationality is almost always *bounded* by customs, morals, and religion. "*Homo oeconomicus"* can also appreciate altruistic preferences, leisure, love, beauty, spiritual bliss, contact

136 Hegel (1822-1832/1970, 49) dubbed this "*List der Vernunft*", whereby there are parallels between Smith's "invisible hand" and Hegels "*List der Vernunft*". To Hegel, reason itself is clever because it makes the human passions work on their behalf. The same relation holds between private interests and public wealth.

to higher powers, *etc.* To humans, feelings (such as risk aversion and anxieties), belongings, bonding, trust, *etc.* matter (Perone 2011). Independent individual utility functions are rare exceptions. If one feels good about other people being happy, as in families or among friends, utility functions mix. We should remember that individual utility functions cannot be summed up to a societal welfare function. A global welfare function over generations is an economic myth.

This model figure "*Homo oeconomicus"* may be helpful to test the hypothesis that there is a human inclination to acquire "more" of material or immaterial goods. There can be, of course, very different entities that a human being wishes to acquire. In prehistoric societies, one may have maximised one's welfare by increasing the number of children. The growth of a family is, perhaps, the original pattern of "good" growth: "Be fertile and multiply" (Genesis 1). God promised Abram descendants as many as stars. If honour and reputation (or role models such as knighthood) are a major currency of personal utility, it might be rational to invest in communal festivities and gifting. If one can convert economic success into political power, the former is a means to reach the latter. Recognition can be also the currency of utility. This is, of course, the problem of whether "potlach" festivities (ceremonies) follow an underlying economic logic, as Graeber and Wengrow (2021) believe.

*Sixth,* HM supposes that economic concepts come to the minds of the participants. These concepts are represented a) in the minds (of the participants) and b) in the theories (of the economists). Economic life came to mind, as servants realised work, merchants realised demand, craftsmen realised commodities, *etc.* In ethnoarchaeology, scientists and people can come into dialogue about emic doings and beings. In prehistory, the emic side of economic life remains conjectural, but historians can conceive indicators. I suppose the emergence of complex economic mindsets. The origins of writings can be taken as indicators for economic counting and calculating. If writing starts with economic documentation and contracts, as in Sumer, economic calculation must be older than writings. There must have been some contracting as well.

*Seventh,* HM combines economic analysis and some evolutionism (better: "emergentism") with denial of superiority (see part 1). There is, however, an economic thought experiment about progress: Would you exchange the life you have in 2024 against the life of Rockefeller in 1910? If not, you appreciate an average academic life in 2024 more than the life of the richest man on Planet Earth in 1910. You can modify the thought experiment with other protagonists: the northern forager, the "big man" in the Iron Age, a Homerian warrior, a pharaoh, a Roman landlord, a medieval duke, *etc.* If you would rather not exchange your life against *any* other "upper-class" life in human history, you should now feel very happy. If one should be happy to live a wealthy modern way of life, one can identify economic achievements which should be kept intact in any future transformation of economic life. Even then, one is not entitled to regard one's life as "being superior" to other lives. Ethics may remind us that one should be grateful for good fortune.

Our conceptual equipment is sufficient to move forward. As we know from part 1, we can always refine and amend the equipment of our economic scaffold.

### 2.7.1 Original egalitarianism

The Marxian term "original communism" might be reconceived as a "pre-economic" way of life. Egalitarianism is lived by simple kinds of hunters and gatherers, some of which exist today (Woodburn 1982). It is highly contested whether the contemporary hunters and gatherers should be taken as role models ("mirrors") for foraging before agriculture. McCaffree (2022, 3-6) argue that contemporary foragers enable us to identify some general features of such a way of life. Such a forager contemporary way of life might be characterised as follows (Woodburn 1982): It is raw and brute (according to our standards), but egalitarian. Life is mobile. Group size is low. Persons have few belongings and there is not much trouble about property rights. The concept of poverty does not apply if there are hardly any differences in wealth. Woodburn's analysis (1982) on contemporary egalitarian nomadic groups (*e.g.* !Kung, Mbuti, Batek and Hadza) shows strong levelling mechanisms against the accumulation of property in such groups as "immediate-return systems". Immediacy in itself is a levelling mechanism, but there are others, too. "Inequalities of wealth, power and prestige are a potential source of envy and resentment and can be dangerous for holders" (*ibid.*, 436). Ambush with poisoned arrows is common among the Hadza. Thus, egalitarian control by killing is as immediate as the economic system itself (*ibid.*, 437). Another levelling mechanism is gambling which makes belongings circulate randomly. Gambling nomads in an immediate return system have hardly any incentive to accumulate. There are no incentives for accumulation in such a way of life. Storage and transport of things is low. There is not hard labour over long hours but foraging, direct consumption, and much leisure (or boredom) to be filled with gambling, gossip, and sex. People have no professions. Randomness and (good and bad) fortune are important features in life. Life expectancy and health status are (very) low. Youth slips away soon and there is no old age waiting. Parasitism is widespread. Dental status is poor. Privacy does not exist. Robberies, assaults, raiders and ambush occur. Note that contemporary hunter and gatherer groups are surrounded by people living different, often modernised lives.

People might not have or have had any concept of scarcity, if they can survive on a daily basis.[137] Such a mode of existence is, however, not "original affluence" (Sahlins 1972/2004), but it is rather a way of life before scarcity, affluence, poverty and wealth. With some likeliness, however, differences between "enough", "less than enough", and "more than enough" matters on the emic side. Starving, thirst, pain, wounds, *etc.* are experienced. There is, indeed, not much labour, but lots of time left for "leisure"[138] and gambling.

Taking a closer look at sharing-meat practices indicates derivation from equal shares. The Hadza do not "place much emphasis on formal meal times" (*ibid.*, 440). The image of large common meals with equal shares among fellows is misleading. These collectives are not "sharing economies", as the hunters consume a large fraction of the meat themselves at the hunting grounds and only bring some meat to the campsite. At the camp (or the kill site), the initiated men consume the best portions in secret. The rest of the meat, if there is any, is called

137 The term "primitive" might transport colonial attitudes, but it also refers to structural characteristics of such a life as egalitarian, simple, repetitive, short, and often on the edge of survival. The term "primitive" is discarded because of its connotations and wrongful suggestions.

138 If we take the thick description of Woodburn (1982) for granted, we may ask whether there is real "leisure" or rather repetitive boredom. The investment of a concept such as "leisure" (Latin: "*otium*") is not self-evident. In the camps of egalitarian groups, there is not much one can do.

"people's meat" (*ibid.*, 441). Meat eating is strongly associated with male fertility. Another "thick" description of meat sharing practices among the Hadza is, however, given by Widlok (2017, esp. chap. 2). He argues that sharing is a different mode of exchange than gifting.

Let us assume that there are still some nomadic tribal communities within which strong levelling mechanisms work against inequality.[139] Let us further assume that immediate-return communities show a lack of commitments compared to our type of society. Such life is "unbound". One has, however, to explain why egalitarian societies have become exceptional and mainly survived in marginal and harsh areas. I see such lives as unbound but not as "free" (in a modern sense of freedom). Following Graeber and Wengrow (2021), I argue that there were many foraging cultures before agriculture which were far more complex than these contemporary egalitarian collectives. I also agree with the following claim: "Any equality worth the name is essentially impossible for all but the very simplest foragers" (*ibid.*, 129). Graeber and Wengrow rely on the distinction between "simple" and "complex" which has an evolutionist subtext. Complexity implies that humans can take different social roles. Note also, that Graeber and Wengrow qualify equality by "worth the name" as complete equality. Thus, equality becomes an "all-or-nothing" affair which is incompatible with contemporary theories of justice which are based on the question "*Equality of what?*".

For concepts of original equality, there is an alternative: Either one a) conceives it as similar to the way of life in contemporary egalitarian collectives. If so, it does not look attractive from the perspective of a Western middle-class citizen. It displays no utopian form. Or b) it denotes a different way of life. Then, the concept of equality vaporises. Complex past foragers are stratified and often engage in raiding and slave trade which are not "sharing" activities. Making captives constitutes radical inequality. The alternative looks fatal for the concept of original equality. If it is not a historical concept, it should not survive as a "zombie"-concept (vision, image, utopia).

## 2.7.2 Foraging among hunters and gatherers

HM sees *foraging* as a proto-economic activity ("economy in the making"), but intentional food production (husbandry, horticulture, agriculture) as a full-blown economic activity.

Palaeolithic foraging was originally mostly performed in open landscapes at daytime. Humans gathered and hunted in banks, on wetlands, in light forests, in rivers, and on savannahs (Hobohm 2021, 6). Foragers perceived something *as* being food or not. Some plants were edible, while some are not. Others were toxic. Food is nourishing. The good feeling of being well-nourished is familiar to (almost) all humans. Humans know that all other humans must eat to survive. This is life-world-knowledge. Eating can take place on a regular basis or it can be volatile. There might be surplus and overabundance one day, while no food is eaten on other days. Since humans can survive for weeks without food, volatile foraging is a way of life in which hunger is often present. As skeletons indicate, children in post-glacial landscapes may have periodically experienced hunger and famine in cold seasons of the year. Being hungry may have been perceived as quite normal.

139 Such communities are clearly attractive from an anthropological perspective since they differ widely from "our" society. Such ethnographic fascination should not be biased in favour of such lives.

According to Scott (2017), humans are inclined to reduce the radius of procurement for a meal. Such a reduction is efficient in terms of calories, and it adds to the embodied wealth: strength and weight. The radius of a meal might be measured by calories being spent for foraging against calories that are acquired. Foraging can be researched under the efficiency-criterion or as "optimal foraging" (Smith 1983). Optimal foraging, from a biological perspective, would mean *ceteris paribus* to maximise the difference between spent and acquired calories. Sociobiology conceives models of efficient (= optimal) foraging based on the assumption of opportunistic behaviour. Efficiency may have deep roots in an inclination for opportunistic convenience. The concept of efficiency means that an agent reaches an objective with least possible effort. All successful strategies to reach an objective are *effective*, but only one strategy is *efficient*. Some philosophers see instrumental rationality as close to economic rationality (Hodgson 2001, chap. 3). Economic activities may reveal such types of rational behaviour.

Foraging models must integrate the fact that food is more than just calories. If some food is more valuable (meat), one has to find an "optimal balance" between "low hanging fruits" and precious and prestigious meals. Some food is tastier than others. Tastiness makes foraging more complex. If there is tasty food at a distance, one may expand the radius in order to reach it. The radius of a meal is related to territories, distance, taste, and risk assessments.

If so, why not assume that gatherers *ceteris paribus* prefer to perform foraging at places where roots, nuts, berries, *etc.* are abundant and easy to pluck. Why *not* assume that humans *ceteris paribus* prefer low-hanging fruits? Of course, there might be reasons to acquire special food at a distance (berries, honey, game, fish). There is no reason *prima facie* to gather non-edible plants. If one, however, picks flowers to attract another person for mating, there is a reason to do so. If plant-abundant places are dangerous because of predators, humans face a trade-off and they have to assess risks of becoming prey before making a choice.[140] One can trust in good luck, but this is not an adaptive strategy in the long run. Will the rest of the band be safe if five adult males go for a hunt far away? A hunter may ask: "Should we leave them alone?" Risk and uncertainty make consequential assessment more complex from within instrumental rationality. In any case, *foraging is connected to practical reasons of how to act.* Such reasons can become standards of prudence.

*Hunting* is a (proto)-economic activity. Chimps go for group hunting, and group hunting is common among humans since the glacial ages (Flannery 2018). Mammoths were hunted. Humans and grey wolves probably had a relationship of mutualism in hunting game. Wolves turned from friends to foes as humans domesticated sheep, goat, and cattle. One should notice that there are clever ways to hunt, such as attracting ants and geese and even game with food ("*anfüttern*"). Half-tame birds are easy to catch. Humans can also make traps and snares (Wadley 2019). Traps and snares are hunting tools which allow humans to "hunt from a distance". Trapping is more effective because most animals flee if they register humans. There are many strategies of where and how to hunt, trap, and gather. Whenever the origins of pitfalls and snares emerged, humans also went hunting with traps which supposes much physical, biological, and technological knowledge.

Humans can debate how to perform such activities. Such speech implies concepts of prey game, effectiveness, effort, distance, timeliness, technologies,

140 See pragmatic evolutionary theories of intelligence, for example, Engels (1989).

(perhaps) support of wolves, yields, taste, nutrition, risk, and likeliness of success or failure. We have to assume that speech acts and deliberation occurred before a hunt, within the performance of a hunt, and after a hunt. If there are speech acts like: "Hunting success is more likely in A than in B. Success is better than failure. Therefore, we should go to A" and some proto-economic thoughts about probabilities, preferences and choice come to mind. Hunters also have to anticipate how to transport prey back to camps. Perhaps, it was risk assessment which made hunting a real economic activity: gain and loss were possible outcomes. Being prey instead of making prey is the worst case. We can suppose *that* complex "hunting deliberations" must have occurred, but we can only speculate *how*.

We can suppose foraging choices among hunters and gatherers under conditions of risk and uncertainty. If Palaeolithic bands may have counted 30-50 people (McCaffree 2022, 8), the numbers of hunters probably amounted to around five persons (Flannery 2018). This makes it rational to hunt large game under the maxim of loss aversion: act in order to minimise the risk of dead or wounded hunters. Common foraging by hunting requires decision-making under conditions of uncertainty. Why not come back to the camp for the evening with some ducks or rabbits than hunt large game in the distance for days? The problem of "good enough" comes to mind, which is reflected in the satisficing-behaviour theory in modern economics. "More" is not always better, if the striving for more consumes time and search costs. Search costs of hunting are high. Satisficing behaviour can take the cultural form of spiritual wisdom: Hunters have to be content with the given and shall be grateful to animal deities if a large animal has sacrificed his life.[141] Clearly, such economic concepts may have been mediated with ideas about taboos, witchcraft, the "givenness" of the animals, territoriality, *etc*. Proto-economic activities have a material and a spiritual side which is represented in cave painting. If there is a spiritual commitment to consume prey animals entirely (including blood, liver, kidneys, *etc*.), there is a reason to stop hunting if this commitment faces limits of resource management. If hunters believe that they will have evil fortunes (diseases, death of children) if they allow meat to go foul, they have a strong reason to stop hunting. Perhaps, the hunters ate as much as they can at the hunt site if transport capacities were limited. Contemporary hunters eat much at the hunting sites.

Common interaction generally constitutes social bonding: harvesting, hunting, cleaning, singing, drinking, feasting, campfire talk, *etc*. This holds for hunting as well. On the social side, common hunting constitutes, perhaps, friendship and comradeship among males. Hunters were ranked according to their capabilities. The extinction of Pleistocene megafauna (Hobohm 2021) indicates all too successful hunting strategies.

There is an (economic) transformation from hunting to husbandry and herding.

> *"It is likely that pastoralism developed, with wolves or dogs as the principal supporter and ungulates as a source of food and materials, thousands of years before agriculture was developed" (Hobohm 2021, 7).*

Russell (2007) argues that domestication had effects not just on animals but also on humans. Domesticated animals were not just tamed, but bred according to human interests. *Breeding* constituted differences to wild variants, as boars are distinct

141 I adopt such wisdom from narratives of the Okanagan-Sylx-nation. See Armstrong (2010). Jeanette Armstrong has been the Okanagan-Sylx "speaker of the land".

from pigs. Darwin was inspired by breeding activities, so breeding belongs to the "context of discovery" of Darwin's theory of evolution.[142] It remains open whether the literal meaning of "domestication" implies that settlement was present before animal keeping (Wilson 2007) or whether the term means "habituate to humans" (Russell 2007). Sedentism is self-domestication of humans which may have been adaptive (in the biological sense of proliferation) (Wilson 1988). Domestication is a great transformation in the ways of human life.

There are two interrelated pathways a) from gathering to horticulture and to agriculture, and b) from hunting over nomadic pastoralism to domesticated animals in corrals and stables. Both agriculture and pastoralism can have more nomadic ("shifting cultivation") and more settled forms. Herding allows people to leave the settlements for some periods and return. Husbandry and herding are crucial steps in economic life since cattle mean wealth and "capital". Cattle[143] are more than just meat, wool and milk, as they have a symbolic and an exchange value. The symbolic value can be actualised in sacrifices, hospitality and festivities, while the exchange value can be actualised in different ways. Cattle markets are important events in contemporary semi-nomadic economies. As it seems, there is an inclination of nomadic herdsmen to increase the number of animals as long as the grazing systems allow for such growth. Herdsmen realise that grazing capacities are the "limiting factor" for herd size. In the Hebrew Bible, this has been documented in the narrative of Abram and Lot (Genesis 13:5-6). "And the land was not able to bear them, that they might dwell together, for their substance was so great, so that they could not dwell together. And there was a strife between the herdsmen" (Genesis 13:6-7). To balance the number of domesticated animals with grazing capacities means to regulate economic activities either peacefully or violently. Abram wishes to avoid conflict and proposes to split. Because humans can negotiate a situation of overgrazing, there is just a tragedy of open access, not a tragedy of the commons. In grazing systems, the concept of limiting factors comes to mind. Facing limiting factors implies that the scarcity of natural resources also comes to mind.

## 2.7.3 Scarcity

Economists are interested in the phenomenon called "scarcity of means", given the many ends humans may wish to reach. Lionel Robbins provided a famous definition:

> *"Economics is the science which studies human behaviour as a relationship between ends and scarce means which have alternative uses" (Robbins 1932, 16).*

There can be as many ends as humans have needs, desires, aspirations, and wishes. Economists take humans as "wishful" beings under boundary conditions of scarcity and embedded in cultural settings and normative orders. The basic economic assumption states that the number of all human wishes always exceeds the means to fulfil them. Even if all wishes of some humans are fulfilled, some

142 Darwin himself refers to breeding as artificial selection to explain his theory of natural selection in his *Origins of Species* (1859). The practical knowledge of breeders was supposed in Darwin's theory.

143 The term "cattle" includes all large domesticated mammals: sheep, goat, bovines, pig, rabbits, camels, *etc*. A good overview about the history and current state of domestication is provided in Cassidy and Mullin (2007).

wishes of some people will remain unfulfilled, always. This predicament of scarcity comes to mind in prehistory.

Cultural economics points to the many encoded ways to deal with scarcity and limitations. Economists concede specific affairs of affluence (*e.g.* eating and drinking at some weddings), but they reject general affluence.[144] Even if no one goes hungry to bed, mansions at lakeshores remain scarce. Even if there are enough alcoholic beverages, old Bordeaux wines will remain scarce. In an epidemic, beds for intense treatment may suddenly become scarce. Scarcity is relative with respect to needs, desires, aspirations, expectations, *etc.* Scarcity comes and goes in degrees for specific groups at specific locations. Scarcity must be perceived as such and it has been experienced throughout history. A hunter may perceive scarcity of arrows. Storage facilities can become scarce in relation to harvests. Timber and fodder become scarce at the end of the winter season. Declining stocks of resources create *prima facie* scarcity. Interestingly enough, the realities of scarcity can be negated by religious doctrines that the fertile earth has plentiful resources by which, in principle, all essential needs of anybody can be fulfilled (see Segbers 2002 for the Hebrew religion). The human lifeworld entails the conviction that scarcity of means continues even if there are moments of saturation and affluence, as in festivities. To economists, a human society in which all persons are "perfectly happy" is wishful thinking. Utopias are, then, a second order of wishful thinking: A wish to live in a world in which all wishes of all humans (or all sentient beings) are fulfilled, all desires satisfied, *etc.*[145] Living within limits may be more humane than trying to realise utopia (part 4).

One might argue that scarcity was unknown to hunters and gatherers because they lived in original affluence. Affluence is conceptually opposite to scarcity. According to Sahlins (1972/2004, 1-41), contemporary hunters and gatherers, such as Kalahari Bushmen, enjoy "a kind of material plenty" without any surplus and storage. Sahlins affirmatively quotes Marshall who praises the Bushmen for not "hoarding" things. Metabolism is direct and immediate from hand to mouth.[146] Egalitarian prosperity means "affluence without abundance" (*ibid.*, 11), and people being "content with few possessions". Has the attribute "content" been rightly chosen? Sahlins' semantic difference between "affluence" and "abundance" is hard to interpret because both terms mean "more than enough". While "affluence" means plenty, "abundance" means hoarding, as I suppose. Sahlins supposes that aboriginal people deliberately chose this way of life "for it is with them a policy, a 'matter of principle' as Gusinde says (1961, 2), and not a misfortune" (Sahlins 1972/2004, 11).[147] Living in plenty without hoarding things (or even money) represents a "good" way of life, as has been suggested by counter cultures since the 1970s.[148] The figure of the hunter looks as if proto-Stoic ethics have been realised: "His wants are scarce and his means (in relation) plentiful" (*ibid.*, 13).

144 If a restaurant offers "as much as you can eat" for a specific price, this offer is not based on affluence, but on calculation how much an average adult can eat.

145 Utopian Marxism (Bloch, Marcuse) rests on the premise that productive forces have increased in such ways as to make such a state beyond scarcity possible.

146 This resonates with Engels (1884, 300): "Das Produkt [...] verläßt ihre Hände nicht".

147 The source is Martin Gusinde "*The Yamana*". This book was originally published in Germany in 1931. Sahlins quotes the translation from 1961. Gusinde did ethnographic research on indigenous people at Tierra del Fuego. Gusinde's biography is provided by Bornemann (1970). It remains doubtful whether this source is credible to warrant Sahlins's claim.

148 Interestingly, Lewis Mumford (1967) imagined such life in Neolithic villages, seen as communities and neighbourhoods.

Hunters and gatherers are not poor, but free (*ibid.*, 14). But is there not some kind of scarcity if wants are scarce? "Scarcity of wants" is an ambiguous concept. It can either mean that some wants never have come to some minds because they are "beyond the horizon", or that some wants have come to mind but have been discarded and suppressed. Sahlins leaves the ambiguity unresolved.

To hunters, material things are burdens. Hunters and nomads must live "lightly", and, perhaps, be "sloppy" with belongings (*ibid.*, 12). They can afford to be lazy and sleepy (*ibid.*, 20). Some are "lazy travelers" (*ibid.*, 29). It seems fair to say that Sahlins's hunters and gatherers look a bit like "hippies", as there were many in the 1970s.[149] Sahlins quotes Lee (1968), who argues that the storage of food "is morally something else again, 'hoarding'" (Sahlins, *ibid.*, 32). Storage of food should run counter to the self-esteem of the hunter (*ibid.*, 32). Even if this may be true for the Kalahari Bushmen, the transfer by way of analogy into former times remains dubious. "Hoarding" seems vicious, but who says so? It is not clear who speaks about "hoarding" (the word is presented in quotation marks): Bushmen themselves, Lee, Gusinde, Sahlins?

> *"Poverty is not a certain small amount of goods, nor it is just a relation between means and ends; above all it is a relation between people. Poverty is a social status. As such it is the invention of civilization" (Sahlins, ibid., 38).*

As matter of fact, however, humans, with very few exceptions, left the "evolutionary base line" (*ibid.*, 40) of hunters and gatherers. Why did they not remain in such original affluence? Why did they exchange "affluence without abundance" against "treadmills of growth without plenty"? Why are contemporary hunters and gatherers marginal groups in harsh environments? Perhaps, these questions are misleading since they, following Sahlins, take contemporary egalitarian collectives as paradigmatic for hunters and gatherers. Graeber and Wengrow (2021, 139) point to Sahlins' "fragile premise" that most collectives before the agricultural transformation lived lives similar to contemporary marginal foragers (Sahlins 1972/2004, 38). This premise does not survive recent findings on complex foragers and their cultures.[150]

It is likely that prehistoric complex foragers realised many kinds of scarcity. Hunters must have realised that the number of arrows was finite and transport capacities were scarce in relation to the weight of a killed mammoth. Within a hunt, time can become scarce. Scarcity is not a state of the world, but a human outlook and perception of realities. Scarcities of different kinds must have come to mind: grazing grounds, food, storage capacities, time constraints, *etc.* Scarcity emerged as an outlook and mode of experience in prehistoric times and it became evident in economic thought. The awareness of scarcity does not diminish but increases with societal wealth. The "original-affluence" thesis, if it ever was more than a polemical retorsion of Galbraith's *Affluent Society* (1958), cannot falsify the TI of scarcity as a basic category in economic life since prehistoric times. Even degrowth economies have to be aware of returning scarcities in a society that move from an ever-lasting "more than before" to a "less than before" (see part 4).

149 The political background of Sahlins was the "French May 1968", when Sahlins was in Paris having lunch with Pierre Clastres on a daily basis. See Graeber and Wengrow (2021, 135-136).

150 Graeber and Wengrow (2021, 139-147) rightly argue that there are many foragers' ways of life, some highly stratified and highly complex such as the very long "Jomon"-period in Japan before rice cultivation started. Some forager cultures placed high value on the accumulation of shell money. Others engaged in raiding and slave trade.

There are three options left: Either a) scarcity is perceived in all economic modes of production, or b) scarcity is a cultural phenomenon, known in many but not all societies, or c) scarcity is a modern ideological invention to legitimise growth. I give more credit to a). By doing so, I assume a sense of scarcity, temporality, and finitude within the human lifeworld (part 4).

From a (Stoic) moral point of view, it remains true that virtuous and voluntary scarcity of wants allows high levels of satisfaction because the difference between satisfied and unsatisfied wants is low. This comes at the price that people have to discard the wants they feel. Economists would concede the possibility of ascetic utility functions but deny that they have been widespread in human history. A historical point of view can take both perspectives into account: On the one hand, it recognises social movements whose members curtail their wants (monks, nuns) while, on the other hand, it sees a dominant economic trajectory of expansion and growth which diminishes some kinds of scarcity for majorities. The mainstream human strategy to combat scarcity was enlargement of the resource base: *expansion and growth*. Even if we wish to overcome this "growth-addicted" strategy, we should not simply deny it (see parts 3 and 4). My historical claim is that expansion and growth have deep roots in human history.[151] Colonialising wild areas (later called "*terra nullius*") has been one way to perform this strategy. Military conquest of territories was another expansionist strategy throughout history.[152] There is an economy of conquest, as in raiding, tribute, defence strategies (walls, fortresses, *etc.*). In the following sections, I abstract away the economy of military conquest and colonialisation and focus exclusively on non-violent economic activities. Widening production ("economic growth") is a civic strategy to reduce scarcity of specific goods without ending scarcity as such in general.[153]

The point about scarcity as an economic phenomenon divides HM from utopian communism, within which the means of production ideally enable the satisfaction of all (legitimate[154]) needs. If original communism is a pre-economical mode of human existence, there was no scarcity yet. If final communism is a post-economical mode, there will be no scarcity any more. Original and final states of affairs coincide at different material levels. Communism is conceived as egalitarian affluence. Real societies, however, will always remain in between. If so, scarcity will remain even in any real society and this will be the case *a fortiori* for a degrowth-society. We should not forget that slightly increasing scarcities in times of pandemic and war (2020-2022) provoked many anxieties. This is why postgrowth-societies must be highly efficient (see part 4).

### 2.7.4 Sedentism

Mobile hunter-gatherer foraging sets rigid limits to growth, while sedentism opens the door to growth. As Sahlins notes, "mobility precludes accumulation" (see also Robb 2013, 666; McCaffree 2022, 7). If a contemporary person values

151 Religious and ethical wisdom can suggest that the reduction of desires is a proper way to satisfaction. The fewer desires, the more can be fulfilled with more ease, as the Stoics have argued. This Stoic ethical solution to the scarcity problem has never been representative for groups, communities, and societies. For the sufficiency problem, see Ott and Voget-Kleschin (2013).

152 Under National Socialism, Germany performed an expansionist "*Lebensraum*" strategy.

153 In the 1960s in Germany, housewives kept an eye on clothing, towels and blankets as they dried outdoors because the risk of theft was high. Such behaviour ended as textiles became less scarce over time. Nobody is inclined to steal cups, pencils and toilet paper at university institutes.

154 Needs stemming from class societies, such as expensive tastes, probably would not count as legitimate ones.

mobility very much, she has a reason not to accumulate possessions. Mobility can be either voluntary or enforced. Migration is an example of the former, while refugees are results of the latter.[155] Mobility of foragers is necessitated by seasonal fruits, migrating wild animals, temperatures, and other pressures. Mobility comes at the price of fewer pregnancies, high infant mortality, and even infanticide (McCaffree 2022, 10). Thus, sedentism (self-domestication of humans) might have been an adaptive strategy which had deep impacts on the overall way of life. Life becomes (more) settled.

There is sedentism before agriculture. There have been many settled complex forager cultures. Sedentism means dwelling or "housing" continuously at a specific place (see critical debate in Bailey *et al.* 2005; Whittle 1997). Housing means having a safe place in permanence rather than searching for resources in vast and often unpredictable and hostile landscapes.[156] Nomadism is a lifeform between hunting and gathering, on the one side, and sedentism on the other side. Nomads move along specific routes between winter and summer camps ("transhumance"). Such regular nomadism allows for more belongings than hunters can achieve, but less than settlers may accumulate. Settlements allow for a DMP and its taskscapes. As we shall see in more detail, sedentism, proliferation, surplus, storage, housing, wealth accumulation, and settlement structures suppose and reinforce each other.

There is much worry why this slow but profound transformation to sedentism occurred at all. Some archaeologists praise the bright sides of nomadic life. Sedentism is seen as self-domestication ("taming") of humans. Sedentism, however, seems to have clear adaptive advantages over nomadism. A house provides shelter from natural forces (rain, storm, snow). It is a location for cooking, sex, fire places, recovery, education, storage, property, crafts, and some luxury items. If gardens belong to the surroundings of houses, another safe place emerges.

Sedentism is *ipso facto* place-making, housing, and dwelling. Material reproduction (foraging, proliferation) becomes localised and quite often rooted in normative ideas about land tenure and other property rights. Houses are material remnants of a "settled" way of human life. Settlements are the material side of dwelling (emic side). I suppose that prehistoric humans also may have endorsed this perspective of dwelling, as findings from houses allow for inferences on behaviour and belief. Sedentism allows for an accumulation of things as stored wealth. From an economic perspective, houses both store and present wealth in terms of precious goods (Wilson 1988). A house itself means wealth. The basements can even be burial places. Sometimes, family lines are identified with "houses". The quality of housing can be increased in space and decoration until, finally, palaces result. The civic palace is the mansion (part 3).

"Being at home" belongs to the lifeworld. It constitutes the difference between an endo- and an exosphere of life. In many cultures, one must not step on the doorstep. Houses are (relatively) safe places. The house is an archetype of the Neolithic village: walls, rooftops, fireplaces, beds, doorsteps are both material and symbolic. The interior of houses may have been full of ornamental decoration and trophies. Humans can lock doors from inside to feel safe at night and sleep well.

If it is true that sleep is different within Palaeolithic camps and settlements, the dreams of humans might have become different in settlements. Bilz (1971)

155 The distinction between refugees and migrants is highly contested in its details within the ethics of migration (Ott and Riemann 2018), but should not be discarded in history and sociology.

156 Note that highly mobile lifestyles are seen as a curse in ancient times. Kain was cursed to a mobile life without safe places (Genesis 1:4).

argues that sleep in Palaeolithic times must have been more open to environmental signals since hostile forces may come at night. If there are predator animals active at night around campsites, sleep is short and waking up is closer because the likelihood of a "fight-or-flight situation" is not negligible. Sleep becomes deeper at safe places. As I speculate, the difference between sleeping and being awake becomes sharper in a sedentary way of life at the expense of "daydreaming". One wakes up in bed from sleep in the morning.

In a settled and domestic mode of production, the difference between work and production becomes established. In her book *Vita Activa oder Vom tätigen Leben,* Hannah Arendt (1960) distinguished work from production. Arendtian work is cooking meals and cleaning houses (or tents) on a regular basis, often performed by females and servants. While work is fugitive, products remain as durable things. The domestic mode of production ("oikos") requires cooking and cleaning on a regular basis, since otherwise a house gets messy and dirty (whatever the standards). Dishes are eaten up rapidly, clean floors get dirty soon again. Work terminates in dirt, waste and garbage, production creates commodities, some of them luxury ones. We must integrate the "work" perspective in PA, which is missing in Marx who was only interested in production. Feminist economy is helpful in this respect. Arendt's definition looks idiosyncratic, but it has a "*fundamentum in re*" and it clearly points to gender roles. It might be an Arendtian question whether there is some evidence in the records that tells us about standards of "clean" houses. Females (housewives) often had to work, males produced. The doings of males are represented in the record, while female work leaves fewer traces. The categories "work" and "production" must have become meaningful to Neolithic people as two kinds of labour. They must have realised that it is not fun if one has to perform hard labour. Labour can be "hard", meaning long, intense, repetitive, dirty, risky, and tiring.[157] A conceptual difference between labour and leisure (later: "*otium*") must have gradually come to mind. This difference is an economic one. In Latin, business is "*negotium*", the negation of "*otium*". Economists would say that – apart from workaholics – most utility functions reveal a preference for leisure over labour. If so, it is a rational strategy to maximise leisure at the expense of enforced and often unfree labour. Slavery existed until modern times and some kinds of labour are still slave-like today (Kabadayi and Reichardt 2007). The opposition between free men who enjoyed leisure time for valuable doings and unfree labouring people was established in Athens.

Sedentism does not imply social hierarchies. There were large, non-hierarchical settlements in Tripolje (4100-3700 BCE) which show few signs of social stratification (Müller *et al.* 2018). There are, however, many regions where hierarchical settlement structures prevailed, for example, in the Fertile Crescent.

> *"Sedentism* [...] *did create the conditions for an unprecedented level of concentration of food and population* [...]. *I choose to call such locations late-Neolithic multispecies resettlement camps" (Scott 2017, 18).*

Scott mentions the presumptive negative side of such settlements: infectious diseases, labour, rules, tributes, and enforcement. Scott argues (2017, 20) that hardly any forager "in most environments would shift to agriculture unless forced

157 See Michael Walzer's chapter on "Hard Work" in his *Spheres of Justice* (Walzer 1983). From a Freudian perspective, humans tend to avoid hard work. They need incentives, gratifications or they must be forced into work. Throughout history, much work was forced.

to by population pressure or some form of coercion". Scott mentions burdens and plagues of agricultural life for non-elites. One may add poor sanitation and a monotonous diet. The coercion-hypothesis, however, may overlook the adaptive sides of sedentism, at least before states emerged. The sympathies with the uncoerced life of the hunters may have a male bias.

If females took a highly active role in hominization in general (Tanner 1981), why not assume a similar role on the way to sedentism. Perhaps, females in their role as mothers of infants are better off in settlements than in mobile campsites. Pregnancies, fertile female years, and birth rates may have increased, child mortality and involuntary abortion might have decreased, periods of sexual abstention might have been shortened. The theory of the Neolithic demographic transition assumes a steady increase in human populations. Scott (2017, 6) estimates that 2-4 million humans existed at 10,000 BCE, while 170 million humans existed at the time when Jesus lived. In the last millennium BCE, population increase was sharp. Thus, sedentism was adaptive. Why not assume that especially women and children profited from sedentism (Mumford 1967)? Why not assume that sedentism makes a *caring* attitude more likely than in a hunter and gatherer way of life. Humans care for other humans, be it children or elders, but they also care for plants in gardens and for domesticated animals, as the archaic image of the "good" shepherd indicates. Sedentism may have made the difference between a rather less caring and a more caring way of life.

New findings indicate that Neolithic life was probably less unhealthy than Scott assumes (Fuchs *et al.* 2019). There is not much evidence of population decline due to infectious diseases in the records. The "great" times of epidemics might have come later, for example, in ancient Roman and medieval times (Harper 2017). The combination of sedentism, complex foraging, horticultures, herding, surplus production, and processing food might have been a successful way of life before states. Taken together with the role of brewing beer since millennia (Morse 1980; McGovern 2020), a narrative on the good, bright, and adaptive sides of sedentism and agriculture seems within reach.

The economic unit of prehistoric villages and towns is the "*oikos*", the household. The Neolithic mode of production was mostly characterised by a DMP. Sahlins (2004, chap. 2-4) argues that a DMP is essentially inert and conservative. I cast doubts on Sahlins's claim.[158] A DMP can spur many innovations and create material wealth. It is an economic location where a division of labour emerges. We see a DMP as production and storage of food, but also as centres of specific crafts. Parts of larger Neolithic settlements were often divided into quarters (= districts) of single professions. Far later, there were still some lanes in town where specific professions were concentrated ("baker street", "butcher lane"). Households are units of work, production, consumption, reproduction, kinship, care, and leisure.

Settlements are constituted by *neighbourhoods* as social relations (Smith 2010; Smith *et al.* 2015). Families, clans, neighbourhoods, and, perhaps, elites differentiate among the inhabitants of settlements. Children explore neighbourhoods. Large settlements are constituted by enclosures provided by natural conditions (rivers, hill tops), or by fences or walls. Living inside housing areas divides "inside" and "outside" life. Which settlement structures allow for social relations

158 First of all, the claim seems to rest on an analogical inference from contemporary pre-state societies to past societies. Such inferences from analogies must be seen critically, but I will not stress this methodological point here.

that we call "(good) neighbourhoods"? In contrast, which settlement structures indicate large inequalities between palaces and prison-like workhouses? How different were housings of free and unfree persons? Were there gardens in prehistoric settlements? If so, which plants were grown? How did people in settlements cultivate fruits? How did ancient and even prehistoric people organise garden life? How was the scent of gardens perceived? How did "pomology" emerge as practical knowledge. Answering such questions contributes to an understanding of daily prehistoric life and its taskscapes.

All *settlements* face specific problems. We might understand prehistoric economies better if we know what counts as waste and garbage for its members. What counts as waste for one person, might not count as waste for another person. One might speculate whether items count as waste for all persons equally in a perfect egalitarian society. In a stratified society, however, the practice of waste-picking is likely. Waste-picking has long traditions in many societies. Were there groups in prehistoric settlements whose members recycled waste and dumped the rest somewhere, as the outcasts in ancient India do? Waste management might have been a basic functional unit of settlements in PA which is of major importance for urban agglomeration in the Anthropocene. It is an illusion that one can "just throw it away".

Settled life is not just the "shining" side of palaces, temples, and necropolises. Eating is just the upper side of metabolism. The lower gut-side of metabolism is defecation that must be located (latrines). One can defecate at common places, somewhere outside of a village, gender-separated. In China, faeces were used as fertilisers even in the 20$^{th}$ century. Settlements must organise mouth-gut-metabolism. This problem is crucial for today's slum dwellers (Davis 2007).

Different settlement patterns emerged. One pattern is agglomeration as a way of settlement growth without a clear centre (Smith and Lobo 2019). Another pattern is hierarchical, such as a castle, palace, and/or temple, which become the (spiritual) centres around which the ordinary houses are located. A third pattern is to establish new settlements at a distance. Different patterns of settlements constitute different public spaces and different ways to perform/present oneself in the public. From rather egalitarian mega-site settlements, more diverse towns emerged with a complex symbolic order, luxury goods, religious and political centres, *etc*. Towns were far advanced at the time of Sophocles' "Antigone" (part 3). "Building a city" (Sophocles) implies many economic and political activities. Plato has registered essential building blocks of a town in the second volume of his "*Politeia*".

## 2.7.5 Territories and "*Landnahme*"

Houses and settlements are located on territories. I see houses as the micro-, settlements and neighbourhoods as the meso- and close territories as the macro-scales of the entire endosphere, which is separated from an (hostile and alien) exosphere (Müller 1987). HM must address the significance of territories (and frontiers) for prehistoric humans. To Marx, the equalising effects of modern industries and urban agglomerations reduced the importance of land in capitalism. Marx was rather disinterested in rural life, agriculture, cattle, forestry, and fisheries. He focused on the system of industrial fabrication. To Marxists, capitalism produces, invests, and distributes within largely urbanised spaces which are subordinated to the imperatives of logistics, transport, trade, advertisement, and shopping. Capitalist modes of production are disinterested in territories, seen as natural/cultural landscapes. Territories are transformed into neutral spaces designed for commerce.[159] Such disinterestedness is reproduced by (post)modern lifestyles in which it does not matter much whether one lives in Hamburg, London, or in Seattle in terms of flats, super-markets, audience halls, restaurants, offices, *etc.* (given a decent salary). Perhaps, the digitalised and urbanised patterns of academic mobility motivate sympathies for prehistoric mobile lives. Post-modern academic nomads show sympathies for migrants, not for farmers.

Prehistoric sedentary lives are localised. One cannot hardly overrate the meaning of territoriality since the Neolithic period. HM must devote due diligence to understand prehistoric modes of territoriality. Settlements imply territorial claims. Territories define the available resource base. Material reproduction must be successful with local and regional resources which cannot be substituted by imports. Reliance on localised resources (subsistence) is key for material reproduction. Since it is localised, reproduction is embedded in vast and changing regimes of natural forces (precipitation, storms, cold winters, droughts, *etc.*) which cannot be controlled but must be coped with. Thus, material and symbolic reproduction must be adaptive to specific territories and resilient to disturbances and (not too) extreme events. Continuity of subsistence and livelihood is not simply given, but must be arranged as soon as settlements have been built. The feeling of security on owned territories is crucial (McCaffree 2022, 13).

European PA must presuppose that humans migrated into unknown and empty postglacial territories with collective intentions to settle down. In Neolithic times, migrating and settling are economic activities. Humans had to take food, seeds, and animals with them to survive the period in time needed to remove forests, cultivate plants, build houses and adapt to new environments (Zimmermann 2007). Migration was a kind of investment in the future. There must have been decisions to settle down based on outlooks on the territories at hand. One may speculate about questions that were posed, for example: "Is this territory promising, rich in resources, fertile, and climatically suitable for settlement, thus not full of disease burdens? Is it a good place to settle down? Or should we move forward?" Perhaps, there is a bountiful bonanza behind the horizon. Perhaps, not.

There are always reasons to move further on and reasons to stay and settle down. Who might have had a say in decision-making? If one believes that women are more prone to sedentism than males, and if they had a say on the matter, they might have voted for settling down if the prospects for livelihood looked decent to them. What might have mattered: freshwater, timber, nuts, berries, grazing systems, game, fish, non-timber forest resources, non-muddy grounds, fertile soils, evenness of ground, abiotic resources such as flint stones, but also some higher points for fortification, *etc*. There is the economic parlance of "rich territory" in terms of the natural resource base: a "bonanza". Prehistoric settlers search for such bonanza-like places.

Migrating into and settling down at a specific territory is "*Landnahme*" (Schmitt 1950). To Schmitt, "*Landnahme*" ("claiming territory" = CT) is a radical title ("*nomos*") from which specific normative orders emerge. CT is to be integrated into HM. CT is different from mere raiding, piracy and robbery. Claiming territory entails claiming land for one's own group. CT is occupation with the intention to settle down. A question of ultimate importance asks whether a given

159 In globalised capitalism, foreign direct investments turn territories into locations of production (as long as transport costs are low). Capitalism mobilises competition between locations as presumptive destinations for investments.

territory counts as a "*terra nullius*"[160] or whether it has been already claimed by other humans. "Is there free access or is there a risk of conflict? Do other humans in the region welcome us or not? Shall we try to accommodate with other people claiming territorial property rights?"

CT can take different (typical) forms. It can take the form of *violent conquest* by which an original indigenous population is evicted, displaced, enslaved, or simply killed. It can take the form of an *invitation* by a ruler (chief, duke, king) to colonialise wild territories that are reigned formally, but not materially. Quite often, rulers were interested in cultivation and provided incentives for settlers. It can be reasonable for them to populate a region with immigrants. There might have been occupation based on invitation. CT can also take the form of *migrating* into wild areas (which are later called "*terra nullius"*) which is "colonialisation". Mixed forms might have been historical realities. In the Hebrew Bible, there is the idea of a promised land which people shall reach after a long trail through the deserts and badlands. This idea has been adopted by the white settlers occupying North America. Today, we see it as colonial ideology.

After the end of the glacial period, there have been CTs all over Europe at different times and territories. To Schmitt, CTs are original factual events ("*factum*" = "being performed"), not intellectual constructs such as the ahistorical constructs of a "state of nature" (as given by Hobbes and Locke).[161] Law is rooted in territorial orderings. Political power is jurisdiction over territory and people. According to Schmitt:

> *"Die Landnahme* [...] *enthält die raumhafte Anfangsordnung, den Ursprung aller weiteren konkreten Ordnung und allen Rechts. Sie ist das Wurzelschlagen im Sinnreich der Geschichte." (Schmitt 1950, 19)* [English translation]: *"It [land appropriation KO] constitutes the original spatial order, the source of all further concrete order and all further law. It is the reproductive root in the normative order of history."* [Translation available at: https://archive.org/details/TheNomosOfTheEarth/page/n47/mode/2up?q=original+spatial+order; last accessed: 6 December 2023].

CTs are always close to ideologies (= doctrines) why some people are (not) entitled to reign and control specific territories. A "*nomos*" is an original constitutive act (Schmitt: "*Ur-Akte des Rechts*"). CT belongs to historical periods in which people were proud to colonialise land.

According to Schmitt, any CT-nomos refers, first, to seasons and rhythms of fertile land which allow for material reproduction, second to lines (walls, fences, dikes, roads, palisades), and, third, to settlements and kinds of buildings (fortresses, castles, assembly halls, megalithic monuments, sacred sites, *etc.*). Schmitt (1950, 13) argues that land is three-fold related to legal orders: a) fruit of labour and property rights, b) borderlines, and c) public order. A "*nomos*" constitutes collective property rights of a community over a territory ("*our* land"). Any "*nomos*" entitles a community to exclude all others. A nomos can be represented by narratives of how the ancestors "won" the land. There are many tales of brave settlers, CT and hard work within settler economies.

---

160 Of course, the Latin wording was not at hand in PA.

161 Not to speak of Rousseau's purely fictious state of nature when people lived mostly in isolation from each other.

According to Schmitt, one should leave aside all modern ideas of how to legitimise normative orders from the factual practice of CT throughout history. A "*nomos"* is prior to any contemporary problem of political legitimacy. A "*nomos"* is not a product of a constitutional assembly, but based on "land grabbing", often violently performed and irreconcilable with our contemporary principles of justice. CT is not a blueprint for current political philosophy, but it constitutes a HM perspective how territories have been won and lost since prehistoric times. Occupying land (= conquest) has an *economical* dimension. It is a primordial macro-economic affair. Territorial claims can be respected or not. I abstract away the martial side of conflict over territories and assume that many peaceful economical activities rely on uncontested territorial claims. Such claims are required for economic prosperity. Pottage (2019, 174) argues that Schmitt's concept of CT is probably the final upshot of a jurisprudence that is patterned by Holocene conditions and the "empty world" of the past: "Schmitt's *Nomos* is in fact the last flourish of 'Holocene jurisprudence'".

Neolithic settlements and ancient cities are surrounded by "barbarian" zones where hunting, gathering, processing food, fur and leather, collecting shellfish, forestry, *etc.* are performed (Scott 2017, 33). The barbarian zones can profit from exchange with settlements, villages, and cities. Settlements are also locations that attract warriors interested in plundering. Barbarians are often raiders. Settlements must be able to defend themselves against attacks. Wealth must be safeguarded by walls and local brigades, since there is no rule of law within large territories before states came into existence. Defence is self-defence, be it successful or not. Interestingly, tributes may often be the lesser evil than war. "Tribute" is an economic concept. Tribute is rather a payment than a gift. It might be better to pay a tribute than to be conquered and enslaved. Tributes require complex economies and they prelude taxes. We must pay attention to early modes of taxation[162] as economic affairs. Plundering is violent, tributes are enforced, while taxes are imposed. The famous slogan: "*No taxation without representation*" opens the historical path to democratic taxation.

Raiding is a kind of a "business model", which may include tributes, enslaving captives and may also turn into mercenaries fighting for despotic states (Scott 2017, 255-256). Invasions by sea-people are a form of naval raiding. I see raiding as a proto-economy of parasitic business models. "Parasitic" means that the products of labour can be appropriated by means of violence (Scott 2017, 238). "Plunder and trade [...] were very effectively combined" by raiders (Scott 2017, 227). In the barbarian zones, there can be successful economic combinations of complex foraging, trading, enslaving, sporadic raiding and claiming tributes for "protection". The economies of the "golden age of the barbarians", however, undermined this way of life. The "chain of predation" for captives strengthened the state as well as the sale of martial skills by mercenaries (Scott 2017, 256). I abstract away these business models, although comparable ones emerge in our present age (see part 4).

162 Today, distributive and compensatory justice are about criteria that define who must pay how much: polluters should pay, beneficiaries should pay, the rich should pay, the poor should be liberated from payments, and so on. In the Anthropocene, matters of justice are often coined in terms of payments. Justice becomes *economised*. Is such economisation of justice just a recent phenomenon?

## 2.7.6 Surplus

Lions eat and leave the rest of prey to other animal consumers. A lion would not understand why humans make a problem out of "what's left after a meal". Animals are disinterested in "what's left", while humans started to take a proto-economic interest in "what remains". As I was told as a boy, one should not waste food. It is always better to "eat it up" than to throw food away. Our current aversions against food waste in private households and supermarkets may have deep roots. Food waste is the negative outcome of a surplus of food. As long as the storage of food is impossible, the hours spent on foraging might be less than labour time in industrialism.[163] Clearly, it does not make sense to collect or hunt more food than can be consumed if it can be neither stored nor exchanged. Hunting rules of tribal collectives demand the consumption of the entire body of a killed animal and forbid killing another animal before the previous one is fully consumed.

Sahlins (1972/2004, 31) touches the crucial topic of *surplus*. He notes (*ibid.*, 23) that bushmen often give surplus to the dogs. To hunter and gatherers, surplus implies a trade-off between storage and mobility (see also Robb 2013). Perhaps, hunters can resolve this trade-off in favour of mobility if "nature has, so to speak, done considerable storage of their own" (Sahlins 1972/2004, 32). Storage may rather constitute a burden than security. Human agents, however, are free to decide such trade-offs differently. They are also free to perceive surplus differently.

Some surplus may remain after the process of immediate daily consumption. Imagine for the sake of argument a situation in an egalitarian community in which everyone's needs for food have been satisfied and something edible remains. To humans, then, remaining food creates an economic problem. One may throw it away, may give it to the dogs, or may think about other and better options. Reason tells that there might be better options than disinterested wastefulness.

Overabundance and surplus, however, remain a random affair to hunters and gatherers within an overall volatile food supply. (Over)abundance may simply have occurred from good luck in hunting and gathering. Active surplus production might have originated gradually from the phenomenon of periodical (over) abundance on the long trail to sedentism. Seasonality is generally important to prehistoric human lives, but seasonality matters differently to hunters and gatherers and people living at least in periodic campsite settlements for some months. Ripe fruits are (over-)abundant for some weeks until the season is over. At some time, there is "too much of x", while most of the time there is a lack of x. A continuity of supply with x looks better than the volatile modes of overabundance and scarcity. Why not process a regular supply with x, if one can? Sedentism improves the options to store surplus. If tribes and bands of the First Nations make a campsite for the winter, there is storage of buffalo meat and dried berries which are at the core of a winter's diet. In Northern latitudes, people store frozen meat in ice cages. There is storage before agriculture, but sedentism makes more room for the interplay of harvesting and storage.

We adopt the claim which Robb (2013, 663) draws from Woodburn (1982):

> *"Economies where food is produced in long-term projects and can be stored are inherently susceptible to accumulating surplus and developing inequality."*

163 This was by no means "affluence", as Sahlins argued. Among hunters and gatherers, life expectancy was very low, child mortality high, humans often fell prey to predators, starvation was widespread, health status was low, *etc*. Life was pervasively exposed to premature death.

Darmangeat (2020) provides an overview on the theories of surplus and the conceptual relations between surplus and storage. He shows that surplus theories often assume that surplus is appropriated by a ruling class. Surplus, however, originated long before class societies. One should better decouple surplus from exploitation. Can one locate surplus in a DMP? Surplus is different from Marx's specific concept of "surplus value", since it remains silent on who does hold property rights over surplus. If we define surplus as "excess of production over what the producers received" (Darmangeat 2020, 63), surplus is conceptually connected to control over labour and exploitation of producers. I prefer a more neutral concept of surplus: "excess (= overshoot) over consumption".

Under conditions of emerging sedentism and DMP, people might have had the clever economic idea that it might be good to produce surplus and store it on a regular basis. Surplus production gradually emerged *as such*. Surplus production does not need states. From a biological perspective, surplus contributes positively to material reproduction, and it might be adaptive from a biological perspective. A regular food supply enhances the fertility of women. The wisdom of the female body registers hunger as an indicator not to become pregnant. From an economic perspective, surplus production within a domestic mode of production is a prudent activity. Surplus is abundance seen with economic eyes: More than enough for the moment, but probably not enough in the longer run. By consent or, more likely, by coercion and command from chiefs of households, domestic surplus production might have been organised. Skills and technologies of storage emerged as prehistoric modes of biotechnology.

Graeber and Wengrow (2021, 128) write:

> *"We need to focus on the very notion of a surplus and the much broader – almost existential – questions it raises. As philosophers realized long ago, this is a concept that poses fundamental questions about what it means to be human. [...] We are creatures of excess, and this is what makes us simultaneously the most creative, and most destructive of all species."*

I perfectly agree. Surplus is a crucial economic category. Is there a peculiar implicit connection between surplus and growth? Why should the prudence of producing and processing some surplus eclipse into excessiveness? Graeber and Wengrow do not tell us. Here, part 3 provides an explanation.

Surplus implies economic choice. One may, for instance, store surplus crops for delayed consumption or take them as seed for widening agricultural production in the next season, may ferment cereals for alcoholic beverages, may organise common festivities (for rank and prestige), may exchange gifts, may arrange weddings, may trade commodities, or may pay a tribute for more security. One can invest surplus for different objectives, but usually not for all objectives simultaneously. Surplus is different from abundance. Surplus is scarce and must be invested prudently. Any choice implies opportunity costs and requires consideration which choice might be "best" under given circumstances, forecasting, and beliefs. Considerations regarding choice may pave the way to concepts of prudence ("*phronesis*"), as in Aristoteles. A reasonable choice should be a well-considered preference based on options being ranked (Hausman 2011). One may also assume economic deliberation between members of a household about options before decision-making. If one holds a strong religious belief, sacrificing surplus to a protective deity is also reasonable. Surplus opens the door to all kinds of exchange (Karatani 2014). It can be perfectly reasonable to share surplus under the expectation that other parties will also share their surplus with me/us. Sharing economies can be societal safety nets long before welfare states. Perhaps, sharing may relieve the costs of the welfare state in the future (part 4).

Storage of surplus further ignites economic ways of thinking. A person may have asked the economic question: "How long can we live from the resources being stored?" This economic question has a clear answer: "It depends on whether we behave wastefully or not". If one has to decide whether to store surplus at home or trade it on a market against another good, one faces an economic choice. If some fraction of cereals must be kept safe as seeds and if another fraction must be eaten up, and if surplus has been produced, one can eat more, devote more for sowing in the next season (widening production), store the surplus as a food reserve, or exchange it. Here, the basic trade-offs between consumption, investments, savings, and trade are entailed in choices to be made. Thus, these economic categories might have come to mind even if the concept of investment was not perfectly clear to people who decided to store a surplus of cereals for seeds in order to expand production in the next cropping cycle.

Surplus, investment (seeds), returns of investment (yields), more surplus, more investment, more return and so on – this is the logic of accumulation ($K \rightarrow K^* \rightarrow K^{**}$). Surplus production may finally terminate in capital. Seeds and soils are clearly agricultural capitals: stocks that yield useful flows. Soil formation in PA by manure might count as capitalising nature. Periods of fallow land are means against degradation. This logic of accumulation differs under different institutions: hierarchical slave-holding societies (as in Mesopotamia and Egypt) or in more heterarchical societies without states and taxes. The logic of accumulation leaves it open as to how wealth was dispersed in different societies, but it makes egalitarian distribution unlikely. Surplus widens the inequality frontier since more patterns of distribution emerge. It runs counter to the liberty, the intelligence, and the inventiveness of prehistoric humans to assume that egalitarian distribution was always seen as the first-best option. From our modern moral point of view, a burden of proof falls upon unequal distribution (Tugendhat 1994). It is, however, unclear whether this moral point of view was held by prehistoric humans. If Nietzsche was right in his genealogy of morals, moral egalitarianism was established in the axial age at the earliest. If so, we should not impose egalitarian morals upon past humans. We should search for indicators whether they conceived distribution in terms of merit, closeness, need, fortune, grace, or destiny.

### 2.7.7 Storage

As I have argued so far, houses are locations of a DMP and of storage facilities (as in pantries). Agriculture brings about surplus on a more regular basis and storage emerges as part of the Neolithic and the Bronze Age economy (Darmangeat 2020). In the first instance, the storage of food is an insurance against an uncertain future. By means of storage, consumption can be delayed. Storage as an enlarged way of foraging supposes the intelligence of risk-aversion with respect to a fragile food supply. Storage is the first safety net in PA. The economy of delayed rewarding starts.

Storage may have originated in smoking or freezing meat and drying fish and berries as it is still practiced today in Northern latitudes. In Northern latitudes, ice is a medium of storage. One can also store food underground, as it is done with vegetables in winter. If one freezes meat after a hunt or processes apples to juice, mousse, or wine, one stores seasonal surplus (abundance, plenty). Oil, wine, and grain can be stored. Cheese is stored milk and cheese production also started in the late Neolithic.[164] Humans also store smells, as in perfume.

The storage of food starts with pantries and is enlarged to caverns and, later, silos. The records indicate food processing activities (cleaning grain). Storage implies laborious (and often boring) processing and vice versa. Processing food is a first step on a long route to contemporary industrialised ways of processing and storing food, ending up with deep-frozen, highly processed convenient food in supermarkets.

Storage is not an exclusive product of an exploitative state economy. In hierarchical societies, storage might be centralised, while it must have been more dispersed in heterarchical ones. In early states in Mesopotamia, surplus production was enforced upon unfree persons (captives, slaves) and appropriated by ruling elites (Scott 2017).

Storage also brings about property rights as a crucial step towards economic life. Who is entitled to consume or exchange stored food – and who is not? Who has access to a pantry – and who has no access? A special case occurs if there are storage facilities, such as pits, which can store food over a long period of time, but the food must be consumed quickly as soon as they are opened. Therefore, to open a pit is an all-or-nothing decision made by command or by deliberation. Who is entitled to open a storage pit – and who is not? The logic of storage implies choice, trade-offs, and decision-making. One important consequence of storage was the search for weights and measures whose signs became prototypes of scriptures.

*Saving* for the sake of saving is not reasonable, but it makes good sense to save in order to pass an *inheritance* to one's descendants. Dealing with savings is clearly an economic activity. Savings can result in initial stocks of capital to be invested in new projects. The origins of investment decisions as a mode of economic choice emerge. The logic of investment requires one to assess presumptive returns of investments (profit) in an uncertain future. Investment in shipping and trade was one risky option. The difference between hoarding and investing became meaningful. To Marx, investing capitalists act more reasonable than persons who hoard money and jewellery (Marx: "*Schatzbildner*"). To Marx, hoarding is mad capitalism. The real spirit of capitalism is a spirit of courageous investment.

Stored food may become an instrument of political power, as the Biblical story of Joseph indicates. Joseph interprets the dream of the pharaoh about seven fat and seven meagre cows as symbolising seven good and seven bad harvests. Joseph also suggests storing food in seven years to come. Twenty percent of good harvests should be taxed away (Genesis 41:33-45) and should be stored in urban centres under the supervision of the pharaoh. Joseph was made the supreme collector of crops and he stored crops "as sand" (Genesis 41:49). As the famine occurs a decade later, Joseph exchanges stored food against money, cattle, land, and future economic income (tributes) on behalf of the pharaoh (Genesis 41:48). The Hebrew Bible tells how stored food can be turned into wealth and power without moralising Joseph's behaviour. In ancient Egypt, storage was organised by the state. The release of stored food becomes output-legitimacy of a political order. Hoarding food in times of famine, however, counts today as vicious specu-

---

164 If most calves were born in spring and summer time, milk was a seasonal product. The strategy was as always: store temporal affluence. Cheese is a result of "surplus storage" via biotechnology. See Balasse *et al.* (2021) for a scientifically based analysis of calving, milk availability, and the origins of cheese production.

lation. This pattern of thought was present in the food crisis in 2008/9 as hedging practices were accused of hoarding at the expense of the global poor. National states store food for times of crisis, as Germany does with 800,000 tons of foodstuffs. The FAO organises the storage of food on a global scale. Today, mankind could be fed for several months from stored food.

Food storage has a relation to yields. If new harvests bring fresh yield and there is still stored food from previous harvests left, exchange may become more rational than further storage. In modern times, a "sale" starts if storage capacities become scarce. If there was a lot of labour invested in the storage of food, economic humans will not waste stored food even if they have harvested fresh food. One might give such food to poor people and receive a positive moral reputation by doing so. One might share it with other groups in order to form coalitions. Reciprocity requires some reward. Sometimes, the animals might be fed. Trade also becomes an option. In the practice of *trade*, commodities are for sale. Initially, a commodity A can be exchanged against a commodity B. If markets are established, the institution of money emerges (as a general equivalent). In trade, things have a price. One can bargain about specific prices, but there cannot be trade without prices. The mechanisms of prices come to mind: offer, demand, scarcity.

The economic choices and trade-offs become more complex: consumption ↔ processing ↔ storage ↔ continued storage ↔ exchange ↔ modes of exchange (gifts, trade). By definition, storage is intrinsic to a given household, while exchange is extrinsic. As economic activities increase, trade-offs between processing and storage, on the one hand, and modes of exchange, on the other hand, become more likely. Exchange means passing something over to another person, household, or collective. Exchange becomes a necessity if there is division of labour. Systems of cooperation are always shaped by modes of exchange (Karatani 2014).

Storage techniques and stored products allow for many past-present-connectivities because some archaic storage technologies are still alive today. Storage connects pre-modern life with modern life. In present times, the moderate zones are full of seasonal harvests which motivate storage. The practices of storage are more common on the countryside but may disseminate in urban regions. Stored food makes households resilient. In the long months of the Corona pandemic (2020-2021), many people rediscovered the value of stored food. In a degrowth and post-Corona-society, storage may regain cultural importance. Storage has "resilience value" even today. Since hierarchical, state-centred storage of essential commodities is prone to political misuse, politics should stimulate a robust combination of private, cooperative, market-driven and state-centred storage. Storage will be needed for a safe Anthropocene (see part 4).

Storage presupposes periodical surplus, and it paves the way for exchange, barter, and, finally, trade, but also for the practice of saving money. *Saving* money is also a kind of storage. It stores purchasing power. Precious metals and money are often stored as hoards at hidden places, as in the Bronze Age. Hoarding precious metals is close to saving money. Saving money is delayed consumption. Storing money at home is, however, risky because it might be stolen or robbed. Material storage was, in part, replaced by monetary savings in the 20$^{th}$ century. Supermarkets and warehouses became locations for material storage, while bank accounts are an abstract monetary pantry.

### 2.7.8 Division of labour

Surplus and sedentism spur a division of labour. If farmers and herdsmen produce surplus, they or other people can specialise in crafts. Thus, a fraction of the population will not primarily produce food, but will produce other goods or services. A division of labour implies a differentiation of skills, specialised production, and craftmanship. In the records from settlements, we find workshops, workplaces, and even special "quarters". Organising production in quarters, where specific professions were concentrated, survived until the 20th century CE. Often, production is organised as hierarchical "command-and-control" chains of value generation. The bright side of the division of labour is the enrichment of human life with goods that are produced by specialised craftsmen. Things are "nice to have", but less nice to make. There must be incentives to produce them. The institutions of exchange provide incentives to produce.

Pottery, metallurgy, butchery, processing of food, leather, fur and textile production, candles, *etc.* are crucial crafts. Crafts and arts coalesced in many admirable ways. Specialists have expertise in skilful "know how" which can be passed over to younger persons within a DMP. Family names often refer to professions (*e.g.* smiths). Given crafts and their products (artefacts, goods, commodities), exchange between them becomes more complex: essential goods versus "luxury" goods, long-lasting goods versus short-lived goods, prestige goods and the like. A special interest should be given to footwear, shoes and shoemakers because shoes and boots contribute to mobility and health.

Settlements, villages, cities and towns are places where a division of crafts and technological innovation gained momentum. If labour is divided, social complexity increases. The division of labour is implicitly present in the concept of a healthy "*polis*", as Plato argued in the "*Politeia*" (book II, 370a-372c). A basic craft is house-building itself, mostly based on timber and, later, bricks. It includes the art of thatching. The blacksmith as the first metallurgic craftsman has attracted attention since Homer.

A division of labour increases productivity. If scarcity of a given commodity decreases, a unit of this commodity is less precious than before. Effects of scales reduce the price of one unit of consumption. Crafts grow to become factory-like industries in the late Roman Empire. "Fabrication" becomes a mode of production which can be scaled-up. Here, the logic of mass production emerges. Producing more X implies that more humans can afford X in the longer run. Supply creates demand and demand stimulates supply. The treadmills of economic growth start running. Arts and crafts become a nostalgic image in the arena of industrial mass production (see Sennett 2009). A division of labour also increases mutual dependencies, at least in the long run. Enhanced productiveness and increasing mutual dependencies are two sides of the same coin (Hegel 1821/1970). Modern societies have become systems of cooperation among specialists.[165] "*Specialize!*" became an imperative and Ricardo's theory of comparative advantages demands specialisation on globalised markets. A division of labour as an economic force originated in the premodern past and it shapes the globalised economy of the Anthropocene (part 4).

Productive crafts are the origins of consumerism that has a long history. Consumerism means that persons, on the average, own continually more material items in their households. Houses store commodities. Settled cultures are

165 Slowly but surely, producing food becomes one specialised profession among others. Meanwhile, there are fewer farmers than students in developed countries.

far richer in artefacts, many of them superfluous, some of them luxurious according to given standards. Self-domestication of humans was rewarded by more artificial and beautiful surroundings since the times of complex foragers. Modern large-scale production by manufactures and industries accelerated the number of commodities for humans. If (most) humans like to hold useful, convenient, beautiful, symbolic, prestigious artefacts in property, then the modern consumer culture does not come as a surprise. Sedentism in conjunction with a division of labour constituted an "empire of things" (Trentmann 2016) which expanded over time. Trentmann (2016) outlines the history of consumerism since 1500 CE in many details. Consumerism is not exclusively a European way of life. From a methodological point of view, one should extend Trentmann's perspective backwards into the Neolithic. The origins of a consumer culture should be researched since the dawn of settled cultures. *Ceteris paribus*, the number of things per household should have gradually increased over the last 8000 years. Although religious movements and other countercultures have rejected consumerism (Ott and Voget-Kleschin 2013), the overwhelming majority of people continues to consume at increasing standards. We may speculate when critique against "luxury" originated. In Christianity, luxuries are sinful if they occupy the soul. In our moral mindset, luxuries are wrong if not all can afford them. Were these also the mindsets of archaic humans? Probably not. Perhaps, former humans would have appreciated and admired our consumer culture. Historical realism runs counter to hopes for a transformation toward anti-consumptive habits and lifestyles in the Anthropocene. It is far more realistic to expect global low-middle-class consumerism than mass-movements for sufficiency (part 4).

A division of labour requires some ideas about how to utilise the labour of other people. How can other persons be made to work for one's own sake? In the Neolithic, labour is a scarce means of production. Children and young adults are helpful hands in domestic modes of production. Quite often, elders profit from labour being carried out by the young (Meillassoux 1981; Geschiere 1985) The family-line (lineage) mode of production should not be described in Marxian terms of "exploitative extraction of surplus value", but in terms of wealth generation across a chain of generations.

Outside households, one can acquire and concentrate labour by enslaving humans or by bringing oneself in a powerful position to command over labour. The difference between free and unfree labour also emerged. Servants and slaves were forced to work. Capturing humans was widespread in premodern times. Captives were enslaved even if some cultures rejected slavery (Graeber and Wengrow 2021). Slavery and other forms of unfree labour might have been supportive for the division of labour.[166] Elites in the coastal communities of the North Pacific Coast used captives as slaves to process fish during the anadromous fish runs (Arnold *et al.* 2016, 481).

Besides slavery, one can also hire labour or let animals work. Economic power emerges as some people ("chiefs") control labour (by commands) and control the technical means of production (by property rights and technological competencies). In principle, large projects (such as megalithic structures), which require the

166 If one takes a closer look into historical case studies, the line between free and unfree labour sometimes becomes blurred. In the case study on ancient Greek textile production, Fischer (2007, 32) quotes John Chadwick: "It is probably unwise to imagine a sharp opposition between slave and free in Mycenaean times". Even if this might be reasonable, one should not abandon the difference. To Marx, proletarian workers are not slaves, but formally free.

coordination of many working persons over long periods of time, might have been realised through a commonly shared belief system or by coercive enforcement and domination (Lund *et al.* 2022). Can one assume a deep-rooted anarchic tendency to escape from being governed and forced to work *and,* nevertheless, believe in large projects made out of common deliberative agreement? One should, perhaps, not overrate the intrinsic (moral or religious) motivations to contribute with hard labour to large-scale building projects. If not incentives, force makes humans work. The tread out of absolute poverty is both incentive and force.

Slaves, servants, labourers, children, women, and animals were forced to work by dominant persons, mostly male "chiefs". If so, we have come close to class societies and to patriarchy. As both the division of labour and the enforcement of labour intensify, economic power and inequalities increase. Control over alien labour spurs inequality. According to our contemporary morals, the dark side of enforced labour shapes economic history.

Mining, metallurgy, and weaponry are "martial" sides of the division of labour with specific economies. Since its origins, metallurgy has been "dual use" technology, also serving the hard core of political power by weaponry production. This holds true despite the fact that the first metal objects were pieces of jewellery. Investments in armed forces can bring about conquest as returns. Conquest is a strategy to expand power over territories since prehistoric times. Armed forces are also constituted by a division of labour: specialists for warfare or professional warriors already appeared in Bronze Age. Warfare technologies become matters of life and death in violent times and they contributed to societal stratification. The specialisation of warriors is a kind of division of labour, too, but it also contributes to violent coercion of other humans. Interestingly, Graeber and Wengrow (2021, 216-219) give scientific credit to the claims made by Marija Gimbutas (1982) that the peaceful "old Europe" came to a catastrophic end in the third millennium BC as extremely warlike people invaded Europe and established patriarchy and warrior elites. Warriors that were equipped with metallic weaponry became invaders, rulers, and forceful military powers in early states. The making of Achilles' shield by Hephaistos, the god of metallurgy, symbolises (in Homer's narrative of Troy) the close connection between metallurgy and warfare. The step from iron to steel (1200 BCE) contributed largely to the military power of empires, such as Assyria. The Roman Empire developed industrial fabrication of steel-based weaponry for its legions.

Metallurgy as craftmanship requires mining. Mining was performed in prehistoric and ancient times in many places. Miners often did not work on a voluntary basis (high confidence). The Roman Empire organised industrial mining with slaves and prisoners who were sentenced "*ad metallas*". Medieval mining towns were centres of capital accumulation. Mining caused local pollution with heavy metals such as lead. Carving into Mother Earth's womb in order to mine gold, silver, copper, and iron for wealth and military power was, however, often seen as a repugnant practice. It continued in colonialism and was upscaled to large-scale industrial mining in the full Anthropocene. Meanwhile, large stocks of materials are incorporated in cities. Such stocks "represent a large resource potential" for future urban mining (Brunner 2011, 339).

### 2.7.9 Modes of exchange

The division of labour and exchange reinforce each other. Exchange refers to different kinds of activities such as presenting gifts, making donations, common consumption at festivals, rituals, and sacrifices, bartering, trading, and demanding and offering tributes. Exchange is always "ideological" and full of cultural meaning. From the records, we can construe distribution maps in order to test hypotheses about paradigmatic modes of exchange. Karatani (2014) correlates social formations and dominant modes of exchange:

1. Pooling (Z[167])
2. Clan and reciprocity, gifting (A)
3. Asiatic, ancient, feudal and plunder and redistribution (B)
4. Capitalism and commodity exchange (C)
5. Utopian communist exchange (vision) (D).

Karatani states (2014, X):

> *"Since Marcel Mauss, it had been generally accepted that the mode of exchange A (the reciprocity of the gift) is the dominant principle in archaic societies."*

Karatani observes an even prior mode of exchange which was dominant in nomadic hunter-gatherer groups: goods were pooled and distributed (or shared) equally, since they could not be stockpiled. This "pooling" mode Z disappeared with sedentism and was replaced by the "gift" reciprocity mode A of clan societies. Many PA scholars assume reciprocity as a basic prehistoric mode of exchange before states and classes emerged. To Graeber (2001, 151), Mauss' theory is the "single most important in the history of anthropology". Graeber argues on the same line as Caillé (2000). According to Graeber and Caillé, we should see "gifting" as a highly complex social category including antagonism, rivalry, *etc*. It would be simplistic to interpret gifting as an activity only based on solidarity and generosity. The gift refers to a social relation: "Gift-giving [...] is a purely voluntary act [...] that nonetheless creates a sense of obligation" (Graeber 2001, 153) on the side of the recipient. *Reciprocity requires reward*. The recipient is committed or compelled to make a return. One should not model the concept of reciprocity within gifting in egalitarian terms. Reciprocity can be equal or unequal. Unequal reciprocity implies mutual recognition of different rank, status, entitling, *etc*. Equal reciprocity can take the forms of love and hate: beloved persons and foes. It can also take the form of bargaining and negotiation among self-interested persons. In any case, we should separate the *theory* of gifting from Mauss' socialistic ideals.

Karatani also envisions a utopian mode of exchange (D). If I understand Karatani correctly, his utopian communist mode of exchange D should be "not the communism of clan society, but that of nomadic society" (Karatani 2014, XI), "the restoration of nomadic society" in a globalised world after capitalism. "D arrives in the form of universal religion" (Karatani 2014, XII). Speculations of a return of original communism seem to be immortal, since D seems to be the return of Z at a higher means of production. The ethics and politics of Karatani's D (see 2014,

167 It is confusing that the mode of pooling/sharing is not indicated with a capital letter by Karatani. I indicate it with Z (for Zero).

302-307) are confusing. The merits of Karatani's book lie in the analyses of the real historical modes of exchange.

*Pooling and sharing* might survive in households since bonds of kinship remain thick. A gift constitutes exchange between parties.[168] An exchange of *gifts* between parties is often performed within a ceremony or during a ritual. The exchange of gifts in the potlach has been taken as paradigm case of gifting. The potlach has attracted the attention of many anthropologists since Boas.[169] From a sober economic point of view, the logic of the potlach is a competition for prestige and rank. A final gift that cannot be answered properly constitutes the winner. One invests property and the return of such investment is "rank". This competitive logic underlies the potlach even if it is also perceived as an eventful festivity by participants and bystanders (Angelbeck and Grier 2012). Graeber and Wengrow (2021, 184) see potlach ceremonies as "manifestations of rivalry between nobles fighting over titular privilege" which "sometimes culminated in the sacrificial killing of slaves" (*ibid.*, 182). Thus, one should not idealise gifting at all just because one dislikes trade as the dominant mode of exchange within capitalism.

The logic of genuine economic exchange (trade) differs from gifting and potlach. For long periods in previous times, *trade* was restricted by transportation costs and by risks such as tempests and piracy. In historical times, water transport has almost always been far cheaper and faster than transport over land. Harbours became locations for marketing long-distance trade. Later, in Venice, merchants agreed to share the risks of long-distant trade. The risks of trade resulted in insurance mechanisms based on calculations of risks.

Trade constitutes commodities, while commodities constitute trade. Trade is exchange for mutual benefit, not competition for prestige. Trade is a voluntary affair presupposing property rights over goods which can be offered as commodities for exchange. Goods have use value and exchange value (= price). Competition happens between producers searching for customers, while trade presumes an improvement of the situation of both parties.[170] We may assume that mutual *trust* is the bedrock of trade. If we see mutual trust as recognition, recognition underlies trade. Trust means expectations of honesty. Decent trade is performed without fraud and cheating, while some persuasion, advertisement, and nudging might be acceptable. Adam Smith hypothesised that humans have a disposition to truck, barter, and trade. Microeconomics starts with a model of an economy of two persons and two goods (grain and fish) assuming that each person (farmer and fisherman) would prefer to have a combination of both commodities. Exchange between goods stops at specific "efficient" points, where further exchange would not be of mutual benefit any more.

In the practice of trade, stored surplus becomes commodities which are for sale. Initially, a commodity A can be exchanged against a commodity B. If the number of commodities that are being traded on markets increases, the emergence of money (as a general equivalent) becomes likely. Some precious commodities or rare metals (gold, silver, copper) take the functional role of a general

168 See, of course, the famous essay by Marcel Mauss "*Essay sur le don*" (1925). Gifts are ways of exchange. We should not moralise the theory of the gift as a demand for a sharing economy or an economy based on ideal commons. It is misleading to associate "gifting" with "making presents".

169 The classical article is based on structuralist models (Rosman and Rubel 1972). See more recently Bill Angelbeck on the potlatch (Angelbeck 2018).

170 A contract is a sober regulation of economic exchange. Even today, contracting parties have a common meal and some drinks to symbolise honesty and mutual trust.

exchange medium.[171] A new mode of commerce emerges with trade: the art of making money (Aristotle). A merchant can be disinterested in the use value of commodities, saying: "I do not care whether I earn money with amber, copper, fruits, or textiles". Despite such an attitude, clever merchants will offer use-values that are demanded by people having some purchase power. By the logic of the market, more use values are thus offered and purchased. People with very low purchase power are excluded from markets.

In historical reality, exchange is influenced by storage capacities: If grain can be stored, but fish cannot, the farmer profits. This might generate incentives to consider how to store fish. Trade provides incentives to think about improved storage – and vice versa. This is a mutual reinforcement. Canned beef became a globalised mass product in the first half of 20th century. The metal can thus combine the storage of food with globalised markets.

Trade has no definite spatial barrier. Long-distance trade exists since prehistoric and ancient times. Amber trade is a famous example. Chinese silk reached Europe in ancient times. The Silk Road trade economy was highly developed (Beckwith 2009). For example, there are Buddhist figurines that have been found in Sweden. Global trade emerged in the 16th century and has sharply increased since the 1950s and the 1990s (the "Great Acceleration") (part 3).

The mainstream modern theory of global trade is Ricardian and based on the concept of comparative advantage which implies a global distribution of labour and institutions that liberate trade (such as the WTO). Since the 1970s, there is political debate on whether the terms of global trade are fair. Here, Neo-Ricardians are in dispute with Neo-Marxists and post-colonial scholars. Exchange and trade belong to our way of life and, therefore, we must take an interest in "fair trade" even if it looks chimerical (Risse and Wollner 2019). The geopolitical realities of trade logistics can be studied in light of the Chinese "Belt and Road Initiative".

Almost all modes of exchange are in some sense *rewarding*. Exchange without reward is true love. If so, PA should become more specific on specific modes of reward that are implied by modes of exchange. The category of reward is the conceptual truth in the "gift". At least, one may test this conceptual TI in PA. Scholars may look for exchange without reward. If they do not find it, the TI holds.

## 2.7.10 Property rights

*Property rights* generally mean that someone is entitled to make decisions about access to, exclusion from, and distribution of (mostly material, but also immaterial) resources. Prehistoric property rights cannot be observed directly but must be inferred. Building houses, storing food, hoarding wealth, breeding animals, gardening, *etc.* correlate with property rights and its opposites, as theft and robbery. To complain about taxes and tributes supposes that presumed properties must transferred to authorities. Private property is one format of property rights among many such as commons. Generally, property rights imply the right to exclude others. They are "exclusive".

With high likelihood, trade presupposes some degree of personal security for merchants, including property rights. Property rights are always "ideological" because they must be legitimised if they are different from brute force used to acquire and possess them (in a Hobbesian state of nature). Peaceful trade (for

171 Far later, theories of money were divided in "nominalist" and "metallurgist" theories. See Moll (1956).

mutual benefit) presupposes safe property rights. Without property rights, no one would transport commodities over long distances in an uncertain world. Trade with property rights is risky, but trade without property rights is an "impossible" activity. Civil trade required contracting between parties. The logic of trade, investment, profit, and contracting required expertise and specific mindsets of merchants. Merchants and their "ethos" played a crucial role on the way to modern capitalism.[172]

If there should be trade, piracy must be rejected as a mode to acquire legal property. Robbery and marine piracy were widespread in ancient times at many locations. Piracy produced commodities including slaves.[173] During the first millennium BCE in the Mediterranean, piracy shifted from heroic to criminal deeds, and pirates turned from noble warriors to criminals. Piracy, however, always kept some anarchic smell and prominent pirates were seen as heroes fighting against rich merchants. The functional imperatives of trade, however, turned out to be the stronger economic forces and piracy vanished from most parts of the ocean. The figure of the noble pirate survives in tales and theatre (*e.g.* the "Störtebecker" festival on Rügen Island or in movies about Caribbean pirates, *etc.*). Merchants, however, did not share the sympathies of anarchistic PA scholars with pirates and robbery partisans. Merchants are less fancy than pirates, but they deserve attention within HM.[174]

## 2.7.11 Inequality

History knows many forms of inequalities among humans. History also knows of large political attempts to minimise inequalities, as in recent socialism (USSR, GDR, China). We assume that inequalities have their origins in the DMP, the accumulation of wealth, the division of labour, conquests, raiding, tributes, trade, migration, and, last but not least, in military power. There are many sources of inequality. All modes of exchange beyond pooling and the division of labour constitute inequalities among persons. Economic inequalities can be converted into political inequalities. Historical inequalities are matters of fact. They can be measured and assessed by different methods (GINI, inequality frontier). Kohler *et al.* (2017) show, for instance, that inequalities in wealth were larger in post-Neolithic Eurasia than in North America and Mesoamerica. Inequality generally increases with the domestication of plants and animals. Large domesticated mammals, which did not exist in America, increased differences in wealth within Eurasian cultures.

Present Western democratic societies, which have *equalised* life prospects in many respects (such as life expectancy, literacy, education, citizenship, equality before the law, gender equality, equality of sexual orientation, *etc.*), have become even more sensitive against remaining economic inequalities (income, wealth, legacies). This is the so-called "Tocqueville paradox": the more egalitarian a society becomes, the more moral complaints about remaining inequalities occur. Economic inequalities are scandalised in terms of distributive justice. This moral sensitivity must be deliberated in the realm of ethics and politics, but it should not shape our historical understanding of past modes of emerging inequalities and how people ar-

172 See Weber (1905/2001) and Hirschman (1977).

173 Today, there is a return of piracy on some coastal areas. Piracy, illegal fisheries and human trafficking might become new maritime business models in the Anthropocene.

174 Graeber's posthumous book is about piracy as a way of life (Graeber 2023).

ranged them. Thus, we should not confuse historical analyses of sources, causes and modes of inequalities with current sentiments for egalitarian distributive justice.

History reveals a plurality of normative orders that process, stabilise, and legitimise different kinds of inequalities.[175] It is a sociological or historical question whether participants perceived inequalities as unjust or whether they held beliefs why (some or all) inequalities are part of a legitimate (theologian or cosmologic or dynastic) order. Did prehistoric people themselves wish to maintain more equality or do archaeologists wish them to be egalitarians? We have to ask the right questions about past economic inequalities. Is it true that inequalities spur violence? Tim Kohler argued (personal communication 2021) that the relationship between violence and inequality is more complex than our intuitions tell us. Lower inequality might induce more violence. An egalitarian distribution of wealth seems compatible with a low level of personal security and with social affairs which look "horrible" to us.

Economic life *as such* constitutes inequalities. This generic claim holds true for the Neolithic. This (inconvenient) claim is in line with the analysis given by Smith, Kohler and Feinman in their "*Studying Inequality's Deep Past*" (2018). Among foragers, wealth is embodied and relational (allies, kin). Foraging does not allow for many belongings.[176] Sedentism is a requirement for an accumulation of goods that constitute disparities. House size is a proxy for wealth, since houses store precious goods. A house becomes a kinship-based household that is an economic unit. In a DMP, some households perform better than others. Inequality in the Bronze Age seems to correlate with households lasting several generations (Mittnik *et al.* 2019a, see also the supplementary material in Mittnik *et al.* 2019b). There is the economic institution of *legacies* in some but not all collectives. An inheritage is a transfer of property rights to descendants (or other parties) in case of death (= legacy). It implies that accumulated wealth can be bequeathed to descendants which may continue wealth generation and accumulation. Legacies constitute family lines and family wealth. If descendants also adopt habits and customs of their parents, they will continue to generate wealth. As a special section in "*Current Anthropology*" has shown, material wealth transmissions are low or moderate among hunters and gatherers, but high or very high among pastoralists and in agricultural societies.[177] If there is trade, the emergence of merchants' capital becomes likely which may accumulate. An anatomy of transformation within PA should be interested in the institution of legacy.

Domestic modes of production become economically integrated family lines over generations which accumulate and transmit wealth if such wealth is not destroyed by natural events, warfare, robbery, or plundering. Some family lines may have accumulated and transmitted wealth, capabilities, and prestige over generations and offspring of such families are likely to reach high societal and political ranks. Wealth can often be converted into influence and political power. Elite families are established. This simple model explains why inequalities must grow under stable conditions if there are no mechanisms and institutions which level them out. Commitments to organise festivities, giving a fraction of one's wealth to the poor,

175 The project of Eric Voegelin was a meta-history of normative orders. See Voegelin (1956). Voegelin based his project on a four-fold conceptual scheme: God, humans, nature, society.

176 To Smith, universal poverty means universal equality in the early stages of history (1776/1976, chap. V.1.b.7).

177 See the special section on *Intergenerational Wealth Transmission and Inequality in Premodern Societies* in Current Anthropology, 51 (1), February 2010.

donations for rituals, *etc.* may reduce inequalities, but they will not change underlying economic structures which constitute and intensify inequalities. Egalitarian movements always wished to abolish legacies (or at least tax them high).

There is a long route (= trajectory) from a simple and egalitarian economic way of life to a wealthier, more complex, and stratified way of life. In "our" society, overall wealth permits the existence of numerous inequalities in terms of professions, lifestyles, careers, wealth, and symbolic capital. In his study on inequality, Milanovic (2016) argues that one can conceive an "inequality frontier" emerging beyond any imagined or real state of initial equality. If "surplus above the subsistence level increases" (Milanovic, 2016, 52), a space for a rise in inequality is opened (*ibid.*, 70). The inequality frontiers reveal how much inequality becomes possible in a society if all its members remain alive (no one is starving to death). Here, I make the TI of the "inequality possibility frontier", hypothesising that they might have expanded within the Neolithic. This TI must be checked against the empirical evidence (see Kohler and Smith 2018).

The record allows for a generalisation: Beyond hunter-gatherer societies, the inequality frontier increases slowly but steadily until ancient times despite periodical equalising events, most of them malign. There are benign and malign ways to reduce inequalities (Milanovic 2016). Wars equalise the losers by making them equally poor. Collapse and decay can have equalising effects. Inequality decreased in the (catastrophic) transformation from ancient to medieval times because overall wealth decreased. With very few exceptions, all persons were equally poor over long uncomfortable centuries (from the 6th to the 11th century CE).

More prosperity allows for more inequality. Economic inequality is the price of overall prosperity. Perhaps, the long-term expansion of the inequality frontier in different societies is revealed as the "locomotion" of economic evolution. Special attention should be paid to intergenerational wealth transmission within clans and family lines (Smith *et al.* 2018) because it touches the moral problem of private legacies. Wealth accumulation may flip into capital.

As European collectives have reached higher layers of economic complexities since the 15th century, the drives of inequality have become more forceful and more diverse. The Kuznets's Curve shows the stylised fact that economic inequality increased from 1800-1900 CE, peaking around 1900. Within the 20th century, inequality decreased due to either malign (war, revolution) or benign forces (taxation, welfare state, education). From a declined level, inequality increased again after the collapse of communism but, with the exception of the U.S., remained (far) lower than in 1900.[178] Today, inequality, as measured by the GINI index, is higher in China, India, and Brazil than in Germany and the EU. It seems noteworthy that rising inequality in wealth and income can coexist with absolute improvements in the quality of life, as defined by HDI parameters (mortality rates at birth, life expectancy, literacy, political participation, health status at a given age, and food security). Inequality is always relational, while absolute measures are about qualities of life. The existence of 1% super rich billionaires does not tell us much about how qualities of life develop within an entire population over long periods of time. It is wrongful to believe that inequality produces absolute poverty and its miseries. Higher inequalities can cohere with less absolute poverty. What is wrong with inequality, as such, if productive but unequal societies can bring about a better life for almost all of its members than static, poor, and egalitarian societies?

---

178 See also Bourguignon (2013).

Historians are not in a position to value equality from "the" moral point of view. The real *historical* problem is how inequalities might have been perceived from the emic side in PA. Did not songs and sagas praise the "big men" as heroes? Did people admire excellence? How did they think about merits and legacies? How strong were commitments to make donations to the poor? Were there rules that one should leave something for others, as in Locke's famous "proviso"? What counted as "more than enough"? Were there sentiments such as envy and resentment? Were inequalities perceived as matters of fortune or matters of justice? Perhaps, we will not know since the moral perception of inequalities requires interpretation and some abductive speculation. Whatever PA may achieve, we should not project "our" moral ideals on distributive justice onto the past.

The ethical and political dispute about how to organise this space of inequalities presents itself in modern democracies. Principles and criteria of distributive justice are ethical investments into this current dispute. There are different theories of distributive justice which allow for more or fewer modes, patterns, and mechanisms of inequality. There is a complex debate about "*equality of what?*". What is meant by "egalitarianism"? I shall return to disputes about distributive justice in part 4.

## 2.7.12 Hierarchies and heterarchies

Economic transformations created new societal structures among complex foragers, in the Stone Age, the Bronze Age and the Iron Age, as well as in early states and empires. We see a multitude of options how to organise a political sphere of life.

Politics is collective decision-making by authorities. From our perspective, we can take this multitude as a historical parade of presumptive political traditions. There is no need to assume that prehistoric people themselves had been aware of this wide range of possibilities. The "sense of social possibilities" (Graeber and Wengrow 2021, 37) is ours and we should be better agnostic on the question whether prehistoric persons were politically "*more* imaginative than we are" (*ibid.*, 73) and were "self-consciously experimenting with different social possibilities" (*ibid.*, 107, see also 113, 115, and 117). I do not assume "experimentation" on the emic side, since ways of life are not experimental. The historical observer, however, is free to face the multitude of possibilities under the correlative ideas of freedom and political self-determination. As I shall argue in part 4, we should adopt the Graeber/Wengrow perspective on the multitude of options and apply it to the situation of the Anthropocene, but must curtail such a multitude by moral principles and traditions. This is to say that historical imagination helps us to think out of the boxes of the Western conventional mindset, while we have to maintain and defend our "best" moral ideas in the tradition of political liberalism (such as liberty, democracy, rule of law, human rights, security, equal opportunities).

Here it suffices to make a TI about an ideal-type alternative. Collectives, communities and societies can be organised in a rather *hierarchical* or a more *heterarchical* manner (Crumley 1995).[179] The framework of HM is compatible with this alternative. HM is not committed to the claim that all stratified class societies are hierarchical and antagonistic.

Both hierarchical and heterarchical societies rest on the qualitative achievements of agricultural transformation and they both contribute to the origins of

179 Articles in the "Special Issue: Heterarchy and the Analysis of Complex Sciences" in the *Archaeological Papers of the American Anthropological Association*, 6 (1) January 1995 display the significance of the concept for the social sciences.

the Anthropocene (part 3). Non-hierarchical, stratified societies have been an option in prehistoric times (Crumley 1995).[180] Here, we see complex foraging, a DMP, reciprocities, and heterarchies as elements of prehistoric ways of life. Heterarchies are "top-less". The hierarchical organisation was implied in the "Asian mode of production". Such organisation is more "imperial".

Some collectives are flexible and may be more hierarchical or heterarchical in different seasons and still remain the "same" collectives (*e.g.* First Nations before and after the buffalo hunt, Inuit in winter and summer). Republican states can allow for limited dictatorship in times of severe crisis (Rome). Broadly speaking, there are two opposite political directions ("trajectories") into which societies may develop. One trajectory is hierarchical. Access to and control over dominant goods[181] (military force, land, economic wealth, control over labour, jurisdiction) is functional in order to acquire other kinds of non-dominant goods (spiritual prestige, mating opportunities, literacy, medicine, *etc.*). In such societies, inequality becomes *hierarchically organised*: Elites control (almost) all kinds of goods because they control the dominant goods. Stratification becomes pyramidal: with a small top and a broad button. Oligarchy and tyranny are two kinds of hierarchical stratification. Historical examples of hierarchical cultures are Egypt, Mesopotamia, China, and the Roman Empire since Augustus. In hierarchical cultures, religion and theology become ideological doctrines which justify the hierarchical structure. Scott (2017) asks whether the walls of early hierarchical states are outer walls against aliens or internal walls to lock the population in, forcing them to work. Hierarchical orders display an imperial style of art.

There are reasons to believe that hierarchies became a centre of attraction from 3000 to 2000 BCE in Mesopotamia, Egypt, and parts of Europe, long after the establishment of agriculture. Violence, patriarchy, weaponry, and steppe invaders belong to this period. John Robb argues that a more egalitarian and peaceful Meso- and Neolithic turned into a hierarchical, violent, inegalitarian society of the Iron Age. Warriors and tax officials are paradigm figures of coercion because they are subordinated parts within a hierarchy. It seems likely that hierarchically stratified societies have often conquered or absorbed heterarchical societies or have defined them as "barbarian peripheries". The hierarchical model is, however, rather unusual in the entire prehistoric past. Robb, Scott, Kohler, Graber and Wengrow seem to agree on this point.

Under a different trajectory, stratification becomes more dispersed. Societies remain more heterarchically structured (Crumley 1995). To take such a heterarchical trajectory into account as one model for archaic societies is not to deny stratification, ranks, authorities, inequalities, and privileges. There might have been inequalities with respect to different kinds of goods which are dispersed over different groups. Economic wealth, spiritual or juridical authority, military power, governmental legitimacy, knowledge and literacy, medical skills, spiritual wisdom, *etc.* are not concentrated around a "top" but are (more or less widely) dispersed. In dispersed (heterarchical) societies, specific social "figures" and roles

---

180 See Müller *et al.* (2018). Mega-sites without hierarchical stratification may have survived for long periods north of the Black Sea. Deliberations might have been an alternative to command-and-control structures. But Müller *et al.* (2018, 258) concede that the political organisation of these mega-sites remains unknown. Property rights of lineages seem likely. Müller *et al.* (2018) assume balanced and multi-faceted identities of individuals. Graeber and Wengrow (2021, 290-297) take the research on these Ukrainian mega-sites as evidence that towns without cathedrals and palaces are always an option.

181 The concept is adopted from Walzer (1983).

emerge: craftsmen, healers, merchants, warriors, judges, priests, artists, merchants, clowns, *etc*. Heterarchical societies have "ranks" based on authority but not on mere violence. There are specific patterns of recognition. Under this trajectory, human capabilities ("beings and doings") are also more dispersed which may have also affected gender relations.

Here, an important archaeologically detectable variable is the degree of concentration or centralisation of political power *vs.* de-centralisation and local autonomy. Concentrated power is also more likely to manifest in personalised ruling institutions (chiefs, kings, governors, district), while decentralised ones more often show corporate forms of organisation such as councils (Carballo *et al.* 2012). All forms of political organisation are potentially multi-dimensional. Heterarchical societies are full of powers (*sensu* Foucault), but they display less domination and coercion (*sensu* Weber) (Lund *et al.* 2022). Heterarchical societies are "rank orders" without supreme tops. Hierarchical systems are systems of command and control, while heterarchical systems are more deliberative and negotiating. The entire cluster of "power" concepts (control, authority, command, rule, coercion, obedience, governance, *etc.*) takes on variable meaning with respect to hierarchical and heterarchical societies.

A second variable affecting our understanding of social inequality with relation to political systems is the degree of integration of political power and access to material wealth. In many cases, political power is built on wealth ("oligarchy"), or is easily converted into it, while in other cases, there are politically powerful individuals or groups with little access to material wealth and *vice versa*. It is an open research question how wealth can or cannot be converted into political power and influence. Do the elites of current capitalism really control politics?

I wish to make the following investment which is at the interface of theory and ethics: Former heterarchical societies may have had parallels with modern societies in that they were stratified according to "spheres" and "functions". As Luhmann (1984) argued, functional differentiation between societal systems was a mode of organisation that emerged in the 18th century CE after a long history of medieval hierarchies and monarchies. To Walzer (1983), complex societies organise different spheres of practical life that are devoted to specific goods and are governed by specific rules. Luhmann's systems and Walzer's spheres point to the option of (post)modern "top-less" heterarchical societies. If prehistoric heterarchical organisations show some parallels (structural and functional analogies) to contemporary ones, there will be options for past-present-connectivities. With some likeliness, both societal models are, *mutatis mutandis*, options for contemporary political orders. Even in modern times, we observe centralised and hierarchical systems (*e.g.* in groups and categories such as the "central committee", "*oberste Führung*", hereditary elites, military despotism) and more heterarchical ones (checks and balances, functional differentiation, functional elites, independency of science, religion, sports, and art, high degrees of self-determination, open public sphere of reasoning). Thus, the archaic difference is still with us. The question remains whether modern Western societies are, in fact, hierarchical or heterarchical. This question falls in the field of general sociology. Marxists believe that capitalism is a hierarchical system. The suggestion made by Graeber and Wengrow (2021) that we are "stuck" in a single mode of existence seems also to suppose an answer in favour of hierarchy. This suggestion might be misleading. I classify modern Western societies as heterarchies and their non-democratic rivals as hierarchies. Marx and Engels conceded that not all historical class configurations must be antagonistic (Flechtheim 1963, 31). This points at the possibility of heterarchical non-antagonistic stratification of modern societies (part 4). If one has reasons to prefer heterarchical over hierarchical orders (as I do), and if archaic ways of life provide examples for heterarchies (as I believe), there might be presumptive *archaic traditions* mirrored in current heterarchies. If so, archaic and modern heterarchies may come in close touch (part 4, section 4.10).

## 2.8 Result: Emergence of economic life and the "thin" Anthropocene

In prehistoric times, we see the transformative emergence of a reinforcing economic logic from foraging, sedentism, surplus, storage, households, domestic modes of production, agriculture, domestication, large settlement, accumulation of wealth, division of labour, exchange, trade, property rights, money, investments, taxes, *etc*. Economic life emerged and it is here to stay. Economic life gives a large pool of reasons how "(prudent) economic humans" should (not) act. We should not impose our standards of economic reasons into the past but may ask what economic reasons (in a very liberal definition) prehistoric humans might have had. Surplus production on a regular basis might have been the prehistoric version of growth orientation.

In any case, economic reasoning becomes a component of the overall pool of reasons which people may have had. The general concept of choice can be specified to economic conceptions of making reasonable choices. If understanding means to understand the reasons that people hold on their emic side of life (see part 1), and if economic reasons belong to the entire pool of reasons, and if economic life, as such, emerges in the Neolithic, our capacity for understanding prehistoric ways of human life increases if we take presumptive economic reasons into account. Such reasons can be about modes of production, consumption and exchange. This is not to claim that all choices are economic ones.

In a Marxian spirit, I claim that economic theories of the most complex economic system we know (advanced market capitalism) provide the scope of theoretical investments in the understanding of prehistoric economic life. If so, we must imagine how richly textured prehistoric economic life must have been. From the HM perspective, we derived specific questions about land tenures, exchange and reward, legacy, inequality, and hierarchy versus heterarchy.

The claim of the transformative emergence of economic life, as such, is complementary to the claim that the Anthropocene emerged in the agricultural transformation as well (part 3). The crucial achievements of the Neolithic period, the eclipse of qualities into ever increasing quantities (see part 3) and the emergence of economic life are correlative. They can be separated for the sake of historical analysis, but they constitute a specific "Western" ("European") way of life. There seems to be a deep entrenchment with respect to increased quantities, expansion, upscaling, acceleration, growth, consumption, gains, "more". Part 3 is about its origins.

# Part 3: Origins of the Anthropocene in the Neolithic

## 3.1 Introduction and outline

To present the thesis of this part straightforward: The concept of the Anthropocene is a theoretical investment (TI) which is helpful ("eye opening") a) as a *diagnostic concept* for the globalised planet in the 21st century CE and b) to make connectivities between prehistoric and ancient times, on the one hand, and the moral and political challenges of the present age on the other hand. This part of the study presents an argument in order to substantiate a risky hypothesis with respect to both a) and b). The hypothesis claims *that the Anthropocene originates in prehistoric times, especially in the agricultural transformation*. This claim was first stated by Ruddiman (2003) and was repeated by Scott (2017).

Paul Crutzen's proposal to coin the recent period of earth's history as the "Anthropocene" has been adopted from a geological perspective (Waters *et al.* 2016; Zalasiewicz *et al.* 2015; 2020; Walker *et al.* 2019, 10) even if the final approval is still missing. As Waters (2022) explains, there has been an abrupt change in the planetary records since the middle of the 20th century. Such change is sufficient to define a new geological epoch even if there is no "Golden Spike" yet. To Waters, the magnitude and speed of change are comparable to the beginning of the Holocene 15,000 years ago. If the polar ice shields were to melt down and the sixth mass extinction of species would accelerate, not just an epoch, but a planetary era would end. An overview of the scientific debate is given in Horn and Bergthaller (2019) and Lane (2023). Flannery (2018, part III) argues that the Pleistocene was replaced by the Anthropocene at the end of the 20th century, because for a very long time there will no longer be any glacial ages. The geological societies, however, have not yet officially agreed on the strati-graphical proposal of the Anthropocene group. Thus, it is still a hypothetical TI. If one entertains this diagnostic hypothesis, it implies a question: When did the Anthropocene originate?

Some historians regard the "Great Acceleration" since the 1950s as the actual origin (Pfister 2010). Radiogenic fallout during the 1950s can also be taken as a criterion of origin (Walker *et al.* 2019). Crutzen argues that the Anthropocene originated in the process of industrialisation since, say, 1750. Some scholars date it back to early forms of globalisation (1500 or 1600 CE onward). Ruddiman *et al.* (2015) favour the Neolithic period because of the deep impacts on natural environments. Scott (2017, 3) sees the Neolithic period as a leap in the human transformation of nature. Smith and Zeder (2013, 8) are even more straightforward:

> *"The initial domestication of plants and animals, and the development of agricultural economies and landscapes are identified as marking the beginning of the Anthropocene epoch."*

Some ecologists see a "very early" Anthropocene originating with the human use of fire, megafaunal extinction, and the arrival of humans on all continents except Antarctica (Corlett 2015).

Scott (2017, 3) distinguishes between a "thin" and a "thick" Anthropocene. "Thin" and "thick" are metaphors for origins and full-blown essence. "Thick" essence and "thin" origins must correspond under a common idea. The emergence of the "thick" Anthropocene is to be taken as an epistemic precondition for research on its presumptive origins.[182] Knowing the essential result is a precondition for genealogical research. If so, we are the first generation of scholars who are able to research the origins, building blocks, patterns, crucial achievements, and the final actualisation (= "*Verwirklichung*" *sensu* Hegel) of the Anthropocene.

Human populations and technologies in the Neolithic and the Bronze Age were not suited to change the global records deeply, regardless of the role of fire.[183] One crucial difference between the prehistoric past and present times is the number of humans. In prehistoric times, the terrestrial sphere was almost devoid of humans. In the Neolithic, the population amounted to less than one person per square kilometre (Zimmermann 2007). Population growth was slow or very slow in the Neolithic and periodic infectious diseases may have reduced populations in urban settlements.

Scott (2017) estimates that there were about 50 million humans alive at 1000 BCE and far fewer beforehand (*e.g.* only 2-5 million worldwide at 10,000 BCE). 50 million prehistoric humans, who were concentrated in some areas (such as the Fertile Crescent, the Indus Valley, Egypt, and on Chinese river plains, *etc.*), were not enough to shape global cycles. Humans shaped regions and might have driven some species to extinction, but they could not create impacts on a global scale. The early "thin" Anthropocene neither changed the climate, polluted the ocean nor did it destroy large primary forests. It originated on a small-

182 This is a Marxian idea. For Marx, capitalism must have emerged fully if research on its origins should make sense at all. One must be familiar with a market economy in order to research its origins (Polanyi 1944/2011).

183 Scott and Ruddiman both emphasise the role of fire. This Promethean legacy originated before the Neolithic. Fireplaces were highly adaptive. Cooking helped digestion. Fire was supportive to human radiation across the globe. To Scott (2017, 42), humans are a fire-adapted species, a "pyrophyte".

scale, not on a large-scale. The origins of the Anthropocene were innovations, not increase. History must point at conditions under which (impressive but also intimidating) scaling effects of a globalised civilisation become possible.

Crutzen's proposal can be traced back into the 19th century (Mauelshagen 2016). Biologist Ernst Haeckel (1870, 347) spoke about an *"anthropozöisches Zeitalter"*.[184] According to Haeckel, the radiation of the genus *Homo* is the beginning of a new major epoch within the organic history of the earth. G. P. Marsh's book from 1864 had the subtitle *The Earth as Modified by Human Action*. Marsh sees humans as disturbing agents on a global scale. Arrhenius claimed in 1896 that releasing greenhouse gases might warm the atmosphere (Uppenbrink 1996). Anthropogenic modifications of nature have been intensified since then within the Great Acceleration. Following Marsh, Thomas (1955) edited an impressive volume on *Man's Role in Changing the Face of the Earth*. Pfister (2010) rightly points at the 1950s syndrome. Much literature was written out of a sense of alarm since the 1960s, most prominently by Rachel Carson in her *Silent Spring* (1962). Philosophers started reflecting upon the ecological crisis in the 1970s (Jonas 1979; Taylor 1986; Rolston 1988; Naess 1989). Thus, we see a finite planet shaped by a rapidly growing human population that is equipped with modern technologies. For centuries, this trajectory was dominated by Europeans, mostly males.

Let us perform a thought experiment. Imagine that humans had never changed the original Palaeolithic way of life as hunters and gatherers. Would it be possible for such hunters and gatherers to produce a direct transformation to the current Anthropocene? According to my assessment, the answer is "clearly not". The abductive implication follows: If we now live in the "thick" Anthropocene, and if (even complex) hunters and gatherers could not have produced an Anthropocene-like state of affairs, and if the agricultural ("Neolithic") transformation constituted a new way of human life (Robb 2013), including economic life (part 2), then it makes epistemic sense to investigate this transformation as a "long-term laboratory" of origins.

The term "Anthropocene" is a *diagnostic*, not an ethical one. It is rather a title over a broad complex diagnosis than a direct (moral and political) recipe of how (not) to act. Thus, such a diagnostic title can be combined with different normative ideas which are often falsely called "implications" of the Anthropocene. The term "Anthropocene" does not imply sympathies for geo-engineering,[185] manned space flight, transhumanism, and artificial intelligence. Nor does it imply "deep ecology" (*sensu* Naess 1989). It only states that human beings, taken collectively as "humankind", now deeply modify most planetary natural cycles. Humans have become very dominant – but are nowadays horrified by their own dominance. Many intellectuals hold the belief that success may eclipse in collapse.

The *method* of the argument is *genealogical*. In this respect, I adopt the idea to discover origins of contemporary challenges in archaic times. I see this idea at work in Horkheimer's and Adorno's *Dialectic of Enlightenment* (1944/1947). They tried to identify the archaic origins of the collapse of enlightenment into barbarism, as in the figure of Odysseus. Two exiled intellectuals, not trained in history

184 Haeckel (1870, 348): *"(Wir) können mit vollem Rechte die Ausbreitung des Menschen mit seiner Cultur als Beginn eines besonderen letzten Hauptabschnitts der organischen Erdgeschichte bezeichnen."* [English translation Ott]: *"We can rightly describe the spread of man and his culture as the beginning of a special last main phase of the earth's organic history."*

185 A radical geo-interventionist strategy is proposed by Reynolds (2021). Reynolds sees Earth System Interventions (ESI) as a "potentially transformative set of innovations in human-Earth system relations". My proposals for a good Anthropocene point in an opposite direction.

and archaeology, tried to explore the archaic origins of the self-destructive dialectics of enlightenment culminating in mass atrocities of total war and genocide (*ibid.*, esp. chapter 1). They outlined how occidental reason collapsed into instrumental rationality (means-ends), how conceptual thinking collapsed into nominalism, how domination over hostile nature collapsed into oppression of inner nature and cruelty against sentient animals. The route from magic to myths, and from myths to reason ("logos") is full of dialectical eclipses. In one crucial chapter, Horkheimer and Adorno portray Odysseus as the prototype of a clever modern subject. His cleverness makes him survive. Finally, however, he acts like a Nazi hangman against female servants in his re-conquered palace.[186]

Horkheimer and Adorno, however, remained far too speculative as they had no expertise in prehistory, ethnography, and archaeology. I only adopt the genealogical perspective of Horkheimer and Adorno and apply it hypothetically to the correlation between "thin" and "thick" Anthropocene. I do not, however, suggest that the Anthropocene must terminate in a "post-modern dark age". Dialectic of enlightenment is not fatalism yet, despite the frightening possibility that "post-modern barbarism" can be an outcome in the Anthropocene. From a historical perspective, however, we should not rule out the inconvenient possibility that the long post-war era (1950-2020) was exceptionally good to European people.

The *logic* of the hypothesis is *abductive*: If "we" humans are now (for better or worse) "makers" ("performers") of a geo-logical and historical period ("age") called the "Anthropocene", there might be some patterns, structures, and mechanisms within the human way of life since the Neolithic which are supportive to such making. If such patterns, spikes, structures, and mechanisms can be identified and historically reconstructed, the upshot of the Anthropocene must be the final outcome, given some supportive circumstances (such as fossil fuels and vaccines). The mainstream counter-thesis runs as follows: The Anthropocene has been constituted by recent developments, such as European globalism (1500 CE onward), industrialisation (1750 CE onward), and the Great Acceleration (1950 CE onward). The second counter-hypothesis claims that the term "Anthropocene" is an ideological one, obscuring the actual and ultimate causes of the present situation: capitalism including colonialism. Given the paradigm of HM (part 2), we shall not deny that the accumulation of large and increasing stocks of capital and the colonial expansion of the West contribute to the rise of the full-blown Anthropocene. The step from wealth accumulation within domestic modes of production to the entrepreneurial spirit of investment and global trade was decisive for the continual growth of capital since 1500. Generally, historical research should focus on the epochs from 1500-1600, 1750-1900, and 1950-present as periods in which the Anthropocene became "thick" and finally exploded. Perhaps, we may identify patterns of acceleration. If one takes the periods from 1618-1650 and 1914-1945 as war-induced backlashes of Western civilisation, one may view the last 500 years in some continuity of transformative expansion.

Capitalism is one moment among many within the comprehensive trajectory towards the Anthropocene. Given the results of part 2, we should critically address but should not demonise the economic affairs surrounding the abstract term "global capitalism". Thus, I do not replace the term "Anthropocene" by the term "capitalocene" as Moore (2016a) does. Moore (2016a, 6) sees capitalism as "a way of organizing nature" and a "world-ecology". Moore "ecologizes capitalism

186 See Schneider (2023).

to a point at which it becomes [...] a geosocial mode of existence" (Pottage 2019, 164). If Moore (2016b, 97) is right, capitalism is the most successful economic system since it does not "act *upon* nature" but develops "*through* the web of life". Moore does not explain how capitalism can both misrepresent nature and is able to develop *through* the web of life. We should not both overrate and demonise capitalism and plea for human innocence. Capitalism is not, as Marxism believes, the ultimate cause of our current situation as there is no ultimate cause but an entire network of efficacies.

Proposals to replace the term "Anthropocene" by "capitalocene", "occidentalocene", "androcene", *etc.* are, however, right in one point: The term "Anthropocene" should neither imply nor suggest that all humans equally contribute to the situation. Environmental impacts of different nations and strata within nations are highly different. The term "Anthropocene" points to the aggregate impacts of our species, while specific sociological investigations should point to the differences between countries, income groups, elites, *etc.* Clearly, environmental destruction caused by poverty and ignorance is different from wealth-induced overconsumption. One should not, however, ignore the different environmental performance of policy-making in different states. Some states may become part of the solution, while others may become part of the problem (part 4).

Generally, it makes sense to distinguish between physical and intellectual "spikes" of the Anthropocene. If my general thesis holds, there must be both material and intellectual spikes of an early ("thin") Anthropocene. In the next section, we shall identify two prominent ancient intellectual spikes. These spikes open lines of analogical reasoning between the past and the present.

If humans a) at present times perform the ongoing proceedings of the Anthropocene at different locations and in different social roles (entrepreneur, farmer, logger, worker, craftsman, trader, consumer, scholar, politician) on a globalised Planet Earth, and b) if there might be prehistoric ("thin") origins of the Anthropocene, then historical understanding of such origins should contribute to the diagnosis of the present, and, perhaps, even give ethical and political suggestions for remedies and therapies. The claim runs counter to widely shared intuitions. Prehistoric and present times seem to be "worlds apart" in terms of technologies, knowledge, wealth, institutions, morals, *etc.* Epistemic claims do not have to conform to shared intuitions. The claim, of course, must not deny the profound differences between prehistoric and modern societies. Origins of X are not necessarily the essence of X. Correspondence is always composed out of similarities *and* differences. Part 1 allows for critical analogical reasoning which is essential to this part. Part 2 has argued that economic life, as such, emerged in prehistoric times. It is in line with the claim. The standard model of Neolithisation (Robb 2013; Zimmermann 2007; Strahm 2006; Scharl 2003, McCaffree 2022, 25-92; Shillington 2019, 23-34 for Africa) is also in line with the claim.

Following these preliminaries, the argument starts by identifying challenges in the next section. Taking a crucial further step, ancient chorus songs are taken as intellectual spikes of the "thin" Anthropocene. The claim itself basically rests on an inverse Hegelian concept: *qualitative achievements eclipse into ever enlarging quantities.* Such quantities finally collapse into a new quality. Claim and model as well as results of part 2 converge to an expansionist scheme: "the more the better". This scheme underlies modern ideas of progress, success, efficiency, large scales, growth, and maximising the good (welfarism). Since theories are research programs (Lakatos 1970), some research questions are finally outlined.

## 3.2 Challenges of the Anthropocene

The physical indicators of the Anthropocene are atmospheric greenhouse gas (GHG) concentrations (roughly 440 ppmv $CO_2$-eq), population growth,[187] urban agglomeration, mass extinction of species, large-scale agricultures, industrialised meat production with billions of animals, extractivism in large mining areas perhaps including the ocean floor in the future, global trade, overfishing, ocean acidification, new radioactive substances (nuclear waste), *etc*. Sea level rise and ocean acidification are among the side effects of GHG emissions (Böhm and Ott 2019). Human activities spread neo-biota around the globe. Humans practice large-scale damming of rivers, mining, and clear-cutting of primary forests. They are fishing down the marine food webs and influence the evolution of fish species. They convert natural systems into agricultural land and (post-)colonial plantations (coffee, palm oil). Groundwater depletion throughout the 20th century contributed to sea-level rise and caused a small drift of the Earth's pole (Seo *et al.* 2023). Humans now settle in mega-cities, many of them located at coastlines of the Global South. The patterns of consumption become more equal despite the fact that the amount of materials and energies being consumed are still higher in the Global North.

The global mean temperature (GMT) is about to increase by at least 2 °C compared to preindustrial times within this century. If emissions of greenhouse-gases (GHG) remain high over the century, the GMT might increase up to 3-4 °C. If so, humankind may leave the temperature range of the mild Holocene, affect tipping points and move toward "hothouse Earth". It will not suffice to stabilise the global emissions. They must be sharply curtailed from now on.

(If there would be extra-terrestrial intelligence observing Planet Earth, they would have to assume that most humans like it hot. The more that humans became aware of anthropocentric climate change (from 1990 at the latest), the more greenhouse-gases they released (from 23 Gt in 1990 to 37 Gt in 2022). From outer space, increasing emissions look like a deliberative collective action to push the planetary thermostat.)

PA may sharpen our minds how volatile and hostile the telluric forces can become. This remains true if humans set them in motion. Our commodified search for safety, pleasure, and comfort may result in threats we impose on other humans, especially future generations and young living individuals. It seems safe to argue that the situation of the Anthropocene, if described properly, constitutes concerns, fears, and anxieties on the side of its "makers", providing some hope for a "new ethics for the Anthropocene" (see part 4).

187 Humans proliferate (over)exponentially in modern times. Demographic patterns (birth and death rates) have changed dramatically since 1800 leading to exponential population growth. At this moment in history, there are 8 billon humans and there will be roughly 9.6 billion people in 2050. A substantial fraction of humans who have ever lived, live now (best guess: 6-10%). When I was born in 1959, the world population counted 2.95 billion humans. Within my lifetime, it increased to 8 billion. Even world wars and epidemics, such as the Spanish influenza, HIV and Corona, are of minor effect upon this trajectory. Population now matters on all parameters: food, housing, transport, electricity generation, *etc*. It is wrong to discard population patterns as "irrelevant". Exponential population growth is a recent phenomenon having deep roots in *proliferation patterns*. Proliferation was "good" in a world where huge regions were almost devoid of humans. The spirit of proliferation was alive in many religions, for example, in the Hebrew Bible. The Anthropocene is a world full of humans, a crowded world. Malthusianism was falsified on the European scale by agricultural progress (Liebig's fertilisers), but it has not been falsified on the global scale today.

## 3.3 Sophocles: The chorus song in the "Antigone"[188]

At the beginning of his *Prinzip Verantwortung,* philosopher Hans Jonas (1979) refers to the chorus song in Sophocles' *Antigone*. To Jonas, this song points to the modern predicament. The tragedy is usually dated between 445 and 435 BCE. The chorus song praises the capabilities of the human being to master a world of nature and to constitute culture. It starts with the potentially gender-neutral *anthrōpos* ("human being", usually translated as man), but it already turns towards the exclusively male term *anēr* in the first antistrophe and repeats masculine participles and pronouns in the last antistrophe. Nonetheless, the focus on "man" is also due to the general gender bias of ancient society – the chorus expects a man to transgress the king's law, but not a woman – and will be ignored in the following.[189] The first sentence: *polla ta deina kouden anthrōpou deinoteron pelei,* especially the word *deinos,* has many translations. There is a deep ambivalence in the word: The online Liddell-Scott-Jones Greek-English Lexicon lists the following as translations "fearful, terrible [...] marvelously strong, powerful [...] clever, skilful". Morton (2016, 64) proposed to translate it as "uncanny". The Greek and the English words agree in the denotation of something that transgresses the expectations and the usual, something supernatural. However, the Greek *deinos* is less restricted and here it is used with its full range of meanings. This younger meaning of the word, including 'astonishment' and 'admiration' – which are all very important in Sophocles' song –, is not denoted by the English word "uncanny" and, thus, the word should be avoided as a translation. Utzinger (2003) explains the use of the word in Sophocles' song in detail.[190] Following Utzinger, one may consider "overwhelming" as one meaning.

*Prima facie,* humans are praiseworthy and their achievements are glorious, overwhelming, striking, and marvellous. I would prefer "extremely striking" as a preliminary translation for the first aspect of the word. *Deinos* has also been translated by "wonders" and "monstrous". Thus, *deinos* denotes pride but it also has connotations of hubris. Praise implicitly suggests a warning not to go too far. Hubris means to overrate one's capabilities and to set oneself on a par with deities. The

---

188 This chapter has been written in collaboration with Laura Schmidt. I am grateful for her help in ancient philology.

189 The contrast between the chorus' expectation and Antigone's entrance and the conflict between men and women as one of the basic problems of this tragedy are recognised by various scholars, cf., *e.g.*, Jouanna (2018) and Griffith (1999). This point about the plot of the tragedy is left aside.

190 According to Utzinger (2003): *"δεινός ist ein Verbaladjektiv zu δείδω, δέος und δεῖμα und heißt primär also so etwas wie "furchtbar, schrecklich". Wenn es sich auf Personen bezieht, dann beschreibt es jemanden, der Autorität besitzt und daher Furcht und Respekt auslöst ("gewaltig, mächtig"). Das sind bei Homer Götter und Heroen. Diese Furcht ist nach antikem Verständnis nichts Negatives: Sie gehörte bis zu einem gewissen Grad zum Respekt. Erst das 20. Jahrhundert hat hier eine Veränderung der Vorstellung gebracht. Im fünften Jahrhundert v. Chr. bekommt das Adjektiv δεινός dann einen neuen Sinn. Es kann jetzt auch den Kundigen, Fähigen bezeichnen. Diese Bedeutung hat sich über den Mittelbegriff des Überwältigenden, Imponierenden herausgebildet. Der Bedeutungswandel scheint sich in diesem Chorlied zu zeigen, da gerade diese neue Bedeutung so farbig illustriert wird. Wie auch sonst bei Sophokles das Wort in allen seinen Bedeutungen vorkommt, so sind hier sogar alle Bedeutungsnuancen miteinander vereint."* [English translation Ott]: *"δεινός is a verbal adjective for δείδω, δέος and δεῖμα and primarily means something like terrible, awful." When it refers to people, it describes someone who has authority and therefore inspires fear and respect ("mighty, powerful"). In Homer, these are gods and heros. According to the ancient understanding, this fear is nothing negative: to a certain extent, it was part of respect. It was not until the 20th century that this idea changed. In the 5th century BCE, the adjective δεινός took on a new meaning. It can now also refer to the knowledgeable, capable person. This meaning has developed via the middle term of the overwhelming, imposing. The change in meaning seems to be evident in this choral song, as it is precisely this new meaning that is so colourfully illustrated. Just as in Sophocles, the word appears in all its meanings, here all the nuances of meaning are combined."*

comparative term *deinoteron* means "more than anything else". This ambivalence in the term *deinos* agrees with the final ambivalence of human activities (second antistrophe): humans can use their skills either for good or for bad, but the skills and the inventions are neither good nor bad *per se*, but humans seem to have the possibility to decide to use their skills either for good or for bad.[191] (The ultimate question of tragedies is, then, about the relation between freedom and fate.)

When the song sets in, the audience will first expect *ta deina* to denote something terrible as in the song of Aeschylus' "*Choephoroe*" (585-586: *polla men gar trephei deina*), but the more positive meanings of *deinos* come forward immediately with the ensuing list of human courage and inventions.[192] As the narrative of the song goes, humans are inventive, creating themselves a portfolio of technologies ("techne") with respect to an uncertain future. Humans can cope with many challenges, but remain mortal. They can do wrong and can fail on moral and political grounds. I give the complete song in Greek with the English translation of Gibbons and Segal[193], not changing the translation of "*deinon*":

Πολλὰ τὰ δεινὰ κοὐδὲν ἀν- στρ. α
θρώπου δεινότερον πέλει·
τοῦτο καὶ πολιοῦ πέραν
πόντου χειμερίωι νότωι
χωρεῖ, περιβρυχίοισιν
περῶν ὑπ' οἴδμασιν, θεῶν
τε τὰν ὑπερτάταν, Γᾶν
ἄφθιτον, ἀκαμάταν ἀποτρύεται,
ἰλλομένων ἀρότρων ἔτος εἰς ἔτος,
ἱππείωι γένει πολεῦον.
κουφονόων τε φῦλον όρ-ἀντ. α
νίθων ἀμφιβαλὼν ἄγει
καὶ θηρῶν ἀγρίων ἔθνη
πόντου τ' εἰναλίαν φύσιν
σπείραισι δικτυοκλώστοις
περιφραδὴς ἀνήρ· κρατεῖ
δὲ μηχαναῖς ἀγραύλου
θηρὸς ὀρεσσιβάτα, λασιαύχενά θ'
ἵππον ὀχμάζεται ἀμφὶ λόφον ζυγῶι
οὔρειόν τ' ἀκμῆτα ταῦρον.
Καὶ φθέγμα καὶ ἀνεμόεν στρ. β
φρόνημα καὶ ἀστυνόμους
ὀργὰς ἐδιδάξατο, και δυσαύλων
πάγων ὑπαίθρεια καὶ
δύσομβρα φεύγειν βέλη,
παντοπόρος· ἄπορος ἐπ' οὐδὲν ἔρχεται
τὸ μέλλον· Ἅιδα μόνον
φεῦξιν οὐκ ἐπάξεται,
νόσων δ' ἀμηχάνων φυγὰς

191 For the ambivalence of *deinos* and the song, see Reitze (2017, 673-684); Utzinger (2003, 24-34, 61-72); Griffith (1999, 179-185); Kamerbeek (1978, 13, 82).

192 The parallel of both songs is noticed by Utzinger (2003, 31); Griffith (1999, 185); Müller (1967, 89).

193 The Greek text follows the edition of Dawe (1996). The translation is taken from the edition of Gibbons and Segal (2008, 33-35).

ξυμπέφρασται.
σοφόν τι τὸ μηχανόεν ἀντ. β
τέχνας ὑπὲρ ἐλπίδ' ἔχων
τοτὲ μὲν κακόν, ἄλλοτ' ἐπ' ἐσθλὸν ἕρπει·
νόμους γεραίρων χθονὸς
θεῶν τ' ἔνορκον δίκαν
ὑψίπολις· ἄπολις ὅτωι τὸ μὴ καλὸν
ξύνεστι τόλμας χάριν·
μήτ' ἐμοὶ παρέστιος
γένοιτο μήτ' ἴσον φρονῶν
ὃς τάδ' ἔρδει.

Translation:

At many things—wonders,
Terrors—we feel awe,
But at nothing more
Than at man. This
Being sails the gray-
White sea running before
Winter storm winds, he
Scuds beneath high
Waves surging over him
On each side;
And Gaia, the Earth,
Forever undestroyed and
Unwearying, highest of
All the gods, he
Wears away, year
After year, as his plows
Cross ceaselessly
Back and forth, turning
Her soil with the
Offspring of horses.
*antistrophe a*
The clans of the birds,
With minds light as air,
And tribes of beasts of
The wilderness, and water-
Dwelling sea creatures—
All these he
Catches, in the close-
Woven nets he
Throws around them,
And he carries them
Off, this man, most
Cunning of all.
With devices he
Masters the beast that
Beds in the wild and

Roams mountains—he harnesses
The horse with shaggy
Mane, he yokes
The never-wearied
Mountain bull.
*strophe b*
He has taught himself
Speech and thoughts
Swift as the wind;
And a temperament for
The laws of towns;
And how to escape
Frost-hardened bedding
Under the open
Sky and the arrows
Of harsh rain—inventive
In everything, this
Man. Without invention he
Meets nothing that
Might come. Only from
Hades will he not
Procure some means of
Escape. Yet he has
Cunningly escaped from
Sicknesses that had
Seemed beyond his devices.
*antistrophe b*
Full of skills and
Devising, even beyond
Hope, is the intelligent
Art that leads him
Both to evil and
To good. Honoring the
Laws of the earth
And the justice of
The gods, to which
Men swear, he stands
High in his city.
But outside any
City is he who dares
To consort with
What is wrong: let
Him who would do
Such things not
Be the companion
At my hearth nor have
The same thoughts as I!

The temporal perspective of the song points from ancient Greece *in retrospect* to previous success stories of humans. At the time of Sophocles, the transformation from the Homerian and the archaic period to the "Athenian" period was in full swing (Glotz 1926).

In later antiquity, it was (falsely) rumoured that Sophocles' father was a blacksmith.[194] Sophocles' interest in the human success story is better explained by a comparison with other authors of his time (Utzinger 2003): During the 5th century BCE, a feeling of admiration and pride in human inventions was increasingly expressed and since about 450 BCE, philosophers and scientists in Athens developed theories about human social and technical evolution. Sophocles – probably a friend of one (Archelaos) and a contemporary of another prominent figure among these thinkers (Protagoras) – seems to reflect on such theories especially in the song *Antigone*.[195] Nevertheless, this play must not be misunderstood as a philosophical treatise or a repetition of specific philosophical opinions. Other contemporary poets (among others, Aristophanes) and rhetors (*e.g.* Gorgias) held similar ideas as well and, thus, we can imagine that these ideas were common, circulated and were broadly discussed in 5th century Athens (Utzinger 2003, 171-229).

Like other texts of this group as well, Sophocles' song only includes a selection of inventions. It mentions neither metallurgy and religious practices nor that humans are the only beings which can control fire at fireplaces where meals can be cooked, with which wild animals can be deterred, and heat provides some comfort against cold nights. Control of fire preceded the Neolithic and was praised in the ancient myth of Prometheus.[196] Thus, Sophocles seems to presuppose the "Promethean" legacy.

Some decades after Sophocles, an unknown poet composed the "*Prometheus Bound*" (*Prometheus Vinctus*), falsely attributed to Aeschylus[197] which also enumerates several technical innovations. I take this song as a corollary to Sophocles. In this song, Prometheus enumerates the inventions he gave as gifts to mankind (436-506) to the chorus:[198]

Πρ. μήτοι χλιδῇ δοκεῖτε μηδ᾽ αὐθαδίᾳ
σιγᾶν με· συννοίᾳ δὲ δάπτομαι κέαρ,
ὁρῶν ἐμαυτὸν ὧδε προυσελούμενον.
καίτοι θεοῖσι τοῖς νέοις τούτοις γέρα
τίς ἄλλος ἢ 'γὼ παντελῶς διώρισεν;
ἀλλ' αὐτὰ σιγῶ, καὶ γὰρ εἰδυίαισιν ἂν
ὑμῖν λέγοιμι· τἀν βροτοῖς δὲ πήματα
ἀκούσαθ', ὥς σφας νηπίους ὄντας τὸ πρὶν
ἔννους ἔθηκα καὶ φρενῶν ἐπηβόλους.
λέξω δέ, μέμψιν οὔτιν' ἀνθρώποις ἔχων,
ἀλλ' ὧν δέδωκ' εὔνοιαν ἐξηγούμενος·
οἳ πρῶτα μὲν βλέποντες ἔβλεπον μάτην,

194 On Sophocles' life, see Jouanna (2018) for his family background. On Sophocles' characterisation of non-elite characters and their relevance for his audience, see esp. Paillard (2017). For a historical placement of Sophocles and his *Antigone* in historical democratic Athens, see Griffith (1999, 1-4).

195 Utzinger (2003); Segal (1964/2019; 1981); Kitto and Hall (1962/2017, xxv-xxvi); Arp (2006, 103-159); Griffith (1999, 38-43).

196 Bosinski (2007, 33) estimates that humans before *Homo sapiens* used fire for more than 1 million years.

197 The Aeschylean authorship is denied by most scholars, see Utzinger (2003, 212-229); West (1979, 1990); Pattoni (1987). Podlecki (2005, 195-200) defends Aeschylean authorship.

198 The text and translation are from Podlecki (2005).

κλύοντες οὐκ ἤκουον, ἀλλ᾽ ὀνειράτων
ἀλίγκιοι μορφῆσι τὸν μακρὸν βίον
ἔφυρον εἰκῇ πάντα, κοὔτε πλινθυφεῖς
δόμους προσείλους ᾖσαν, οὐ ξυλουργίαν,
κατώρυχες δ᾽ ἔναιον ὥστ᾽ ἀήσυροι
μύρμηκες ἄντρων ἐν μυχοῖς ἀνηλίοις.
ἦν δ᾽ οὐδὲν αὐτοῖς οὔτε χείματος τέκμαρ
οὔτ᾽ ἀνθεμώδους ἦρος οὔτε καρπίμου
θέρους βέβαιον, ἀλλ́ ἄτερ γνώμης τὸ πᾶν
ἔπρασσον, ἔστε δή σφιν ἀντολὰς ἐγὼ
ἄστρων ἔδειξα τάς τε δυσκρίτους δύσεις.
καὶ μὴν ἀριθμόν, ἔξοχον σοφισμάτων,
ἐξηῦρον αὐτοῖς, γραμμάτων τε συνθέσεις,
Μνήμης ἀρωγὴν, μουσομήτορ᾽ ἐργάνην.
κἄζευξα πρῶτος ἐν ζυγοῖσι κνώδαλα,
ζεύγλησι δουλεύσοντα σάγμασὶν θ᾽, ὅπως
θνητοῖς μεγίστων διάδοχοι μοχθημάτων
γένοινθ᾽, ὑφ ἅρμα τ᾽ ἤγαγον φιληνίους
ἵππους, ἄγαλμα τῆς ὑπερπλούτου χλιδῆς.
θαλασσόπλαγκτα δ᾽ οὔτις ἄλλος ἀντ᾽ ἐμοῦ
λινόπτερ ηὗρε ναυτίλων ὀχήματα.
τοιαῦτα μηχανήματ᾽ ἐξευρὼν τάλας
βροτοῖσιν, αὐτὸς οὐκ ἔχω σόφισμ᾽ ὅτῳ
τῆς νῦν παρούσης πημονῆς ἀπαλλαγῶ.
Χο. πέπονθας αἰκὲς πῆμ᾽: ἀποσφαλεὶς φρενῶν
πλανᾷ, κακὸς δ᾽ ἰατρὸς ὥς τις εἰς νόσον
πεσὼν ἀθυμεῖς, καὶ σεαυτὸν οὐκ ἔχεις
εὑρεῖν ὁποίοις φαρμάκοις ἰάσιμος.
Πρ. τὰ λοιπά μου κλύουσα θαυμάσῃ πλέον,
οἵας τέχνας τε καὶ πόρους ἐμησάμην·
τὸ μὲν μέγιστον, εἴ τις εἰς νόσον πέσοι,
οὐκ ἦν ἀλέξημ᾽ οὐδέν, οὔτε βρώσιμον,
οὐ χριστόν, οὐδὲ πιστόν, ἀλλὰ φαρμάκων
χρείᾳ κατεσκέλλοντο, πρίν γ᾽ ἐγώ σφισιν
ἔδειξα κράσεις ἠπίων ἀκεσμάτων,
αἷς τὰς ἁπάσας ἐξαμύνονται νόσους·
τρόπους δὲ πολλοὺς μαντικῆς ἐστοίχισα,
κἄκρινα πρῶτος ἐξ ὀνειράτων ἃ χρὴ
ὕπαρ γενέσθαι, κληδόνας τε δυσκρίτους
ἐγνώρισ᾽ αὐτοῖς ἐνοδίους τε συμβόλους,
γαμψωνύχων τε πτῆσιν οἰωνῶν σκεθρῶς
διώρισ᾽, οἵτινές τε δεξιοὶ φύσιν
εὐωνύμους τε, καὶ δίαιταν ἥντινα
ἔχουσ᾽ ἕκαστοι, καὶ πρὸς ἀλλήλους τίνες
ἔχθραι τε καὶ στέργηθρα καὶ συνεδρίαι,
σπλάγχνων τε λειότητα, καὶ χροιὰν τίνα
ἔχουσ᾽ ἂν εἴη δαίμοσιν πρὸς ἡδονὴν
χολή, λοβοῦ τε ποικίλην εὐμορφίαν·
κνίσῃ τε κῶλα ξυγκαλυπτὰ καὶ μακρὰν
ὀσφῦν πυρώσας δυστέκμαρτον εἰς τέχνην

ὥδωσα θνητούς, καὶ φλογωπὰ σήματα
ἐξωμμάτωσα πρόσθεν ὄντ’ ἐπάργεμα.
τοιαῦτα μὲν δὴ ταῦτ’· ἔνερθε δὲ χθονὸς
κεκρυμμέν’, ἀνθρώποισιν ὠφελήματα,
χαλκόν, σίδηρον, ἄργυρον χρυσόν τε, τίς
φήσειεν ἂν πάροιθεν ἐξευρεῖν ἐμοῦ;
οὐδείς, σάφ᾽ οἶδα, μὴ μάτην φλύσαι θέλων.
βραχεῖ δὲ μύθωι πάντα συλλήβδην μάθε·
πᾶσαι τέχναι βροτοῖσιν ἐκ Προμηθέως.

PROMETHEUS
Don’t think I am silent from snobbishness
Or stubborn pride; my heart is rent with brooding
As I see myself treated thus outrageously.
And yet the honours these new gods possess,
Who else but I divided them definitively?
But I keep silent about this, for I would be telling you
What you already know. But listen to me tell
Of humans’ sufferings, how I made them, mere infants
Before, intelligent and possessed of minds.
I’ll speak, not out of reproach for humans,
But to explain the grounds of goodwill for what I gave them.
At first they looked about them, but looked in vain;
Hearing they did not hear, but like mere shapes
Of dreams they led their long lives randomly
And in total confusion. They did not know how to build
Houses of brick against the sun, nor carpentry,
But they lived underground like scurrying ants
In the dark and sunless recesses of caves.
They had no sure sign, either, of winter
Nor of flower-fragrant spring, nor of fruitful
Summer, but they carried on entirely
Without rational thought, until I showed them
The stars’ risings and settings, difficult to discern.
And more: number, that mental feat par excellence,
I discovered and gave them, and the combining of letters,
Memory’s helper, hardworking mother of the arts.
I, too, was the first to put beasts in yokes
To endure servitude with yoke-straps and saddles
So as to relieve mortals of their hardest toils.
I also made horses docile for drawing chariots,
A delight to be indulged by luxurious wealth.
And none but I discovered a way for sailors
To roam the sea in vessels with linen wings.
Though I invented such contrivances for humans,
In my wretchedness now I have no clever device
To get myself out of my present misery.
CHORUS-LEADER
Your mistreatment is shameful. You’ve taken leave of your senses,
And like some inferior doctor who’s become ill

You're in despair and are unable to discover
By what medicine you yourself can be cured.
PROMETHEUS
When you hear the rest from me you'll be more amazed,
What sort of skills and methods I devised.
The greatest was, if anyone fell ill,
There was no remedy, either to be eaten,
Or rubbed on, or drunk, but because of lack
Of medicine they wasted away, until
I showed them how to blend soothing remedies
By which to defend against all diseases.
And I sorted out many ways of prophecy
And first determined what must follow after dreams
When the dreamers awake, and I helped them understand
Omens in obscure utterances and on journeys,
And I defined clearly what the various flights of crook-taloned
Birds meant, which ones were by nature favourable,
Which unlucky, the meaning of their different
Ways of life, their enmities, loves, associations,
As well as the smoothness of the entrails, and what colour
The victims' gall-bladder would have to have
To be pleasing to the gods, and what constituted
An attractive, variegated liver-lobe.
By roasting bones covered with smoking fat
And the long chine, I directed mortals towards
The obscure art of prophecy, and equipped with eyes
The previously cloudy signs in burning offerings.
So much for that. As for metals hidden
Inside the earth that might benefit humans –
Bronze, iron, silver, and gold – who
Could claim to have discovered their use before me?
No one, I know, not wanting to be called a babbler.
Listen to a succinct summary of my whole account:
Humans have all technical skills from Prometheus.

Interestingly, Prometheus omits the gift of fire, the most prominent gift connected to him. However, it is mentioned in the tragedy as his gift and the origin of every *technē* (7, 109-111, 249-260). Behind the evaluation of the past time as bad and a description of an animal-like life of mankind lies the idea of the human being as a deficient being. The term "*Mängelwesen*" has been coined by Arnold Gehlen, but the idea can be found in various ancient texts (Utzinger 2003, 97-167 and 212-229). This is probably one of the most obvious differences to Sophocles. To Sophocles, there is no bad past as a driving force for human inventions, rather they originate from the inventive nature of humankind.

The differences between the two presented tragic passages can partially be explained by the plot and subject matter of the respective plays: *e.g.* in *Prometheus Vinctus,* Prometheus wants to emphasise the importance of his gifts to humankind, and the description of their animal-like past, their nearly complete passivity in the process and the positivity of the outcome – its ethical or qualitative value for mankind is not questioned – displaying effectively the difference to their current state and the effectivity of Prometheus' gifts. Sophocles is more interested in the *deinon*-aspect of mankind: the wonderous power of humans, but also the moral ambivalence and potentially hubristic outcome of their deeds. He concentrates on major achievements, human daring, intelligence, activity and freewill. This concentration on the *human* as an agent of his own social and technical development makes the song of the *Antigone* more important for the present study.

I interpret Sophocles' song as retrospection into archaic times, being full of "wonders", that is: achievements that brought about the societal life of ancient *poleis*. The Athenian period had been often seen as a "laboratory of modernity". The "*polis*" way-of life includes, beside city building itself, a division of labour, arts and crafts, long-distance trade, money and commerce (Aristotle: "*chrematistike*"), stratification including slavery, colonialisation, sportive games, rhetoric-agonistic democracy, and philosophy. Protagoras (490-411) stated: "*anthrōpos metron hapantōn*". The "*metron*" (Protagoras) and the "*deinoteron*" (Sophocles), taken together, suggest high levels of self-esteem. The "polis"-way-of-life, however, did not fall from heaven. The chorus song points at crucial material requirements (enabling conditions) of such a way of life. Humans could not have leaped from a hunter-gatherer way of life into the "polis" way of life. The period in between two distinct modes of human life can be seen as a transition period with reinforcing upswing mechanisms.

Contemporary scholars who are equipped with methods of PA and ethnoarchaeology can (and should) adopt this backward perspective concerning requirements. According to Sophocles, humans are hunters, catchers of birds, fishermen, seamen, farmers, settlers, carpenters, physicians, architects, seers, priests, and citizens. They go by ship. They domesticate wild animals and breed them. They plough the fertile soils, sow seeds, and bring in harvests. They live a sedentary life in common within settlements, finally building cities. They make normative orders to organise their own cultural, economic, and political life. Sometimes, they revolt and rebel – and may fail.[199] The difference between evil and good is still with us in political life. This difference should not be eliminated by the (dangerous) belief to know "the right side of history".

As Sophocles suggests, no other being on Earth can compete with humans in any of these "*deinon*" respects. Humans perform activities that catapult the species far beyond nature although they, as individuals, remain embodied mortal beings.[200] One line of the song reminds of mortality as an inescapable human predicament despite all medical achievements. The finitude of the individual human being and visions about an afterlife, however, are not at the heart of the song. Irrespective of its mortal existence, humans are gorgeous but also precarious beings. They are dangerous to other living beings, including other humans, but are also endangered and fragile.

Sophocles' song as well as Prometheus' monologue highlight the commonalities between archaic and present times. They compile what humans have been capable of since former times. We take the two texts paradigmatically as intellectual markers of the early "thin" Anthropocene. Neolithic achievements still shape our modern lives. They are, so to say, "still close with us". Thus, we have common-

199 The tragedy of Antigone is a dilemma resulting from a failed rebellion. The modern ways of rebellion, revolt, and revolution are outlined by Albert Camus in *L'Homme révolté* (1953).

200 The chorus song has some parallels with the story of Genesis in the Hebrew Bible which presents the human being as having been created in the image of God, but I will remain silent on such presumptive parallels. See Hardmeier and Ott (2015) for a new interpretation of Genesis 1.

alities with archaic people in our lifeworld. Perhaps, a Hegelian idea can finalise this point: Humans enrich their own world with achievements (tools, knowledge, institutions) which remain and are continued by generations. They are, so to say, "eternalised" by way of practices being performed. The Neolithic achievements have sustained.

## 3.4 The eclipse of qualities into quantities

Neolithic achievements may have paved the way towards the thick Anthropocene. An *achievement* is actualisation and persistence of a clever inventive idea with transformative force. Persisting ideas become knowledge ("*know that*") and practices ("*know how*") (Ryle 1949). Achievements are, so to say, cultural Baldwin-effects. They emerge from learning processes. Learning occurs before humans in the animal kingdom (see Weber and Depew 2003). In human life, learning supposes curiosity, cleverness, and creativity. If achievements emerge and are actualised, they persist and endure. Thus, they are *transformative achievements*. Given the older meaning of "revolution" in astronomy and the younger meaning of "revolution" as a change of an institutional order (Ott 2017a), transformative achievements are *not* revolutionary, but profound transformations. A political revolution may not change human affairs as profoundly as transformations of entire ways of life.

Note that in Kuhn's (1962) *The Structure of Scientific Revolutions*, the term "achievement" indicates scientific transformations. Chemistry without "phlogiston", biology with mutation, selection, and evolution, and physics with time-speed-space-relativity is different compared to *status quo ante* in all three sciences. Scientific achievements are irreversible as long as the project of science continues.

In the humanities, the term "achievement" belongs to a cluster of concepts indicating improvements.[201] Improvements are always comparative with respect to some *status quo ante*. Achievements are gains that resulted out of struggling (striving, longing) for a better life. "Better" may mean "more" of something "good" or "less" of something "bad" to humans. Evaluations, such as "easier", "more comfortable", "more convenient", "less burdensome", "less precarious", "less painful", "less brief", are used in this context. Achievements are past novelties which reasonable persons would not like to miss any more at any point in time. Technological, cultural, political and moral achievements are something we wish to keep and wish to continue as traditions. Thus, *ceteris paribus*, achievements are valuable and progressive. If one registers achievements, one may ask, what kind of reasons a presumptive abolition movement might have. Abolition might be demanded by some moral theories, as in the case of current animal rights movement, but I do not see any real voluntary abolition of such achievements through human history. Thus, abolition is not a real option to humans.

Achievements persist, spread, disseminate, and stabilise in the longer run. Slowly, quantities and scales increase. Achievements become expansive over long spans of time.[202] The domestication and breeding of animals, crop agriculture,

201 Western scholars living a digitalised, comfortable, decent academic life with nice salaries should not become ignorant about achievements and improvements which are taken for granted in the "thick" Anthropocene. They should not forget how miserable human life has most often been.

202 Darwin recognised that his theory of evolution had to presuppose a very long geological age of Planet Earth. See Gould (1987). Braudel et al. (1986) pointed at "long duration" in history. In a similar sense, we suppose millennia for the origins of the thin Anthropocene. Such time spans are supposed in the argument.

irrigation (as in Egypt and China) and dealing with seeds, food storage, fisheries with networks, shipping and long-distance trade, settlements, urban centres of commerce (trade) and religion, a division of labour and metallurgies are essential Neolithic achievements. Following Robb (2013), we can define a "Neolithic package" of achievements which transformed societal order. In the following, Robb's theory of European neolithisation is presupposed.

By way of hypothesis, a dialectical transformation ("eclipse") of specific qualitative achievements occurs into an unlimited increase in quantities (expansion, growth).[203] A quality denotes a "how" ("*qualis*"), while a quantity denotes a "how much" ("*quantus*"). In Hegel, an increase in quantities can transform into a new quality, as sand gradually transforms into a dune. The essential Neolithic achievements have no *intrinsic* limitations. They can expand in their quantities on different spatial and temporal scales until they reach planetary boundaries. The expansion is driven by technological progress. Finally, a new quality of scale with new effects is reached.

Let us scaffold a simple scheme: A qualitative achievement (Q-1) might, first, expand over time into ever increasing quantities (Q-2) and, later, collapse into a new quality with many negative side effects and risks (Q-3). Now, the slow origins and the rapid upshot of the Anthropocene since industrialisation and the Great Acceleration can be perceived as an eclipse of basic Neolithic achievements (Q-1 "qualities") into increasing Q-2 quantities which have collapsed in a new Q-3-quality since industrialisation, colonialism, and the Great Acceleration. Q-1 and Q-3 can differ from an evaluative point of view. Q-1 is, by definition, something "good to have". Q-1 is an achievement. Abolition of Q-1 would affect our ways of life profoundly: no shipping, no domestication, no medicine, no urban life, *etc.* Q-2 has been a long period of "more of the good" which seems to equal "better". If x is good, x+1 is better than x, x+2 is better than x+1 – *ad infinitum*. This is the utilitarian logic of maximising the good. In utilitarianism, a unit of good always adds to welfare, and if one wishes to make the world a better place, the good should be maximised and the bad should be minimised. This is a highly tempting pattern of thought and a basic economic model: maximise (discounted) utility. Such a pattern is linear, not dialectic. Linearity demands "more of the same" and it restricts problem solving to "usual remedies". It precludes transformations. Q-2 has been passed throughout historical waves (the Neolithic, antiquity, 1500 CE, 1800 CE, 1950 CE). The eclipse of Q-2 into Q-3 terminates in a state of crisis and grave concerns about the future (part 4). Recently, concerns terminate into apocalyptic anxieties about climate catastrophes. Q-3 is the situation we are facing: the Anthropocene. If so, there is a quest for another transformation from Q-3 to some non-existent Q-4. Such a transformation cannot be a continuity of Q-2 ("growth"), but should not abolish Q-1 ("achievement"). Q-4 is a better way (mode) of doing Q-1 and it should help to escape the present state of crisis (part 4).

The relation (Q-1 → Q-2) is a *past-past*-relation. It can be filled with many historical studies and narratives. The relation (Q-1 → Q-3) is a *past-present*-relation. The relation (Q-1 → Q-2 → Q-3) is a *past-past-present*-relation. The relation (Q-3 → Q-4) is either prospective or prescriptive (or both). Q-4 would be a "good" Anthropocene. The search for such a "great transformation" towards Q-4 unites the third

203 The transition from quantity to new qualities has been seen as a mechanism of social evolution by Carneiro (2000) who follows Hegel, Marx, and Engels. I invert this mechanism. There were qualities in low numbers which expanded into quantities and, far later, eclipse into another quality which is different from the first one.

epistemic culture of concerned scholars, including PA, because we need to understand origins (Q-1) and Q-2 histories in order to have informed discourse on good and viable (Q-3 → Q-4) transformations. From an ethical point of view, intellectual proposals about "Q-4" states are evaluative and/or normative investments entailing concepts such as sustainability, resilience, justice, degrowth, *etc.* (part 4).

The relation (Q-3 → Q-4) should not abstract from (Q-1 → Q-2 → Q-3). There is a bulk of recent literature on this "Great Transformation" (Q-3 → Q-4) which are ignorant of history. If one adopts a HM perspective, then the perspective called "the moral point of view" may also be transformed. The moral point should not be conceived as the ideal peak of practical reason. Such a peak becomes highly demanding, but it loses contact with the modes of life which have been shaped by enduring achievements. The proposed alternative is to navigate through (Q-1 → Q-2 → Q-3) in some detail *before* addressing (Q-3 → Q-4) from the moral point of view. The macro-history would be composed from (Q-1 → Q-2 → Q-3 → Q-4): *origins and achievements (Q-1), expansion and growth (Q-2), eclipse and crisis (Q-3), future solution (or failure)* (Q-4). This macro-historical scaffold coheres with the DPSIR scheme. The (Q-2 → Q-3) trajectories are drivers and pressures, Q-3 are states and impacts, while Q-4 is about response.

Following Sophocles and his anonymous colleague, the following subsections present some instances for these qualitative/past and quantitative/present connectivities between a "thin" (Q-1) and a "thick" (Q-3) Anthropocene which have long historical Q-2-periods in between. Past-present-analogies are presented. Q-4-transitions are outlined but not argued yet, as this will be done in part 4. In the following, we can simply follow the enumeration of Sophocles.

### 3.4.1 Shipping

Humans cross the sea by ships. That is something marvellous. *Shipping* is an achievement made by terrestrial humans who are able to swim and dive, but unable to live in the waters for long. Going by boat or ship enlarges mobility, migration, transport, and trade. Shipping is a human practice and the ship has become an archetype for adventure, courage, piracy, journey, conquest, but also trade and a route to an afterlife. Ships are vessels (gr.: *ochema*, as in the poem of Prometheus). The sea has been often symbolised and there are many ocean narratives. Navigation was seen as art in ancient Greece.[204] Shipping along coastlines was augmented in a long Q-2 period by shipping routes across the open sea. Shipping along coastlines means to hold contact with terrestrial space. The next step was to navigate into the "high" sea. The risk of drowning never stopped shipping. The ancient Greek myths are narratives of heroes and adventures on shipping routes.

Shipping became a crucial force for European expansionism since the 14th century.[205] If one dates another historical spike towards the Anthropocene in the times of Magellan, Columbus, and Drake, shipping across the ocean is a key activity of European globalism (Spain, England, Netherlands), including

204 The importance of shipping for ancient Greek culture is beyond doubt. The great myths deal with shipping to distant places such as the Black Sea, Crete, Cyprus, and Asia Minor. See contributions in the nice collection edited by Richter and Stupperich (1999), especially those by Chrysos, Karageorghis, Pöhlmann and Stupperich. See also Schmidt *et al.* (forthcoming 2023). The sea is dialectical, since it separates and connects.

205 See Kollert (2000) for Portuguese expansionism. Kollert argues that modern marine technologies and the spirit of late medieval knights may explain this expansionism of a rather small nation.

slave trade and overseas agrarian industries (sugar, cotton).[206] The crew of Magellan circumnavigated the planet by ship (1519-1522). 18 survivors returned. Drake (1577-1580) and Cavendish (1598-1600) also rounded the planet by ship. "Classical" Eurocentrism divided the terrestrial "old" world from the colonies of the "new" world and from the open maritime space (Schmitt 1950). The "freedom" of the ocean became a crucial topic in interstate law within the tension of "*res nullius*" and "*res communis*". Grotius' "*Mare liberum*" was published in 1608. The opposition of two different spaces, land and sea, constituted European inter-state law ("*jus publicum Europaeum*", see Schmitt 1950). Later, England became the first maritime naval power which outcompeted its rivals. It "ruled the waves" and, by doing so, it conquered a global empire. Its outposts were nods from Gibraltar to Malta, Cyprus, Egypt, and Aden to India. Geopolitical discourse emphasised the role of sea power for colonialism and expansion (Werber 2014). Alfred Mahan (1897) was the most prominent proponent of sea power. Thus, there is a long Q-2 trajectory to the contemporary state of an ocean crowded with ships of different types (far more than 100,000 each day). The "blue planet" is full of ships.

Today, more than 90% of global trade is performed by shipping. Global trade has multiplied since decades reaching nine billion tons in 2017. Maritime transport costs dropped due to container technologies. Given the magnitude, it does not matter that several thousand containers go overboard each year. Shipping is a key driver of globalisation. Locations of production and consumption can have any distance. Harbours mobilise trade and increase tourism. Ship-building was always about larger transport capacities ("tonnage"). Vessels grew. Today, huge container ships force harbours to expand. Ferries transport cars, vans and even railways. Cruising ships have become swimming hotels with several thousand inhabitants shipping across different routes. The former luxury of cruising has become affordable for middle-class people. Sailing yachts have become luxury commodities with distinctive advantages ("positional goods" *sensu* Bourdieu). Meanwhile, some destinations of the growing number of large cruising ships wish to regulate "overtourism" (Venice, Barcelona, some fjords in Norway).

Naval forces are still strategic means of contemporary geopolitics. Main shipping routes are of paramount geopolitical interest and become "securitised". The ship is a Q-1 achievement which eclipsed into the aircraft carrier which combines sea power and air force.

All in all, the innovative idea to go by ship across the sea has eclipsed into "gigantic" quantities which must be governed. A political Q-4 task of the Anthropocene is to regulate shipping according to the spirit of the Sustainable Development Goal 14 (SDG 14). One may think of speed limits, noise reduction, engines made from sails and solar panels, sharp regulation on overtourism, marine protected areas, sea route planning, ban on whaling, recovery of fish stocks. Roberts (2012) demands a "New Deal" for the ocean. With contributions from Kiel scholars, some papers have been recently published on maritime sustainability and governance (Neumann *et al.* 2017; van Doorn 2021; Franke *et al.* 2020; Ott *et al.* 2022). The (Q-3 → Q-4) transition with respect to shipping would have to replace the "classical" *mare-liberum* approach by a "common-heritage-of-mankind" (van Doorn 2021) providing an alternative approach for a marine Q-4 framework. One "planetary" idea is to tax shipping in order to finance ocean recovery and restoration projects.

206 There was slave trade between Sub-Saharan Africa and Arab countries over centuries, but only the Europeans organised colonial industries based on slavery until 1865. Slavery was a profitable large-scale business model within a maritime triangle (England, France, West-Africa, Caribbean, U.S.).

### 3.4.2 Fishing with nets

Fisheries are a special case of shipping. Some mammals catch fish, such as bears that catch salmons with their paws. Some Indonesian apes catch small fish in rivers. Prehistoric humans also caught fish in rivers, wetlands, estuaries, and coastal zones. Salmon (*Salmo trutta labrax*) was caught in Palaeolithic times (Bosinski 2007). Fishing is a crucial foraging activity in many complex hunter-gatherer societies, for example, on the Pacific West Coast. Fish contributes positively to a healthy diet.

Fish, however, are quick and slippery. How can fish be caught best? Bears have no alternatives, humans can consider the problem "at hand". Hands, spears, and artificial barriers in creeks may do the job. Humans even use captive birds for fishing, as they use falcons for hunting. One can also catch fish from the riverbank by a fishing rod, but this practice requires patience and does not bring a high catch. The most innovative and clever idea, however, is the *net*. With some likelihood, nets originated in the Mesolithic. Perhaps, the nets of spiders served as a bionic inspiration. Fishing with nets is far more effective than fishing with spears, hooks, or by hand. The technological idea of the net is "inescapability for (bigger) fish". The combination of threads and knots does the job. Since nets must be produced in advance, they are investments in productive forces from a HM perspective. Repairing nets takes much time and is clearly labour. Catch is delayed reward. Nets are mobile and easy to transport. The size of the ancient nets are just some square meters. The combination of a human being, a boat, and a net constitutes the traditional figure of a fisherman.

Today, fisheries have moved from artisan coastal fisheries in rivers, lakes, and coastal zones (in a long Q-2 period) to advanced high-sea factories and industrialised aquacultures (Q-3). Leaving aquacultures aside, we see a (Q-2 → Q-3) trajectory from boats to high-sea factory fishing. At present, nets of a globalised fishing fleet have become even larger, often resulting in overfishing, in by-catch, in collateral damage of seabirds and dolphins, and in seafloor dragging. The net of the trawler "*Margiris*" is, for instance, 600 meters long, 200 meters broad and can catch up to 250 tons of fish per day (Deutsche Stiftung Meeresschutz 2022). An eclipse from a Q-1 achievement into Q-3 quantities constitutes problems of overfishing worldwide. If fishing fleets and fish stocks are complementary goods (Daly 1996), sustainable fishery must take care of the stocks and regulate fisheries.

Humans will not abandon nets and they have good dietary reasons to consume fish. Even if fish seem to be sentient beings, I would not abolish fishing because I do not apply rights to fish. Perhaps, we will have to draw the permission line somewhere between sardines, herring, cods, and sharks. At a moral minimum, Q-4 should be a steady state of sustainable fisheries at any scale. From a sustainability perspective, we have to regulate fisheries by means of law and have to restore (replenish) degraded fish stocks rather than improve fishing fleets. Open access structures and unregulated catches should be banned and combatted. There is an ongoing debate of how to redesign nets from which young fish may escape, which may not kill dolphins or turtles (as by-catch), and may not scatter ocean floors. Thus, in the Anthropocene humans have to regulate fisheries. The concept of "safe biological limits" for reproductive fish stocks is a Q-4 objective.

*Aquacultures* as a combination of fisheries and domestication are not mentioned by Sophocles but should be also considered. Humans can domesticate and breed fish in containments. Aquacultures have a millennia-long tradition in

China. Wittfogel (1931, 473-478) mentions the tradition of tamed fish in ponds as a category of domestication. My abduction speculates on origins of aquacultures in wetlands. Collecting shrimps, crabs, frogs, and even snails combines gathering with hunting animals. Originally, Mesopotamia was a large wetland and a bonanza for foraging. Collecting snails was an activity of poor strata in premodern China (Wittfogel 1931, 474). According to Wittfogel, aquacultures were an investment decision made by wealthy peasants. Since the 1980s, investments in export-oriented shrimp farms industrialised aquacultures at the expense of mangroves. Currently, 50% of "marine" food stem from aquacultures, mostly from Asia. Aquacultures can be also used for cosmetics and pharmaceutical products. We should construe smart multi-tropical aquacultures (see Ott *et al.* 2020) in order to relieve pressure from wild fish stocks. We should consider options for sustainable aquacultures on African wetlands (Ott and Kalu 2020). There have been traditional rice-fish-duck-systems in China which are now proposed as Globally Important Agricultural Heritage Systems (Dai and Xue 2019).

In principle, there can be "good" Q-4 aquatic food in the Anthropocene and humans can continue the traditions of fisheries as ways of foraging which supported the farming way of life in the Neolithic (Terberger *et al.* 2018). In the Gospel, fish goes along with bread.

### 3.4.3 Husbandry and domestication

Most human like to eat meat either sporadically or on a regular basis. Hunting is foraging for meat. In hunter-and-gatherer collectives, humans consumed large portions of meat if there was periodical abundance of meat. The gallbladder was adaptive.

> *"Meat contains creatine* [...] *which improves muscular strength, size, and physical and neural performance.* [...] *Meat has a more complete profile of amino acids than do plant-based proteins" (Love and Sulikowski 2018, 1-2).*

There is a strong male-meat association among contemporary hunter-gatherer societies (Love and Sulikowski 2018). Meat eating symbolises physical strength, predatory attitudes, and fitness.[207]

The domestication of animals has been a crucial inventive achievement (see Cassidy and Mullin 2007). *Humans stored domesticated animals for food and they made animals work on their behalf.* Domestication probably starts with fencing and taming from where it moved to breeding. "Two (woven or wooden) fences were set up in a V shape. Animals were driven in and a third fence, a gate, closed the triangle" (Wilson 2007 with reference to Russel 1988). Wilson (2007, 107-108) sees husbandry as a consequence of human self-domestication. The domestication of animals is co-evolution. Herding is a pastoral way of semi-nomadism and half-way sedentism. Original domesticated mammalian species included dog, goat, sheep, later also pig, donkey, and cattle. Horses have been domesticated since roughly 3000-2200 BCE. Humans also domesticated birds, as chicken and pigeons.

Hunting game is time consuming, exhaustive, and uncertain. Conducting husbandry means control over living meat resources which also produce eggs, milk, and wool. Milk production originated and cheese was a consequence. Per-

207 This prehistoric image is, of course, inacceptable as a symbol of "hetero-normativity" for Western feminist scholars.

forming husbandry is an achievement in terms of availability of fats and proteins. In the (Q-1 → Q-2) transition, the herdsman became a civilised figure compared to the hunter. This transformation has been symbolised in the Biblical story of Jacob and Esau. The civilised shepherd acquires his father's blessing via cheating. Esau, the hunter, looks brute and somewhat stupid. The Hebrew Bible does not admire hunting, but tolerates it (Genesis 27; Deuteronomy 12:15-16, 22-25).

In Greek mythology, meat eating belongs to the lifestyle of masculine warriors, as the behaviour of the comrades of Odysseus indicates. In the Hebrew Bible, meat consumption is tolerated by God because it is recognised as a strong human inclination. It is not, however, fully appreciated. In the Hebrew Bible, the human diet should be more vegetarian. To consume milk and honey in freedom is better than to eat meat in Egyptian serfdom ("Exodus"). Nevertheless, meat eating belongs to rituals, hospitality, and feasting. To the Hebrew Bible, meat eating is the extraordinary part of the diet.

In prehistory and ancient times, large herds meant prosperity. The growth of one's herds counted as a blessing in the Hebrew Bible. The economic logic seems alive in contemporary herdsmen. Growing herds increase the numbers of animals. Natural boundary conditions, however, set limits to husbandry. The Hebrew Bible was aware of overgrazing. In the story of Abram and Lot (Genesis 13:1-10), one family line (clan) had to split into two groups because the meadows could not sustain the grazing of the large number of sheep and cattle. Overgrazing caused trouble between the herdsmen of Abram and his nephew Lot (see part 2, subsection 2.2).

Domestication spread over the Fertile Crescent and Europe. We see a long (Q-2 → Q-3) trajectory. Domesticated animals could be used for riding, ploughing, dairy products, wool production, *etc*. Ploughing the earth with the help of animals (oxen, horses) intensifies agriculture. The domestication of animals and crops reinforces itself. Breeding animals is at the heart of domestication and agriculture. Breeding splits "wild" from "domesticated" species lines such as boars from pigs. Breeding constitutes artificial species as "bio-facts" (Karafyllis 2004). Humans succeeded in breeding mules from donkeys and horses. They bred across species lines producing an artificial animal with both horse and donkey traits. There is another (Q-1 → Q-3) pathway from mules to genetically modified animals.

The numbers of acres and animals indicate degrees of wealth in agricultural and pastoral societies. Horses indicated wealth. There is a long Q-2 period of expansive domestication. In Europe, pigs played an important role in cold medieval times. A decisive step to large-scale cattle breeding occurred in the U.S. since beef could be canned. In the 19$^{th}$ century, Chicago became the real symbol of "gigantic" slaughterhouses. Slaughter became an industrial practice and large-scale effects made meat an affordable mass product (Giedion 1948, part IV).

The current expansion of livestock and slaughter ("factory farming") is a Q-3 eclipse into quantities on global scales: pigs (1.5 billion/year), cattle (300 million/year), poultry (55 billion/year).[208] Both Americas are meat-eating continents. China has sharply increased meat consumption since 2000. Brazil, for instance, produces beef for China, enlarging cattle grazing in the Amazon region

208 The "top" countries are Australian and New Zealand (121 kg/person/year), U.S. (117), Austria (106), Argentina (101), Brazil (93), France (89), Germany (88). Roughly 20% of the eatable meat is not consumed but thrown away (lung, brain, kidney, tongue) or used to feed dogs and cats. These 20% are ignored in the statistics on meat consumption. In Germany, meat consumption has dropped in recent years due to cultural change. In 2022, average net consumption was 52 kg. This is the lowest average since 1989.

at the expense of primary forests. Denmark and Germany have become meat-exporting countries despite large domestic consumption. Meat consumption on a daily basis has been perceived as a kind of social equity. Prices for meat dropped with the help of scaling-effects. The body weight of all humans and domesticated mammals compared to wild mammals has a fraction of 96% to 4%.

Large-scale industrial meat production has severe consequences on ecosystems and climate and it looks morally repugnant from an animal ethics perspective. Today, animal rights activists demand the abolition of domestication – except pets. Some would give even political rights to pets but deny any entitlement of humans to utilise animals. In any case, large-scale meat production is one moment of the Anthropocene. An ethics of the Anthropocene must include a statement on the future of animal domestication. By intuition, we should replace containments and should return to sustainable and diverse grazing systems, including sheep and goat herding in the open landscape. In a globalised sustainable economy, it might be possible to concentrate husbandry on grasslands which are not suited for agriculture (Mongolia, Argentina, mountainous meadows in Europe). Nomadic herdsmen have come to the brink of extinction since most herds now live in containments. Such processes might be reversed in a (Q-3 → Q-4) transition. Q-4 would be closer to early herding than to industrial meat production. Why not combine electronic combustion in small cars with horses and mules that are used in forestry and for transportation? *If* one favours an animal-welfare approach over an animals-rights-approach in animal ethics, humans do not have to abolish domestication for human purposes. Humans have to pay due respect to the well-being of domesticated animals and must not overburden them, but are permitted to take a superior role. Animal rights activism, however, will argue for a (Q-3 → Q-4) transition which finally ends with the abolition of domestication except pets. Thus, animal-welfare- and animal-rights approaches conceive the (Q-3 → Q-4) transition differently. I will address this problem in more detail in part 4.

### 3.4.4 Agriculture

Gatherers took wild plant seeds, grounded them by rocks, made powder into paste, and were nourished (Zabinski 2020, 8). The origins of agriculture are hard to detect in the records since cropping plants did not leave traces. Agriculture originated roughly 13,000 years ago in the Fertile Crescent. There might have been a common origin of agri- and horticulture which was later divided into fields and gardens. A field is originally a small patch in the wild devoted to cropping. There is much semi-agriculture in the transition from wild growing plants to crops. The inventive Q-1 idea is to reserve a patch for, ideally, only one species of a crop plant, removing all other plants and combating pests. The ideal is a monoculture that allows for high crop yields which can be stored. Cropping is highly labour-intensive, but it contributes to food security in complex foraging. Stored grain reduces the radius of a meal to some steps from the pantry to the kitchen. Such reduction counts in cold and rainy seasons. 2.5 ha might have fed a Neolithic household (8-9 persons) a year, given additional food sources. The plough, which appeared at 3500 BCE in Central Europe, became the technological symbol of agrarian cultures. There are some areas in Germany which have been ploughed for 5000 years. The combination of ox and plough survived in Europe until the 20$^{th}$ century.

For the farmer, agriculture made fertile land a stock of capital which has to be treated with care. One can invest in fertility of soil by manure, but also by planting trees to prevent erosion. Property rights over land were established: ownership, leasing, payments for lease, legacy, *etc*. High crop yields allow for both storage and taxation. As Scott (2017) argues, rice, barley, and wheat could be taxed by agencies of emergent early states.

Zabinski (2020) tells the ecological-cultural narrative of wheat from a wild grass to a mega-crop of the Anthropocene. Others crops, such as millet, arrived from East Asia to Europe where it amplified the crop package, enriched diets, could be used as fodder, and might have served as an insurance crop in bad years since it grows on poor soils and ripens fast (Kirleis *et al.* 2022). After millet arrived in Ukraine at 1600 BCE, it dispersed quite quickly to Bohemia (1500 BCE) and to Lithuania, where, as a C-4 plant, it gradually came to its limits. We also consider emmer, wheat, rye, and barley and we also see a conjunction of millet with beer brewing and bread baking. Cereal-based diets became common in the temperate zones.

Agriculture is not just meant for baking bread. Alcoholic fermentation was humankind's first biotechnology originating probably 8000 years ago in China (Guerra-Doce 2020; McGovern 2020). The production of alcoholic beverages (brewing) is also a Q-1 achievement.[209] Brewing is a complex "multistage process" of malting and fermentation which required "large quantities of surplus" (Guerra-Doce 2020, 62). It is well-established in Mesopotamia. In Bronze Age graves, there were buckets with fermented beverages, probably beer sweetened with honey. Death (1887/2013) speculated that the desire for beer spurred the domestication of cereals. This hypothesis was revived in the 1950s. Guerra-Doce (2020) investigates whether some sites in Neolithic Europe from Iberia to Britain had been breweries. The innovative idea is to have access to alcoholic beverages on a regular basis (McGovern 2020, 85). Under archaic conditions of polluted water, fermented beverages had positive effects on health. Consuming alcohol in common was a medium of social bonding. Drinking is an embodied material culture and may count as a paradigm instance of a "total social fact" (*sensu* Mauss 1925) which has repercussions throughout different spheres of societal life, including identities (Dietler 2020). Guerra-Doce (2020, 74) infers a pattern of "male warrior feasting structured around the consumption of alcoholic drinks" from Bronze Age drinking equipment. Getting drunk together was a common practice of young men in ancient Greece. One should remember the initial scenery in Plato's "*Symposion*" (176a-e) where a group of young men felt sick after excessive drinking during the previous night. In Northern sagas, there is much drinking in the afterlife. Petersen (1782) wrote a history of drinking in Germany.

There is a long (Q-2 → Q-3) narrative about fermenting, wine making, brewing, and distilling all over the world. Breweries, wine making and distilleries have become large-scale industries in the Anthropocene. The Q-1 achievement eclipsed into globalised Q-3 alcoholic industries. Drinking produces negative health-effects and many alcohol-addicted persons.[210] Thus, some countries regulated the consumption of alcohol in the common interest, such as Sweden, while other countries accepted (or even promoted) the toxic effects of drinking alcoholic beverages on their population such as Russia. A comparison between the Swedish and the Russian case is given by Schrad (2014). Q-4 should reduce the

---

209 See alcohol production in Göbekli Tepe at DOI:10.1017/S0003598X00047840.

210 A very special case is vodka politics in Russia. See Schrad (2014). He shows how the Russian state made much profit from the intoxication of its population.

social costs of alcohol abuse, but should not abolish alcohol consumption. The Swedish model may serve as "best practice" for regulation.

In agriculture, fields and farms increased continually. Since 1800 CE, there is a strong push to larger farm units in Europe which intensified throughout the 19th and 20th centuries. The conquest of North America by white settlers ("*Landnahme*") introduced agriculture and a farming way of life which was praised in Jefferson's *Notes on the State of Virginia* (1787). The prairies were subjected to ploughing, whereby farming became industrialised (Gideon 1948). Socialist agriculture also wished to collectivise and industrialise agriculture. In the U.S., soil erosion escalated to "dust bowls" which ruined many farmers in the Midwest in the 1930s (Worster 1979) and motivated Aldo Leopold to conceive a "land ethics" (Leopold 1949/1989).

At present, cereals (barley, wheat, rice, maize) are produced on 600 million hectares. Global harvests have tripled since the 1950s. As a matter of fact, cereals are *the* global staple food. On the one hand, industrialised agriculture is a success story: In Germany, one farmer feeds 120 people which have to pay less than 15% of their average income for food. Food has become abundant in the west. On the other hand, the productive forces of industrialised Q-3 agriculture out-compete peasant farmers in low-income countries, whereas high-input-large-scale agriculture has negative environmental impacts. Food security of many African countries relies on imports of cereals. Russian warfare against Ukraine (2022) suddenly made visible how states in Sub-Saharan Africa and the Near and Middle East have become dependent on cereal imports from northern states. Cereals may become political weapons in the Anthropocene, as it happened during the Russian war against Ukraine in 2023. This is a strong case for closing yield gaps in Africa, including decent large-scale agricultural investments from which local peasant farmers might also profit (Reichert and Ott 2021).

The (Q-3 → Q-4) transition would turn towards more organic farming in Europe and to diversified diets which may reduce the fraction of meat, processed potatoes (chips, fries) and cereals (Kortetmäki 2022). We should combat the business model of highly processed ("convenient") food which is reminiscent of the Mesopotamian monotonous cereal-based diet resulting in poor health status compared to complex foraging. Thus, prehistory should make us aware about the broad spectrum of human diets. There are reasons to believe that mixed diets (fruits, vegetables, fish, nuts, poultry, mushrooms, cereals) are healthier than a diet based on cereals and meat. The achievement of cropping might diversify away from cereals. PA can reveal humans as dietary flexible omnivores. An ethics of the Anthropocene must include an agro-diet ethics (part 4).

### 3.4.5 Urbanism

The chorus in the "*Antigone*" sings about towns and cities ("poleis"). It is contested whether "*astynomous*" means sedentism or city-building. Utzinger (2003, 32) and Reitze (2017, 676) argue in favour of city-building. The latter presupposes sedentism and housing (part 2), but city life constitutes a new way of life (Mumford 1970). Cities become three-dimensional as buildings grew higher. Modern metropolitan areas appear as silhouettes of skyscrapers from the distance. A majority of humans will live urban ways of life, but urban life in the Anthropocene will differ from "classical" European city life. The logic of urbanism has moved toward (metropolitan) agglomeration, including slum-dwelling for many. Archaeologists have contributed to a better understanding of urban settlement trajectories (Lobo *et al.*, 2019; Fletcher 2020; Smith and Lobo 2019). Ortman *et al.* (2020, 151) argue that PA is necessary or at least very helpful for a supposed general theory of urbanization that deals with "general laws that seem to govern cities everywhere" (Batty 2019, 998). Other approaches research the intrinsic logic ("*Eigenlogik*", see Berking and Löw 2008) of urban development at the level of single cities, particular city-cultures (as harbour cities or mining cities), and urbanism in general. The triadic structure of singularity, particularity, and universality seems more appropriate to urbanism than general formal models. The ancient song points to the worrisome prospects of an urbanised Anthropocene.

Houses are single units of cities. One crucial achievement of housing is the clever idea that the roof can become a second floor. In oriental cities, rooftops are locations of dwelling and gardening. Rooftops are the highest floor. Within houses, floors are connected by stairways and ladders. In ancient times, houses with more than one floor are called "towers". In light of the clever idea to have a second floor, only building technology set the limits to vertical settlements. If one can have a second floor, why not a third one? The Q-1 achievement turns into a long Q-2 story about verticality in architecture. As technologies improved, a Q-3 period of "skyscrapers" and "skylines" emerged which now dominates urban spaces on a global scale. Modern architects, such as Le Corbusier (1930), designed vertical settlements. Vertical housing moved from architectonic utopia over prestige to necessity in densely crowded areas. The highest recent building (Burj Khalifa) is 828 meters high.

### 3.4.6 Cutting forests

I wish to add one practice to the list of human practices which is not emphasised in Sophocles' song. The author of "Prometheus" mentions timber and wood as materials for craftmanship. In the full-fledged Anthropocene, forests are under pressure, especially tropical primary forests. Although the idea of sustainable forestry was already coined in 1713 (Carlowitz 1713/2013), clearing, converting and removing forests remained an ongoing activity with deep roots. Archaic and ancient humans were not "friends of the forests".

The myth of Gilgamesh entails a story about killing the demon of the large forest and clearing the forest (George 2003). Gilgamesh makes timber out of trees. In the Hebrew Bible, cedars and firs of Lebanon became timber for King Salomon's palace (1 Kings 5: 6-10). The myth of Heracles symbolises the relation between a human hero and an old-grown forest. Forests provide timber which becomes fuel for the pyre of the dying hero.[211] Cutting the oak trees of Oeta becomes "the last victory of the great civilizational hero who, in his death, clears the slopes" (Kliszcz and Komorowska 2017, 54). In the tragedy *Hercules on Oeta*, falsely attributed to Seneca the Younger, the final demand of the hero is to (1483f.): "*caedatur omnis silva et Oetaeum nemus succumbat* – Let all the forest be cut and the grove of Oeta shall be overcome." The large pyre for the hero's funeral is more important

211 Ovid (Met. 9.229ff.) writes about this event: *At tu, Iovis inclita proles, arboribus caesis, quas ardua gesserat Oete, inque pyram structis,* [...] *dumque avidis comprenditur ignibus agger, congeriem silvae Nemeaeo vellere summam sternis".* [English translation]: *"But you, illustrious son of Jove, cut down the trees which grew on lofty Oeta, built a huge funeral pyre [(...] And as the pyre began to kindle with the greedy flames, you spread the Nemean lion's skin on the top of the pile of the forest."* [Translation available at: https://www.loebclassics.com/view/ovid-metamorphoses/1916/pb_LCL043.19.xml; last accessed: 6 December 2023].

than a sacred grove of old oaks. It seems that such descriptions were a literary motif in Roman literature that were provoked by the historical deforestations of Caesar and Octavianus (Leigh 1999).

Humans "clear" (German: "*roden*") forests, starting with "slash-and-burn" practices. Small groups performing slash and burn only create a patch in the midst of large primary forests. This practice, however, escalates within history. Humans convert forests into meadows and fields and/or they utilise timber for ships, houses, fires, vehicles, *etc*. To clear a forest brings a double advantage: timber and space for agriculture and husbandry. It also brings about an emotional advantage: reduction of fear, since large forests appear as "old, unfriendly forces to be approached with utmost discretion" (Kliszcz and Komorowska 2017, 54). Crossing large forests remained a dangerous adventure for a long time. In many legends and fairy tales, forests were seen as locations for beasts and witchcraft. In ancient times, they are regarded as "*loca horrida*".

Despite this human inclination to remove forests, forest cover remained high over many millennia. Archaic collectives which settled in mixed step-forest landscapes hardly overexploited the timber supply of forests. Later, increasing populations and improved technologies reduced forest cover in ancient and medieval times (Q-2). There was heavy deforestation in the Mediterranean Basin during Roman times. The long Q-2 story on forestry, including the normative idea of sustainability, is beyond the scope of this section. Some Hegelian ideas about ecological forestry in times of climate change are given in Ott (2021c).

Similar short stories might be told about other human achievements that are enumerated by Sophocles and in the "Prometheus": hunting game, teaching and education, medicine, legislation, numbers and letters, interpretation of dreams, and metallurgy. Such stories might be added to make the "big picture" of human inventiveness more complete. Modern medicine might be the greatest success story ever.

## 3.5 Preliminary results

*If* these crucial instances of eclipses from inventive Q-1 ideas over expansionist Q-2 routes to highly worrisome contemporary Q-3 quantities are convincing, the Anthropocene has deep and under-researched roots in the Neolithic. Qualities expand into large-scale quantities, be it the number of knots in a net, transport capacities of ships, shipping routes, cleared forests, size of agricultural fields, floors in houses, number of domesticated animals, breeding practices, storage of crops in silos, trade volumes, and even medicine. These Q-2 numbers ("volumes") may be researched over all relevant historical times to quantified time series. Techniques of economic time series can be applied. Here, "big data" might be helpful for such macro-histories which may reveal patterns. Such macro-histories are in line with HM.

We may speculate that the origins of the Anthropocene (part 3) and the origins of economic life (part 2) reinforced each other via many feedbacks. The basic achievements can be seen with economic eyes. This perspective reinforces the eclipse from qualities into increasing qualities. What Marx (1863, 167) writes about capitalism is true in a more generic sense: There are no intrinsic measures ("*Maß*") for increases in quantities. There are only technological constraints. By shifting such constraints, new frontiers of production emerge. Humans drain mires, convert forests, perform deep sea mining, and explore outer space.

If so, there is a deep entrenchment of human ways of life since the Neolithic with respect to increased quantities, enlargements, expansion, acceleration, growth, excessiveness, *i.e*, "more". "The more, the better" is (or has been) an emblematic slogan even today. Conventional economic wisdom tells us that there are no absolute limits. I generalise Graeber and Wengrow (2021, 274), who make the point of an "explosive growth potential" of a specific "European" constellation. This ever-lasting longing for "more" might now be hypothesised as a past-present-connectivity which can abductively be inferred from part 2 and part 3. If this hypothesis holds, we can see the *tragedy* of the "thick" Anthropocene: There are sound reasons to overcome this growth-addicted trajectory, but the records from the Neolithic origins to the Great Acceleration point to growth and expansion as a deeply entrenched behavioural strategy. I leave it as an open question whether this strategy is widespread "human" or particularly "European", but claim that it reveals itself in European modes of thought and modes of life. It seems possible to correlate patterns of economic thought with the achievements praised by Sophocles into a perspective on the emergence of modern "European" technological and industrial civilisation. The list of achievements includes engineering projects on the continental scale (van Laak 1999). The U.S. appears as a liberalised variant of the European spirit (Hughes 1989). The modernisation projects in the USSR and China aimed at wealth generation by liberating productive forces in socialist modes of production. To Lenin, socialism was soviet power plus electricity. Socialism continued the project of mastery of nature. The USSR wanted to make great Siberian rivers flow to the south where they should irrigate the deserts. However, cotton production in Turkmenistan made the Aral lake fall dry.

The external effects of ever-enlarging industrialised Q-3-quantities on natural environments are undeniably huge: climate change, loss of biodiversity, eutrophication, pollution, *etc.* As a huge bulk of literature argues, these impacts should be reduced to sustainable levels within human-defined planetary boundaries (Rockström *et al.* 2009). As historians know, there can be "boom-and-bust" trajectories. 50 years ago, the Club of Rome (Meadows *et al.* 1972) warned against "boom and bust", but the bust has not been realised yet despite further growth. Perhaps, the period of the boom has been prolonged by environmental reforms, but the bust has come close now via climate change. Since decades, concerned earth-system scientists blow the whistle that humankind is on a trajectory leaving the geological comfort zone of the mild Holocene. The Anthropocene abbreviates the Holocene. The "cold" Pleistocene was replaced by the "mild" Holocene only 15,000 years ago which now might be replaced by the "warm" or even "hot" Anthropocene. The modern creators of the Anthropocene will probably make life less comfortable for their descendants.

There are strong prudential reasons of precaution to remain within a modified Holocene/Anthropocene. Remaining within the "Holocene-window" implies to restrict the increase of the global mean temperature to "well below 2 °C" (Paris Agreement) or, better, to 1.5 °C (as compared to pre-industrial periods). The 1.5°C target is a first defence line against run-away climate change (Schellnhuber 2021). If this line cannot be held, there remain other defence lines in the range between 1.5 °C and 2 °C, such as adaptation, negative emissions, such as bioenergy with carbon capture and storage (BECCS), and natural climate contributions (NCC). BECCS would, however, need much fertile land, and an ocean alkalinity increase and enhanced weathering would require large-scale mining. Climate engineering at global scales are prolongations of the upscaling attitude that we should better overcome. Hubris in a technological era may mean that humans overrate their capabilities to control deliberative technological intervention in planetary records, such as solar radiation. Solar radiation management (SRM) is a high-risk strategy (Ott 2018b; Neuber and Ott 2020; Tang and Kemp 2021). Some options of climate engineering point to the repugnant side of "*deinon*" and "*Prometheian*" thinking.

Right now, humankind is in a situation of how to successfully adapt to ongoing climate change. Humans must become highly responsive to a paramount challenge.[212] Most modern humans, however, might be still trapped in industrialised ways of life and modes of thought. It looks as if we should not go further but can neither stop nor return. Here, I generalise Graeber and Wengrow again: "We are stuck", or so it seems. In contrast to their diagnosis, Graeber and Wengrow place freedom at the heart of their normative suggestions. The emphasis on freedom replaces a commitment to egalitarianism. This is a move from Marx to Hegel which I dearly endorse. Persons, who see themselves as both stuck in something evil but realise their freedom in a situation of challenge, must reflect upon presumptive transformations. Such reflection will entail ethical topics.

212 The option to migrate on a densely populated planet will be supported by cosmopolitans under the headline of "climate refugees". Cosmopolitan utilitarianists (Khanna 2021) wish to relocate large fractions of humankind into northern latitudes. I see this migratory option highly critically (see also Keyserlingk 2018), but will abstract this topic from the present analysis. See Ott (2016b).

# Part 4: Prehistoric archaeology and contemporary ethics: Prospects for a "good" Anthropocene

*Wo aber Gefahr ist, da wächst*
*Das Rettende auch.*
(aus: Friedrich Hölderlin, *Patmos*, V. 2-4)

*But where there is danger,*
*the rescue also grows.*
(from: Friedrich Hölderlin, *Patmos*, v. 2-4)
[English translation: Ott]

## 4.1 Diagnosis

PA is successful in reconstructing a European trajectory of the agricultural transformation. The TPCL approach (part 1) allows us to research, understand, explain, and narrate details of this trajectory on different scales of transformation. This trajectory is one of the great transformations in human history. On the economic side of the economy-culture divide (Robb 2014), HM reconstructs the origins and emergence of economic life as such which has become apparent at the emic side (part 2). While TPCL supposes human agency in general, HM is about economic agency in particular. There are reasons to believe in an early "thin" Anthropocene in the prehistoric European way of life (part 3). As we have seen in part 3, crucial qualitative innovations and achievements (Q-1) eclipsed into ever increasing quantities (Q-2 → Q-3). Economic life became growth-oriented. The steps from hoarding material wealth to investing capital occurred. Earning (more) money became a supreme principle of ancient market economies (Aristotle). We see long-term patterns of a growth-trajectory without intrinsic limitation mechanisms. Contemporary economic rationality demands a maximisation of either personal or overall utility. The accumulation of capital and the GDP as a standard measure and a crucial indicator for welfare are modern upshots of a growth trajectory starting with surplus production and storage. Following a very slow onset, a rapid take-off can be noted after 1820 (Aghion *et al.* 2021).

One cannot deny the dominant role of European civilisation in the actualisation of a contemporary "thick" Anthropocene. Weber (1905/2001), Eisenstadt (1965), and Nelson (1977), among others, have argued about the role of European rationalism, the mastery of nature, and expansion. In some sense, the collapse of the Western Roman Empire (Meier 2020) and the very slow recovery in the so-called "medieval" period were interruptions within the larger transformation to industrialisation and, finally, to the "thick" Anthropocene. The word "medieval", as coined in the 17th century, is not completely misleading. The Renaissance opened the route again which had been blocked by the disastrous decay of the catastrophic 6th century CE. The reverse of the growth-trajectory in times of pandemics, little ice ages, and warfare was experienced by most people as a disaster and a decay (Fried 2016). Recovery proceeds after 1648.

Economic life regained dominance in modern times. A long-lasting ethical discourse justified calm economic interests over uncontrolled passions (Hirschman 1977). Markets became mechanisms of social integration (Polanyi 1944/2011). There was pride and hope in economic success among the new class of entrepreneurs. There was hope, since wealth could, especially in Calvinism, be taken as indicator of God's grace (Weber 1905/2001). In philosophy, Francis Bacon (1982) integrated modern empirical and experimental science, inventive technology, and industries which produced commodities for expanding markets. The Royal Society was an epistemic community that had promoted a "Bacon-project" since the 18th century (Fischer 1923; Musson 1972). The British enlightenment (Locke, Hume, Hutcheson, Smith) combined moral theory, political philosophy, and economics. Economists became worldly philosophers (Heilbroner 1953/1999). Hegel (1821/1970) outlined the patterns of modern societies under the idea of freedom. Economic life was realised within all of Europe and as Hegel and Marx foresaw, since the 15th century CE, Europe occupied and colonised large parts of the planet. In the first section of the "*Communist Manifesto*", Marx and Engels praised the triumphs of capitalism over feudalism as well as over Asian modes of production, before they claimed that capitalism is bound to fail according to its own contradictions. In the 19th century, European colonialism and imperialism reached their zenith (Friedjung 1919; Mommsen 1979; Shillington 2019). The 30 years from 1914 to 1945, including two world wars and the intermittent period between them, was a deep moral and political catastrophe, culminating in the Holocaust. The former British colonies (U.S.) continued this imperial project after they became a superpower in 1945 and, for some years at least, a hegemonic power after 1989. The competition with the Soviet Union was not just a contest between political systems, but also a competition between different growth strategies. Socialism wished to "overtake" capitalism in terms of productive forces. The "Great Acceleration" since the 1950s was fuelled by coal, oil, and nuclear energy (Pfister 2010). The oil fields of Saudi Arabia and the nuclear reactors became both realities and symbols of energy abundance. Despite the risks of nuclear deterrence, the "nuclear age" was praised (Bluhm 1999) since it promised electricity "too cheap to meter".

The Anthropocene is here to stay. Humans do not live *within* the Anthropocene as other species have lived within other geological epochs. They are its "makers". The Anthropocene is a human "factum". The Anthropocene conceptually entails some abstract human responsibility (Jonas 1979; Ott 2018a). Such responsibility is anticipatory, deeply concerned, but unspecific. If humans, out of transcendental necessity, have to conceive themselves as reasonable agents (part 1), and if agency means accountability and liability, and if this conceptual implication also holds on the aggregate ("humankind"), then ("we") humans are collectively responsible for how ("we") they (do or do not) act in the Anthropocene. Such collective responsibility must be specified since nobody is responsible for anything. Responsibility is not a moral principle, but a concept by which liabilities and duties can be specified and attributed. Philosophers may help to attribute specific responsibilities and liabilities. Thus, the Anthropocene is dominated by a species whose members are, in principle, free, responsible, and reasonable, but have to organise collective action under established Q-3 conditions in order to reach "better" Q-4 positions. The mechanisms of globalised markets and value chains have integrated large parts of humankind into an emerging world society.[213] A global "we" (humankind, global demos, family of humans[214]) is, however, moral hope at best.

The Anthropocene perspective intertwines the *globe* (and globalisation), on the one hand, and the *planet* (and planetary finitude) on the other hand (Chakrabarty 2020[215]; Bonneiul 2020). The planet has been an object of study for the geosciences and now becomes an object of study for the social sciences and for the humanities (Chakrabarty 2015; 2020). To Chakrabarty, this brings about a new connectivity between the historical and the natural sciences. Economic globalisation has become a topic for earth system analysis. Such epistemological shifts may shatter the modern system of disciplines and may form a "third culture" beyond the classical divide (Snow 1961) between science and humanities (Ott 2014a). In this "third culture", PA may take a role which connects the past and the present. Ethics, as a reflective discipline, might be of some help in determining the role of PA in such a "third culture".

From a sociological point of view, there are eight billion individuals divided into many different particular entities, such as groups, clans, corporations, parties, states, regimes, cultures, *etc.* which (re)produce the Anthropocene. I do *not* claim that all humans equally contribute to the major risks of the Anthropocene. There is not just agency, but also victimisation. Individuals, countries and continents are unequal in terms of income, wealth, and power. For some countries, such as those of sub-Saharan Africa, a post-colonial situation seems to prolong without end. Retrospectively, the former colonial powers have better coped with the loss of colonies than the former colonialised regions. Sub-Saharan Africa has remained the poorhouse of the planet. The list of failed or fragile states has grown.

---

213 In the theory of international relations, the more realistic schools of thought deny "humankind" as a political agent. The term "world society" was coined by the English School whose members gave more credit to hopes for global solidarity. See Dunne *et al.* (2013), especially Dunne on world society. See also Hurrell (2007).

214 See Edward Steichen's great exhibition "*The Family of Man*" (1955). I was deeply influenced by this collection of pictures showing familiarity among members of our species.

215 Chakrabarty relies on Heidegger and he comes close to Schmitt's (1950) *Nomos der Erde*.

Inequalities motivate demands for redistribution at different scales, although the relationship between inequalities and injustice is far from clear (Frankfurt 2015). It is easy to blame the Western way of life for being "imperial" since, at least in its current modes, it cannot be universalised. The Western way of life is, however, a blueprint for a growing global middle-income class (Rosling 2018) whose members strive for a better material life. The role model of growth globalises. There is a "bottom billion" (Collier 2008) stuck in absolute poverty, but there is also a strong tendency at the global scale towards Westernised or "glocalised" modes of consumption. Absolute poverty, illiteracy, and child mortality have been reduced, average life expectancy has increased. Rising inequality within and in between countries is compatible with more economic prosperity for billions. Despite the threats of climate change, many middle-income countries in the Global South carbonise their economies (Marz *et al.* 2022).

There are reasons to believe that this century matters. Environmentally, it matters in terms of climate change, biodiversity, ocean acidification, forest cover, *etc.* Politically, it matters in terms of migration, democracy, UN-regimes, and, last but not least, peace. It was the philosopher Hans Blumenberg (1986) who argued that people in some periods perceive their brief mortal lives as connected to a decisive situation in world history. Apocalyptic anxieties as well as revolutionary hopes result from such perceptions. Today, a young generation feels endangered by climate change and sees "the world on fire". Many intellectuals blow the whistle and demand a "great" transformation comparable to the Neolithic and to the industrial transformation. Such a transformation should be both great and sudden. Since all great transformations in history have been unintentional and have been recognised as such retrospectively, the anticipated "great transformation" (WBGU 2011) is conceived as the first intentional and deliberative one. A "great" transformation "by design, not by disaster", as the slogan tells. Perhaps, an intentional "great transformation" by design might be moral hubris. And who would be its designers and masterminds? In such a troubling situation, ethics matters. Even if one should recognise the limits of Western academic ethics, including environmental ethics, in changing the world (Williams 1986), one can and should give philosophical ethics a voice in the quest for a good Anthropocene. Such a voice should, however, not just repeat current moral demands. Ethicists should refuse to take the role of global moral masterminds.

## 4.2 Program and claim

In part 4, I wish to explain, first, why *normative investments* must be part of the Anthropocene debate (part 4, section 4.3). Second, I argue for "thin" *moral universalism* which is not disrespectful against particular cultures (part 4, section 4.4). Third, I make my *ethical framework* explicit (part 4, section 4.5). Fourth, I reflect on outlooks for a second axial age which should not just be a cosmopolitan expansion of the first axial age (part 4, sections 4.6 and 4.7). This section might be the most provocative one. I will, fourth, outline a *method* of how results from previous parts of the book can become reasons by which we can debate both past-present-connectivities *and* "good" and "right" (Q-3 → Q-4) transformations (part 4, section 4.8). Finally, I wish to present *paradigm cases* for such debates (part 4, section 4.9) and draw some conclusions of how to live in the Anthropocene (part 4, section 4.10).

Ethics generally reflects upon moral intuitions, emotions (such as guilt, compassion, anxiety), and (deep) convictions about right and wrong as well as good and evil. Humans are moral agents, "*scientes bonum et malum*". Ethics must bring moral convictions and moral principles into a *reflective equilibrium* which allows for reasonable and considered moral judgements.[216]

Since the Age of Enlightenment, European ethics is *secular* in method and *universal* in scope, but most humans still live in "thick" cultural communities. For moral sociology, Western universalism is only one option among many. Religions still play a major role in moral life in many regions. Nationalism is on the rise in right-wing ("populist") movements in the EU. There are neo-imperial doctrines flourishing outside the Western world ("Russian world", "rise of the dragon", "ummah"). Ethics operates under conditions of moral and ethical pluralism. In metaethics, one distinguishes *moral* pluralism (first-order pluralism of moral belief systems) and *ethical* pluralism (second-order pluralism of competing ethical theories). Taken together, the quest for moral or ethical agreements might likely be in vain.

## 4.3 Normative investments

In part I, we investigated epistemic investments in theoretical scaffolding of PA. Theories about past moral belief systems and past ethical doctrines are *epistemic* investments. The investments about prehistoric economic life (part 2) are epistemic investments as well. This holds true for the explanatory side of the claim that the Anthropocene originated in the Neolithic (part 3). This claim, however, makes room for past-past-present connectivities and outlooks on possible (Q-3 → Q-4) transformations. At these points, prescriptiveness enters the stage. In some sense, ethics is pragmatically implied in the "*deinon*" because this six-letter word entails the idea that "something can go (terribly) wrong". Humans can fail in ways no animal can (Ricoeur 1971). The concept of sin in the Hebrew Bible points to the same human predicament as Sophocles' chorus, especially in the tale that the first human who ever died was slain by his brother (Genesis 4). The "*deinon*" is not just "uncanny", as Morton (2016) believes. The chorus points to the potentials for moral corruption, failure, and evil. There is the dark side of "*deinon*" at work in political affairs, but also in the eclipse of achievements into ever-lasting growth. The many Q-3 trajectories suggest that humans have "gone too far" in mastering and subduing nature. The political "*deinon*" can take many forms, such as aggression, conquest, civil war, ambush, hunting for captives, sacrificing, mass atrocities, torture, terrorism, *etc.*

If there is such deep ambivalence in the "*deinon*", and if one cannot be ignorant against the nasty sides of Q-3 growth, and if one participates in the enterprise of the Anthropocene, one cannot remain in the position of a neutral observer of human history. If so, past-present-connectivities must entail prescriptiveness. If this century matters, we must find pathways into an Anthropocene that can be qualified as "good" and/or "right". At present, there is a tendency to present recipes: post-modernism, cosmopolitanism, neo-communism, transhumanism, neoliberalism, geo-engineering, post-colonialism, degrowth, *etc.* There are philosophers who wish to compost humans and create human-animal hybrids (Haraway 2016) or wish to mobilise Gaia-fighters (Latour 2017). We have to sidestep these many voices. Ethics will not present recipes, but it can clarify how to

216 Overviews on ethical reasoning and ethical theories are given in Ott (2005) and Werner (2021).

check validity claims that are entailed in *prescriptive investments.* Prescriptive investments can refer to universality, particularity, and individuality.

There are different prescriptive investments to be made in a (Q-3 → Q-4) transformation discourse about how humankind, particular collectives, and individuals can and should live well in the Anthropocene. In ethics, one distinguishes axiology from deontology. *Axiology* is about values which are prescriptive in a *weak* sense. Values define tasks to actualise them. The actualisation of values is constituted of material goods and intellectual traditions. Goods can be combined with patterns of distribution and with property rights. Since values have no strict hierarchical order, concepts of a good life must be plural. One can devote one's own life to pleasure, wealth, beauty, fame, science, or religion.

*Deontology* is about obligations which are prescriptive in a *strong* sense: normativity. Obligations can be distinguished in broad commitments and specific duties. I focus, first, on normative investments before I analyse how normative and axiological investments can be combined with historical knowledge to abductive inferences about how to make the Anthropocene good and sustainable.

A first cluster of normative investments is about supreme principles and general moral duties (Rawls 1971, 114-117: "natural duties"). A second cluster of normative investments is about entitlements of humans in terms of capabilities and/or rights. Such entitlements can either apply to all humans or to citizens of particular collectives. A third cluster of normative investments is about ecological constraints (boundaries, limits) that people have to respect. The planetary boundaries (Rockström *et al.* 2009) are a paradigm example. A fourth cluster is about the moral status of non-human beings (= demarcation problem). A fifth cluster is about specific responsibilities (duties, liabilities). Other clusters of normative investments may be about types of justice, for example, political, distributive, and compensatory justice. There is a multitude of claims for (global) justice. From within Western academia, the Western way of life is often accused of being colonial, racist, masculine, capitalistic, commercialised, alienating, *etc.* These accusations are widespread in PA and in cultural anthropology. Via this politicised vocabulary, ethical and political disputes trickle down into PA via many value-laden theories (part 1). I regard such claims as normative investments which deserve ethical attention. Some investments can be subsumed under the concept of recognitional justice (Schuppert 2014). Colonial and masculine attitudes fail to recognise others as equals. These accusations are, however, not self-evident, but require substantiation.

A *sceptical* type of normative investment sees the human faculty of moral and altruistic behaviour as limited. From a sociobiological perspective, humans have some dispositions to behave myopically and perform altruistic behaviour mainly within small groups of kinship, bands, and neighbourhoods. Wilson (1975/2000) argued that there is *strong* altruism based on genetic kinship and *weak* altruism based on cooperation for mutual benefit. Beyond both kinds of altruism, humans are no moral heroes. Most of them are not inclined to support others if there is no reward. As an African proverb says: "Nobody cracks palm kernels with his teeth for another" (Gyekye 1997, 40). Aliens are often seen as foes. According to Dunbar (1993) and Kelly (2013), prehistoric humans lived in expanding circles (family, extended family, bands, periodic aggregation of bands, tribal populations), whose outer circles included 500-2500 people (McCaffree 2022, 8). Given such a way of life over most periods in human history, a "family of humankind" and a "global demos" are moral ideals at best (or even illusions). This holds true for hopes that there might be economies based on sharing. Most humans are not moral saints. They often feel overburdened by moral demands. There is a gap between insight and motivation and there are deficits in compliance. Ethics should be different from a mere denial of such limits of moral behaviour. It rather should recognise that most humans are neither saints nor moral heroes.

## 4.4 Universalism and particularism

*The three basic logical categories of the individual, the particular, and the universal are not just realised in types of history (part 1), but in types of ethics as well.* Some ethicists believe that moral beliefs are individual perspectives and there are as many morals as there are individuals (Stegmaier 2008). Other ethicists have argued that moral beliefs are always embedded in cultures and are meaningful only as part of cultures (MacIntyre 1984). These approaches are dubbed "communitarianism". Universalism must claim that some principles are valid for all moral agents and, in some sense, superior to particular cultures. The number of such universal principles must be low.

To HM (part 2), morals belong to the superstructure that reflects (Marx: "mirrors") economic affairs. To adopt HM (part 2) seems to imply economic-cultural relativism. But even an anti-capitalistic belief system will be ideological, because concepts, such as "surplus", "alienation", "exploitation", "class struggle", "revolution", "party doctrine", *etc.*, do not belong to a sphere of pure practical reason, but to a specific historical antagonism. This problem has been debated by ethicists who wished to reconcile Kantianism and Marxism at the end of the 19th century (sources in Sandkühler and de la Vega 1974, interpretations in Holzhey 1994). It was alive in the question on which normative foundation a critical theory of modern society may rest (Habermas 1984). I hold that HM must be made compatible with moral universalism. This is to say that some moral beliefs are *insights* rather than ideologies.

Ethical approaches can be distinguished according to the three logical categories:

*Universalism:* The collective "humankind" is, in general, responsible for the predicament of planetary nature and, by implication, for its own future. There is a need for universal principles ("global ethics"). *Global* universalism asks for principles of global morals and of global justice,[217] while *planetary* universalism ask for environmental principles. Both kinds of universalism may conflict.

*Particularism:* Particular collectives are cultural units with specific doctrines, world-views, cultural customs, political orders, concepts of good life, *etc.* Ethical particularism (= parochialism) claims that any ethical universalism is ideological in as far as it is biased by a specific culture. This holds true for the Western doctrine of liberty, democracy, gender equality, and human rights as well. Universalism is either an illusion or a betrayal. Ethical parochialism denies both global and planetary universalism. Clashes of cultures are likely and there is no God's eye perspective to settle them. There is no benevolent spectator above cultures. According to this view, the global political order in the Anthropocene will be dominated by several hegemonic regimes which pursue geopolitical strategies for their own sake.

217 The relation between morals and justice is contested. Some ethicists identify morals and justice. This seems wrong. Others see justice as a subset of morals while others, including myself, see justice at the intersection between morals and politics.

*Individualism*: Ethical individualism can take two forms. It, first, can claim that every individual constitutes a moral perspective of her/his own. This is Nietzschean individualism. Individualism can also become *normative individualism*. Single humans (or sentient beings) are the final locus of all commitments, responsibilities and entitlements. According to the current European doctrine, all individuals are bearers of human rights and "have" dignity as individuals. From such a humanitarian doctrine, a strong tendency flows to expand the set of human rights.

In part 1, it was argued that there must be three kinds of history according to these three logical categories. This structure is repeated in ethics: universalism, particularism, individualism. Ethical debates can be reconstructed as a contest between three logical categories. The debate about "universalism/communitarianism" was about how to correlate both categories. Normative individualism can form a strong coalition with universalism. Historians and archaeologists should, on reflection, become aware about these affinities between kinds of history and kinds of ethics.

Often, historians and cultural anthropologists are sceptical against moral universalism since they are faced with a parade of particular moral belief systems. To them, moral beliefs are embedded in cultural frames. There is no free-standing moral principle above cultures, and all cultures remain particular ones. Particular moral belief systems are inherently complex as they entail role-based virtues, clan loyalties, kinship-based altruism, religious taboos, regulations of sex and gender, and images. If, for instance, a stranger is adopted as a guest in specific cultures, he is equipped with food and shelter, but if the status of a guest is denied, s/he may be killed. Strong moral duties against members of one's own collective correspond to permission to treat aliens as one pleases. Care for beloved children coexists with infanticide and sacrificing captives and servants. There is sexual mutilation and burning of widows. Captives might be either adopted or tortured to death. Honour plays an important role in many cultures. Very often, holy scriptures prescribe moral behaviour. Cultures display moral diversity, but such diversity entails practices which look repugnant or overtly horrible to European minds.

Ethicists are uneasy with an uncritical adoration of moral diversity. The ethical idea to overcome particularism has stayed alive in contemporary ethics because there was a fatal backlash to moral particularism in nationalism, racism, and fascism in the 20$^{th}$ century. Moral diversity as such is not good in itself since moral beliefs often lie at the edge of fanatism and terrorism. Historians and anthropologists may come in moral trouble if they sharply oppose European slave trade without realising that hunting for captives, slavery, and slave trade was common among many prehistoric and indigenous cultures. Can slavery (colonialism, warfare, *etc.*) be opposed in culture A, while simply taken as a social affair in culture B? Only very few cultures have established the moral institution of human rights. Can one complain that human rights are disrespected if no such rights are assumed.[218] If no universal investments are made, no historian is in a position to complain about historical and cultural affairs. Given such problems, historians should not oppose ethical universalism too quickly.

Historians might also realise that the so-called Golden Rule ("Treat others as you wish to be treated") is common to many cultures and to different religious codes. Recognising this, why not give some credit to ethical theories which wish to make a valid universal principle out of the general idea behind the Golden Rule, as Kant (1785) did? To Kant, the categorical imperative is a moral principle which can

---

218 In Islamic countries, human rights must conform to the rules of sharia. See Talesh (1991) for Saudi-Arabia.

be made intelligible in the sphere of pure practical reason. It is unconditional and formal. It remains close to the Golden Rule as it constitutes a procedure of checking one's own maxims (subjective rules) according to the questions whether they might qualify as a basis for a common law. The capability to perform such intellectual procedures makes human beings "autonomous" in a strong sense and it transforms humankind ideally into a "kingdom of ends" in perpetual peace (Korsgaard 1996, especially part 1). Kant's elaborate ethics includes many particular elements stemming from Prussian and Protestant traditions, as in his virtue ethics (Kant 1797), but the formal core of his ethics presumes validity to all reasonable beings, be they human or not. Thus, Kantian ethics might be a refined version of the common moral sense of the Golden Rule. The Golden Rule is about universal moral reciprocity, and discourse ethics (next section) follows the Kantian tradition.

Even if historians and anthropologists are critical against Western universalism, they often implicitly hold some universal principles as, for instance, "respectfulness against all cultures", or an "anti-colonial non-domination principle" or "global justice". Graeber and Wengrow (2021, 47) argue in favour of a "certain minimal, 'baseline' communism which applies to all societies". The all-quantifier denotes universalism. Such "communism"[219] is decent altruism in case of emergencies and needs. Graeber and Wengrow (2021, 503) also claim three human liberties: freedom to leave one's community, "freedom to shift back and forth between social structures", freedom to "disobey authorities without consequences". They give these three basic liberties the following wording (2021, 503):

> *"1. The freedom to move away or relocate from one's surrounding; 2. the freedom to ignore or disobey commands issued by others; and 3. the freedom to shape entirely new social realities, or shift back and forth between different ones."*

There are two points to be made. The first point is about the normative status of these normative investments. Graeber and Wengrow are universalists if and only if they give both normative investments (minimal communism, three liberties) universal scope. The second point is about *content and justification* of the validity claims being made. Let us start with "minimal communism". The "all"-quantifier seems to indicate that "minimal communism" is common to all societies. Such commonality is not ethical grounding, since there might be widespread commonalities which should be morally rejected. To prove God "*ex consensus gentium*" does not work. Perhaps, Graeber and Wengrow might reply that they suppose a Humean approach to moral sentiments with empathy as a basic sentiment. Empathy is not just common among humans, but it is good in itself. Even if such empathy-morals would be supposed, the content remains unclear. Graeber and Wengrow (2021, 47) comment on such minimal communism: "What varies is just how far it is felt such baseline communism should properly extend". The "just" discloses a can of worms, because duties to help and assist are imperfect ones (Hill 1971). Moreover, whose feelings establish the proper extension of imperfect duties? Such feelings vary widely among individuals and collectives. "Baseline communism" remains unclear in both status and content.

The three freedoms (= liberties, rights) are not widely accepted, since many political orders factually do not accept a general freedom to refuse orders. Some countries did not even allow citizens to leave the country (such as the German

219 This is highly unusual wording. Altruism and duties of assistance and support belong to moral behaviour, while communism usually refers to an economic order beyond capitalism.

Democratic Republic). Are these three liberties just demanded by two Western academic anarchists or do they have some solid ethical grounding? The *first liberty* might be seen as a freedom a) to move freely within the borders of one's state and b) to leave a political collective. If so, both freedoms have been stated by the UN Declaration of Human Rights (Article 13). To my mind, this should suffice as justification. This freedom might, however, be expanded to unrestricted global mobility even if the wording ("relocate from one's surrounding") does not indicate such expansion. If the liberty is expanded, Graeber and Wengrow would adopt the so-called "cantilever" argument made by Carens (2014, 237-245). This argument expands the freedom to move to the global scale ("worldwide") and it implies the case for "open borders". This argument is, however, highly contested in the ethics of migration and I do not endorse it (Ott 2016b). The *second liberty* is unwarranted. Whether one should (not) follow orders and rules, depends on their legitimacy. A soldier has a right to disobey any command whose execution would violate human rights. Under German constitutional law, all citizens have a right to resistance if some forces violently attack the democratic order. The rights to disobey and resist are strictly conditional. A general freedom to disobey orders and rules would presuppose that there is no legitimate legal, economic, and political order from which authorities derive their entitlements to give orders and commands. Is the second freedom meant to be unconditional? Graeber and Wengrow comment on the second freedom with respect to First Nations of North America. Even if it might have been the case that members of First Nation collectives were entitled to ignore orders given by "playkings", it remains unclear whether Graeber and Wengrow (2021, 503) generalise this particular ethnological fact as they write: "The same would go for any other hierarchy of offices or system of authority". This generalisation is unwarranted. The second liberty ignores the moral difference between conditional and unconditional liberties in cases of disobedience. The *third liberty* is the "more creative one" (*ibid.*, 503) which supposes the two other liberties. It is divided into two parts: a) shaping new realities, b) moving between different realities. With respect to a) there might be a liberty to *imagine* different social arrangements, including utopian ones. But from imaginations it does not follow that there is a right to realise them against the will of others. Other citizens might see such imaginaries as horrible phantasmagorias. It is political Romanticism to demand that we should bring phantasy and imagination into political power ("*Phantasie an die Macht*"). The word "shaping" seems to be ambiguous and may motivate fallacies of ambiguities. With respect to b), it might be the case that political orders in some cultures may shift according to seasons, warfare, carnival times, *etc.* If one great buffalo hunt has to be organised which is essential for survival in winter, there are reasons to respect organising authorities strictly. In Roman times, the republican order could be replaced by military dictatorship in times of severe crisis, but dictatorship was restricted for one year only. In case of severe emergencies, authorities might gain additional competences even in democracies. Should we generalise such phenomena to shift between normative orders? Is there a freedom to switch between legal codes, constitutional law, regimes of property rights, codes of conduct, as one likes? Can any individual do so? What kind of social order would this imply? Graeber and Wengrow (2021, 503) regret that these liberties have "gradually retreated" and have become unintelligible to most modern humans. Ultimately, they claim that any social order should rest on these liberties (and on baseline communism). Since I see many ethical flaws in these normative investments, I wish to present an alternative.

## 4.5 Ethical framework

At the heart of my approach in ethics is a synthesis of *discourse ethics* (and its implications, such as deliberative democracy, see Lafont 2020) and *environmental ethics* (and its implications, such as strong sustainability, see Ott and Döring 2011). This synthesis presumes to reconcile universalism with the particular sides of life and with ecological constrains. Within the nutshell of part 4, I only present the essential ethical investments and point to the literature.

### 4.5.1 Discourse ethics

Discourse ethics continues the Kantian project of transcendental practical reason within the "linguistic turn" of modern philosophy (Hönigswald 1937; Habermas 1983; Apel 1979). The basic idea is that conditions of moral validity are anchored in basic commitments of moral discourse which cannot be denied without performative self-contradiction.[220] Discourse ethics derives a discourse principle of normative validity as an outcome of transcendental reflection upon the role of being a participant in the commonly shared practice of reasoning called "discourse" (Ott 1997; 2017b). There are some commitments of arguing, which pragmatically entail principles of mutual recognition (Humboldt 1829/1979). The system of the personal pronouns allows to interchange between the roles of an "I" and a "you". "I" and "you" are united under the idea of giving and taking reasons as equal peers in discourse. The system of personal pronouns constitutes reciprocity within speech. It overcomes the lingual contingencies of semantics, grammar and "lingual world views" (Whorf 1956). The divide between particularism and culturalism has an equivalent in the philosophy of language: The concept of a "lingual world view", which also can be found in Humboldt ("*sprachliches Weltbild*"), is particular, while ethical reflection upon the system of pronouns reveals basic reciprocity and tends to universalism. Linguistic particularism argues that moral semantics and the grammars of moral language differ widely. It is impossible to argue about morals if others speak a very different language. Universalism claims that to talk and to listen to others pragmatically implies some kind of reciprocity which is more profound than the reciprocities of gifting. Reasoning can be seen as specific gifting: give and take reasons. An ethics of discourse has deeper roots than any ethics of cultural gifting can have.

Universalism must assume that moral claims can be translated. Universalism is in line with the idea of speech acts and the option to affirm ("Yes") or deny ("No") validity claims (part 1). From this lingual-pragmatic universalism, some obligations might be derived: a) respect all other persons as presumptive peers in moral dispute ("*discursive egalitarianism*"), b) do not give primacy to violence and coercion over the force of better arguments ("*non-violence*"[221]), c) do not make others believe what you want them to believe ("*honesty*"). More moral substance can be integrated stepwise within such a framework by way of reasoning. Univer-

220 An overview on different attempts to justify discourse ethics is given in Gottschalk-Mazouz (2000). The function and role of transcendental arguments in ethics are analysed in Brune *et al.* (2017).

221 The non-violence principle is close to pacifism as lived by Jesus and Gandhi. It allows self-defence against aggressors who violate the principle.

salism expands, for instance, the scope of the moral community further, taking future individuals into account ("future ethics"), and, perhaps, it includes even sentient animals.

With respect to *history*, discourse ethics sees the "objects" of historical research, namely past human beings, *counterfactually* as virtual members of historical discourse which, if they were still alive, would be entitled to comment on historical statements (explanations, narratives) with "Yes" or "No" in a similar way as in oral history and in ways as members of indigenous cultures are entitled to comment on statements by cultural anthropologists. All history must presuppose counterfactually that statements should have been agreed from the emic side. Apel (1979) argues that history is tied to the transcendental ideal of a universal community of interpreters. The critical community *among* historians and anthropologists substitutes the impossible direct communication *between* historians and their subjects under study. The "No!" from another historian presumes to represent the "No!" from the side of the humans under study. This holds true for historical narratives and "thick descriptions" as well.

Historians often take the role of advocates of past humans who had been victimised. Such moral advocacy is alive in all "history from below" which addresses the lives of slaves, women, servants, beggars, *etc*. If theoretical anarchism focuses "on how local societies through cooperative means can withstand or challenge the emergence of coercive power and centralization" (Lund *et al.* 2022, 8), members of local resistance groups must, in principle, have been able to give reasons why they wished to escape coercive powers. If anarchism in PA rests on the idea that power should be nothing but justified authorities and democratic rule of law, the ideals of anarchism are not far from discourse ethics and deliberative democracy (or Arendtian ideas of power, see Lund *et al.* 2022).

Habermas (2009) argued that morality is rooted in *anthropology*. Moral rules are a fragile equivalent for lost instincts against killing members of one's own species. An obligation not to kill other humans (without very strong reasons) is at the heart of most moral doctrines. As the Bible demands: "*Thou shall not kill*". Throughout history there emerges, by way of moral experience, a deep moral lifeworld-knowledge about violence, bloodshed, torture, killing, war, and atrocities since humans are able to kill, wound, rape, and enslave each other. Humans often had to face moral evils (Kekes 1990). There is failure, corruption, "sin" (Ricoeur 1971). Humans have made moral experiences which have been stored as convictions within the human lifeworld. Moral convictions are like "sediments" of past moral experiences. A test of the categorical imperative and such moral experiences often comes to the same result about what counts as moral evil.

Bernhard Gert (1988) has argued that rational wishes (for example not to be killed, betrayed, assaulted, harassed, hurt, *etc.*) in combination with a discourse principle of public reasoning can warrant a set of universal *prima facie* obligations. This set is acceptable to Kantians, contractarians, and even rule-consequentialists. This set of *prima facie* obligations entails an obligation not to kill, not to hurt or wound, not to lie and betray, not to steal and rob. The final rule is about role-obligations which define codes of conduct for parents, professionals, consumers, and even politicians. Gert's rules are duties of omissions. An ethically far more difficult set of duties entails obligations to help, to assist, to support, *etc*. Such obligations belong to each doctrine of the axial age, as in the narrative of the helpful Samaritan, but they must have some limits because nobody can help everybody who needs help. One should not inflict harm upon others and should not live at the expense of others, but one cannot personally heal all harm and suffering on any larger scale. This problem haunted Kant (Hill 1971) and I will not try to present a solution here. As I have argued in the previous section, Graeber and Wengrow (2021, 47) face this problem in their concept of "minimal communism": "What varies is just the question how far it is felt such baseline communism should properly extend." The "just" discloses a large can of moral worms about help, assistance, and solidarity in a globalised world.

The layer of universal moral principles and commitments must be a "thin" one. Universalism is an intellectual enterprise, while particularity is seated in practical life. We may think universal, but continue to live in particular and individual settings. Cultural ways of life remain "thicker", as they incorporate daily routines, values, customs, traditions, taste, spiritual habits, *etc*. Even if we may hold some universal principles (as we should), we continue to live in particular settings. Humans cannot live on the moral point of view. We should respect some universal principles, but we love particular humans and appreciate particular places as our homes (Scruton 2014). *We can and should neither deny nor downplay this particular side of human life ethically.* We should respect the insight of universalism itself that universalism is a "thin" layer that emerges from the "thick" layer of cultures.

This relation between both layers has been conceived by Rawls (1988) as the primacy of the (thin) deontological "rightfulness" over the (thick) axiological "goodness". "Primacy" means that in case of conflict rightfulness *overrides* (= trumps) goodness. The "thin" trumps the "thick". The "right" constrains permissible ways of life. From a cultural perspective, however, the concept of overridingness might be seen as a "top down" imposition. One may ask: "Where does this moral demand stem from? Whose justice is this?" Not all moral demands are, as such, overriding. A reasonable concept of cultural goodness may trump an unwarranted or contested moral demand. The requirements of overridingness are bound to the quality of reasons being given in favour of a moral claim.

Herder's concept of "humanity" should reconcile historical thinking and cultural diversity with moral universalism (Habermas 2019, II, 430-439). To Herder, human beings can *learn* morally within history. Under a formal supreme Kantian principle, by way of learning from moral experience, and by way of discourse, a directed evolution of moral traditions becomes possible. One can also learn from moral defeats and moral catastrophes. In this sense, Adorno (1966, 358) argues that a new categorical imperative obliges all humans to prevent Shoah-like events. Even Kant (1795) drew some lessons from history, as he argued in *Perpetual Peace* how to combat the causes for war. Kant argued that free republican states hesitate to go to war – and history has proven him right. This example shows how moral principles against warfare can be combined inferentially with historical "lessons" to judgements of how (not) to act.

Hegel (1821/1970) argued that moral rightfulness should be *actualised* in the "thick" ethical[222] life of different collectives. Ethical life cannot be as universal as a categorical imperative, but, at least in some lucky periods in history, it can be shaped by moral principles. Perhaps, there can be *deliberative ways of ethical life* in times of peace, liberty, and prosperity. Or so I hope.

Discourse ethics is *evolutionistic,* as it supposes a historical perspective on long-term learning processes in the realm of practical reason (Habermas 2019). If Kantian ethical universalism, Herder's learning culturalism, and Hegel's mac-

222 The term "ethics" has two different meaning. Mostly, it means "theoretical reflection upon morals", while with respect to Hegel, it means a comprehensive rightful and decent way of life ("*Sittlichkeit*").

ro-history of "progress in the spirit of freedom" define a specific philosophical constellation at the turn to the 19th century, this constellation is repeated *within* discourse ethics (Habermas 2019). This raises the question of whether one can reject teleology in history, but accept moral learning processes. If learning processes already occur within natural history, as the theory of Baldwin-effects assumes (Weber and Deprew 2003), why should we not see ourselves as beings being able to learn and keep "lessons learned" in our collective memory? Forgetfulness does not improve morality. There is rather a moral commitment to remember the past.

Moral learning requires historical situations and geographical locations in which firm doctrines are shattered. Moral reflections are more likely at specific situations and locations. They are situated. As Graeber and Wengrow argue (2021, 207), there are "cultural areas" within which moral belief systems are firmly rooted in cultural ways of life. Such differences in morals come to mind to people who do *not* live within such cultural areas, but at the interfaces between different cultural areas and feel free to judge different cultures. Boundary areas are locations of innovation (McCaffree 2022, 24). At those boundaries and interfaces, questions emerge about "better" and "worse" ways of societal life and its regulations. The conscious refusal of slavery by some tribal collectives on the Pacific West Coast might have been a result of such reflective questioning. Locations, such as the coastlines of Asia Minor in the 6th century BCE or Hellenistic Egypt, were also cultural melting pots where ethical reflection emerges.[223] In our globalised world, there are many interface-locations of moral and political reasoning, universities among them. We are now in a position to conceive PA as an academic "cultural area" where Kantian (Golden Rule, discourse, and reciprocity), Hegelian (ethical life), and Herderian (humanitarian learning) modes of thought can be combined with past-past-present-connectivities and ideas about how a "good" Anthropocene beyond Q-3 growth might be actualised. Debates about "minimal communism" and basic liberties (Graeber and Wengrow 2021) can find proper places within this discourse-ethical framework.

### 4.5.2 Environmental ethics

An ethics of the Anthropocene would be incomplete without environmental ethics. Within the field, I favour a concept of *deep anthropocentrism plus X* (Ott 2010; 2016a; 2020a; 2020b). This concept is an interpretation of the overall universe of environmental discourse. There are strong reasons to overcome a mere instrumental attitude toward nature. Deep anthropocentrism highlights the many human eudemonic, biophilic, and even spiritual values, encounters, and interactions with nature. Non-instrumental attitudes have deep roots in the Western tradition from Roman times until the Romantic movement (Glacken 1967; Schama 1995). Eudemonic values (= cultural ecosystem services) shape one's attitude to biophilic ways of being alive (Ott 2016a). Nature has transformative values upon one's attitudes and one should cultivate the dispositional attitude of biophilia (Wilson 1984; Kellert 1997). It seems appropriate to feel deep admiration, awe, and reverence for the "blue Planet Earth" as a cosmic jewel. Such emotional attitudes can also be articulated from within religious traditions, as in the case of the Bible (Hardmeier and Ott 2015). Thus, a mastery of nature is

223 Note that radical scepticism against morals can also be a result of ethical reflection, *e.g.* as it happened in ancient Greece. To Hegel, scepticism results from half-way reflection.

not the only rational attitude towards nature. Care, reverence, admiration, awe, playful interactions, embodied joy, biophilic and spiritual encounters, *etc.* are other modes of life with/in nature.

My conception also demands *fair intergenerational legacies* with respect to all such attitudes and the natural goods and so-called ecosystem services that they refer to (Ott and Reinmuth 2021). Rawls (1971, § 44) argued in favour of a principle of justice that holds between different generations: a fair bequest schedule augmenting the principles of liberty, equality, and safe minimum. This principle can be regarded as a general sustainability principle (Ott 2014b). All societies should adopt this principle, but there remains political freedom to specify it to decent transgenerational legacies within different cultures in democratic ways. The principle will be chosen behind a veil of ignorance, while specific conservation policies require empirical (geographical, ecological) knowledge about particular environments. Some cultures may preserve and restore traditional landscapes, while others may realise large re-wilding projects, protect symbolic sites, care for parks and gardens or design new ecosystems with neo-biota. There are many ways to act on behalf of nature in the Anthropocene.

Since there are three categories (universal, particular, individual), future ethics should not just expand the category of humankind to following generations ("posterity" in general), but should also conceive future ethics through the concept of diachronic cultural communities (De-Shalit 1994) and family lines. If one starts with the individual, there are *descendants*: children, grandchildren and unborn descendants. Here, one is usually deeply inclined to protect and support one's own descendants. On the middle-ground of particulars, there are new cohorts of children and young adults: *young compatriots and future fellow citizens.* Here, the solidarities and loyalties are still quite strong, but there are also legitimate expectations that young compatriots may continue our traditions of nature conservation. On the universal, there is *posterity* in general: future humankind. Here, one cannot know about the individuality of future persons ("future individual paradox", see Parfit 1982). The term "future human generations" represents this level of abstraction. The feeling of responsibility runs counter to increasing distance in space and time. Motivation to help and assist decreases from the individual to the general, while universal morality teaches that it makes no difference at which point in time harm occurs, rights are violated, and units of utility pop up. Universalism is intellectual, particularism is practical. Even if we will not discard universalism in theory, motivation, knowledge, solidarity, and advocacy are stronger on particular and on kin layers (Scruton 2014). If so, environmental future ethics should not ignore the minor and particular scales of action. As Jacob *et al.* (2022) argue, sustainability policies must operate on minor scales as well. Acting on behalf of future generations may focus regional and national scales, even if humankind must combat climate change on the global scale.

The unspecific addition to deep anthropocentrism ("plus X") refers to the moral puzzle of the demarcation problem: the attribution of *inherent moral value to non-human beings*. Discourse ethics is not committed to anthropocentrism (Hendlin and Ott 2016). The non-instrumental attitudes mentioned above, however, are not strictly moral ones. The resolution of the demarcation problem always rests on ontological assumption (Ott 2008; Lie 2016). Since I have no preference for desert landscapes in ontology, my ontology is a "*scala naturae*". Ontological differences are of moral relevance. Given the many ontological differences in nature, which result in highly different capabilities of natural beings (stones, bacteria, jellyfish, leopard), it seems quite strange to attribute inherent moral value to (some or all) natural beings in an egalitarian manner (Ott 2008). Plants can share information, higher animals display gestures and voice, but only humans display speech acts and can argue. Some animals are sentient, but humans are discursive and logical beings. Animals are singular, but humans are individual beings. The basic and the negative anthropology (part 1) both imply that humans are free, as Herder said: "*die ersten Freigelassenen der Schöpfung*". [English translation Ott]: "*the first freedmen of creation*". They are "*deinon*" (Sophocles, part 3) and, as we have seen in part 2, they are economic agents. For better or worse, humans are exceptional creatures. With high likeliness, they have gone too far in subduing nature, but they may be able to correct their own excessiveness. After a long voyage through each and any option of how to solve the demarcation problem,[224] I take the human being as the only free and reasonable (logical) living being. From the exceptional form of human life, one can "decline" (Schelling: "*depotenzieren*") to other forms of life.

Such a decline sees many commonalities in organic life. In modern times, many scientifically educated humans have underrated the capabilities of animals, plants and other organisms by far. Higher animals are sentient, can make choices, are conscious, can express emotions, can communicate within and among species, *etc*. Dolphins can name each other and share drug-like substances. Whales "sing". Some apes come close to personality and can learn sign language. Thus, we should respect different sentient animals for what they are capable of doing. With respect to non-vertebrates, I would not kill or hurt animals without reason which, perhaps, are perceptive beings (snails, dragonflies, bees, *etc*.). Plant life can also "communicate" in the sense of exchanging information by biomolecules. It is marvellous to be surrounded by plant life in grasslands, forests, and gardens.

Deep anthropocentrism allows for different solutions of the demarcation problem, but it requires all solutions to allow for *moral grading*. There is, first, no conceptual implication between inherent moral value and egalitarianism. Second, a "*scala naturae*" ranging from bacteria to humans cannot abstract away all ontological differences from moral discourse. Ethics must make differences visible, not abstract them away. *Distinguamus*! Third, grading shows more respect for different non-human forms of life. It seems wrong to suggest that grading rests on disrespectfulness. We should respect moss *as* moss, and shellfish *as* shellfish, and rhinos *as* rhinos. This approach "respect X as such" may initially come at the price of biases and prejudices, but it ought to result in a self-correcting and learning outlook regarding nature. Studies in animal behaviour can teach us how to respect specific animal species as such.[225]

Giving full account to the striking capabilities of non-human beings makes one even more aware of the spectacular mode of human life (Neuweiler 2008). The more one recognises and respects capabilities of animal and plant life, the more one should appreciate and admire human capabilities, such as humour, music, dance, cooking, sport, art, science, and religion. To take the "*deinon*" (Sophocles) seriously, implies that "we" are somewhat different from all other organisms (=

224 The major positions (sentientism, biocentrism, ecocentrism, holism) are analysed in articles within the *Handbuch Umweltethik* (Ott *et al*. 2016).

225 See contributions in Kappeler (2010).

exceptionalism). Only humans "*exist*".[226] Humans can even fail in ways that other living beings cannot. Exceptionalism, however, should move from hubris to humility. If there can be such a project as "making peace with nature", humans may realise such a project only if they address themselves as logical, moral, and exceptional beings. They should not see themselves on a par with animals, plants, and ecosystems.

Deep anthropocentrism allows the continuation of practices of domestication, breeding, agriculture, forestry, fishing, aquaculture, and hunting if and only if these practices are performed in decent, respectful, and sustainable ways. From a historical and cultural point of view, there are many ways to respect domesticated and wild animals and plants. There is much to learn from the history of domestication if we wish to correct our dominionistic industrialised style of utilising nature. Humans can and should *re*-learn how to interact respectfully and sometimes even playfully and generously with a non-human world. They can try to restore the many cultural landscapes which are under pressure from homogenising forces (Zerbe 2022). Re-learning implies that we can and should take pre-industrial and even tribal ways of doing agriculture, forestry, husbandry, aquacultures, *etc.* more seriously. Perhaps, pre-industrial ways of living with/in nature can be turned into post-industrial ones (Q-2 → Q-4). Thinking about such (Q-2 → Q-4) connectivities can be governed by the principle of sustainability.

### 4.5.3 Strong sustainability

Following the work of Daly (1996), I argued for *"strong" sustainability* (Ott and Döring 2011; Ott 2014b). Sustainability is a principle of the long-term political economy of natural resources, goods, and services, inclusive the cultural practice of nature conservation. The concept of strong sustainability demands to hold remaining stocks and funds of natural capital intact over time and to restore degraded natural environments. At the planetary scale, this has to be done on behalf of the entire future of humankind whose individual members are entitled to find a similar "wonderful" green-blue planet as we and our ancestors did. The model of "safe space for humankind" (Rockström *et al.* 2009) addresses the planetary scale, but minor scales remain important (Jacob *et al.* 2022). Planetary and global sustainability require compliance at different particular scales. If the intellectual enterprise of moral universalism, the abstract notion of "future humankind" and the global scale are conjoined, the resulting ethics will become lofty. Not just epistemic social theories, but also ethical approaches can fly very high. Strong sustainability must be realised at different scales. Therefore, democratic national states remain important.

Strong sustainability distinguishes the guidelines of a) physical degrowth (less input, less output, less waste), b) resilience of all major land use systems, and c) sufficiency in lifestyles. The concept of strong sustainability has been applied to climate ethics (Ott 2021a), a Chinese river (Ott *et al.* 2016), coastal areas (Neumann *et al.* 2017), and forestry (Ott 2021c). Restoration means interventions on behalf of nature which may become focal practices to local communities (Zerbe and Ott 2021). Humans can act on behalf of nature, which can become focal practices

226 I adopt the term "existence" in a way close to Heidegger (1949/1981). "*Das Stehen in der Lichtung des Seins nenne ich die Ek-sistenz des Menschen.* [...] *Der Mensch allein ist, soweit wir erfahren, in das Geschick der Ek-sistenz eingelassen*" (*ibid.*, 15). [English translation Ott]: *"I call standing in the clearing of being the ex-sistence of man.* [...] *Man alone, as far as we experience, is involved in the destiny of ex-istence."*

(Borgmann 1984) and even "beautiful actions" (Naess 1993). Success stories of restoration and recovery give hope that humans may be able to design and compose new ecosystems and landscapes ("post-industrial landscapes") within the Anthropocene which become habitats for many adaptive species, including non-invasive neo-biota. *Why not imagine the Anthropocene as a coming age of re-learning, care, protection, restoration and recovery?* Such vision may pass the test of discourse and may be conceived as sets of interconnected transformative scenarios and options of how to live.

Such scenarios can include past-past-present relations and, especially (Q-3 → Q-4) relations. Humans would have to recognise their deep-rooted inclination for "more" (growth) (parts II and III) in order to overcome it. We should not deny our susceptibilities and should not model ourselves as moral heroes, but should recognise many peaceful and joyful modes of exchange with nature for mutual benefit and reward. A great transformation requires people who also perform "great", not in a sense of societal hierarchies and making money, but in terms of environmental virtue ethics (Cafaro and Sandler 2011). Humans, then, would still be "*deinon*", but (slightly) different. It is easy to demand that humans should live *completely* different, but it is hard to determine the "slight" differences that actually make the difference.

Both deep anthropocentrism (ethics) and its practical implication of strong sustainability (political economy) point to the contemporary relevance of cultural practices which have deep roots in prehistory (gardening, foraging, hunting, sailing, fishing, forestry, aquacultures, *etc.*). Here, I see high potentials for past-present relations. As I will argue in some detail, we are, thanks to the progress in PA, now in a position to overlook and assess the many options to organise human metabolism with nature and perform many flourishing human-nature interactions under different environmental conditions including climate change. By cultural-ethical renewals of such prehistoric practices, we may stepwise escape the destructive sides of the Anthropocene. At this decisive point, I wish to mobilise the dialectics between "being free" and "being stuck" found in Graeber and Wengrow (2021). We are still stuck inside the system of industrial fabrication and consumerism which has reigned the Western world for centuries. Environmental movements have become aware of the destructive sides of this growth-oriented system since decades. Most citizens will not jeopardise the advantages and achievements of "our" European way of life. Environmental policy making has been mostly incremental so far. These incremental reforms have brought us in a position to go for more profound ones.

As political agents, we are, in principle, free to perform a further "great" transformation. Such a transformation can take many routes in terms of politics and economy, some of which are riskier than others. In modern times, our collective sense of social possibilities has been stripped. To Graeber and Wengrow (2021), we move within a large historical pool of options. We cannot simply shift between them, but must select according to reasons. Not options as such, but reasons to select between options indicate real freedom. No great historical transformation, however, has ever been made out of reason or by way of discourse. *If so, we are exceptional creatures in an exceptional situation.* And, as the slogan goes, no one should be left behind in the great transformation. Is this a "mission impossible"?

### 4.5.4 Political philosophy and deliberative democracy

In *political theory,* I combine Rawlsian principles of a well-ordered society with Habermasian deliberative democracy and a political sympathy for anti-hierarchical, positively put: *heterarchical* societies which give room for many spheres of justice (Walzer 1983). While Rawls (1971) establishes principles of basic institutions of a well-ordered (modern) society, Walzer (1983) gives leeway to cultural variations in different spheres of life. A well-ordered society needs a) a basic political constitution, b) major institutions, and c) heterarchical spheres of life (science, arts, sports, education, religion, private sphere). While hierarchical regimes wish to command and control all other spheres of life, heterarchical orders protect spheres of life against the colonising forces of politics and commerce. Heterarchical societies disperse power, authority, and decision-making widely among such spheres. There can be specific authority and expertise as well as restricted and balanced political governance ("checks and balances") but there is, strictly speaking, no supreme authority. There are complex patterns of inequalities, but economic inequalities should not be converted into political power. The rich can be powerless and *vice versa*. In heterarchical societies, there are many things which money cannot buy. Checks, balances, and civil society must protect politics from oligarchic ambitions.

In well-ordered societies, freedom becomes real in a system of liberty rights, legal security, fair chances to reach attractive positions, and some material security (Rawls 1971; Habermas 1992; Pettit 2014). In political philosophy, Habermas (1992) has made a strong claim that citizens who wish to regulate their social life democratically by means of law must grant different types of rights to each other. Such rights include liberty rights, protection by law, rights of political citizenship, and rights to basic decent livelihoods. Such systems of rights should be established in each and any national state as long as there is no international order which guarantees these rights to all persons. Thus, democracy and human rights suppose each other. In his *A Theory of Justice* (1971), Rawls made a strong case for a reflective equilibrium between the ideals of the French Revolution (liberty, equality, solidarity) and principles of justice that free and reasonable persons would choose under a veil of ignorance. "We" Europeans cannot deny such principles without a denial of the political traditions "we" hold precious. From within these traditions, we can conceive international relations as confederations or even covenants of free republican states.

This idea can be specified to concepts of *deliberative democracy* (Lafont 2020; Habermas 1992). Thus, I see democracy as a way of self-government which in modern territorial states must be organised in representative, parliamentarian ways. Deliberative representative democracy can be opened for participatory formats, such as citizen juries, but they cannot be replaced by local and direct democracy. We should withstand such illusions which are presented in anthropological literature.[227]

The case against hierarchical regimes might be the political and moral motive for *anarchism* in PA (Lund *et al.* 2022; Graeber and Wengrow 2021; Scott 2009). I see anarchism, in the first instance, as a political philosophy that had some prominent representatives in the 19th century (Bakunin (1869a, b/1972)[228], Kropotkin 1902) and some heroic moments in the Spanish civil war (1936-1939). The primary aim of political anarchism was to combat the state, including its representatives. Contemporary PA anarchism is opposed to the repressive order of early states such as Mesopotamian ones. Fair enough. I share the aversion against all despotism, be it "oriental" or not, but I do not share a general aversion against "the" state, because there is not "the" essence of statehood, but there are many forms of states which are typed from Aristotle until Rawls. A distrust against a "Leviathan" belongs to political liberalism, but even liberals concede that complex modern societies require states for many purposes. The modern democratic welfare state is less fearsome than its absence, and rule of law is far better than anomic affairs, as failed states demonstrate. Thus, political anarchism in a literal sense is not an option. The decent intuition of anarchism is a deep aversion against being forced and being dominated by others. If humans experience themselves as free, such an aversion against domination (and different kinds of governmentality) may have deep historical roots. From Graeber and Wengrow (2021), I hypothetically adopt a general human inclination with an "aversion against being forced", but I draw a distinction between brute force and the forceless force of the better argument (Habermas1981). Moreover, there are many moral and legal commitments which do not rest on force. The general idea of freedom becomes actual if one can accept reasonable commitments without being forced and dominated.

## 4.6 Why and how a second axial age should be different

Universalism continues the legacy of the *axial age* (Jaspers 1955). Jaspers' concept of the axial age implies that a cluster of universal moral doctrines emerged independently from each other within a specific period of time (from the 8th until the 3rd century BCE) in different parts of the world, including Buddhism, Confucianism/Daoism, the Hebrew Bible, and Greek philosophy. Christianity continued the axial age in the Roman period and beyond.[229] These doctrines have been later laid down in scriptures and formed large bodies of literature such as

227 Given an idiosyncratic definition of democracy as "self-rule by ordinary people", the egalitarian hunter and gatherer groups become the "true democrats of human history" (Reiter 2021). The Palaeolithic groups are modelled as original campfire democracies. Reiter presents a stylised affirmation of such societies which "remained democratic and egalitarian, ruling themselves collectively to this very day". Reiter claims that true democrats do not settle down, but hide in forests and jungles, or retreat to mountain regions. By implication, evading statehood is real democratic practice. It becomes, by implication, doubtful whether there can be a political entity as a "democratic state". As Reiter speculates, original campfire democracy was established by African village democracy. Such original democracy should have reached Europe from Egypt, "from where Greek civilization originated" (Reiter 2021, 6 with reference to Bernal and Diop). The same tendency to see African villages as locations of true democracy is to be found in Graeber and Wengrow (2021). It is highly doubtful, whether Diop (1974) is a credible author.

228 Bakunin (1869a/1972) demanded complete destruction of the present order. He also argued (1869b/1972) that one should learn from bands of Russian robbers. Robbers are seen as heroes who defend the ordinary people against representatives of the state.

229 The concept of the axial age has been adopted by Habermas (2019), but has been rejected by Assmann (2018).

Kabbalah, Buddhism, and Patristic and Scholastic theology. The doctrines of the axial age represent the first wave of moral universalism, serving as a measure (Jaspers: "*Maßstab*") for moral evolution. These doctrines have been counter-projects to prehistoric and ancient ways of life. Compared to the universal doctrines of the axial age, moral belief systems within PA remained particular in all tribal, pre-state, and early-state societies (Bellah 2011, chap. 3-5). To Jaspers, archaic history ends as the intellectual adventures of the axial age start.

According to Jaspers, within a small Eurasian strip of land, ethical reflection about how to live as a human being may have started. There might have been "*Gunsträume*" not just for agriculture but also for moral reflection (Graeber and Wengrow 2021). Graeber and Wengrow (2021, 450) note that the axial doctrines "emerged in precisely those cities which had recently seen the invention and widespread adoption of coined money". Universal morals and general economic equivalents emerge in parallel. If we do not believe in randomness, we should ask for an explanation. Why might the exchange mode of monetary trade and universal recognition of the other emerge in parallel? My abduction speculates about parallels between modes of economic exchange and modes of moral discourse. One can offer a commodity for sale as one can offer an argument for debate. I will not follow this line of thought further.

The doctrines of the axial age, such as Buddhism, are not rigidly anthropocentric. Early Christianity, however, had to oppose all kinds of paganism in order to gain a moral and religious profile in the Roman Empire. Within this profile, nature became marginal. Since Roman times, the Genesis narrative was falsely regarded as divine command to subdue nature ("*dominium terrae*"). The trajectories of growth (part 3) have been legitimised by a misreading of the Genesis narrative. Lynn White (1967) rightly argued that the axioms of this misreading were secularised in modern philosophies, for example, in Descartes and Bacon. The industrial age was a Baconian project (Schäfer 1993). As I can say with confidence (Hardmeier and Ott 2015), the original narrative of creation has a different moral message. Humans should take the earth under their feet ("*kavash*") as representatives of an instance being praised as "God" who blessed them. Moreover, humans should become attentive and sensitive to the wonderful ways a natural world has been established (as "creation"). Wherever humans show up, they should represent the divine spirit of world making. They should give due respect to fertile earth and the co-creatures of sea, air, and land. This implies a very strong sense of stewardship. If this reading is close to the original, a second axial age in which the Biblical tradition continues should proceed from this reading in its environmental ethical dimensions.

Jaspers (1955) was not interested in analysing and comparing the religious "axial" doctrines in detail. He was interested in the general structure of world history. His noble vision (Jaspers 1955, 35-37) is given in a metaphor and a resulting scheme. To Jaspers, history of humankind takes, metaphorically speaking, two deep "breathes" (Jaspers: "*Atemzüge*"). The first breath leads from archaic history over early states to the first axial age. The second breath should be taken by industrial civilisation that was based on science and technology and it may, perhaps, lead to a second axial age of real humanism. To Jaspers, the difference between the first and the second "axial" breath is this: While the first breath was dispersed at several locations (China, India, Persian, Israel, Greece), the second axial breath should be taken by humankind in its entirety.[230] The outlined scheme of world history (Jaspers 1955, 37) shows a speculative terrain above the globalised industrial age. An arrow pointing to the future could be titled "*Die eine Welt der Menschheit des Erdballs*". History moves between the invisible origins of the species and the invisible second axial age, being the "*telos*" of world history. Jaspers' metaphor and scheme put archaic history into the grey and dark zones of history. Archaic history remains largely unknown and, as seen from the breakthrough of the axial age, deserves not much attention. If so, a second axial age might ignore prehistoric archaeology as well. Or it may not. *Hic Rhodos, hic salta.*

Contemporary ethicists argue that humanity needs a "second axial age" in the Anthropocene, or, at least, a new era of ecological enlightenment (Pelluchon 2021). If one gives credit to this tempting idea, such a "second axial age" can be, however, conceived differently. Ethical universalism, seen as the legacy of the first axial age, can be either *expanded* to cosmopolitanism or it can be *reconciled* (mediated, balanced) with legitimate particularism and even localism, especially with respect to environmental practices. This is a difference which deserves a closer look. Jaspers' scheme and its interpretation suggest a cosmopolitan expansionism directed at a globalised society.

Universalists share the intuition that a second axial age would have to expand the principles that were coined within the original axial age. If Christianity essentially implies a "pro-poor" option, Christian cosmopolitanism would opt for global pro-poor solutions. To Jesus, rich people cannot enter the "*basileia tou Theou*". The Christian aversion against commerce would flourish. If Buddhism is about mercy with all suffering beings, Buddhist cosmopolitanism would try to minimise suffering in the animal kingdom also. Humans should interfere in wild food nets in order to minimise suffering (Horta 2017). Perhaps, even Platonism returns in concepts of "ideal" justice and "ideal world supposition" (Carens 2014). Such concepts of a second axial age adopt and continue expansionist tendencies in moral reasoning. Such reasoning takes the moral point of view as a supreme point of practical reason. As a result, modern societies are, at any point in time, overcrowded by moral demands that are presumed to stem from the ultimate moral peak. In recent years, political philosophy has also become highly normative as: "normative political philosophy".

In such a second axial-age outlook, there can be a strong cosmopolitan coalition based on the categories of individuals and universals. The individual is mostly represented by *normative individualism*: Rights and the well-being of individuals are the final locations of all moral assessments. Normative individualism gives equal moral worth to all human individuals or all sentient "subjects of a life" (Regan 1986): Everyone counts for one and nobody for more than one. The singularity of individuals is combined with universal qualifiers: "all individuals", "all subjects of a life". Individuals are seen as bearers of rights. Universalism and normative individualism converge toward cosmopolitanism via the expansion of the set of entitlements which transforms into moral and, at least in demand, legal rights. The ethical difference between right-based morality and utilitarian welfarism will shrink because many material endowment rights are integrated into the "full set of the human rights": right to food, freshwater, housing, energy,

---

230 I quote this crucial point in Jaspers (1955, 35) in German: "*Während der eine Atemzug gleichsam zerspalten war in mehrere nebeneinander hergehende, ist der zweite Atemzug der der Menschheit im Ganzen*". [English translation (Jaspers 1953)]: "*Whereas the first breath was, as it were, split up into several parallel ones, the second breath is being taken by mankind as a whole.*"

health services, education, shelter, asylum, *etc.* The aversion against being forced can be integrated in claims for a perfect welfare state, including an unconditional basic income. Demands for endowment rights (= rights to be supplied with x") flourish. In this coalition, there is a global society living on a common planetary terrain consisting of individuals being equipped with a full set of rights.[231]

Most ethicists would regard the set of rights that a human person holds as "trumps" that are independent from the numbers of humans. Numbers do not matter if rights are rights. Nussbaum's (2000) ten capabilities with ambitious thresholds implies 80 billion demanding entitlements. If the human population amounts to about 8 billion, it makes a difference whether the full set of rights includes 20 or 40 rights. In the first case, there are 160 billion right-based entitlements, in the second case there are 320 billion entitlements to be fulfilled by some duty bearers. The more rights there are, the more impairments of rights are likely. Such expansionism of rights is fuelled by the strategy to dress any political demand into the language of rights. This strategy is attractive, because it transforms political debates into moral discourse. This logic turns rights into political weapons (Bopp 2019). This critical perspective of the expansion of human rights is silent about a valid full set of human rights and which status or role such a set may have within an ethics of the Anthropocene. It only provides some reflective scrutiny against the expansion of rights.

*There is much growth-orientation in moral demands as well.* Moral demands are an engine of growth. The concept of the good demands "more of the good". For example, the utilitarianism demand to *maximise* the difference between good and bad states of the world. As an economic philosopher, Lisa Herzog (2018, 68) writes that social justice means to make all kinds of liberties for all citizens *as large as possible*. This is clearly an expansive ideal: maximise all L for all P. Expansion of the full set of human rights, expansion of the moral community, expansion of duties of assistance, expansion of social welfare transfers in different directions, redistribution of wealth, increasing standards of education, mobility, health care services, retirement pensions, *etc.* Some demand a maximum of social diversity with a minimum of inequality, as if one can easily have both. Upon first look, moral demands are, by content, critical against existing capitalist market economies, while, upon a second look, they follow the underlying logic of expansion and growth ("more"). Moral demands coalesce with monetary demands to demands for retributive transfers.[232] Justice becomes "financed" and it is supposed that more money can buy more justice. If so, ethics must reflect upon expansive tendencies *within* moral reasoning.

---

231 This "great" institution of human rights originated in the Age of Enlightenment, it was at the heart of revolutionary constitutions (1776, 1793) and it was established worldwide via the UN Declaration of Human Rights in 1948. Hannah Arendt (1955) speaks of a "right to have rights" as the main trait of normative individualism. Many moral theories within political liberalism are right-based. Rights are "trumps" (Dworkin 1977). Rights bearers have a strong claim that rights are to be respected and fulfilled by duty bearers. The very logic of the institution of human rights is expansive, overriding and hierarchical. More rights, more overriding trumps. The logic of expansion is applied to the full set of the human rights which constantly expands. New rights are claimed in permanence. On psychological grounds, it is hard to oppose rights claims because nobody wishes to be blamed to be a "foe of human rights". Meanwhile, there are four generations of rights: a) liberty rights, b) political rights, c) material endowment rights ("social rights"), and d) solidarity rights. Moreover, the institution of rights is enlarged e) to group rights for indigenous people and, last but not least, f) to sentient animals. Animal rights activists campaign even for political rights of animals. "More rights for more beings".

232 A paradigm instance is given by Piketty (2022), who demands a basic inheritance of about 120,000€ for each and any young adult.

In the expansionist outlook of a second axial age, *particularity*, being the third ethical category, is stripped of its moral significance by verdicts of irrelevance. The coalition between ethical universalism and normative individualism crushes particularity. Therefore, we lack ethical philosophies of cultural practices, daily life, metabolic reproduction, customs, and territories which point to the particular sides of life. This is one reason why ethics and history have lost contacts. This situation should be overcome. The situation of the Anthropocene cannot be addressed if we abstract away the particular sides of life.

My claim is that an ethics of the Anthropocene should not just *expand* the universal principles to be found in the original axial age. It should not be a mere extrapolation of universal principles, but a prudent reconciliation of all three logical, historical, and ethical categories. It should not be disrespectful against particular sides of ethical life and it should give more emphasis to "good" interactions with a more-than-human world. This is not to reject universal principles. Modest universalism adopts commitments of arguing (Habermas 1983), the Golden Rule and the Categorical Imperative, a set of moral duties (Rawls 1971; Gert 1988), a *prima-facie*-aversion against being forced (Graeber and Wengrow 2021), Rawlsian principles of justice (Rawls 1971), and a set of basic individual rights (Habermas 1992) which actualise the idea of freedom (Hegel 1821/1970). From environmental ethics, deep anthropocentrism "plus X" and strong sustainability should be added. Strong sustainability recognises boundaries, finitude, scarcity, and ecological constraints at different scales. From the theory of international relations, some principles for a law of peoples can be established (Rawls 1999) which follow Kant's idea of "*Perpetual Peace*" (1795). Humans should, in general, be peaceful. *Such "thin" moral universalism is "thick enough"*. Under these universal principles, history in general and PA in particular may resurrect the particular sides of ethical life.

The question remains whether PA might be of some help in such a reconciliation. If it were, we would have to read Jaspers' scheme differently. The post-industrial age should dig retrospectively in the deep well of PA, making such ways of life visible for post-industrial societies. To Jaspers, the locations of the axial age were "lighthouses" ("*Lichtinseln*"; Jaspers1955, 33) in a dark archaic world. PA has identified many other interesting cultural locations and lifestyles. Here, I adopt the general spirit of Graeber and Wengrow (2021). We should shed light on the many cultural options that are stored in past ways of life in order to make decent livelihoods in the Anthropocene.

*History, including prehistoric archaeology and (ethno)archaeology, might fill intellectual territories about particular livelihoods which contemporary ethics has left.* PA points to the particular and localised sides of life: foraging, settlements, pantries, quarters, dwellings, childhood, gender, work and labour, land, hunting grounds, grazing systems, landscapes, trails, gardens, borders, palisades, music, dance, festivities, and burials. Here, individuals are embedded in particular families, environments, languages, customs, *etc*. In history, individuals are instances of particularities. Individuals are transitory mortal entities which mostly remain anonymous. Thus, the historical perspective on individuals is different from the moral one, since it situates people in particular ways of life.

These particular sides of ethical life cannot be grasped by the semantics of utility, interests, and rights. Particular sides of ethical life point to loyalties, religious commitments, rituals, worship, customs, merits, affiliations, emotions, bonds, honour, and decency. These semantics are more familiar to historians. The particular sides of life include environmental and ecological relations which primarily take place at minor territorial scales (local, regional, national). Since prehistoric times, individuals live their lives in concentric circles, starting with kinship, bands, clans, buddies, neighbourhoods, village and township communities, acting as guests, strangers, foes, *etc*. The planetary scale is beyond the horizon of prehistoric humans despite long-distance trade and transport of knowledge. Even today, nature conservation and restoration will remain a territorial and "localised" enterprise that is based on particular traditions as in U.S. traditions of "wilderness" and in German traditions of "cultural landscape".

PA may also work as a corrective against wishful thinking that the most viable escape routes from the destructive forces of the Anthropocene will bring about a convenient, comfortable, cosy, safe and amusing way of life for all. Perhaps, PA will present more inconvenient truths about transformations, but it can also reveal how prehistoric humans solved problems *without* writings, states, and money (see next section).

If so, the "great" vision quest is open for feasible (Q-3 → Q-4) transformations. The qualifier "feasible" indicates the political side of transformations in mass democracies whose populations have been accustomed to high and even excessive standards of material wealth over decades.[233]

## 4.7 "Greening" the Anthropocene with the help of prehistoric archaeology (PA)

Let us face the Anthropocene from an environmental ethics perspective. By the growth trajectories from Q-1 qualities via long-term Q-2 processes into current large-scale Q-3 quantities (part 3), the many negative sides of increasing quantities (external effects, loss and damage, moral evils, waste, emissions, pollution, mass extinction of species, *etc.*) have become visible to the inhabitants of the Anthropocene whose large majority, however, would like to keep Q-1 achievements and some Q-2 quantities to have "enough".[234]

The visibility of environmental destruction during industrialisation gave rise to nature conservation movements in the 19th century (Ott *et al.* 1999). The visibility of environmental pollution in the post-war period of economic growth and consumerism triggered new "Green" movements (Engels 2006). The laments against growth-oriented industrial civilisation have dominated intellectual debates since the report on the limits to growth in 1973 (Rathfelder 2023). There have been many degrowth perspectives since then. After a first wave in the 1970s, there was a second degrowth-hype around 2010. In some sense, I see myself in the non-communist degrowth-camp (Ott 2012). I must explain my position in brief.

## 4.8 On degrowth theories

Cosme *et al.* (2017), Kallis (2018), Muraca (2014), Schmelzer and Vetter (2019), among others, propose a deep transformation out of a growth-addicted economy. In Ott (2012), I endorsed three of four variants of degrowth: 1) critique against GDP as a measure of happiness and political success, 2) strong sustainability including

233 It did not come as a surprise to me that governments took huge credits in years of crisis (2020-2023) to buy previous normality back since anxieties about returning scarcities were widespread.

234 Some animal rights theorists (Regan 1986), egalitarian biocentrism (Taylor 1986), radical ecocentrism (Callicott 1980), and holism (Gorke 2003) might be willing to abolish some Q-1 achievements – at least in theory.

a system of rules to keep natural capitals and ecosystem services intact over time, and 3) deep cultural change in our daily ways of life. I rejected, however, a fourth variant of degrowth: *neo-communist concepts*. Some degrowth-concepts rely on utopian communist modes of thought. For example, Muraca (2014) relies on Ernst Bloch. Utopian thinking and degrowth-concepts are, however, strange bedfellows.[235] Neo-communist degrowth theorists see a sharp contradiction between strong sustainability and capitalistic modes of production and suggest an "either-or" choice out of this presumed contradiction. The contradiction is often derived theoretically from Marx's (cellular) commodity analysis and the logic of (returns of) investment. The mechanism of (re)-investments implies accumulation of capital which is growth without end (Marx 1863). Such degrowth theories have a simplistic picture of capitalist modes of production and markets as locations of commodity exchange which both are demonised by a self-reinforcing rhetoric. They overlook the potentials to redirect investments and launch long waves of "greening" capitalism and consumerism. Stocks of capital should be better spread and relaunched but not destroyed. Thus, there is a deep divide between reformists and revolutionaries within the degrowth movement.

The revolutionary concepts wish to replace the current political and economic system by another one. They propagate to abandon large parts of the apparatus of industrialised societies and hope to shrink stocks of capital in magnitude from 30% to 90%. They promise that there would be a high quality of life for all despite a reduced standard of life (Schmelzer and Vetter 2019). Economic inequalities would be sharply curtailed. There would be a redistribution of wealth on different scales. There should, for instance, be a radical reduction of working hours without a reduction of salaries for low ones. Such a strategy implies, according to conventional economics, a high increase in salary per working hour (= growth). In the middle-term, there would be sharp conflicts over distribution because redistribution must be realised within a shrinking economy. The standards of the welfare state, public transport, health services, quality education, science and culture, transfers to the Global South, *etc.* should be increased while the economy should shrink. I cast doubts on the feasibility of such strategies, because one cannot have an increase of both scarcity and affluence.

One "great" lesson of the 20th century was the disaster and failure of communism. Communism made many great promises which were never kept. Communism demonised capitalism but it collapsed into demonic politics itself (Stalinism, Maoism, "Brother No. 1"). Communism was never democratic and it never respected liberty rights of citizenry. I would not subscribe to the parlance that communism is, in principle, a good idea that, regretfully, once failed in application, but now deserves a second chance. Communism might be immortal as a moral ideal, but its historical failure (and my biographical experiences with a ruined post-GDR society) make me highly risk-averse to new socialist experiments. One should remember Harich (1975) who envisioned communism without growth as a rigid egalitarian and centralised distribution of scarce goods without markets: food stamps, square meters of rooming, rationing energy, standard

235 Utopian thinking (Bloch 1975) rests on an ontology which allows for paradise-like collective ways of life, while degrowth recognises scarcity and limitations on a finite planet. Bloch (1977, II, 775) wishes to melt down the ice-shield of Greenland by nuclear energy ignoring sea-level rise. According to Bloch, nuclear energy should make Siberia and Antarctica to Mediterranean regions. Bloch's chapter on medical utopias preludes transhumanism. Jonas (1979) was right in criticising Bloch's utopianism.

textiles. Since I rejected the imaginary of original communism (part 2), there is nothing left within communist ideology to attract me morally, economically, and politically. Therefore, I take a seat in the reform-oriented degrowth-camp.

## 4.9 Outline of the method: Historical laboratories and "do-it-yourself" strategies

Universal principles and environmental ethics rightly demand that humans should re-direct their lifestyles to more sufficient and sustainable ones, but principles and objectives might be too abstract to tell them *how*. At this crucial point, PA might be of relevance and help. Boivin and Crowther (2021) wish to mobilise the remote past to shape a better Anthropocene. They remain unspecific about the normative qualifications that they suppose ("better, greener, more sustainable, more equal"), but since they use the term "sustainable", they might agree to strong sustainability. The impressive article points to 243 references from different fields of historical, archaeological and ethnographic inquiry. Boivin and Crowther (2021) suppose that the deep past "provides insights into how we emerged as a planet-transforming species". This is in line with part 3. Moreover, they see history in general and PA in particular as repertoires of cultural and technological practices, whose success and failure can be critically evaluated. Graeber and Wengrow would agree. Learning can also mean to avoid repeating mistakes. This historically saturated perspective points to practices that can "be locally managed, and have been tested, often over centuries or even millennia" (Boivin and Crowther 2021). PA does contribute to practical knowledge that is stored in Q-2-practices. What, for instance, did prehistoric humans know about natural environments, diets and cuisines, technologies, breeding and gardening practices, as well as manure and soils. Boivin and Crowther (2021) highlight some fields for such a "better" Anthropocene, but they do so rather arbitrarily.

In his article *"The Future Neolithic"*, Robb (2014) wishes to present a new research agenda for PA, especially the Neolithic, which moves beyond the old frontlines of former science wars between scientific processualism and post-modern culturalism and between a rigid economy-versus-culture divide. Robbs concept of *material practices* mediates between economics and culture. From an epistemological perspective (part 1), the "new vocabularies" (Robb) are topics for theoretical investments (part 1). From a HM perspective (part 2), the concept on material practices overlaps with the concept of economic life.

I see a common trend in Robb (2014) and Boivin and Crowther (2021), despite a different focus of interest. While Robb (2014, 27) is interested in a profound understanding of the Neolithic, Boivin and Crowther (2021) focus on presumptive past-present relations for a good Anthropocene. Taken together, they point to practices and bodies of knowledge which connect the "thin" and the "thick" Anthropocene. Degroot *et al.* (2021) also wish to uncover pathways of successful adaptation strategies in history. The scholarship "History of climate and society" (HCS) is a nice example how to present challenges that provoke historical research.

> *"The past does not reveal that societies and communities inevitably succumbed when confronted with climate change and variability." (Degroot et al. 2021, 547).*

To Degroot *et al.* (2021, 547), history might be helpful in order to identify "overlooked examples of resilience". The past can also identify adaptation capabilities. Smith *et al.* (2021) wish to address urban sustainability by identifying the determinants of settlement persistence. They outline a research agenda (*ibid.*, 6-7) to improve the longevity of cities.

Taken together, these approaches can define a comprehensive agenda for research on feasible (Q-3 → Q-4) transformations. The "sense of social possibility" (Graeber and Wengrow 2021, 37) can stimulate our imagination on how to perform such transformations. The better we understand the Neolithic, the more profound we can consider our current options and *vice versa.* By doing so, we sharpen the lenses to see what, for us, is really "important and interesting about the Neolithic" (Robb 2014, 28).

This provides reasons to study the many ways that humans pursued to cope with challenges in order to learn from them. How did prehistoric humans cope with drought? How did they store water if there are dry seasons? How can northern latitudes be re-settled in sustainable ways? How can we cope with sea-level rise combining dikes, flood plains and, perhaps, house-boats? How can we arrange public parks in cities to make outdoor living more attractive? Can we revitalise domestic modes of production? How can we become "prosumers"? How shall we perform gardening? How can we deal with neo-biota? How may seasonality become more significant again to our lives?[236] This "we" is never all of humanity, but always particular collectives.

Responsive humans will have to realise *a multitude of localised small-scale defence lines* against climate change and its impacts: restoration policies, keeping waters and moisture in the landscapes, creating safe spaces, recreating gardening, the storage of food, caring for fertile soils, re-forestation, and re-inventing cooperative neighbourhood strategies. With respect to such small-scaled systems of adaptive, resilient, and restorative defence lines, PA can be of great help. The multitude of particular ways of cultural life, including prehistoric ones, should become a repertoire of practical knowledge of *how* to change. In the sense of Graeber and Wengrow (2021), PA may identify the many options to cope with changing environmental conditions. We have to limit climate change to "well below 2 °C" (Ott 2021a) *and* have to adapt in the spirit of strong sustainability. We should do so with the attitude of radical hope (Lear 2008). Even if the outcome would be an increase of 2-2.5 °C GMT in this century, we might be able to pass this warm bottleneck and remove carbon from the atmosphere in centuries to come. There are reasons to be concerned, but no reasons to panic.

There might be many overlooked and underrated options to maintain the coupled nature-human system within Holocene conditions for as long as possible. On the long route from Q-1 over Q-2 to Q-3, there was also forgotten practical knowledge with respect to human-animal-plant-landscape interactions which might be relaunched for the (Q-3 → Q-4) transition into a "good" Anthropocene. We may and should look back on the long Q-2 periods for practices in fisheries, forestry, gardening, horti- and aquacultures, manure, husbandry, storage, settlements, *etc.*, which look attractive with respect to the (Q-3 → Q-4) transformations. Given the definition of transformation, transitions from Q-3 to Q-4 should endure. Even if Q-3 is not sustainable, not all negations of Q-3 will be sustainable. It is wrong to claim that if X(¬S) then ¬X(S) because there can be states of affairs such

236 Since industrial and urban modes of production, work, consumption, and leisure have levelled out seasonality, we might re-learn how seasonal ways of life might be both viable and attractive. Seasonality might constitute new patterns of indoor/outdoor life with increased time spent outdoors. In Europe, mild winters are not terrifying.

as ¬X(¬S). If a transition transforms X(¬S) into ¬X(¬S), the situation may become even worse.[237] Reformism must be aware of ¬X(¬S) failures. There are lessons from history how people made things worse despite good moral intentions. If so, we must search for really feasible transformative (Q-3 → Q-4) trajectories.

*Q-2 from prehistoric times onward is now to be seen as a "historical laboratory" for practices which look attractive for responsive and adaptive strategies.* History and PA become such a "laboratory" in a metaphorical sense. We do not make experiments with past humans, and past humans did not make experiments with their lives (in a scientific sense of the word). The term "historical laboratory" means that persons, who are interested in a good Anthropocene, are enabled to look curiously into a large repertoire of options which former free and reasonable humans have adopted for better or worse, success and failure. If religions are storehouses of moral wisdom (Habermas 2005), prehistoric practices may be seen as storehouses for strategies of how to survive and perform decent livelihoods. Here, the epistemological idea that humans are united under agency and reason (part 1) gets a fresh twist. If we have reasons to search for adaptive and responsive strategies, and if prehistoric humans successfully coped with similar challenges, post-industrial and prehistoric reasons come in touch. (One may think of Gadamer's (1965, 288-290) "fusion of horizons" with respect to practical life.)

Prehistoric humans, however, had to solve problems *without* the help of writings, money and a state which did not exist. They could not scream for help, assistance, and financial support from states which may take credits on international finance markets in times of crisis. Prehistoric collectives could not mobilise finances and had no alternative to self-reliance. Deficit spending was not an option. If one wishes to draw any lesson, or better: inspiration from prehistory for contemporary problem solving, one has to take seriously into account that such an inspiration is based on *non-writing, non-state, and non-monetary strategies.* If legal codes suppose written documents, there was only customary law. The main modern cybernetic mechanisms of formal law, money, and states were non-existent in prehistoric times. *Therefore, prehistoric ways of life can primarily teach us "do-it-yourself" strategies.* "Do-it-yourself" strategies do not suppose individualism, but they have been self-reliance strategies in social units up to several thousand people, for example, at mega-sites. Prehistoric people could not buy normality and resilience by money, even if there were tributes against raiding. One big question in prehistoric life must have been: "How can we help (rescue, defend, feed) ourselves?" Thus, we see a large repertoire of strategies and capabilities of adaptive self-reliance. A grain of truth in PA-anarchism might be a focus on self-reliance and its virtues, such as courage and stubbornness. In modern times, this repertoire of action can be revitalised in our daily life, even if some strategies may look inconvenient and uncomfortable. The point about "*do-it-yourself*" strategies remains of importance even if modern democratic welfare states and industries will continue to fulfil essential functions within the great transformation. "Do-it-yourself" strategies can never substitute the state but may complement it. The nice slogan applies: "*Be the change you want to see*". Without doubt, such strategies

237 If a normative order O is not perfectly just, and one wishes to transform O into a more just order O*, it may happen that the real outcome O** is less just than the original O. Good intentions, if not prudently applied, may make things worse. Then there will be a search for scapegoats.

cannot substitute law and policy making. Policies and such strategies must accommodate each other. Connectivities matter.

Finally, we are now in an epistemic and ethical position to conceive a *methodic* approach from our theoretical building blocks. Given the diagnosis and origins of the Anthropocene, given both epistemic and normative investments (an ethical framework), given economic life, and given our (Q-1 → Q-2 → Q-3 → Q-4) scheme (and the DPSIR scheme), we can address all crucial fields which are mentioned in the Sophocles chorus successively, seeing humans as "*deinon*". How can we remain on the bright side of "*deinon*"? The question is *governed* by universal principles, but it cannot be *answered* by those principles. How can strong sustainable and feasible (Q-3 → Q-4) transformations be made in shipping, fisheries, agriculture, domestication, urbanism, and medicine? To provide answers, Q-2 routes serve as historical records and a laboratory for feasible "do-it-yourself" strategies.

## 4.10 Ways ahead

It is beyond the scope of part 4 to address all these questions in detail. Some suggestions about how to re-direct Q-3 quantities into Q-4 constellations have been given in part 3. It must suffice to show how this method *may* work based on some paradigmatic topics mentioned by Robb (2014) and Boivin and Crowther (2021).

### 4.10.1 Animals and animal economies

Even if animals are finally eaten, "raising is a project" (Robb 2014) and an economic-cultural practice. Zooarchaeology should draw up the "social view of the animal economy" (Halstead 1981, quoted in Robb 2014). Today, we have to integrate animal ethics into our ways of treating domesticated animals. How should animal domestication be continued? Within contemporary animal ethics there is a divide between two ethical approaches. One approach wishes to improve the lot of domesticated animals but wishes to continue the prehistoric project of husbandry. Animals should have good lives, but single animals can be replaced by other ones, according to the difference between animal singularity and human individuality. Single animals are receptacles of pleasure and pain, but almost all animals (except, perhaps, great apes and marine mammals) are not persons. Meat consumption should be reduced, but not made illegal. There should be cultural leeway for animal husbandry and breeding, for herding, hunting, and fisheries, and to use animals for transport and work, *etc*.

The animal rights camp goes further since it applies the institutions of rights at least to mammals being "subjects of a life" (Regan 1986). From a metaethical point of view, this transfer of rights to the animal kingdom is far from being self-evident, since Regan's argument only results in an entitlement of (elder, normal) mammals to be treated with respect. Regan expands his argument to a right not to be killed. This, by pragmatic implication, results in abolitionism of domestication with the exception of pets. The animal rights movement runs counter to what humans have done for many millennia. Animal rights activists will argue that the mere duration of a given practice is irrelevant from the moral point of view. I agree, but one is not committed to Reagan's argument. If not, humans can ask about careful animal economies in the Anthropocene. The contributions in Cassidy and Mullin (2007) may serve for inspiration. The many past human-animal interactions may inspire future ones. Religious traditions of the axial age tell that humans should not be cruel to animals.

There are many sound arguments to phase out industrial meat production and to reduce meat consumption, but no stringent arguments against meat-eating in general. A degrowth strategy would reduce the number of animals worldwide and would reduce the number of animals in containments. We should also reduce the numbers of pets since dogs and cats must be fed with meat (Mullin 2007).[238] Strong sustainability would open the landscape for animals even if some sheep would be, despite all fencing, consumed by wolves. In the northern hemisphere, we should stop devoting large tracts of farming land for animal fodder production. Animals should graze on land that is not well-suited for agriculture. Finally, we have to consider non-cruel slaughter. "Compassionate slaughter" is not a contradiction in terms.

Why not breed fewer pigs, but more rabbits, goats, mutton, and doves? Rabbits can be fed by grass from the roadside. If boars have high fertility rates in times of climate change, hunting is necessary for forest ecology. Why not breed camels again in Europe? Thus, animal economies would enrich human diets as they did in the age of complex foraging. Dairy products have been included in animal economies for millennia. Cows that are fed from grazing systems give less milk but can live longer in better health conditions than "super-cows" which are degraded to short-lived machines converting maize into milk. We can also expand reindeer keeping in Scandinavia, as the Sami people still do.

## 4.10.2 Food, dishes, cuisine

PA research should take the step from a "Neolithic diet" to a "Neolithic cuisine". "Cuisine" entails storage, processing, spicing, cooking, arranging, and celebrating meals. It is far more than the intake of calories. The difference between ordinary and extraordinary meals must have emerged because festivities are extraordinary events with much common eating and drinking. Cooking by fire was originally adaptive, but it also paved the way to the diversity of cultural cuisines, such as Chinese, Indian, Mediterranean, and African cuisines. Common meals may include alcoholic beverages which have accompanied human life for millennia (Hockings and Dunbar 2020). Common drinking can be seen as a "total social fact" (Dietler 2020, 119). There is a debate between anthropologists and physicians about alcohol: If common drinking constitutes friendship, and if friendship contributes positively to health, one has to balance these benefits with the health-related risks. If life expectancy is rather low, alcohol consumption might have (had) a fitness benefit (Hockings and Dunbar 2020, 5).

A focus on cuisine might correct the Christian belief that bread (cereals) is needed on a daily basis to stay alive, but food has less importance in life than caring for the eternal soul. Medieval Christian theology was suspect against the vices of gluttony (Latin: "*gula*"). There are reasons to believe that the recent economic success of "fast food" and highly processed "convenient" food points back to the Christian disregard for cuisine. Meanwhile, there are strong tendencies in

238 The overall market is valued at 46 billion $ in the US only. Mullin (2007, 285) points to the tendency that pet keepers wish to purchase pet food that looks similar to the food they eat themselves. Therefore, human vegetarians buy organic meat to feed their pets. Such practices may look decadent from a more prehistoric perspective from which dogs should be given carcasses and cats should prey on mice. Why should zoos cease showing carnivore-feedings?

favour of "abstract" high-caloric food in a digitalised environment. Many people have de-learned cooking. Against Christian morals, we should rediscover fun and joy in foraging and cooking. In a sustainable degrowth-society, there would be far fewer "fast-food"-stations.

We should re-learn taste for (common) dishes which nourish us well in tasty ways. Cooking skills should be relearned. We should return to regional dishes which can be combined with different distant styles of cooking. Personally, I like to combine Baltic fish with Japanese traditions to prepare raw fish. In the age of climate change, northern dishes become more "southern", as there are great combinations of Danish and French dishes. We should hold strong to the SDG objective that, in general, there should be no hunger, but we should also experiment with more archaic ways of foraging: gathering in the outdoors, sharing food in neighbourhoods, storing seasonal abundance, growing spices and vegetables in gardens and on balconies, baking long-lasting bread, fermenting cabbage, *etc.* Our kitchens should become laboratories of cuisines. These prospects are different from a mere return to "palaeo-diets" of hunters and gatherers.

### 4.10.3 Gardening

Gardening was, on the one hand, "Neolithic people's largest source of calories" (Robb 2014, 25) but it was also a social practice of using space, seasons, schedules, harvests, smell, beauty, care, *etc.* There was gardening before agriculture (Mumford 1967; Bogaard 2005; Graeber and Wengrow 2021) and small-scale cultivation has "facilitated the spread of agriculture to Europe" (Bogaard 2005, 177). Gardening and "play agriculture" (Graeber and Wengrow 2021) might have been in touch. Gardening and its results, gardens, have found attention in archaeology (see Malek 2013) and are philosophically addressed in a special issue (Zentgraf *et al.* forthcoming). Gardening is a human practice which connects prehistoric, ancient and modern ways of life. Contemporary (good) gardeners are the heirs of prehistoric horticulturalists, connected to a prehistoric past of complex foraging that they sometimes may "feel" while gardening. Some garden devices have not changed much since ancient and archaic times. Tilling the ground, digging, composting, watering plants, removing weeds, arranging flowers, harvesting berries, spices, salads, and vegetables, feeding some chicken and rabbits, *etc.* can be performed today in ways which are quite similar to prehistoric and ancient practices. Gardens point to the deep background of humanity ("lifeworld") even if there are some collectives which do not practice gardening. If there is only one human lifeworld, gardens and gardening are, despite all cultural garden styles, locations of the lifeworld.

Gardening is a way of *dwelling* (Heidegger 1951/2022). As Kettering (1987, 257-262) argues, dwelling in a Heideggerian sense means "ethos" in the original Greek wording. Good gardeners perform the localised practice of dwelling. Gardens provide many material and immaterial ecosystem services such as garden scents (Draycott 2015). As enclosures, they provide shelter and security. While the wilderness can become frightening, one usually does not perceive garden life as frightening. Thus, gardens are locations to affiliate with natural beings, mostly plant life, in safe ways. In prehistoric and ancient times, such joy might have revealed biophilic inclinations such as caring for single plants. Gardens are suited for nursing and many children take their first steps in gardens. In gardens, one can realise biophilic affiliations with nature in the mode of dwelling in shelter

("*Geborgenheit*").[239] A garden ethics is close to plant ethics (see Kallhoff *et al.* 2018; Cooper 2006). While plant ethics reflects the moral status of plants irrespective of context, garden ethics focusses on the pragmatic context and the role and virtues of the "good" gardener (Kallhoff and Schörgenhumer 2017). With some likeliness, a gender topic is revealed since gardening was often regarded as female practice. The division of labour between males and females should be properly understood. While males had to perform hard, enduring, boring, stupid, and dusty field-work, females could devote labour to more technological advanced, fine-grained work in the domestic sphere (Tietz 2015, 111). Females might have been the experts on how to dwell between houses and gardens. Since not all humans own private gardens in our urban environments, urban areas must devote areas for public parks and greeneries. Private gardens and public parks are complements (Olmsted 1870/1997).

### 4.10.4 Domestic modes of production

It was a modern development to make the household an economic unit that is specialised on consumption. The archaic mode of "oikos" was transformed into a private sphere. The taskscapes of the housewives were reduced. Economy became the male-dominated art of earning money outside the household. A transformation towards sustainability would overcome the modern split between a sphere of commerce and a sphere of consumption as well as the split between labour and leisure by new taskscapes in the spirit of "*vita activa*". Households can and should rediscover practices of production, such as gardening, repairing and fixing, and, perhaps, non-commercialised exchange within neighbourhoods. Storage contributes to resilience, be it private, communal, commercial or state-centred. Households may become units of gifting within neighbourhoods and local communities (Ott 2023). Such ideas are circulation in the do-it-yourself variants of degrowth (Paech 2014) which sometimes come close to "survivalism". Survivalism seems to be a weird idea in modern societies where death rates are low, food is abundant and hospitals are close. Prehistoric people, however, may ask: "What's wrong with survival?" We should, perhaps, also rediscover the concept of embodied wealth for our time and conjoin it with recent ideas on a truly individualised medicine in the tradition of "*cura sui*" (Ott and Fischer 2015, following Foucault).

### 4.10.5 Agriculture

Probably the most urgent field of action is agriculture as *the* crucial legacy of the Neolithic. It took humans 3000 years to learn how to produce plant-based food in gardens and on fields. Many humans lived for millennia in an agricultural universe ("*cultura*") as peasant farmers in a combination of agriculture and other ways of foraging. Today, 50% of the German territory is devoted to agriculture (fields and green lands). There has been an increase in field size and yields due to improved crops and artificial fertilisers. By way of modern agriculture, Malthusian anxieties

239 Gardens were seen as safe and peaceful spaces because of the seclusion. Although gardens have erotic appeal, they are not locations of violence and rape.

became pointless for Europe.[240] Agriculture has been intensified over two centuries. In Germany, now less than 2% of the working population works directly in farming. A small fraction of the population nourishes the overall population at cheap prices. An average German household spends less than 14% of its income for food (Hampicke 2018). As prices for food increased in 2022 roughly 10% due to the Russian aggression against Ukraine, this fraction increased to 15.4%, but prehistoric anxieties of food shortage popped up soon.

Modern agriculture is a success story, but it comes at the price of external effects on the environment. Many urban people accuse agro-industries despite all its productivity. While non-Western people see supermarkets as magical places of a permanent overabundance of all kinds of food, many people in the West gradually oppose the global logistic chains which offer strawberries from Peru in winter. There are sound reasons to oppose globalised agro-business, but such opposition can be differently conceived.

Timothy Morton (2016, 38) opposes "agrilogistics" as a kind of "palaeopathology" and even as "*an original sin*". Morton relies on Cohen and Armelagos (2013), who edited a volume on *Paleopathology at the Origins of Agriculture*. This volume, however, does not support Morton's criticism against agriculture. Morton just takes the title but ignores content. To Morton (*ibid.*, 42), agrilogistics is "toxic from the beginning to humans and other lifeforms, it operates blindly like a computer program". Almost all of us are mental "Mesopotamians", continuing the disaster and misery of agrilogistics blindly. Agrilogistics is a kind of Heideggerian "*Ge-Stell*" (Heidegger 1962) that we are caught in like in Plato's cave. Morton's associations and accusations are highly superficial with respect to all the serious problems of industrialised agriculture. Morton does not reflect on how 10 billion people should survive without high-yield agriculture. For the urban agglomeration of the Global South, intense agriculture is needed which nourishes many people who have to buy food. If yields per acre would not have increased after the 1950s (due to the "Green Revolution"), there would be famines in many regions. Agricultural yields have to increase parallel with population growth if diets do not change and if there should be food security for all. Morton seems disinterested in food security as he writes that agrilogistics "is performed *for its own sake*" (*ibid.*, 44-5, italics in the original) as if there would be no food production.

As we have seen in part 3, the inventive idea to produce plant food on fields has eclipsed into industrialised agriculture as a Q-3 system. The first states were based on cereals which could be taxed (Scott 2017). The way of farming in the U.S. is paradigmatic in this respect (Giedion 1948, part IV). As it is now, this system is unsustainable. But abolishing modern agriculture is not a viable option. There are, however, more organic ways of farming that have been implemented since archaic times. There has been playful agriculture (Graeber and Wengrow 2021) and there is horticulture as well as small homestead farming, market gardening, urban gardening[241], agro-forestry, some approaches in "sustainable intensification", *etc.* Such organic options should dominate agricultural (Q-3 → Q-4) transformations. Agriculture should become more "cultural" since many ways of cultivating plants can be observed in past and present times. In a balanced healthy diet,

---

240 The horrible famines in the 20th century have been politically induced by Stalinism (Applebaum 2017) and Maoism (Jisheng 2012). As Sen argues, there are no famines in democracies. In present India, a critical public sphere pays attention to local famines.

241 Included here are experiments with vertical urban farming. On vertical farming, see Despommier (2010).

cereals and meat do not have to dominate any more. If gardening and orchards would contribute a higher yield proportion to our diets, fields may become more "organic", making agrobiodiversity flourish. Perhaps, we can integrate prehistoric Mexican ways of combining maize and beans in our European vegetable-production. Enhancing soil fertility by manure, developing resistant crops, exchanging seed, preserving wild relatives as genetic reserves, practicing organic farming, implementing grazing systems, applying multi-trophic integrated aquacultures, *etc.* are promising options. In this respect, food and diets are key. At this point, past-present relations are crucial that highlight dietary alternatives to the dominance of cereals and meat. We should, however, not forget that organic agriculture is labour-intensive. Schools could also be locations for food production to teach children that food does not fall from heaven into supermarkets.

### 4.10.6 Biodiversity and biophilia

The combination of climate change, deforestation, and industrial agriculture has resulted in the sixth mass extinction of species in planetary history. Even if biodiversity recovered from each of the first five mass extinctions, the recoveries took millions of years. The exact number of species going extinct each year is uncertain because it is assumed that most extinctions eliminate species which have not been taxonomically registered. The numbers are speculative as they rest on assumptions about species composition and the rates of deforestation of primary tropical forests (as well as the degradation of coral reefs). Even if all numbers are speculative, one can state with confidence that the rate of extinctions is rising and almost all extinctions are due to human activities. In the 1980s, prominent biologists coined the term "biodiversity" to draw attention to the loss of species, but also to the loss of genetic variability and ecosystem degradation (Takacs 1996).

"Biodiversity" is a hybrid concept with an epistemic and a normative dimension. In the epistemic dimension of biodiversity, there are the levels of genes, populations, species, ecosystems, and biomes (landscapes). In the normative dimension, the focus lies on the objectives of conservation, sustainable use, fair access and benefit sharing. Combing both dimensions into a matrix (Jetzkowitz *et al.* 2017, 6-7), one sees many strategies for measures and policies. Here, the history of cultural landscapes and restoration ecology can be coiled for adaptive policies at the landscape level. At minor scales, one may think about gene pools, assisted evolution, restoring ecosystem functions, and the like. Conservation biology is about measures of how to protect species "*in situ*" or "*ex situ*".

As Ceballos *et al.* (2015) argue, it is still possible to avert a dramatic decay of biodiversity if conservation and restoration projects would intensify, but authors also add that the window of opportunity is closing. Climate change will increase the risk of going extinct for many species, but there will also be evolution and migration under conditions of climate change. There has always been landscape change since the last glacial age. In the original post-glacial landscapes of Europe, there was far less biological diversity than in pre-industrial agricultural landscapes. The Little Ice Age (from the 14th to the 18th century CE) reduced biodiversity.

Under conditions of climate change, there will be new biotopes. If Alpine mountain glaciers melt down, new mountain habitats emerge. Species compositions will inevitably change and humans must become familiar with neo-biota. It is rather good news that, from a historical perspective, Eurasian plant species do not possess a higher adaptation to agro-pastoralism than non-Eurasian species (Bellini *et al.* 2022). Palaeo-botany might also be of help to dampen unfounded anxieties against neo-biota. Neo-biota can be aggressive against indigenous species, especially on islands, but the wording of "fertile invaders" sometimes also has political associations against immigrations of humans (Eser 1999). Biological wording should not support xenophobia.

European *forestry* will have to experiment with different mixtures of tree species to make forests more resilient to pests, fires, and storms. Reforestation and some afforestation are possible. In the age of climate change, periods of drought increase risks of fires, as we have seen in Russia, Indonesia, Greece, Australia, California, and France in recent years. Prehistoric humans performed deforestation by intentionally igniting fires, but now, humans have to prevent the risks of forest and peat fires. Fire management includes the ecohydrological strategy to maintain moisture in landscapes. Soils, plants, mires, forests, even gardens should be kept wet.[242] Ecological forestry is the best protection strategy against forest fires. We should prepare for forest fires by remote sensing, but we should also trust in forest ecology telling us that natural forests are hard to ignite. We should allow forests to remain wet, even if this might make logging more difficult. Landscapes should be sponges rather than drainage systems. Wetlands should be preserved and restored. Strawberry production at the expense of wetlands, as in Spain, should be curtailed. If climate change makes the land more arid, humans should do their best to keep it wet. This generic maxim must be realised at many particular places.

We can and should implement more agroforestry systems, protect soils by hedgerows, keep the landscape wet over dry seasons, and bring animals back into the landscape. We should study and restore traditional cultural landscapes worldwide (Zerbe 2022). There are options to re-wild some peripheric parts of Europe and bring back megafauna such as bears, wolves, wisent, Konik-horses, and elks (Flannery 2018, chap. 43-44).[243] There are several recent success stories in zoological species conservation and re-wilding in Germany (lynx, wild cat, owl, wolf, bearded vulture, among others).

With respect to biodiversity, including neo-biota and forestry, one can coil PA with new ideas on *biophilic cohabitation* of humans and non-human species. In environmental ethics, it is hard to argue why humans should preserve all kinds of entities that fall under the broad concept of biodiversity (Ott 2015; 2021b). Since prehistoric times, there has been much fluctuation within biodiversity at particular locations. Humans favoured species, bred genetic varieties, interfered in ecosystems, *etc*. By doing so, they either increased or decreased alpha-, beta-, or gamma-biodiversity. Without doubt, tendencies to reduce biodiversity have been dominant worldwide for some centuries. There is, however, much biodiversity left which might be enhanced. Interestingly, there has been a long-term increase of biodiversity after each mass extinction in natural history. Since humans are responsible for the ongoing mass extinction (whatever the exact numbers of species extinction), they should see themselves as stewards for the remaining biodiversity. Stewardship can be realised in species-poor environments and in biodiversity "hot spots" which are all located in (sub)-tropical zones. Palaeobiology can tell us how to respond under conditions of climatic change.

---

242 See Ziegler (2020) for the prospects of "wet" agricultures ("paludicultures").

243 Flannery also mentions technologies of deliberate introduction of neobiota, re-breeding and even de-extinction. In a warming continent, he imagines rhinos and elephants in some European wilderness areas in the not too distant future.

Stewardship may profit from biophilic motivations. Human history was always cohabitation and by such cohabitation the human disposition of biophilia may have emerged (Wilson 1984). Does PA give support to the biophilia hypothesis? There were many kinds of ways to be affiliated with nature in prehistoric times. The hostile side of nature in prehistoric times is beyond dispute. Former humans could become prey and the phenomenon of being prey has been described in environmental ethics (Plumwood 1995). Prehistoric hunts were often dangerous and unsuccessful. The buffalo hunt of the First Nations, who inhabited the plains of North America, was performed without horses for a long time and it was extremely risky for individuals who, for example, had to direct the stampedes towards the rims of a cliff. Prehistoric humans also drove large game to extinction. Prehistoric cave painting symbolised interactions between humans and animals, mostly in hunting scenes. There were ceremonies of tribal communities which were performed so that young adults could each detect "their own" animal. Often, young adults had to retire to special wild places to become aware of "their" animal in magic moments. Symbolic expressions of human-animal-interactions indicate that many prehistoric encounters with nature were not instrumental. Fertility was celebrated in ceremonies, often by sacrifices. Other kinds of affiliation with nature are interactive. Riding a horse, hunting with falcons, common hunting with wolves, assisting the birth of sheep, swimming in lakes, diving for shellfish, smelling flowers, eating berries, and catching salmon in rivers may count as examples. Even today, children like to play with animals and to climb on trees. PA should research the biophilia hypothesis (Wilson 1984; Kellert 1997) with respect to prehistoric ways of life.

### 4.10.7 Treatment of waste

Societal metabolism with nature creates products, livelihoods, but also residuals: waste. If metabolism with nature is an eternal predicament of human existence (Marx), there will always be waste. The "tool making animal" is also a waste producing animal. But humans also reuse tools.[244] Waste may come into existence at all stages of production and consumption: knapping, foraging, mining, fabrication, transport, sale, storage, consumption, and waste-treatment. Waste is a by-product. In our current globalised economy, artificial substances are transported all over the planet. They disperse and become waste at many different locations. Littering is common at many sites, be it public parks or coastal zones. There is debris in outer space and there are centres of floating waste in the midst of the ocean. By intuition, we fear a world full of waste.

There are many historical ways to treat waste which can and should be studied in history, sociology, and archaeology. Waste is a material companion of human life and it tells societal, cultural, economic, and even moral stories. If waste is part of the archaeological record, it can be used as a material basis for inferences about societal and economic life.

A cultural theory of modern waste is presented by Thompson (1979/2017). He argues that most intellectuals, including economists, are not interested in waste. We discard it, place it outside our dwellings and mind-sets. Waste apparently belongs to a minor sphere of life and persons treating waste are of minor status.

244 Brumm *et al.* (2021, 150) argue that there was "scavenging and reuse of stone artefacts by Lower Palaeolithic hominins". Brumm *et al.* also identify recycled artefacts and propose a terminology of how to speak about re-use, repair, recycle, and repatination in Palaeolithic times.

We do not place trash cans at the centre of our dining room and we do not like to remove the waste of other people.

Waste is a topic for historical investigation on how it is perceived, processed, organised, and regulated. From the HM perspective, one can learn much about human practices, customs, technologies, gender roles, *etc.* if one studies the treatment of waste. Waste treatment can be either anomic (irregular) or regulated and organised. In different societies, there can be a regulation of some waste while other kinds of waste remain unregulated. As a result, there are different "wastescapes" at different times and locations to be studied in PA.[245] It is a topic for historical investigations how waste is perceived, processed, organised, and regulated.

In ancient times, the Roman "*cloaca maxima*" is a famous example for wastewater recharge. Wastewater was used to clean latrines. This technology was part of the overall water supply system of Rome. There was an official "*curator aquarum*" who had to manage the system, including the storage of water in underground cisterns. Under conditions of climate change, there might be the need to rediscover such technologies since the modern strategy of building large dams has many disadvantages (waterborne diseases, high evaporation rates, eviction of humans, *etc.*) (Jobin 1999). Irrigation by large canals induced the disaster of the Aral Sea.

Humans will have to treat freshwater as a scarce resource which should remain unpolluted. In arid areas, we may remember non-flush toilets. Some wastewater might go into aquacultures for algae production or might be used for urban gardening irrigation. Ancient Rome and medieval Islamic cities may be seen as laboratories for dealing with (scarce) freshwater resources and wastewater. Urban water supplies and discharge systems have been researched recently (Chiarenza *et al.* 2020). Research reveals a great deal of ingenuity in bringing water into cities and removing wastewater.

In principle, there are two major routes for the treatment of waste. It can either be retained and re-used or it can be disposed of (= removed). If kept, it is not "really" waste, but remains within the sphere of economic production because there is still some use value and even exchange value of waste. For example, if a farmer pays for manure, excrements have exchange value. The same holds for metals and textiles. But if waste is removed as such, it might be burned, deposed of above ground or underground, channelled into rivers, lakes, and the ocean, *etc.* Removing waste can be performed in anomic or in organised, controlled, and regulated ways. If there is open access to environments, one can just throw anything anywhere according to the motto: "Out of sight, out of mind". Such a maxim might be perfectly reasonable in large natural environments, if almost all waste is organic (ashes, bones, eggshells). Why should a person not throw away the remnants of an apple somewhere in Siberia? As I speculate, waste was not a big problem in nomadic hunter and gatherer collectives. One could leave waste behind. If human collectives, however, settle down and live in larger units, for example, in villages or towns, the treatment of waste *may* become organised. This "may" is not a strict "must", since collectives may also adapt to and cope with waste in their immediate surroundings. Waste can be perceived of as a problem to be solved, but also as a given state of affairs. Problem solutions can be organised at the level of single households, production sites, and entire settlements.

245 "Wastescapes" can be seen as analogies to "soundscapes" and "smellscapes" which have become objects of study in cultural anthropology and social history.

Waste has been a crucial topic in the environmental movement in a first wave of "social hygiene" since the 1870s and in a second wave since the 1970s. In the first wave, municipalities and representatives of social medicine wished to reduce the so-called "urban penalty", namely the risk of infectious diseases and unhealthy as well as toxic working and housing conditions. This first wave can be viewed as successful "biopolitics" (*sensu* Foucault) with a focus on freshwater consumption and discharge. Foucault (1979, 169) conceded that the biopolitics that accompanied industrialisation had positive effects on life expectancy and health status. The "social hygiene" movement had impacts on water sewage, but also on public parks, architecture, trade union policies, food safety, and the like.

A century later, the second wave had a focus on toxic and risky chemicals which had become abundant in the post-war period (such as heavy metals, asbestos, and DDT). It also addressed air pollution, water pollution, and chemical residuals in food. The sheer amount of waste of different kinds and different sources was (and still is) a crucial component of the "Great Acceleration" which constitutes the full-blown Anthropocene. Some waste remains invisible to most inhabitants of Western societies since it is produced in mining areas somewhere in the Global South. Just remember toxic accidents with respect to gold mining. In the Fordist period of industrial capitalism, it was "business as usual" to externalise waste products (emissions) into the air, water, soil, forests, *etc.* Rivers became wastewater canals and the ocean became the final sink for waste. Japanese fisher cultures were contaminated with mercury and women gave birth to highly handicapped children. In Germany in the 1980s, there were recommendations to reduce the consumption of herring caught in the Baltic Sea because of contamination with heavy metals. Highly toxic waste had to be disposed of in underground repositories, while "normal" waste was dumped, often illegally, or burned. Early waste burning facilities were emitters of toxic substances because the temperature of such burning was too low to destroy them. Moreover, there was a strategy to export waste to countries in the Global South and severe accidents occurred such as in Bhopal. The environmental justice movement in the U.S. claimed that people of colour and First Nations people were victimised because dirty industries and waste repositories were often placed close to their settlements but rarely near to the white suburban towns where consumer waste was produced. While economic theory demands the internalisation of negative external effects (polluter pays principle), economic practice made externalities to "business as usual" as long as there was no protest. There was and still is much waste on the consumer side as well, for example, the consumption of products of planned obsolescence, the use of wrapping and packaging material, and the disposal of food as well as pharmaceutical waste, *etc.* Affluent societies were and are "throw-away societies". There has been a solid coalition between consumers and producers in this respect. The models of the Club of Rome supposed that pollution would run parallel to economic growth and, if so, waste and pollution would increase without end.

The environmental motives, political protest, and bleak predictions about waste and pollution created impacts on policy making since the 1970s. Such policies originated as prudent technocrats realised that dispersal strategies will not work. For instance, "dilute-and-disperse" strategies failed prominently in the case of acid rain being an adverse effect of "high-chimney" policies. Slowly but surely, industrial societies improved waste management technologies and, by doing so, constituted new industries and business models. Capitalism operated as it always does: It transforms a problem into a business and makes a profit out of its own deficiencies. Consumers started to separate waste for recycling (glass, paper, plastic, or organic) and they were nudged to reduce their waste volume by price incentives. Some littering problems were resolved by economic incentives (beer cans). Companies were enforced to take back old and broken devices, creating incentives against planned obsolescence. Some toxic substances were prohibited by law or phased out by substitutes. Burning facilities were improved. Thus, the treatment of waste in general did rather follow the so-called "Environmental Kuznets Curve", although the particular problem of radioactive waste remains unresolved in most countries. Theoretical concepts, such as "cradle-to-cradle" (Braungart and McDonough 2002), conceive outlooks for a "zero-waste" economy. The protagonists of the "cradle-to-cradle" concepts argue that humans should invent many things anew. PA may help to look at things differently under the prescriptive idea to minimise waste. Past-present-connectivities might be made on the way to a full non-waste culture.

In prehistoric settlements, there were strategies of recycling materials in a "down-use" process. Broken ceramics were used for nets or as toys. Old textiles were used as production supports. Former storage bins were re-used as deposits for waste. Some waste was dropped in wetlands to avoid dust.

In the emerging post-Fordist period of capitalism, the perception, regulation, and treatment of waste are undergoing a deep transformation which is still in progress. Recycling should become the new mainstreamed normality. In our ongoing transformative period, there are cultural experiments as well. Sharing economies and flea markets can reduce the amount of waste. A nice symbol of transformation is the ban of some plastic products, for example, drinking straws (which were not made from straw). Should a local authority remove litter bins in public parks, bus stations, and coastal zones, hoping that people will take their waste back home, or should one enlarge the number of such bins in order to avoid nasty wastescapes in the surrounding of the remaining ones? Should we place things outside of our houses as takeaway gifts or do we create a new litter problem?

In our aging societies, houses have become huge storage bins of material commodities over long decades of consumerism. There is a material legacy of the post-war growth societies which is "more than just waste". Post-growth business models might prevent many commodities from ending up as waste. Post-growth policies may profit from ceramics, leather, furniture, textiles, books, records, *etc.* being stored during the period of consumerism. Archaeology of modern times may discover basements and attics as discovery sites.

From the raw materials to disposal, waste has been globalised. If there are "trickling down effects" with respect to commodities, waste will end up in poorer countries. If a used car goes from Germany to Poland, and from Poland to Georgia, it will end as waste somewhere in Central Asia. Similar effects occur if used computers, printing machines, screens, TVs, and electronic devices are traded from, say, Japan to South East Asia. The trade with used commodities is hard to control. An innovative way to deal with such a repugnant mechanism might be to make countries of the Global South manufacturers for recycling, upgrading, and export. Why not create fancy clothing for young adults with the branding "recycled from Western textile waste in Sierra Leone"? Why not manufacture bicycles from bamboo and old metals for post-modern urban professionals? Beyond the many demands for global, post-colonial justice, we should also think about innovative business ideas for a "green" global entrepreneurship which recycles former waste. Waste allows for "do-it-yourself" recycling activities. Urban mining might be a prospect for the longer run.

Strictly speaking, there cannot be a "post-waste" society. "Cradle-to-cradle" is a "Vision Zero Ideal". There will always be some type of waste in the Anthropocene. Humans, however, are inventive and can engage in practical discourse on waste, being informed by historical knowledge. We can and should proceed according to the maxim: "Reduce, refine, replace, recycle". Advanced countries, such as Germany, can become cultural labs for the post-industrial treatment of waste under the "Vision Zero" ideal of "cradle to cradle" (Braungart and McDonough 2002). Our patterns of recognition should shift, making the social reputation of waste managers as high as the reputation of novel writers, architects, legal scholars, physicians, professors, and priests. Post-modern societies might, for the first time in history, upgrade the social esteem of waste-work, seen as a cultural practice.

## 4.11 Results and outlooks: System and lifeworld

### 4.11.1 Looking back to previous parts

Finally, theoretical ideas can be harboured. The idea that the contexts of discovery within scientific history are based on practical interests (part 1) can now be specified. With Benjamin (1940/1974), we can "jump" back into PA in order to shape pathways into a "good" Anthropocene. As we have seen in the previous section, there are many threads to be coiled in past-past-present-connectivities and presumptive (Q-3 → Q-4) transformations. Prehistory can and should be seen as a "laboratory" for adaptive and responsive change. We connect the prehistoric and ancient past with the futures we wish to bring about. In doing so, we rely on PA as an historical enterprise which profits from scientific methods (Kristiansen 2022; Pollard *et al.*, 2023) and has a broad conceptual and theoretical horizon (part 1).

In part 2, I did not invent the wheel anew but reloaded HM in order to explain why and how economic life, as such, emerged in the Neolithic transformation. I rely on a materialistic standard model of the agricultural ("Neolithic") transformation. Since economic life must have become apparent since then, a comprehensive and practical self-understanding of the human being must not downplay the economic sides of life. We should not be afraid of being economic agents. From Marx, I adopted the epistemic idea that the economic theories, which have been designed to model the most developed economic system, namely globalised industrial market-capitalism, are needed to understand and explain prehistoric and ancient economies. Surplus is key. Emerging economic life from surplus, storage, a domestic mode of production, and a division of labour onward has had a strong intrinsic tendency to increase material wealth in terms of useful and consumable things. The HM economic perspective can be sharpened according to effects of post-growth (Q-3 → Q-4) transformations on land-use systems, husbandry, gardening, waste, *etc.* If historical materialists are interested in land-use and waste, their mindsets become less utopian and more pragmatic. They do not, for instance, believe that fabrication can become almost completely automatic and labour might shrink to some hours per week. HM has to accept the predicament of scarcity despite all increases in wealth and it recognises the expansion of the inequality frontier as a driver of stratification. In addition to part 2, I see a property-owning democracy with a broad dispersal of wealth as a decent option (Rawls 2001). A balanced mixture of a solid welfare state providing a Rawlsian safe minimum, opportunities for upward mobility, broad dispersal of wealth and taxation may and should limit inequality. I leave open for further debate whether the alternative of liberal and democratic socialism is viable.

In part 3, the chorus song of "*Antigone*" was taken as an intellectual spike of the "thin" Anthropocene, because it looks back from ancient into prehistoric times. Basic innovations, which formed the Neolithic package, are seen as achievements whose *qualities* are to be affirmed, but whose *quantities* can be increased without intrinsic measure ("*Maß*"). There is an excessive eclipse from quality into expanding quantities which in the very long run terminated into the present situation of the "thick" Anthropocene. "Anthropocene" is taken a diagnostic geo-historical term which must be combined with normative investments. In the previous section of part 4, I explained the logic of (Q-1 → Q-2 → Q-3 → Q-4) transitions and transformations. To repeat the basic idea: Q-1 is the innovative achievement whose origins can be researched. (Q-1 → Q-2) are long periods of increase before modern times, while (Q-2 → Q-3) are more recent periods which terminated in the "acceleration" since the 19th century or the 1950s. (Q-1 → Q-2 → Q-3) are objects of historical research. The (Q-3 → Q-4) transitions are about the near future, while the remote future is behind our horizon. If one sees (Q-3 → Q-4) as a merely *descriptive* enterprise, one may take the attitude of a "historian of the present time" and perceive this ongoing century as a great spectacle within human history whatever the results. This is a "stoic" solution: trying to remain unaffected by being beyond fear and hope as well as beyond good and evil. This, however, highly stylised and artificial position is not an option for an ethicist who takes an interest in practical reasoning. If so, one must take a more prescriptive, ethical (and hopeful) attitude toward (Q-3 → Q-4) transitions. To qualify them as "good", "proper", "rightful", "decent", "sustainable", *etc.* requires prescriptive investments. Part 4 makes such normative investments ethically explicit.

In section 4.6 of part 4, I defend a "thin" universal discourse ethics, but leave room for "thick" particular cultural ways of life which should be deeply reformed. The coalition between universal principles and normative individualism should not become an ethical stalemate which crushes particularities. The outline of my ethical concept implies that (Q-3 → Q-4) transitions cannot be qualified without investments from environmental ethics and sustainability discourse. Such investments cannot dispense with the particular, cultural, customary, and localised sides of life which are generally important in ethical life (Hegel: "*Sittlichkeit*", see Ribeiro 2021). The customary sides of life constitute common moral decency on a daily basis (Michéa 2007). Therefore, I conceive a second axial age not merely as an *expansion* of universalism to cosmopolitanism but rather as a *reflection* back into particular ways of ethical life and into the deep well of historical cultures, including prehistory. I do not discard universalism, but restrict universalism to a "thin" layer of principles. I dub this position "sufficient universalism". A second axial age, then, should be more than crowding the moral point of view with numerous principles. Instead, our system of practical belief should look upon a repertoire of particular ethical ways of life which history reveals. We should consider the many historical options of how to perform sustainable ways of ethical life. Here, I agree with Graeber and Wengrow (2021). "Our" European universal principles serve, of course, as constraints against cultural ways of life that "we" cannot accept. My ethics combines, so to say, a "thin" universalism with a "thick" cultural dimension ("*Sittlichkeit*") and a "deep" historical memory function. It tries to find middle-ground between the poles of cosmopolitanism and parochialism.

Some anthropological investments have been made in part 1. Humans are exceptional beings in the kingdom of animals, but they are made from crooked wood (Kant). Humans are practical beings long before they start theorising the world. They have to cope with challenges, face scarcity and trade-offs, experience competition and contest, but also boredom, disease, old age, *etc*. There also is rivalry, work, labour, frustration, trouble, anxiety, routine, stress, *etc*. The immediate fulfilment of desires, longings, and aspirations is, as Sigmund Freud (1930) argued, exceptional in all cultures. Cultures are systems of delayed reward. Since the Neolithic, we are adapted to delayed reward as part of our way of life. Individual human life is organic and, by implication, fragile and mortal. To carry out human life on Planet Earth comes with the price of some struggling. To emphasise "struggling for life" does not imply a revival of Social Darwinism as it was conceived at the end of 19th century. It is rather close to the idea of "*vita activa*" (Arendt 1960).

## 4.11.2 Rethinking complexity and evolution

Decades ago, prehistoric lives were regarded as "primitive" (see, for example, Barnes 1948). This image of primitivism has been rightly discarded by recent PA research. On the side of modern lives, it has been argued that societal complexity might increase in industrialism, but individual lives have impoverished and are dominated by forces they cannot control. This bleak picture of *modern* primitivism (wage labour, consumption, death) has been painted by Critical Theory, especially Marcuse (1964).[246] Graeber and Wengrow (2021, 519) follow this line as they want to make us believe that "we are stuck in just one social reality". At the end of their book (*ibid.*, 2021, 519), they remember Franz Steiner's (1949) concept of "pre-servile institutions" which restrict basic liberties.[247] The underlying message of the book *The Dawn of Everything* seems to be that inhabitants of modern societies are one-dimensional servants of dominant powers (capital, state) rather than free citizens. Most contemporaries do not even realise that they are "stuck" in a primitive modern way of life. It remains doubtful whether Graeber and Wengrow (2021, 523) include Western democracies into the class of "free or relative free societies". If there might be such a suggestive message (and the motif is repeated throughout the book), it is not argued for in terms of a general sociology of modern societies.

The "possibilities for human interventions" (*ibid.*, 2021, 524) and creative innovation within modern societies are far greater than Graeber and Wengrow want to make us believe.

The previous sections (part 4, sections 4.7 and 4.8) pointed at a vast landscape of possible (Q-3 → Q-4) transitions. We are not "stuck" in a stalemate. To make this argument against Graeber and Wengrow, one has to repeat the state of the art in the general sociology of modern societies which rely on some evolutionist concepts.

In part 1, three types of doing history were established. The right of doing micro-history is without doubt. Part 1 endorsed middle-range theories as TI. The

246 A very thoughtful, but sharp critique against Marcuse is to be found in MacIntyre (1970).

247 Steiner's PhD thesis is mentioned on p. 519-520, but is not to be found in the bibliography of "*The Dawn of Everything*".

epistemic legitimacy of macro-history is more contested, and so is evolutionism. Evolutionism is associated with the danger of smuggling flawed ideas of European supremacy into history. The dangers of implicit supremacy suggestions are, however, not a sufficient epistemological reason to discard evolutionary thinking completely. From an epistemological perspective, doing universal history (part 1) should not be discarded (Habermas 1976). Such a type of history transcends the paradigm of ordinary historical narratives from within since it must be more theoretical. Thanks to the "Global History Databank", social scientists and historians can support theoretical models with data. Societal evolution can be hypothetically conceived in terms of complexity[248] and learning processes.

In some sense, modern Western societies are the preliminary result of a long-lasting tendency of increasing societal complexity (Turchin *et al.* 2017). As Turchin *et al.* argue (*ibid.*, 2017, 6), huge masses of data "indicate a shift toward more complex societies over time in a manner that lends support to the idea of a driving force behind the evolution of increasing complexity". Turchin *et al.* resonate with Perreault's (2019, 165) idea of macro-scale patterns and processes which only become visible over time scales longer than $10^3$ years. These are scales of transformations which are only identified by an evolutionary perspective and cannot be perceived on the emic side. A task-based approach of measuring an increase in complexity from individuals, groups, teams and partitioned tasks has been proposed by Barrientos and Sanjuàn (2021). The approach has a theoretical background in ergonomics and has been applied to prehistoric archaeology with respect to the construction of monuments in Iberia. This approach fits well to HM. As Turchin *et al.* (2017) clearly state, a measure of increasing complexity does not imply any normative judgement: "more complex societies are not necessarily 'better' than less complex societies" (Turchin *et al.* 2017, 5). But also not necessarily worse. The durable cohesion of an extremely complex modern society is somewhat striking and should not be taken for granted. Complexity paves the way to individual freedom, but it comes at the price of inequality.

Complexity can be ordered in hierarchical and non-hierarchical ways. Increasing complexity may run counter to hierarchical orderings. In the longer run, hierarchies (command-and-control, central planning) may become dysfunctional for complex societies. Since the Age of Enlightenment, European societies refigured themselves in a long process. There was a transformation from (monarchic) hierarchy to (liberal) heterarchy. French absolutism was the last actual hierarchy before this transformation.

Habermas (1981) conceives modern societies as a dynamic correlative interplay between the *lifeworld* and different *social systems*. We shall address both sides in turn. With respect to the *systemic* side, Habermas relies on Luhmann's functional system theory which Luhmann presented some years later in elaborated form (Luhmann 1984; 1986). According to Luhmann, modern societies are both highly complex and functionally differentiated. Specific systems are specialised with various tasks. Science, politics, economy, education, law, health, sports, religion, and art are functional systems which are internally stratified. Modern societies

248 "Complex" means a dynamic autopoietic composition out of a high number of heterogenous entities, relations, and operations which cannot be predicted in detail. One should read Sahal's "classical" article anew (Sahal 1976). A definition is given by Luhmann (1984, 46): A coherent set of elements is complex if not all single elements can be combined with each other single element anymore. Given the definition, a band of hunters and gatherers is not complex. In modern societies, complexity reproduces at higher layers. See also Barton (2014) who argues that all human collectives are complex.

are "top-less" and heterarchical. Within single systems, there are rankings according to expertise and there are functional elites, but single systems operate independently from political and morals doctrines. Elites are not hereditary even if sons and daughters of elites have better prospects. Realities are, as always, more complex, since political administration, industries, social movements, *etc.* wish to create influences on the autopoietic operations within the systems that can either accept or reject such external influences. Political and monetary power should, however, not become dominant forces within such systems (Walzer 1983). This also represents the minimal morals of system theory not letting money and politics become intrusive into the basic functions of a system. This is why scientific truth and sentences at court are not for sale. Is it true that the "totalitarian" logic of capitalism is disrespectful against the autonomy of science, law, art, religion, and politics?

Whatever the details, modern societies reproduce themselves by the outputs of such systems. As Luhmann (1984) argues, widespread criticism against alienation, exploitation, inequality, "being stuck", *etc.* does not recognise that modern societies bring about more liberties, more security, more individual diversity and even more love and care[249] than other ways of life. While democratic elections constitute "input"-legitimacy, functional systems produce "output"-legitimacy. The modern way of life cannot be simple any more since we have to perform the different roles of economic agents, members of families, legal persons, political citizens, followers of aesthetic traditions, and the like. We are trained to switch between different roles which are not "play roles" but modes of modern life. We cannot escape the complexities of such a way of life. Müller (2022) has shown the intrinsic complexity of the role of consumers.

There are interesting parallels between modern functional differentiations and premodern heterarchies. As it has been argued (parts I and II), heterarchic stratification has been an alternative to hierarchical stratification throughout history. The archaic figures of the judge, the healer, the merchant, the craftsman, the fisherman, the shaman, the political duke, and the "*strategos*", *etc.* have parallels in modern functional elites. We can compare modern and premodern heterarchies from the lenses of complexity and freedom.[250] The question remains whether heterarchical societies are in a better position to cope with the challenges of the Anthropocene. Luhmann (1986) asked this question because the ecological crisis requires all functional systems to represent nature within their autopoietic operations.

According to Luhmann (1984; 1986), all systems have a fixed binary code which should be kept intact. Within the systems, however, there are flexible programs open for re-programming. The collective commitment to sustainability requires re-programming law, science, education, economy, even politics. In the longer run, reprogramming creates impacts on practices which are located outside the systems such as daily ethical life. Luhmann's theory has limits and shortcomings, since it cannot properly conceive daily life, moral discourse, a public sphere of reasoning, and habits of social characters. This brings us to the second side: the *lifeworld*.

The concept of the lifeworld has found different interpretations since Husserl (1936/2012). It has been conceived as daily life, as a reservoir of deep convictions, and as a cultural background. Lifeworld knowledge is an inexhaustible

249 See Luhmann (2008).

250 In recent years, Luhmann's theory has attracted interests of historians. In March 2022, Alois Winterling and colleagues organised a conference under the title: "*Systemtheorie & Antike Gesellschaft*". See Hinsch (2022).

horizon beyond all cultural and epistemic bodies of knowledge. Such a lifeworld horizon can only come to mind partially, but not in its holistic entirety. We are now, however, in an epistemic position to shed historical light into the different domains of the lifeworld, *because all sets of concepts (part 1) refer to domains of the lifeworld.* Taking the lifeworld-perspective, PA can be focused on agencies, practices, taskscapes, reproduction, natural environments, speech act knowledge, symbols, economic affairs, normative orders, and, last but not least, (Hegelian) ethical life. If we make TI in PA, we disclose domains of the lifeworld with respect to the past *and* the present. If so, we improve our self-understanding (Habermas 1965). By making past-present-relations with respect to single domains of the lifeworld, we *ipso facto* navigate in discursive pools of *options* and correlative pools of *reasons*. If so, we are united with prehistoric and ancient humans by the lifeworld horizon of practical reasons. With prehistoric humans, we share some experiences about the "good things" in life and we share some conviction about evil. PA can also make us reflect upon adequate expectations and beliefs in the deep background of the lifeworld.

The question remains whether the *"deinos"* (part 3) can be integrated in the lifeworld. Since the lifeworld is generally open for integration and revision, this might be the case, even if it takes time. Ethics should consider how the *"deinos"* might be adequately represented in the lifeworld. Humans should both admire and fear themselves (Jonas 1979). If so, we should not model humans as "smooth" and "soft" beings.

### 4.11.3 Social systems, heterarchy, and freedom

Even if stratification is unavoidable in all complex societies, we face political alternatives. An aversion against hierarchical top-down command and control systems is pragmatically implied in the idea of freedom (Pettit 2014). Since we have reasons to believe that this aversion against being forced has been alive since prehistoric times (Graeber and Wengrow 2021), humans are united under the idea of freedom. Westerners have no monopoly on this idea, but can identify traces of freedom within history.[251] It was Hegel's great idea that the sphere of objective spirit should be governed only by freedom and by commitments which can be freely endorsed. Hegel placed political freedom over moral autonomy. It was, however, Hegel's mistake to see freedom as a (more or less) exclusive European project.

Graeber and Wengrow (2021, 495) see the political idea of the enlightenment as "self-conscious projects for reshaping society in accord with some rational ideal". Thus, the project of enlightenment resonates with their third liberty. There is, however, no enlightenment without the recognition of its dialectics, regressions, and perils (Horkheimer and Adorno 1944/1947).[252] European societies were not immune against political doctrines which implied a denial of freedom. Freedom is fragile (Fromm 1941/2011), and so are democracies. Transformations must take care of both.

---

251 To Hegel (1821/1970), general freedom was a privilege of Western modernity. As Hegel argues, in ancient states, only the monarch was free, in ancient Greek poleis, male citizens were free, while in modern societies, all humans are, in principle, to be recognised as free individuals. Hegel, however, had a very narrow picture of history. Contemporary Hegelians will appreciate any longing for a free human life wherever its location in space and time.

252 The real rupture within this transformation was the German attempt to re-establish a strict and violent hierarchical order (*"Führerprinzip"*) under a parochial and racist moral doctrine (*"arische Volksgemeinschaft*). But such an attempt was not a transformation since the new order did not last a thousand years (as a *"1000jähriges Reich*), but had to be defeated to unconditional surrender.

There is much freedom within more complex and heterarchical societies throughout history.

PA and anthropology demonstrate that there are many ways for a free and dignified human life. Even Marxian scholars may accept that heterarchical non-antagonistic stratification of liberal modern societies are an option in the repertoire of societal orders. This coheres with Rawls' (2001, 140) concept of a "property owning democracy" that disperses the ownership of property widely throughout the populace. From a political point of view, we should consider the presumptive attractiveness of this option which gives due respect to the historically established institutions of property and legacies.

### 4.11.4 The lifeworld and its colonisation

As Habermas (1981) argues, it may happen that some mindsets and beliefs "colonise" the lifeworld. They are integrated in the reservoir of deep beliefs, although they are distortive. Such a colonisation can, in principle, occur at any time in history. In a commercialised society, commercialised mindsets may distort ethical life. We[253], then, perceive a life as a career, a person as an "entrepreneur of oneself", and nursing a child as a "baby break". We may falsely convert moral problems into technological ones. To identify such "colonisations", which occur *within* the lifeworld, we need some elementary knowledge to explain what is going wrong and why.

May we identify the "growth"-orientation (parts II and III) as an instance of such a (distortive and deceptive) colonisation of the lifeworld *or* is this growth mindset ("the more the better") a legitimate component of lifeworld knowledge since prehistoric times? This question haunts us in the ongoing debates about how to overcome growth. On the one hand, the "more" has deep roots: more descendants, more food, more cattle, more storage, more rooms, more servants, more soldiers, more money. On the other hand, there is wisdom stored in religions and philosophies that one should be content with "enough" and should not aspire to "more". If one follows Sahlins (1972/2004), the hunters and gatherers may have agreed with the ancient and medieval monks that one should not have many belongings. There is some lifeworld logic in the economies of more and some lifeworld wisdom in restraint. If so, in daily life we face economic incentives *a fronte,* while the lifeworld gives different advice *a tergo*. We cannot simply *decide* to eradicate the growth-orientation from the lifeworld. If we represent both the "*deinos*" and some lessons from environmental ethics in the lifeworld, we may, however, constitute an ethical asymmetry between the "more" and the "enough". Perhaps, we can "de-colonise" the growth-orientation from the lifeworld, but we should not believe that humans can simply "make" a decision to live simply and frugally.

### 4.11.5 Mirroring ourselves in prehistoric lives

One idea about critical history and ethnology is that the process of understanding the other in its alterity can and should have a flip side: One becomes reflective upon oneself and becomes alien to oneself. If we come close(r) to prehistoric lives, we see

253 From now on, the "we" does not refer to specific groups (collectives, generations, or strata). It is used in an appellative way: "To whom it may concern". It refers to common mental habits which I see as widespread.

ourselves as if from a distance.[254] Immersion into prehistoric archaeology sheds a different light upon our contemporary world. We may become surprised about our way of life and our mental habits, including our morals. We may discover different "colonial" intrusions into the lifeworld which do not stem from commerce, but from the (technologically shaped) comfort zones of modern life itself (Borgmann 1984). We may become critical against all-too-easy convenience and comfort and against highly demanding morals. As Habermas (1981) argues, colonisation of the lifeworld hides itself in matters we simply take for granted and in expectations about life.

By mirroring ourselves reflectively in prehistoric lives, we may see current Western expectations as demanding, if not excessive, including, for example, prolonged youth, having a perfect body, making steep careers, having great journeys, living in fancy apartments, following a life-work-balance, reaching sexual satisfaction, owning digital equipment, appreciating social security, receiving delivered consumption goods, and enjoying much fun. Our universities should become "safe spaces" and no one should be left behind in the great transformation. These expectations do not only stem from commercial advertisements, but also evolve from standards of life in which food and shelter are taken for granted.[255] The baselines of expectations have been shifted. In the long decades of peaceful growth, we de-learned how to face hardship in life. We ramped up insurance systems against hardship – and rightly so. By doing so, we became highly sensitive against subtle forms of emotional suffering and discrimination.

The "growth" attitude has shifted to intellectual demands. There is much talk on "degrowth" among intellectuals, but real political demands are based on the logic of "more". Moral philosophy and concepts of (global) justice have become intellectual engines of demands for "more". Included in this logic are, for example, improved schooling, inclusion and integration, free kindergartens, quality education, nice infrastructures, higher grants, more academic positions without time limits, unconditional basic income, more streetworkers, increases in transfers, improved social security systems, more means to integrate minorities, more health care, more money for climate adaptation financing and for (strictly additional) development assistance, more compensation for burdens, *etc.* Implicitly, almost all of these demands are demands for "more money". Morals becomes "monetised" and we tend to believe that money can buy justice and infer that more money will buy more justice. We may overlook the many pitfalls in making finance the medium of moral progress after virtue.

Perhaps, a look into the deep well of prehistory may become a cure against such colonisation of the lifeworld. PA teaches that human lives can flourish and be dignified without scriptures, money, states, modern infrastructures and insurance systems. Prehistoric lives, however, were not cosy and humans had to face many hardships as well. PA will not downplay the rigid and harsh sides of prehistoric life, but it can also help us to appreciate the many good things in life we simply take for granted. Prehistoric lives were not primitive, poor, stupid, and sad. There are many activities to appreciate and to re-learn. There was, is, and will be husbandry, gardening, sailing, fishing, foraging, storing, feasting, dancing, making music, dreaming, cooking, brewing, fixing, joking, caring, loving, teaching, debating, hiking, sportive games, friendship, play, and, last but not least,

254 This idea has been explored by Kögler (1992). Understanding the other implies to come into a distance to one's own mindsets, attitudes, and values which are harboured within the lifeworld.

255 The 20th century has been a social-democratic welfare state capitalism century in many Western states (Esping-Andersen 1989). Thus, there are established welfare state mindsets.

worship. All these practices were present in archaic times and our post-modern lives would be impoverished if they were completely missing. They are still part of our daily ethical life. We should continue to appreciate them and should become more attentive about how much goodness there is in life.

If one wishes to adopt some practices from prehistoric times, it must be practices which can, in principle, work without writing, without money, and without a state. Since we cannot abolish the cybernetic mechanisms of writing, money, and the state, "*do-it-yourself*" strategies could enrich and diversify modern ways of life. They define new "taskscapes", but it might be doubtful whether we really are willing to take the tasks.

Mirroring ourselves in prehistoric lives might help to detect the deficits that we would have to overcome if we should really perform a great transformation. We do not suffer from a lack of moral principles and moral sensibilities, but rather from a lack of motivational strength and a rigour of readiness. We have reasons to transform our societies. Reasons are necessary but not sufficient for motivation. The ancient problem of "*akrasia*" is redefined as a "motivation-gap". If one reflects upon deficits of motivation and a rigour of readiness, "rigour of readiness" means decisiveness. The nice slogan applies again: "*Be the change you want to see*", or: "*Act as if persons matter!*"

Practical life itself might become a catalyst for a transformation to post-growth attitudes.[256] Environmental practices (gardening, forestry, agriculture, ecological restoration, dealing with waste, *etc.*) are now to be regarded as decisive transformative practices. Such practices are laboratories of (Q-3 → Q-4) transitions from which a transformation may emerge. Moreover, Q-2 becomes the epistemic historical laboratory which may inspire single (Q-3 → Q-4) transitions that sum up to a "great" transformation. *Finally, we are in a position to face a new constellation and dialectical interplay of how prehistoric, but transformative lifeworld practices may contribute to a programmatic renewal of our societal systems and the ways of interferences in nature.*

Ethical lessons from PA will be lessons of how to live well in the Anthropocene in a transformative degrowth culture. "We" (whatever the scope of the "we") should protect and create a multitude of idyllic places in our natural environments. In our lives, dwelling should come first and journeys should be rare, but better as they are within commercial tourism. Cruising and "all inclusive" tourism should have no future. We should rediscover the domestic mode of production and consumption, including gardening (Aristotelian "oikonomia"). We should adopt "green" hobbies such as keeping pigeons and bees, cooking, making wine and vinegar, gardening, walking, riding bicycles, *etc.* We should rediscover omnivore diets and overcome our reliance on "Mesopotamic" staple food (cereals) and its modern additives (sugar, fat, salt). Diets should serve embodied wealth and resilient health. We should take care of our bodies (Foucault: "*cura sui*") and should be aware of finitude. We should re-learn environmental dwelling within particular territories and landscapes. We should engage in local and organic horti- and agriculture. We should plant groves, forests, and perform new ways of agro-forestry. We should restore nature at any scale and combine nature conservation, restoration, adaptation to climate change and carbon-sequestration via so-called "natural climate solutions" (Seddon *et al.*

256 „*Alles gesellschaftliche Leben ist wesentlich praktisch. Alle Mysterien, welche die Theorie zum Mystizism(us) veranlassen, finden ihre rationelle Lösung in der menschlichen Praxis und im Begreifen dieser Praxis*" (Marx 1845, 8). [English translation]: "*All social life is essentially practical. All mysteries which lead theory to mysticism find their rational solution in human practice and in the comprehension of this practice.*" [Translation available at: https://www.marxists.org/archive/marx/works/1845/theses/theses.htm; last accessed: 6 December 2023].

2020). We should recycle materials and relearn how to fix things. Perhaps, there can be low-density urbanism in the future. Our modes of exchange can shift toward gifting and pooling, even if such modes will not replace monetary exchange on markets. At some occasions, we should learn to be content with the given. Most of these ways of practical lives rely more on attitudes and virtues than on money and support by the state. A "great" transformation requires actions, practices, and attitudes which can be recognised as being "great".

Finally, a heterarchical, non-antagonistic, and deliberative societal order, on the one hand, and (Q-3 → Q-4) transformations of cultural lifestyles, on the other hand, are correlative under the idea of freedom. There are trails ahead.

### 4.11.6 Going public

Given such perspectives, PA should go public and disseminate its findings into a public sphere of reasoning. If modern society cannot do without a "memory function", PA should take this role. PA should "give the public other histories to think with and about" (Robb and Pauketat 2013, 5). This supposes that there is still a sphere of public reasoning from which the inhabitants are able and willing to think about such histories not for the sake of history only. Robb and Pauketat (2013, 33): "There is a void to be filled". If there is a void, it will be filled by some narratives, be they scientifically credible or not. The digital media operate without many checks and control (Habermas 2022). It is populated with archaic figures such as imagined Celts, Druids, Aryans and Fred Feuerstein. Thus, there is a moral responsibility for PA and other historians as well not to leave the battle-ground of historical narratives and exhibitions. If so, one has to join the new media whether one likes them or not. Dissemination is time-consuming and does not bring many rewards for academic careers.

In Germany, history at school focusses on the past two centuries. Teachers have to rush through European ancient and medieval history in order to devote attention to the atrocities of the 20th century. Prehistory is hardly taught at schools. The popular images of "cave dwellers" are worlds apart from the epistemic state of the art. The "Indiana Jones" movies have produced a wrongful public image of what archaeology is all about.

Exhibitions may move even more from being collections of things to presentations of practices. They should be interactive. One should try to have visitors crack nuts, row a boat, ride a mule, cook with fire, cut a tree with an axe, shoot with a bow and arrow, and, perhaps, even kill an animal. At the end of their inspiring article, Boivin and Crowther (2021) suggest the following tasks for PA:

The study of how archaeology can contribute to "shape a better future" should become a "regular feature of mainstream archaeology". PA knowledge must be disseminated to a broader public. There is still a widespread image of "primitive" prehistoric humans, living in caves, eating raw meat, being stupid, *etc*. The idea to make (Q-3 → Q-4) transitions will only work if such images are overcome.

PA should concentrate more on the systematic research and assessment of past "solutions, practices and sustainability" in inter- and transdisciplinary ways. PA should engage beyond academia at the "Anthropocene front lines". As part 3 suggests, the front lines are the Q-3 upshots and the (Q-3 → Q-4) transitions. Such a transdisciplinary mode of doing PA is, of course, unusual to PA and time consuming. It may, however, bring PA closer to us as we learn to integrate the practical wisdom of prehistoric modes of life into contemporary transformations. Didactic experts may consider how to disseminate the knowledge gained with PA about practices, solutions and sustainability.

# References


Adorno, T.W., 1966/1980. *Negative Dialektik*. Frankfurt/M.: Suhrkamp.

Aghion, P., Antonin, C., Bunel, S., 2021. *The Power of Creative Destruction*. Cambridge: Belknap Press.

Angelbeck, B., 2018. *"Flatten the enemy", "Fighting with Property", "Interest-Bearing Investments": A consideration of Potlach interpretations with Indigenous views of the gifting ceremony*. Canadian Anthropological Society (CASCA) Conference.

Angelbeck, B. and Grier, C., 2012. Anarchism and the Archaeology of Anarchic Societies Resistance to Centralization in the Coast Salish Region of the Pacific Northwest Coast. *Current Anthropology*, 53, 547-87.

Apel, K.-O., 1979. *Die Erklären:Verstehen-Kontroverse in transzendentalpragmatischer Sicht*. Frankfurt/M.: Suhrkamp.

Applebaum, A., 2017. *Red Famine*. New York: Doubleday.

ArchaeoGLOBE Project, 2019. Archaeological assessment reveals Earth's early transformation through land use. *Science*, 365, 897-902.

Arendt, H., 1955. *Elemente und Ursprünge totaler Herrschaft*. Frankfurt/M.: Deutsche Verlags Anstalt.

Arendt, H., 1960. *Vita activa oder Vom tätigen Leben*. Stuttgart: Kohlhammer.

Armelagos, G., Goodman, A.H., Jacobs, K.H., 1991. Origins of Agriculture: Population Growth during a Period of Declining Health. *Population and Environment*, 13 (1), 9-22.

Armstrong, J., 2010. *Constructing Identity:* Syilx Okanagan Oraliture and tmixwcentrism. Dissertation, Universität Greifswald.

Arndt, E.M., 1820. *Ein Wort über die Pflege und Erhaltung der Forsten und der Bauern im Sinne einer höheren, d.h. menschlichen Gesetzgebung*. Schleswig.

Arnold, J.E., Sunell, S., Nigra, B.T., Bishop, K.J., Jones, T., Bongers, J., 2016. Entrenched Disbelief: Complex Hunter-Gatherers and the Case for Inclusive Cultural Evolutionary Thinking. *Journal of Archaeological Method and Theory,* 23, 448-499.

Arp, M.J., 2006. *Pre-Socratic thought in Sophoclean tragedy*. Doctoral dissertation, University of Pennsylvania.

Arponen, V., Dörfler, W., Feeser, I., Grimm, S., Groß, D., Hinz, M., Knitter, D., Müller-Scheeßel, N., Ott, K., Ribeiro, A., 2019b. Environmental determinism and archaeology. *Archaeological Dialogues,* 26 (1), 1-9.

Arponen, V., Grimm, S., Käppel, L, Ott, K., Thalheim, Bl., Kropp, Y., Kittig, K., Brinkmann, J., Ribeiro, A., 2019a. Between natural and human sciences: On the role and character of theory in socio-environmental archeology. *Holocene,* 29 (10), 1671-1676.

Arponen, V., Müller, J., Hofmann, R., Furholt, M., Ribeiro, A., Horn, C., Hinz, M., 2016. Using the Capability Approach to Conceptualise Inequality in Archaeology: The Case of the Late Neolithic Bosnian Site Okolište c. 5200–4600 BCE. *Journal of Archaeological Method and Theory,* 23 (2), 541-560.

Assmann, J., 2018. *Achsenzeit*. München: Beck.

Austin, J., 1955/1962. *How to do Things with Words*. New York: Oxford University Press.

Bacon, F., 1982. *Das neue Organon*. Berlin: Akademie Verlag.

Bailey, D., Whittle, A., Cummings, V., eds., 2005. *(Un)settling the Neolithic*. Oxford: Oxbow.

Bajohr, H. and Edinger, S., eds., 2021. *Negative Anthropologie*. Berlin: De Gruyter.

Bakunin, M., 1869a/1972. Die Prinzipien der Revolution. *In*: M. Bakunin. *Staatlichkeit und Anarchie*. Berlin: Ullstein, 100-105.

Bakunin, M., 1869b/1972. Die Aufstellung der Revolutionsfrage. *In*: M. Bakunin. *Staatlichkeit und Anarchie*. Berlin: Ullstein, 95-99.

Balasse, M., Gillis, R., Živaljević, I., Berthon, R., Kovačiková, L., Fiorillo, D., Arbogast, R.-M., Bălăsescu, A., Brèhard, S., Nyerges, É.Á., Dimitrijević, C., Bánffy, E., Domboróczki, L., Marciniak, A., Oross, K., Vostrovská, I., Roffet-Salque, M., Stefanović, S., Ivanova, M., 2021. Seasonal calving in European Prehistoric cattle and its impacts on milk availability and cheese making. *Scientific Reports,* 11, No. 8185.

Barnes, H.E., 1948. *Historical Sociology: Its Origins and Development. Theories of Social Evolution from Cave Live to Atomic Bombing*. New York: Philosophical Library.

Barrett, J., 2016. Archaeology after interpretation. *Archaeological Dialogues,* 23 (2), 133-137.

Barrett, J.C., 2021. *Archaeology and its discontents: Why Archaeology Matters*. London: Routledge.

Barrientos, G. and Sanjuán, L., 2021. Measuring the Complexity of Past Social Systems: A Task Analysis Approach to the Study of Late Prehistoric Monumentality in Iberia. *Journal of Archaeological Method and Theory,* 28, 1058-1105.

Barton, C.M., 2014. Complexity, Social Complexity, and Modelling. *Journal of Archaeological Method,* 21 (2), 306-324.

Bataille, G., 1985. *Aufhebung der Ökonomie*. Berlin: Matthes & Seitz.

Batty, M., 2019. On the Confusion of Terminologies. *Environment and Planning B: Urban Analytics and City Science,* 46, 997-998.

Beckermann, A., ed., 1985. *Analytische Handlungstheorie. Bd. 2. Handlungserklärungen*. Frankfurt/M.: Suhrkamp.

Beckwith, C., 2009. *Empires of the Silk Road*. Princeton: Princeton University Press.

Bell, M. and Blais, J., 2021. Paleolimnology in support of archaeology: a review of past investigations and a proposed framework for future study design. *Journal for Paleolimnology,* 65, 1-32.

Bellah, R., 2011. *Religion in Human Evolution. From the Paleolithic to the Axial Age.* Cambridge/Mass: Belknap.

Bellini, G., Erfmeier, A., Schrieber, K., 2022. No Support for the Neolithic Plant Invasion Hypothesis: Invasive Species from Eurasia Do Not Perform Better Under Agropastoral Disturbances in Early Life Stages Than Invaders From Other Continents. *Frontiers in Plant Science,* 13, Article no. 801750.

Benjamin, W., 1940/1974. *Über den Begriff der Geschichte*. Gesammelte Schriften. Bd. I/2. Frankfurt/M.: Suhrkamp, 691-704.

Benjamin, W., 1940/1974. *On the Concept of History.* No. XVI. Transl. D. Redmond. Available at: https://www.marxists.org/reference/archive/benjamin/1940/history.htm.

Berking, H. and Löw, M., eds., 2008. *Eigenlogik der Städte.* Frankfurt/M.: Campus.

Bernbeck, R., 1997. *Theorien in der Archäologie*. Tübingen: Francke.

Bevan, A., 2015. The data deluge. *Antiquity,* 89, 1473-84.

Bezzel, C., 1996. *Wittgenstein zur Einführung*. Hamburg: Junius.

Bilz, R., 1971. *Paläoanthropologie*. Frankfurt/M.: Suhrkamp.

Binford, L.R. 1962. Archaeology as Anthropology. *American Antiquity,* 28 (2), 217-225.

Binford, L.R., 1981. Behavioral archaeology and the "Pompeii premise". *Journal of Anthropological Research*, 37, 195-208.

Bintliff, J.L., 1993. Why Indiana Jones is smarter than the Post-Processualists. *Norwegian Archaeological Review,* 26, 91-100.

Bintliff, J. and Pearce, M., eds., 2011. *The Death of Archaeological Theory?* Oxford: Oxbow.

Bird-David, N., 2017. Before Nation. *Current Anthropology,* 58 (2), 209-226.

Blackbourn, D., 2006. *The Conquest of Nature*. London: Random House.

Bloch, E., 1975. *Experimentum Mundi*. Frankfurt/M.: Suhrkamp.

Bloch, E., 1977. *Das Prinzip Verantwortung.* 3 Vol. Frankfurt/M.: Suhrkamp.

Bluhm, H., 1999. Das Atomzeitalter. *In*: K. Fischer, ed. *Neustart des Weltlaufs. Fiktion und Faszination der Zeitwende*. Frankfurt/M.: Suhrkamp, 203-224.

Blumenberg, H., 1986. *Weltzeit und Lebenszeit*. Frankfurt/M.: Suhrkamp.

Böhm, F. and Ott, K., 2019. *Impacts of Ocean Acidification*. Marburg: Metropolis.

Bogaard, A., 2005. 'Garden Agriculture' and the Nature of Early Farming in Europe and the near East. *World Archaeology,* 37 (2), 177-196.

Boivin, N. and Crowther, A., 2021. Mobilizing the past to shape a better Anthropocene. *Nature Ecology and Evolution*. DOI:10.1038/s41559-020-01361-4.

Bonetto, S., 2006. Race and Racism in Hegel - An Analysis. *Minerva,* 10, 35-64.

Bonfantini, M., 2000. Die Abduktion in Geschichte und Gesellschaft. In: U. Wirth, ed. *Die Welt als Zeichen und Hypothese*. Frankfurt/M.: Suhrkamp, 235-247.

Bonneiul, C., 2020. Der Historiker und der Planet. *In:* F. Adloff and S. Neckel, eds. *Gesellschaftstheorie im Anthropozän*. Frankfurt/M.: Campus, 55-92.

Bookchin, M., 1977. *Die Formen der Freiheit*. Asslar-Werdorf: Büchse der Pandora.

Bopp, C., 2019. *Rights as Weapons. Instruments of Conflict, Tools of Power*. Princeton: Princeton University Press.

Borgmann, A., 1984. *Technology and the Character of Contemporary Life*. Chicago, London: Chicago University Press.

Bornemann, F., 1970. D. Martin Gusinde S.V.D. (1886-1969). *Anthropos,* 65 (5/6), 737-757.

Bosinski, G., 2007. Die Entwicklung des Menschen bis zum Ende des Altpaläolithikum. *In*: A. Jockenhövel, ed. *WBG-Weltgeschichte, Band I: Grundlagen der globalen Welt. Vom Beginn bis 1200 v. Chr.* Darmstadt: WBG, 13-53.

Bourguignon, F., 2013. *Die Globalisierung der Ungleichheit*. Hamburg: HIS Verlag.

Bradtmöller, M., Grimm, S., Riel-Salvatore, J., 2017. Resilience theory in archaeological practice – An annotated review. *Quaternary International,* 446, 3-16.

Brandom, R.B., 1998. *Making It Explicit. Reasoning, Representing, and Discursive Commitment*. Cambridge/Mass.: Harvard University Press.

Braudel, F., Duby, G., Aymard, M., 1986. *La Méditerranée*. Paris: Flammarion.

Braungart, M. and McDonough, W., 2002. *Cradle to Cradle. Remaking the Way We Make Things*. New York: North Point Press.

Brozio, J.P., Müller, J., Furholt, M., Kirleis, W., Dreibrodt, S., Feeser, I., Dörfler, W., Weinelt, M., Raese, H., Bock, A., 2019. Monuments and economies: What drove their variability in the middle-Holocene Neolithic? *Holocene,* 29 (10), 1558-1571.

Brück, J. Stutz, L.N., 2016. Is archaeology still the project of nation states? An editorial comment. *Archaeological Dialogues,* 23 (1), 1-3.

Brumm, A., Pope, M., Leroyer, M., Emery, K., 2019. Hominin Evolution and Stone Scavenging and Reuse in the Lower Paleolithic. *In*: K. Overmann and F. Coolidge, eds. *Squeezing Minds from Stones*. Oxford: Oxford University Press, 149-178.

Brune, J.P., Stern, R., Werner, M., eds., 2017. *Transcendental Arguments in Moral Theory*. Berlin: De Gruyter.

Brunner, P., 2011. Urban Mining. *Journal of Industrial Ecology,* 15(3), 339-341.

Bunch, T., LeCompte, M.A., Adedeji, A.V., Wittke, J.H., Burleigh, T.D., Hermes, R.E., Mooney, C., Batchelor, D., Wolback, W.S., Kathan, J., Kletetschka, G., Patterson, M.C.L., Swindel, E.C., Witwer, T., Howard, G.A., Mitra, S., Moore, C.R., Langworthy, K., Kennett, J.P., West, A., Silvia, P.J., 2021. A Tunguska size airburst destroyed Tall el-Hammam a Middle Bronze Age City in the Jordan Valley near the Dead Sea. *Scientific Reports,* 11, Article no. 18632.

Burckhardt, J., 1905. *Weltgeschichtliche Betrachtungen*. München: DTV 1978.

Butler, J., 1991. *Gender Trouble*. London: Routledge.

Byrne, R.W., 2007. Animal Cognition: Bring Me My Spear. *Current Biology,* 17(5), 164-165.

Cafaro, P. and Sandler, R., eds., 2011. *Virtue Ethics and the Environment*. Springer: Netherlands.

Caillé, A., 2000. *Anthropologie du don*. Paris: Desclée de Brower.

Callicott, B. 1980. Animal Liberation. A Triangular Affair. *Environmental Ethics,* 2 (4), 311-328.

Camus, A., 1953. *L'Homme révolté*. Paris: Gallimard.

Carballo, D.M., Roscoe, P., Feinman, G.M., 2012. Cooperation and Collective Action in the Cultural Evolution of Complex Societies. *Journal of Archaeological Method and Theory,* 21, 98-133.

Carens, J., 2014. *The Ethics of Immigration*. Oxford: University Press.

Carlowitz, H.C. von, 1713/2013. *Silvicultura oeconomica*. München: Oekom.

Carneiro, R.L., 2000. The transition from quantity to quality: A neglected causal mechanism in accounting for social evolution. *PNSA,* 97 (23), 12926-12931.

Carson, R., 1962. *Silent Spring*. Mariner Books.

Cassidy, R. and Mullin, M., eds., 2007. *Where the Wild Things are Now. Domestication Reconsidered*. Oxford: Berg.

Cassirer, E., 1923/1964. *Philosophie der symbolischen Formen*. Darmstadt: WBG.

Cebalos, G., Ehrlich, P., Barnosky, A., Pringle, R., Palmer, T., 2015. Accelerated modern human-induced species loss: Entering the sixth mass extinction. *Science Advances,* 5, e1400255.

Chakrabarty, D., 2015. *The Human Condition in the Anthropocene*. Tanner Lectures on Human Values. Utah.

Chakrabarty, D., 2020. Der Planet als neue humanistische Kategorie. *In:* F. Adloff and S. Neckel, eds. *Gesellschaftstheorie im Anthropozän*. Frankfurt/M.: Campus, 23-53.

Chapman, J., 2000. Fragmentation in Archaeology: People, Places and Broken Objects in the Prehistory of South Eastern Europe. New York: Routledge.

Chapman, R. and Wylie, A., 2016. *Evidential Reasoning in Archaeology*. London: Bloomsbury.

Chiarenza, N., Haug, A., Müller, U., eds., 2020. *The Power of Urban Water*. Berlin: DeGruyter.

Childe, G.V., 1936. *Man Makes Himself*. London: Watts.

Childe, G.V., 1951. *Social Evolution*. London: Watts.

Cohen, M. and Armelagos, G., eds., 2013. *Paleopathology at the Origins of Agriculture*. Orlando: University of Florida Press.

Collier, P., 2008. *The Bottom Billion*. Oxford: Oxford University Press.

Cooper, D.A., 2006. *A Philosophy of Gardens*. Oxford: Oxford University Press.

Corlett, R., 2015. The Anthropocene concept in ecology and conservation. *Trends in Ecology and Evolution*, 30 (1), 36-41.

Cosme, I., Santos, R., O'Neill, D., 2017. Assessing the degrowth discourse: A review and analysis of academic degrowth policy proposals. *Journal of Cleaner Production*, 149, 321-334.

Crumley, C., 1995. Heterarchy and the Analysis of Complex Societies. *Archaeological Papers of the American Anthropological Association*, 6 (1), 1-5.

Dai, R. and Xue, D., 2019. Of rice, fish, ducks and humans. *The UNSECO Courier*, 2019-1.

Daly, H., 1996. *Beyond Growth*. Boston: Beacon.

Danto, A., 1965. *Analytical Philosophy of History*. Cambridge: University Press.

Darmangeat, C., 2020. Surplus, storage, and the emergence of wealth: pits and pitfalls. *In:* L. Moreau, ed. *Social inequality before farming?* Cambridge: McDonald Institute for Archaeological Research, 59-81.

Darwin, C., 1859. *On the Origins of Species*. London: Murray.

Davidovic, A., 2018. On Melting Grounds: Theories of the Landscape. *In*: A. Haug, L. Käppel, J. Müller, eds. *Past Landscapes. The Dynamics of Interactions between Society, Landscape and Culture*. Leiden: Sidestone Press, 53-72.

Davis, M., 2007. *Planet of Slums*. London: Verso.

Dawe, R., 1996. *Sophocles 'Antigone'*. Boston: Bibliotheca scriptorum Graecorum et Romanorum Teubneriana.

Death, J., 1887. *The Beer of the Bible*. Reprint EOD Bavaria 2013.

Degroot, D., Anchukaitis, K., Bauch, M., Burnham, J., Carnegy, F., Cui, J., de Luna, K., Guzowski, P., Hambrecht, G., Huhtamaa, H., Izdebski, A., Kleemann, K., Moesswilde, E., Neupane, N., Newfield, T., Pei, Q., Xoplaki, E., Zappia, N., 2021. Towards a rigorous understanding of societal responses to climate change. *Nature*, 591, 539-549.

Descola, P., 2005. *Par-dela nature et culture*. Paris: Gallimard.

Descombes, V., 2001. *The Mind's Provisions: A Critique of Cognitivism*. Princeton: Princeton University Press.

De-Shalit, A., 1994. *Why Posterity Matters*. London: Routledge.

Despommier, D., 2010. *The Vertical Farm: Feeding the World in the 21st Century*. New York: Thomas Dunne Books.

Dessauer, F., 1927. *Philosophie der Technik*. Bonn: Cohen.

Deutsche Stiftung Meeresschutz, 2022. *EU-Supertrawler*. Internet-Blog 12. January 2022.

Devereux, G., 1985. *Baubo. Die mythische Vulva*. Frankfurt/M.: Syndikat.

Dietler, M., 2020. Alcohol as Embedded Material Culture: Anthropological Reflections on the Deep Entanglement of Humans and Alcohol. *In*: K. Hockings and R. Dunbar, eds. *Alcohol and Humans*. Oxford: Oxford University Press, 115-129.

Dilthey, W., 1910/1981. *Der Aufbau der geschichtlichen Welt in den Geisteswissenschaften*. Frankfurt/M.: Suhrkamp.

Diop, C.A., 1974. *The African Origin of Civilization: Myth or Reality?* Los Angeles: A Cappella Books.

Dobres, M.-A. and Robb, J., 2000. *Agency in Archaeology*. London, New York: Routledge.

Dobres, M.-A. and Robb, J., 2005. 'Doing' Agency: Introductory Remarks on Methodology. *Journal of Archaeological Method and Theory*, 12 (3), 159-166.

Doorn, E. van, 2021. *Legal Implication of the 'Common-Heritage'-Principle for Atlantic Bluefin Tuna*. Berlin: Duncker & Humblot.

Dray, W., 1957/1964. *Laws and Explanation in History*. 3rd ed. Oxford: University Press.

Draycott, J., 2015. Smelling trees, flowers and herbs in the ancient world. *In:* M. Bradley, ed. *Smell and the Ancient Senses*. London: Routledge, 60-73.

Droysen, J.G., 1882/1974. *Historik*. Darmstadt: WBG.

Dunbar, R., 1993. Coevolution of Neocortial Size, Group Size, and Language. *Behavioral and Brain Sciences,* 16 (4), 681-694.

Dunne, T., Kurki, M., Smith, S., eds., 2013. *International Relations Theory*. 3rd ed. Oxford: Oxford University Press.

Dworkin, R., 1977. *Taking Rights Seriously*. Cambridge/Mass.: Harvard University Press.

Earle, T., Olsen, A.-L., Eriksen, B., Henriksen, P., Kristensen, I., 2022. Everyday Life at Bjerre Site 7, a Late Bronze Age House in Thy, Denmark. *European Journal of Archaeology*, 25 (3), 1-24.

Eggert, M., 2012. Prähistorische Archäologie. 4th ed. Tübingen, Basel: Francke.

Eisenstadt, S.N., 1965. *Essays on Comparative Institutions*. New York: John Wylie and Sons.

Elias, N., 1980. Über den Prozeß der Zivilisation. Frankfurt/M.: Suhrkamp.

Engel, C., 1942. Die Ausweitung unseres Geschichtsbildes durch die Vorgeschichte. Rektoratsrede am 2. Juni 1942 an der Ernst-Moritz-Arndt Universität Greifswald. *In:* G. Mangelsdorf, ed. *Zwischen Greifswald und Riga*. Stuttgart: Steiner, 307-316.

Engel, C., 1945. Erinnerungen an die letzten Kriegstage und die kampflose Übergabe Greifwalds. *In:* G. Mangelsdorf, ed. *Zwischen Greifswald und Riga*. Stuttgart: Steiner, 317-329.

Engel, C., 2007. Zwischen Greifswald und Riga. Tagebücher. Stuttgart: Steiner.

Engels, E.M., 1989. *Erkenntnis als Anpassung?* Frankfurt/M.: Suhrkamp.

Engels, F., 1845. *Die Lage der arbeitenden Klasse in England*. MEW 2, Bd. 25, 224-506.

Engels, F., 1884. Der Ursprung der Familie, des Privateigentums und des Staates. *In:* K. Marx and F. Engels, *Ausgewählte Schriften in zwei Bänden.,* Moskau: Verlag für fremdsprachliche Literatur, Bd. II, 159-318.

Engels, J.I., 2006. *Naturpolitik in der Bundesrepublik*. Paderborn: Schöningh.

Eser, U., 1999. *Der Naturschutz und das Fremde*. Frankfurt/M.: Campus.

Esping-Andersen, G., 1989. *The Three Worlds of Welfare Capitalism*. Princeton: Princeton University Press.

Evans, C., 1998. Historicism, chronology and straw men: situating Hawkes' 'Ladder of Inference'. *Antiquity,* 73, 398-404.

Evans-Pritchard, E.E., 1937/1976. *Witchcraft, Oracles and Magic among the Azande*. Oxford: Oxford University Press.

Falter, R., 2006. *Natur prägt Kultur*. München: Telesma.

Feeser, I. Dörfler, W., Kneisel, J., Hinz, M., Dreibrodt, S., 2019. Human impact and population dynamics in the Neolithic and bronze age: Multi-proxy evidence from north-western Central Europe. *Holocene,* 29 (10), 1596-1606.

Feyerabend, P., 1975/1993. *Against Method.* 3rd ed. London: Verso.

Fischer, J., 2007. Freie und unfreie Arbeit in der mykenischen Textilproduktion. *In:* M.E. Kabadayi and T. Reichardt, eds. *Unfreie Arbeit.* Hildesheim: Olms, 3-37.

Fischer, K., 1923. *Francis Bacon und seine Schule.* Heidelberg: Carl Winter.

Flaig, E., 2018. *Weltgeschichte der Sklaverei.* München: Beck.

Flannery, K. and Marcus, J., 2012. *The Creation of Inequality.* Harvard: Harvard University Press.

Flannery, T., 2018. *Europe. A Natural History.* Melbourne: Text Publishing.

Flechtheim, Ossip K., 1963. *Von Hegel zu Kelsen. Rechtstheoretische Aufsätze.* Berlin: Duncker & Humblot.

Fletcher, R., 2020. Urban Labels and Settlement Trajectories. *Journal of Urban Archaeology,* 1, 31-48.

Foley, R., 1995. *Humans before Humanity.* Oxford: Blackwell.

Foucault, M., 1975. *Surveiller et punir.* Paris: Gallimard.

Foucault, M., 1979. *Sexualität und Wahrheit. Der Wille zum Wissen.* Frankfurt/M.: Suhrkamp.

Fouquet, G., 2022. Die Pest in Lübeck und Schleswig-Holstein während des 14. Und 15. Jahrhunderts. *In:* U. Stephani, K. Ott, C. Bozzaro, eds. *Die Corona-Virus Pandemie und ihre Folgen.* Kiel: Kiel University Publishing, 269-295.

Franke, A., Blenckner, T., Duarte, C., Ott, K., Fleming, L., Antia, A., Reusch, T., Bertram, C., Hein, J., Kronfeld-Goharani, Dierking, J., Kuhn, A., Sato, C., Doorn, E. van, Wall, M., Schartau, M., Karez, R., Crowder, L., Keller, D., Engel, A., Hentschel, H., Prigge, E., 2020. Operationalizing Ocean Health: Toward Integrated Research on Ocean Health and Recovery to Achieve Ocean Sustainability. *One Earth,* 2 (6), 557-565.

Frankfurt, H., 2015. *On Inequality.* Princeton: Princeton University Press.

Freeman, D., 1983. *Margaret Mead and Samoa: The Making and Unmaking of an Anthropological Myth.* Cambridge: Harvard University Press.

Freud, S., 1930. *Das Unbehagen in der Kultur.* Studienausgabe Bd. 9, 193-270.

Fricke, C. and Schütt, H.-P., eds., 2005. *Adam Smith als Moralphilosoph.* Berlin: De Gruyter.

Fried, J., 2016. *Dies Irae. Eine Geschichte des Weltuntergangs.* München: Beck.

Friedjung, H., 1919. *Das Zeitalter des Imperialismus.* Berlin: Neufeld & Henius.

Fritz, J. and Plog, F., 1970. The Nature of Archaeological Explanation. *American Antiquity,* 35 (4), 405-412.

Fromm, E., 1941/2011. *Escape from Freedom.* Ishi Press.

Fuchs, K., Rinne, C., Drummer, C., Immel, A., 2019. Infectious diseases and Neolithic transformations: Evaluating biological and archaeological proxies in German loess zone between 5500 and 2500 BCE. *Holocene,* 29 (10), 1545-1557.

Furholt, M., Hinz, M., Mischka, D., 2018. Putting Things into Practice: Pragmatic Theory and the Exploration of Monumental Landscapes. *In:* A. Haug, L. Käppel, J. Müller, eds. *Past Landscapes: The Dynamics of Interactions between Society, Landscape and Culture.* Leiden: Sidestone Press, 87-106.

Gadamer, H.-G., 1965. *Wahrheit und Methode.* 2nd ed. Tübingen: Mohr.

Gadamer, H.-G. and Vogler, P., eds., 1974. *Neue Anthropologie. Band 7: Philosophische Anthropologie, Zweiter Teil.* Stuttgart: Thieme.

Galbraith, J.K., 1958. *The Affluent Society.* Houghton & Mifflin.

Gallay, A., 1990. L'ethnoarchéology. *Coloquio international arqueologica hoje,* 1, 282-302.

Gallie, W.B., 1955. Essentially contested concepts. *Proceedings of the Aristotelian Society,* 56, 167-198.

Gao, C., Ludlow, F., Matthews, J., Stine, A., Robock, A., Pan, Y., Breen, R., Nolan, B., Sigl, M., 2021. Volcanic climate impacts can act as ultimate and proximate causes of Chinese dynastic collapse. *Communications Earth and Environment,* Vol. 2(1), article id.234.

Geertz, C., 1973. *The Interpretation of Culture.* New York: Basic Books.

Gehlen, A., 1944. *Der Mensch. Seine Natur und seine Stellung in der Welt.* 3rd ed. Berlin: Junker und Dünnhaupt.

Gehlen, A., 1986. *Urmensch und Spätkultur.* Wiesbaden: Aula.

George, A.R., 2003. *The Babylonian Gilgamesh epic: introduction, critical edition and cuneiform texts.* Oxford: Oxford University Press.

Gerber, D., 2012. *Analytische Metaphysik der Geschichte.* Frankfurt/M.: Suhrkamp.

Gert, B., 1988. *Morality. A New Justification of the Moral Rules.* Oxford: Oxford University Press.

Geschiere, P., 1985. Applications of the Lineage Mode of Production in African Studies. *Canadian Journal of African Studies,* 19, 80-90.

Gewirth, A., 1978. *Reason and Morality.* Chicago: Chicago University Press.

Gibbon, E., 1776-1788/1952. *History of the Decline and Fall of the Roman Empire.* New York: Viking.

Gibbons, R. and Segal, C., 2008. *Antigone (Greek Tragedy in New Translations).* Oxford: Oxford University Press.

Giddens, A., 1979. *Central Problems in Social Theory: Action, Structure, and Contradiction in Social Analysis.* London: Macmillan.

Giddens, A., 1984. *The Constitution of Society: Outline of the Theory of Structuration.* Cambridge: Polity Press.

Giedion, S., 1948. *Mechanization Takes Command.* Oxford: Oxford University Press.

Gill, R., Mayeswki, P., Nyberg, J., Haug, G., Peterson, L., 2007. Drought and the Maya Collapse. *Ancient Mesoamerica,* 18, 283-302.

Gimbutas, M., 1982. *The Goddesses and Gods of Old Europe.* London: Thames and Hudson.

Ginzburg, C., 1979. *Der Käse und die Würmer.* Frankfurt/M.: Syndikat.

Glacken, C.J., 1967. *Traces on the Rhodian Shore.* Berkeley: University of California Press.

Glotz, G., 1926. *Ancient Greece at Work.* London: Kegan Paul. (reprint Hildesheim: Olms).

Golley, F.B., 1993. *A History of the Ecosystem Concept in Ecology. More than a Sum of the Parts.* New Haven, London: Yale University Press.

Gorke, M., 2003. *The Death of our Planet's Species: A Challenge to Ecology and Ethics.* Washington D.C.: Island Press.

Gosden, C., 2023. Foreword: Archaeological Science and the Big Questions. *In:* A.M. Pollard, R. Armitage, C. Makarewicz, eds. *Handbook of Archaeological Sciences.* 2nd Edition. Hoboken and Chichester: Wiley, xvii-xviii.

Gosselain, O.P., 2016. To hell with ethnoarchaeology! *Archaeological Dialogues,* 23 (2), 215-228.

Gossen, H. H., 1888. Entwicklung der Gesetze des menschlichen Verkehrs und der daraus fließenden Regeln für menschliches Handeln. 2nd Edition. Berlin.

Gottschalk-Mazouz, N., 2000. *Diskursethik.* Berlin: De Gruyter.

Gould, S.J., 1987. *Time's Arrow – Time's Cycle.* Cambridge, Mass: Harvard University Press.

Graeber, D., 2001. *Toward an Anthropological Theory of Value.* New York: Palgrave.

Graeber, D., 2011. *Debts: The First 5000 Years*. New York: Melville House.

Graeber, D., 2015. Radical Alterity is Just Another Way of Saying 'Reality'. *HAU: Journal of Ethnographic Theory*, 5 (2), 1-41.

Graeber, D., 2023. *Pirate Enlightenment, or the real Libertalia*. New York: Farrer, Straus and Giroux.

Graeber, D. and Wengrow, D., 2021. *The Dawn of Everything. A New History of Humanity*. New York: Farrer, Straus and Giroux.

Griffith, M., 1999. *Sophocles. Antigone*. Cambridge: Cambridge University Press.

Groß, D. Piezonka, H., Corradini, E, Schmölcke, U., Zanon, M., Dörfler, W., Dreibrodt, S., Feeser, I., Krüger, S., Lübcke, H., Panning, D., Wilken, D., 2019. Adaptation and transformations of hunter-gatherers in forest environments: New archaeological and anthropological insights. *The Holocene*, 29 (10), 1531-1544.

Grotius, H., 1608/1916. *Mare liberum sive de iure quod Batavis competit ad indicana commercia*. Translated by R. van Deman Magoffin. The Freedom of the Seas. New York: Oxford University Press 1916.

Guerra-Doce, E., 2020. The Earliest Toasts: Archaeological Evidence of the Social and Cultural Construction of Alcohol in Prehistoric Europe. *In:* K. Hockings and R. Dunbar, eds. *Alcohol and Humans*. Oxford: Oxford University Press, 60-80.

Guratzsch, H. and Carnap-Bornheim, C. von, 2005. *Wege ins Jenseits*. Neumünster: Wachholtz.

Gusinde, M., 1961. *The Yamana: Life and Thought of the Water Nomads of Cape Horn*. New Haven: Human Relations Area Files.

Gyekye, K., 1997. *Tradition and Modernity. Philosophical Reflection on the African Experience*. New York: Oxford University Press.

Haber, W., 2016. Landschaft. *In:* K. Ott, J. Dierks, L. Voget-Kleschin, eds. *Handbuch Umweltethik*. Stuttgart: Metzler, 26-30.

Habermas, J., 1965. Erkenntnis und Interesse. *In:* H. Albert and E. Topitsch, eds. *Werturteilsstreit*. Darmstadt: WBG 1979, 334-352.

Habermas, J., 1976. *Zur Rekonstruktion des Historischen Materialismus*. Frankfurt/M.: Suhrkamp.

Habermas, J., 1981. *Theorie des kommunikativen Handelns*. Frankfurt/M.: Suhrkamp.

Habermas, J., 1983. *Moralbewußtsein und kommunikatives Handeln*. Frankfurt/M.: Suhrkamp.

Habermas, J., 1984. *Der philosophische Diskurs der Moderne*. Frankfurt/M.: Suhrkamp.

Habermas, J., 1992. *Faktizität und Geltung*. Frankfurt/M.: Suhrkamp.

Habermas, J. 2005. Religion in der Öffentlichkeit. *In:* J. Habermas, *Zwischen Naturalismus und Religion*. Frankfurt/M.: Suhrkamp, 119-154.

Habermas, J., 2009. *Treffen Hegels Einwände gegen Kant auch auf die Diskursethik zu?* Studienausgabe Bd. 4. Frankfurt/M.: Suhrkamp, 116-140.

Habermas, J., 2019. *Auch eine Geschichte der Philosophie*. Berlin: Suhrkamp.

Habermas, J., 2022. *Ein neuer Strukturwandel der Öffentlichkeit und die deliberative Politik*. Berlin: Suhrkamp.

Haeckel, E., 1870. *Natürliche Schöpfungsgeschichte*. Berlin: Reimer.

Halbwachs, M., 1985. *Das kollektive Gedächtnis*. Frankfurt/M.: Fischer.

Halstead, P., 1981. Counting Sheep in Neolithic and Bronze Age Greece. *In*: I. Hodder and N. Hammond, eds. *Patterns of the Past*. Cambridge: Cambridge University Press, 307-337.

Hampicke, U., 2018. *Kulturlandschaft*. Berlin: Springer.

Haraway, D., 2016. *Staying with the Trouble: Making Kin in the Chthulucene*. Durham and London: Duke University Press.

Hardmeier, C. and Ott, K., 2015. *Naturethik und biblische Schöpfungserzählung*. Stuttgart: Kohlhammer.

Harich, W., 1975. *Kommunismus ohne Wachstum*? Reinbek: Rowohlt.

Harper, K., 2017. *The Fate of Rome. Climate, Disease, and the End of an Empire*. Princeton: University Press.

Haug, A., Käppel, L., Müller, J., eds., 2018. *Past Landscapes: The Dynamics of Interactions between Society, Landscape and Culture*. Leiden: Sidestone Press.

Hausman, D., 2011. *Preference, Value, Choice, and Welfare*. Cambridge: Cambridge University Press.

Hawkes, C., 1954. Archaeological Theory and Method: Some Suggestions from the Old World. *American Anthropologists*, 56 (2), 155-168.

Hayden, B., 2009. *The Proof Is in the Pudding: Feasting and the Origins of Domestication. Current Anthropology*, 50, 597-601.

Hayden, B., 2014. *The Power of Feasts*. Cambridge: Cambridge University Press.

Hegel, G.F.W., 1821/1970. *Grundlinien der Philosophie des Rechts*. Werkausgabe, Bd. 7. Frankfurt/M.: Suhrkamp.

Hegel, G.F.W., 1822-1832/1970. *Vorlesungen über die Philosophie der Geschichte*. Werkausgabe, Bd. 12. Frankfurt/M.: Suhrkamp.

Hegel, G.F.W. 1845/1958. *System der Philosophie. Dritter Teil. Die Philosophie des Geistes*. Jubiläumsausgabe (ed. Glockner), Zehnter Band. Stuttgart: Holzboog.

Heidegger, M., 1927/1979. *Sein und Zeit*. 15th ed. Tübingen: Niemeyer.

Heidegger, M., 1949/1981. Über den Humanismus. Frankfurt/M.: Klostermann.

Heidegger, M., 1951/2022. *Bauen, Wohnen, Denken*. Stuttgart: Klett-Cotta.

Heidegger, M., 1962. *Die Technik und die Kehre*. Pfullingen: Neske.

Heilbroner, R., 1953/1999. *The Wordly Philosophers*. New York: Touchstone.

Heinz, M., Eggert, M., Veit, U., eds., 2003. *Zwischen Erklären und Verstehen?* Tübinger Archäologische Hefte, Bd. 2. Münster: Waxmann.

Hempel, C.G. and Oppenheim, P., 1948. Studies in the Logic of Explanation. *Philosophy of Science*, 15, 135-175.

Hendlin, Y. and Ott, K., 2016. Habermas on Nature: A Postnormal Reading Between Moral Intuition and Theoretical Restrictiveness. *Environmental Ethics*, 38 (2), 183-208.

Henrich, K., 2003. *Biodiversitätsvernichtung*. Marburg: Metropolis.

Herder, J.G., 1784/1976. *Ideen zur Philosophie der Geschichte der Menschheit*. Darmstadt: Melzer.

Herder, J.G., 1793-1797/2022: *Briefe zur Beförderung der Humanität*. Berlin: Holzinger.

Herzog, L., 2018. *Freiheit gehört nicht nur den Reichen*. München: Beck.

Hill, T., 1971. Kant on Imperfect Duty and Supererogation. *Kant-Studien*, 62, 55-76.

Hinsch, M., 2022. Tagungsbericht 'Systemtheorie und antike Gesellschaft. *H-Soz-Kult*, 23.5.2022.

Hirschman, A.O., 1977. *The Passions and the Interests: Political Arguments for Capitalism before Its Triumph*. Princeton: Princeton University Press.

Hobohm, C., 2021. Environmental History. *In:* C. Hobohm, ed. *Perspectives for Biodiversity and Ecosystems*. Switzerland: Springer Nature, 3-16.

Hobsbawn, E. and Ranger, T., 1992. *Inventing Traditions*. Cambridge: Cambridge University Press.

Hockings, K. and Dunbar, R., eds., 2020. *Alcohol and Humans*. Oxford: Oxford University Press.

Hodgson, B., 2001. *Economics as Moral Science*. Heidelberg: Springer.

Hönigswald, R., 1937. *Philosophie und Sprache*. Basel: Haus zum Falken.

Holzhey, H., ed., 1994. *Ethischer Sozialismus*. Frankfurt/M.: Suhrkamp.

Honing, H., 2018. Musicality as an Upbeat to Music: Introduction and Research Agenda. *In:* Honing, H., ed. *The Origins of Musicality*. Cambridge: MIT Press, 3-20.

Honing, H., ed., 2018. *The Origins of Musicality*. Cambridge: MIT Press.

Horkheimer, M., 1937/1968. Über traditionelle und kritische Theorie. *In:* M. Horkheimer, *Kritische Theorie II*. Frankfurt/M.: Fischer, 137-191.

Horkheimer, M., 1937/1972. Critical Theory. Selected Essays. Transl. by M.J. O'Connell *et al.* New York: Continuum, 227. Available at: https://criticaltheoryworkshop.com/wp-content/uploads/2018/03/horkheimer_traditional-and-critical-theory.pdf.

Horkheimer, M., 1947. *Eclipse of Reason*. New York: Oxford University Press.

Horkheimer, M. and Adorno, T.W., 1944/1947. *Dialektik der Aufklärung*. Frankfurt/M.: Fischer.

Horn, E. and Bergthaller, H., 2019. *Anthropozän zur Einführung*. Hamburg: Junius.

Horstmann, R.-P., 1984. *Ontologie und Relationen*. Königstein: Athenäum.

Horta, O., 2017. Animal Suffering in Nature: The Case for Intervention. *Environmental Ethics*, 39 (3), 261-279.

Hughes, T.P., 1989. *American Genesis*. Viking Penguin.

Huizinga, J., 1938/1949. *Homo Ludens*. Basel und Köln: Pantheon.

Humboldt, W. von, 1829/1979. Über die Verschiedenheiten des menschlichen Sprachbaus. Werke Bd. III. Darmstadt: WBG, 144-367.

Huron, D., 2018. Affect Induction through Musical Sounds: An Ethological Perspective. *In:* H. Honing, ed. *The Origins of Musicality*. Cambridge/Mass: MIT Press, 309-322.

Hurrell, A., 2007. *On Global Order: Power, Values and the Constitution of International Society*. Oxford: Oxford University Press.

Husserl, E., 1936/2012. *Die Krisis der europäischen Wissenschaften und die transzendentale Phänomenologie*. Hamburg: Meiner.

Ingold, T., 2017. Taking taskscape to task. *In:* U. Rajalla and P. Mills, eds. *Forms of Dwelling. 20 Years of Taskscapes in Archaeology*. Oxford: Oxbow, 16-27.

Jacob, D., Birkmann, J., Bollig, M., Bonn, A., Nöthlings, U., Ott, K., Quaas, M., Reichstein, M., Scholz, I., Malburg-Graf, B., Sonntag, S., 2022. *Research priorities for sustainability science. Position Paper German Committee Future Earth*. Hamburg: DKN.

James, W., 1907/1975. *Pragmatism: A New Name for Some Old Ways of Thinking*. Cambridge/Mass.: Harvard University Press.

Jaspers, K., 1953. The Origin and Goal of History, translated by M. Bullock. New Haven: Yale University Press, 25.

Jaspers, K., 1955. *Vom Ursprung und Ziel der Geschichte*. Frankfurt/M: Fischer.

Jefferson, T., 1787. *Notes on the State of Virginia*. London: Stockdale. Electronic Text Center. University of Virginia Library [Last access: November 2022].

Jetzkowitz, C., van Koppen, K., Lidskog, R., Ott, K., Voget-Kleschin, L., Wong, C., 2017. The significance of meaning. Why IPBES needs the social sciences and humanities. *Innovation: The European Journal of Social Science Research,* DOI:10.1080/13511610.2017.1348933.

Jisheng, Y., 2012. *Grabstein*. Frankfurt: Fischer.

Jobin, W., 1999. *Dams and Disease: Ecological Design and Health Impacts of Large Dams, Canals and Irrigation Systems*. London: Taylor & Francis, Routledge.

Jockenhövel, A., ed., 2009. *WBG-Weltgeschichte I: Grundlagen der globalen Welt. Vom Beginn bis 1200 v. Chr*. Darmstadt: WBG.

Johnson, M., 1989. Conceptions of agency in archaeological interpretation. *Journal of Anthropological Archaeology*, 8, 189-211.

Jonas, H., 1970. *Wandel und Bestand. Vom Grund der Verstehbarkeit des Geschichtlichen.* Frankfurt/M.: Klostermann.

Jonas, H., 1979. *Das Prinzip Verantwortung.* Frankfurt/M.: Insel

Jouanna, J., 2018. *Sophocles. A Study of His Theater in Its Political and Social Context.* Princeton: Princeton University Press.

Jung, C.G., 1981. *Symbole der Wandlung.* Collected Works 5. Olten: Walter.

Kabadayi, M.E. and Reichardt, T., 2007. *Unfreie Arbeit. Ökonomische und kulturgeschichtliche Perspektiven.* Hildesheim: Olms.

Kallhoff, A. and Schörgenhumer, M., 2017. The Virtue of Gardening: A Relational Account of Environmental Values. *Environmental Ethics,* 39 (2), 193-210.

Kallhoff, A., Di Paola, M., Schörgenhumer, M., eds., 2018. *Plant Ethics.* London: Routledge.

Kallis, G., 2018. *Degrowth.* Newcastle: Agenda.

Kamerbeek, J.C., 1978. *The Plays of Sophocles. Commentaries 3: Antigone.* Brill: Leiden.

Kant, I., 1781. *Kritik der reinen Vernunft.* Werke III (ed. Weischedel), Frankfurt/M.: Suhrkamp 1982.

Kant, I., 1783. *Prolegomena zu einer jeden künftigen Metaphysik.* Hamburg: Meiner 1976.

Kant, I., 1783/2017. Prolegomena [= Preliminaries] to any Future Metaphysic that can Present itself as a Science. Transl. J. Bennett. Available at: https://www.earlymoderntexts.com/assets/pdfs/kant1783_3.pdf.

Kant, I., 1785. *Grundlegung zur Metaphysik der Sitten.* Werke VII (ed. Weischedel) Frankfurt/M.: Suhrkamp 1982.

Kant, I., 1795. *Zum ewigen Frieden.* Königsberg: Nicolovius. Stuttgart: Reclam.

Kant, I., 1797. *Metaphysik der Sitten.* Werke VIII (ed. Weischedel), Frankfurt/M.: Suhrkamp 1982.

Kappeler, P., ed., 2010. *Animal Behaviour: Evolution and Mechanisms.* Heidelberg: Springer

Karafyllis, N., 2004. *Biofakte.* Paderborn: Mentis.

Karatani, K., 2014. *The Structure of World History. From Modes of Production to Modes of Exchange.* Durham: Duke University Press.

Kaulbach, F., 1982. *Einführung in die Philosophie des Handelns.* Darmstadt: Wissenschaftliche Buchgesellschaft.

Kekes, J., 1990. *Facing Evil.* Princeton: Princeton University Press.

Kellert, S., 1997. *Kinship to Mastery: Biophilia in Human Evolution and Development.* Washington: Island Press.

Kellerwessel, W., 1995. *Referenztheorien in der analytischen Philosophie.* Stuttgart: Frommann and Holzboog.

Kelley, J.H. and Hanen, M.P., 1988. *Archaeology and the Methodology of Science.* Albuquerque: University of New Mexico Press.

Kelly, R.L., 2013. *The Lifeways of Hunter-Gatherers: The Foraging Spectrum.* Cambridge: Cambridge University Press.

Kerig, T., Bröker, J., Ohlrau, R., Schreiber, T., Skorna, H., Wilkes, F., 2023. An archaeological perspective on social structure, connectivity, and measurement of social inequality. *In*: J. Müller, ed. *Connectivity Matters!* Leiden: Sidestone, 93-114.

Keßler, L. and Ott, K., 2017. *Nec provident future tempori, sed quasi plane in diem vivant* – Sustainable Business in Columella's De Re Rustica? In: C. Schliephake, ed. *Ecocriticism, Ecology, and the Cultures of Antiquity.* Lanham: Lexington, 197-216.

Kettering, E. 1987. *Nähe. Das Denken Martin Heideggers.* Pfullingen: Neske.

Keyserlingk, J.G., 2018. *Immigration Control in a Warming World.* Exeter: Imprint Academic.

Khanna, P., 2021. *Move.* New York: Scribner.

Kirleis, W., 2018. The Cultural Significance of Plants. *In:* A. Haug, L. Käppel, J. Müller, eds. *Past Landscapes. The Dynamics of Interactions between Society, Landscape and Culture.* Leiden: Sidestone Press, 169-182.

Kirleis, W., Dal Corso, M., Filipovic, D., eds., 2022. *Millet and What Else?* Leiden: Sidestone.

Kitto, H.D.F. and Hall, E., eds., 1962/2017. *Oxford World's Classics: Sophocles: Antigone; Oedipus the King; Electra.* Oxford: Oxford University Press. Published online May 2017.

Klein, W., 2009. Conceptions of Time. *In:* W. Klein and P. Li, eds. *The Expression of Time.* Berlin: De Gruyter, 5-38.

Kliszcz, A. and Komorowska, J., 2017. Glades of Dread: The Ecology of *loca horrida. In:* C. Schliephake, ed. *Ecocriticism, Ecology, and the Cultures of Antiquity.* Lanham: Lexington, 45-60.

Kluckhorn, K., 1951. Values and Value-orientations in the Theory of Action. *In:* T. Parsons and E. Shils, eds. *Toward a General Theory of Action.* Cambridge: Harvard University Press, 388-433.

Kluckhorn, K., 1961. The Study of Values. *In:* D. Barrett, ed. *Values in America.* Notre Dame: Notre Dame University Press, 17-45.

Kneisel, J., Dörfler, W., Dreibrodt, S., Schaefer-Di Maida, S., Feeser, I., 2019. Cultural change and population dynamics during the Bronze Age: Integrating archaeological and paleoenvironmental evidence for Schleswig-Holstein, Northern Germany. *The Holocene,* 29 (10), 1607-1621.

Kögler, H.-H., 1992. *Die Macht des Dialogs. Kritische Hermeneutik nach Gadamer, Foucault und Rorty.* Stuttgart: Metzler.

Kohler, T. and Smith, M., eds., 2018. *Ten Thousand Years of Inequality.* Tucson: University of Arizona Press.

Kohler, T., Smith, M., Bogaard, A., Feinman, G., Peterson, C., Betzenhauser, A., Pailes, M. Stone, E., Prentiss, A., Dennehy, T., Ellyson, L., Nicholas, L., Faulseit, R., Styring, A., Whitlam, J., Fochesato, M., Foor, T., Bowles, S., 2017. Greater post-Neolithic wealth disparities in Eurasia than in North America and Mesoamerica. *Nature,* 551, No. 24646, 619-622.

Kollert, G., 2000. *Der Gesang des Meeres. Die portugiesischen Entdeckungsfahrten als Mythos der Neuzeit.* Frankfurt/M.: Insel.

Korsgaard, C.M., 1996. *Creating the Kingdom of Ends.* Cambridge: Cambridge University Press.

Kortetmäki, T., 2022. *Agriculture and Climate Change. Ethical Considerations.* Bern: ECNH.

Kosso, P., 1991. Method in Archaeology: Middle-Range Theory as Hermeneutics. *American Antiquity,* 56 (4), 621-627.

Krader, L., 1976. Einleitung. *In*: K. Marx, 1976. *Die ethnologischen Exzerpthefte.* Frankfurt/M.: Suhrkamp, 9-122.

Kralemann, B. and Lattmann, C., 2013. Models as icons: modelling models in the semiotic framework of Peirce's theory of signs. *Synthese,* 190, 3397-3420.

Krause-Kyora, B., 2022. Epidemien als Motor der Entwicklung seit der Steinzeit. *In:* U. Stephani, K. Ott, C. Bozzaro, eds. *Die Corona-Virus Pandemie und ihre Folgen.* Kiel: Kiel University Publishing, 241-267.

Kretschmer, I., 2015. *Demographische Untersuchungen zu Bevölkerungsdichten, Mobilität und Landnutzungsmustern im späten Jungpaläolithikum.* Rahden: Leidorf.

Kristensen, P., 2004. *The DPSIR Framework.* National Environmental Research Institute. Department of Policy Analysis. Denmark.

Kristiansen, K., 2014. Towards a new paradigm? The third science revolution and its possible consequences in archeology. *Current Swedish Archaeology*, 22 (1), 11-34.

Kristiansen, K., 2022. *Archaeology and the Genetic Revolution*. Cambridge: Cambridge University Press.

Kristiansen, K. and Larsson, T.B., 2005. *The rise of Bronze Age society: travels, transmissions and transformations*. Cambridge: Cambridge University Press.

Kristiansen, K., Allenthoft, M.E., Frei, K.M., Iversen, R., Johannsen, N.N., Kroonen, G., Pospieszny, L., Price, T.D., Rasmussen, S., Soegren, K.-G., 2017. Re-theorising mobility and the formation of culture and language among the Cord Ware Culture in Europe. *Antiquity,* 91, 3343-47.

Kropotkin, P.A., 1902. *Mutual Aid: A Factor in Evolution*. Reprint Project Gutenberg E-Books, No. 4341.

Kruse, A., 1997. *Geschichte der volkswirtschaftlichen Ideen*. 6th ed. Berlin: Duncker and Humblot.

Kruse, F., Nobles, G., Jong, M., Bodegom, R. van, Oortmerssen, G. van, Kooistra, J. Berg, M. van den, Küchelmann, H., Schepers, M., Leusink, E., Cornelder, B., Kruijer, H., Dee, M., 2021. Human-environment interaction at a short-lived Artic mine and the long-term response of the local tundra vegetation. *Polar Record,* 57 (3), 1-22.

Künzli, A., 1986. *Mein und Dein. Zur Geschichte der Eigentumsfeindlichkeit*. Köln: Bund Verlag.

Kuhn, T.S., 1962. *The Structure of Scientific Revolutions*. Chicago: Chicago University Press.

Laak, D. van, 1999. *Weiße Elefanten*. Stuttgart: DVA.

Lafont, C., 2020. *Democracy without Shortcuts*. Oxford: Oxford University Press.

Lakatos, I., 1970. Falsification and the Methodology of Scientific Research Programme. *In*: I. Lakatos and A. Musgrave, eds. *Criticism and the Growth of Knowledge*. Cambridge: Cambridge University Press, 91-195.

Lane, C., 2023. Quaternary Geochronological Frameworks. *In*: A.M. Pollard, R. Armitage, C. Makarewicz, eds. *Handbook of Archaeological Sciences*. 2nd Edition. Hoboken and Chichester: Wiley, Vol. 1, 7-24.

Latour, B., 2017. *Kampf um Gaia*. Berlin: Suhrkamp.

Lear, J., 2008. *Radical Hope*. Harvard: University Press.

Le Corbusier, 1930. *Precisions. On the Present State of Architecture and City Planning*. Cambridge/Mass: MIT Press 1991.

Lee, R., 1968. What Hunters Do for a Living, or, How to Make Out on Scarce Resources. *In*: R. Lee and I. DeVore, eds. *Man the Hunter*. Chicago: Aldine, 30-48.

LeGoff, J., 1988. *Wucherzins und Höllenqualen*. Stuttgart: Klett-Cotta.

Leigh, M., 1999. Lucan's Caesar and the Sacred Grove. Deforestation and Enlightenment in Antiquity. *In:* N. Esposito and L. Nicastri, eds. *Interpretare Lucano*. Naples: Arte Tipographica, 167-205.

Lenneberg, E., 1967. *Biological Foundations of Language*. New York: Wiley and Sons.

Leopold, A., 1949/1989. *A Sand County Almanac. And Sketches here and there*. Oxford: Oxford University Press.

Leroi-Gourhan, A., 1980. *Hand und Wort*. Frankfurt/M.: Suhrkamp.

Levy-Bruhl, L., 1930/1956. *Die Seele der Primitiven*. Darmstadt: WBG.

Lévy-Strauss, C., 1962/1981. *Das wilde Denken*. Frankfurt/M.: Suhrkamp.

Lie, S., 2016. *Philosophy of Nature*. London: Routledge.

Lobo, J., Bettencourt, L.; Smith, M., Ortman, S., 2019. Settlement scaling theory: Bridging the study of ancient and contemporary urban system. *Urban Studies,* 57 (4), 1-17.

Lombard, M., 2019. On the Minds of Bow Hunters. *In:* K. Overmann and F. Coolidge, eds. *Squeezing Minds from Stones*. Oxford: University Press, 473-496.

Loos, C., 2021. Ludwig Feuerbachs Kritik an ‚theologischen und anthropologischen Ungeheuerlichkeiten und Unverträglichkeiten'. *In:* H. Bajohr and S. Edinger, eds. *Negative Anthropologie*. Berlin: De Gruyter, 103-124.

Love, H. and Sulikowski, D., 2018. Of Meat and Men: Sex Differences in Implicit and Explicit Attitudes Toward Meat. *Frontiers in Psychology*, 9, article no. 559.

Lowe, A., 1965. *On Economic Knowledge*. New York: Harper and Row.

Luhmann, N., 1984. *Soziale Systeme*. Frankfurt/M.: Suhrkamp.

Luhmann, N., 1986. Ökologische Kommunikation. Opladen: Westdeutscher Verlag.

Luhmann, N., 2008. *Liebe*. Frankfurt/M.: Suhrkamp.

Lund, J., Fuhrholt, M., Austvoll, K., 2022. Reassessing power in the archaeological discourse. *Archaeological Dialogues*, DOI:10.1017/S1380203822000162, 1-18

Lyotard, J.-F., 1987. The Postmodern Condition. *In:* K. Baynes, J. Bohmann, T. McCarthy, eds. *After Philosophy*. Cambridge/Mass: MIT Press, 73-94.

MacIntyre, A., 1970. *Herbert Marcuse*. London: Collins & Co.

MacIntyre, A., 1984. *After Virtue*. Notre Dame: Notre Dame University Press.

Mahan, A., 1897. *The Interest of America in Sea Power, Present and Future*. Boston: Little, Brown and Co.

Maier, M., 2019. *Geschichte der Völkerwanderung*. München: Beck.

Maine, H.S., 1876. *Village Communities*: East and West. London.

Malafouris, L., 2013. *How Things Shape Minds. A Theory of Material Engagement*. Cambridge/Mass: MIT Press.

Malek, A.-A., ed., 2013. *Sourcebook for Garden Archaeology*. Frankfurt: Peter Lang.

Marcuse, H., 1955. *Eros and Civilization*. Boston: Beacon Press.

Marcuse, H., 1964. *One-Dimensional Man*. Boston: Beacon Press.

Marrou, H.-I., 1973. Über die historische Erkenntnis. Freiburg: Alber.

Marsh, G.P., 1864. *Man and Nature. The Earth as Modified by Human Action*. New York.

Martinón-Torres, M. and Killick, D., 2014. *Archaeological Theories and Archaeological Sciences*. Oxford Handbooks Online. Oxford University Press.

Marx, K., 1844. *Auszüge aus James Mills Buch "Élémens d'économie politique"*. MEW Ergänzungsband 1, Berlin: Dietz, 445-463.

Marx, K., 1845. *Thesen über Feuerbach*. MEW 3. Berlin: Dietz, 5-7.

Marx, K., 1859. *Zur Kritik der Politischen Ökonomie*. MEW 13, Berlin: Dietz, 3-160.

Marx, K., 1863. *Das Kapital*. Erster Band. MEW 23 Berlin: Dietz.

Marx, K., 1972. *The Ethnological Notebooks* (ed. Krader). Assen: Van Gorcum & Comp. B.V.

Marx, K. and Engels, F., 1846. *Die deutsche Ideologie*. MEW 3, Berlin: Dietz, 9-530.

Marx, K. and Engels, F., 1848. *Manifest der kommunistischen Partei*. MEW 4, Berlin: Dietz, 459-493.

Marx, K. (ed. F. Engels), 1894. *Das Kapital*. Dritter Band. MEW 25 Berlin: Dietz.

Marz, J., Ayhan, S., Gavard, C., Schenker, O., Sievert, M., Will, U., Winkler, M., 2022. *Capital Markets, Institutions and Distributional Effects: Towards Ambitious Climate Policy in Low- and Middle-Income Countries*. Background Paper Forum Climate Economics No. 9. IFO-Institute.

Maslow, A.H., 1943. A Theory of Human Motivation. *Psychological Review*, 50, 370-396.

Mauelshagen, F., 2016. Der Verlust der biokulturellen Diversität im Anthropozän. *In:* W. Haber, M. Held, M. Vogt, eds. *Die Welt im Anthropozän*. München: Oekom, 39-56.

Mauss, M., 1925. Essai sur le don. Forme et raison de l'éxchange dans les socíetés archaiqué. *Annee sociologique*, 1 (series 2), 30-186.

Mbembe, A., 2016. *Ausgang aus der langen Nacht*. Berlin: Suhrkamp.

McCaffree, K., 2022. *Cultural Evolution: the empirical and theoretical landscape*. New York: Routledge.

McGovern, P., 2020. Uncorking the Past: Alcoholic Fermentation as Humankind's First Biotechnology. *In:* K. Hockings and R. Dunbar, eds. *Alcohol and Humans*. Oxford: Oxford University Press, 81-92.

McGranaghan, M., 2017. Ethnographic Analogy in Archaeology: Methodological Insights from Southern Africa. *Oxford Research Encyclopedia of African History*, online access.

McGuire, R.H., 1992. *A Marxist Archaeology*. San Diego: Academic Press.

McGuire, R.H., 1993. Archaeology and Marxism. *Archaeological Method and Theory*, 5, 101-157.

Mead, G.H., 1910/1987. Soziales Bewußtsein und das Bewußtsein von Bedeutungen. *In:* G.H. Mead, *Gesammelte Aufsätze 1*. Frankfurt/M.: Suhrkamp, 210-240.

Mead, G.H., 1934. *Mind, Self and Society*. Chicago: University Press.

Mead, M., 1928. *Coming of Age in Samoa*. New York: William Morrow & Co.

Meadows, D., Meadows, D., Randers, J., 1972. *Limits to Growth. A Report for the Club of Rome's Project on the Predicament of Mankind*. New York: Universe Book.

Meier, M., 2020. *Geschichte der Völkerwanderung*. München: Beck.

Meillassoux, C., 1981. *Maidens, Meal and Money: Capitalism and the Domestic Community*. Cambridge: Cambridge University Press.

Merton, R.K., 1949. On Sociological Theories of the Middle Range. *In:* R.K. Merton, *Social Theory and Social Structure*. New York: Free Press 1968, 39-72.

Merton, R.K., 1968. *Social Theory and Social Structure*. New York: Free Press.

Meuter, N., 2014. Narration in Various Disciplines. *In:* P. Hühn, J. Pier, W. Schmid, W. Schönert, eds. *Handbook of Narratology*. Berlin: De Gruyter.

Michéa, J.-C., 2007. *L'empire du moindre mal. Essai sur la civilisation libérale*. Paris: Flammarion.

Miera, J., ed. 2023. *Narrating the Past: Archaeological Epistemology, Explanation and Communication*. Archaeolingua Series 46. Budapest: Archaeolingua Foundation.

Mikkelsen, M., 2020. Slaves in Bronze Age Southern Scandinavia? *Acta Archaeologica*, 91 (1), 147-190.

Milanovic, B., 2016. *Global Inequality*. Cambridge, London: Belknap.

Mill, J.S., 1871/1909. Principles of Political Economy. (ed. Ashley) London: Longman, Greene and Co.

Mittnik, A., Massy, K., Knipper, C., Wittenborn, F., Friedrich, R., Pfrengle, S., Burri, M., Carlichi-Witjes, N., Deeg, H., Furtwängler, A., Harbeck, M., Heyking, K. von, Kociumaka, C., Kucukkalipci, I., Lindauer, S., Metz, S., Staskiewicz, A., Thiel, A., Wahl, J., Haak, W., Pernicka, E., Schiffels, S., Stockhammer, P., Krause, J., 2019a. Kinship-based social inequality in Bronze Age Europe. *Science*, 10.1126/science.aax6219.

Mittnik, A., Massy, K., Knipper, C., Wittenborn, F., Friedrich, R., Pfrengle, S., Burri, M., Carlichi-Witjes, N., Deeg, H., Furtwängler, A., Harbeck, M., Heyking, K. von, Kociumaka, C., Kucukkalipci, I., Lindauer, S., Metz, S., Staskiewicz, A., Thiel, A., Wahl, J., Haak, W., Pernicka, E., Schiffels, S., Stockhammer, P., Krause, J., 2019b. Supplementary Material for Kinship-based social inequality in Bronze Age Europe. *Science*, 3-68. 10.1126/science.aax6219.

Mizoguchi, K., 2015. A future of archaeology. *Antiquity*, 89, 12-22.

Mizoguchi, K. and Smith, C.E., 2019. *Global Social Archaeologies: Making a Difference in a World of Strangers*. London and New York: Routledge.

Moll, B., 1956. *Logik des Geldes*. Berlin: Duncker and Humblot.

Mommsen, W., 1979. *Der europäische Imperialismus*. Göttingen: Vandenhoeck & Ruprecht.

Moore, J.W., 2016a. Anthropocene or Capitalocene? Nature, History, and the Crisis of Capitalism. *In:* J.W. Moore, ed. *Anthropocene or Capitalocene?* Oakland: PM Press, 1-11.

Moore, J.W., 2016b. The Rise of Cheap Nature. *In:* J.W. Moore, ed. *Anthropocene or Capitalocene?* Oakland: PM Press, 88-113.

Moreland, J., 2001. *Archaeology and Text*. London: Duckworth.

Morelly, È.-G., 1755/1964. *Gesetzbuch der natürlichen Gesellschaft*. Translation Ernst Moritz Arndt. Berlin: Dietz.

Morgan, L.H., 1877. *Ancient society or, Researches in the line of human progress from savagery through barbarism to civilization*. Chicago: C. H. Kerr.

Morina, C., 2017. *Die Erfindung des Marxismus*. München: Siedler.

Morse, R.A., 1980. *Making Mead (Honey Wine): History, Recipes, Methods, and Equipment*. Ithaca: Wicwas.

Morton, T., 2016. *Dark Ecology*. New York: Columbia University Press.

Müller, G., 1967. *Sophokles. Antigone. Erläutert und mit einer Einleitung versehen*. Heidelberg: Carl Winter.

Müller, J. and Diachenko, A., 2019. Tracing long-term demographic changes: The issue of spatial scales. *PLoS ONE,* 14 (1), e0208739.

Müller, J. and Kirleis, W., 2019. The concept of socio-environmental transformations in prehistoric and archaic societies in the Holocene: An introduction to the special issue. *The Holocene,* 29 (10), 1517-1530.

Müller, J., Hofmann, R., Ohlrau, R., Shatilo, M., 2018. The social constitution and political organizations of Tripolye mega-sites: hierarchy and balance. *In:* H. Meller, D. Gronenborn, R. Risch, eds. *Surplus without the State – Political Forms in Prehistory*. Halle: Landesmuseum, 247-262.

Müller, K. E., 1987. *Das magische Universum der Identität*. Frankfurt/M.: Campus.

Müller, S., 2022. *Die Grenzen des Konsums*. Frankfurt/M.: Campus.

Müller, U., 2016. Epochenübergänge und Zäsuren. Transformationen im Mittelalter. *In:* T. Kühtreiber and G. Schichta, eds. *Kontinuitäten, Umbrüche, Zäsuren*. Heidelberg: Universitätsverlag Winter, 43-79.

Müller, U., 2017. Get Up – Stand Up: The Historical Archaeology of Resistance. *In:* S. Hansen and J. Müller, eds. *Rebellion and Inequality in Archaeology*. Bonn: Habelt, 303-331.

Mullin, M.H., 2007. Feeding the Animals. *In:* R. Cassidy and M. Mullin, eds. *Where the Wild Things are Now. Domestication Reconsidered*. Oxford: Berg, 277-303.

Mumford, L., 1944. *The Condition of Man*. London: Secker & Warburg.

Mumford, L., 1967. *The Myth of the Machine: Technics and Human Development*. New York: Harcourt.

Mumford, L., 1970. *The Myth of the Machine: The Pentagon of Power*. New York: Harcourt.

Muraca, B., 2014. *Gut leben*. Berlin: Wagenbach.

Musson, A.E., ed., 1972. *Science, Technology, and Economic Growth in the Eighteenth Century*. London: Methue.

Naess, A., 1989. *Ecology, Community and Lifestyle*. Cambridge: Cambridge University Press.

Naess, A., 1993. Beautiful Actions. *Environmental Values,* 2 (1), 67-71.

Nahum-Claudel, C. 2016. Feasting. *In:* F. Stein, ed. *The Open Encyclopedia of Anthropology,* Online. https://www.anthroencyclopedia.com/.

Nelson, B., 1977. *Der Ursprung der Moderne*. Frankfurt/M.: Suhrkamp.

Neuber, F. and Ott, K., 2020. The Buying Time Argument within the Solar Radiation Management Discourse. *Applied Science*, 10 (13), 4637. DOI:10.3390/app10134637.

Neumann, B., Ott, K., Kenchington, R., 2017. Strong sustainability in coastal areas: a conceptual interpretation of SDG 14. *Sustainability Science*, 12, 1019-1035.

Neuweiler, G., 2008. *Und wir sind es doch – die Krone der Evolution*. Berlin: Wagenbach.

Nietzsche, F., 1874. *Vom Nutzen und Nachteil der Historie für das Leben. Zweite unzeitgemäße Betrachtung*. Werke in zwei Bänden. München: Hanser, Bd. 1, 113-174.

Nussbaum, M., 2000. *Women and Human Development: The Capabilities Approach*. Cambridge: Cambridge University Press.

Nussbaum, M., 2014. *Die neue religiöse Intoleranz*. Darmstadt: WBG.

Oakeshott, M. 1960. *Introduction*. *In*: T. Hobbes, Leviathan or the Matter, Form and Power of a Commonwealth Ecclestical and Civil. Oxford: Blackwell, v-lxvi.

O'Brien, P., 2006. Historiographical traditions and modern imperatives for the restoration of global history. *Journal of Global History*, 1 (1), 3-39.

Olmsted, F.L., 1870/1997. Public Parks and the Enlargement of Towns. *In*: C. Beveridge and C. Hoffman, eds. *The Papers of Frederick Law Olmsted*. Supplementary Series 1. Baltimore: Hopkins University Press, 171-205.

Olszewski, D.I., 2020. *Archaeology and Humanity's Story*. Oxford: University Press.

Ortman, S., Smith, M., Lobo, J., Bettencourt, L., 2020. Why Archaeology is Necessary for a Theory of Urbanization. *Journal of Urban Archaeology*, 1, 151-167.

Ostrom, E., 1990. *Governing the Commons*. Cambridge: Cambridge University Press.

Ott, K., 1991. *Menschenkenntnis als Wissenschaft. Über die Entstehung und Logik der Historie als der Wissenschaft vom Individuellen*. Frankfurt: Haag and Herrchen.

Ott, K., 1997. *Ipso Facto*. Frankfurt/M.: Suhrkamp.

Ott, K., 2005. *Moralbegründung zur Einführung*. Hamburg: Junius 2005.

Ott, K., 2008. A Modest Proposal of How to Proceed in Order to Solve the Problem of Inherent Moral Value in Nature. *In:* L. Westra, K. Bosselmann, R. Westra, eds. *Reconciling Human Existence with Ecological Integrity*. London: Earthscan, 39-60.

Ott, K. 2010. *Umweltethik zur Einführung*. Hamburg: Junius.

Ott, K., 2012. Variants of De-Growth and Deliberative Democracy: A Habermasian Proposal. *Futures*, 44, 571-581.

Ott, K., 2014a. SuWaRest, the 'Third Culture' and environmental ethics. *In:* G. Cirella and S. Zerbe, eds. *Sustainable Water Management and Wetland Restoration Strategies in Northern China*. Bolzano: Bolzano University Press, 11-26.

Ott, K., 2014b. Institutionalizing Strong Sustainability: A Rawlsian Perspective. *Sustainability*, 6 (2), 894-912.

Ott, K., 2014c. Ob die Klimatheorie auf den Weg der Wissenschaft gebracht werden könne. *Zeitschrift für Kulturphilosophie*, 8 (2), 381-389.

Ott, K., 2015. *Zur Dimension des Naturschutzes in einer Theorie starker Nachhaltigkeit*. Marburg: Metropolis.

Ott, K., 2016a. On the Meaning of Eudemonic Arguments for a Deep Anthropocentric Environmental Ethics. *New German Critique*, 43 (2), 105-126.

Ott, K., 2016b. *Zuwanderung und Moral*. Stuttgart: Reclam.

Ott, K., 2017a. Philosophical Problems of how to Think Revolutions. *In:* S. Hansen and J. Müller, eds. *Rebellion and Inequality in Archaeology*. Bonn: Habelt, 59-78.

Ott, K., 2017b. Normative Pragmatics: Approach, Promise, Outlook. *In:* J.P. Brune, R. Stern, M. Werner, eds. *Transcendental Arguments in Moral Theory*. Berlin, Boston: De Gruyter, 213-229.

Ott, K., 2018a. Verantwortung im Anthropozän und Konzepte von Nachhaltigkeit. *In:* R. Sierra and A. Grisoni, eds. *Nachhaltigkeit und Transition: Konzepte*. Frankfurt, New York: Campus, 141-188.

Ott, K., 2018b. On the Political Economy of Solar Radiation Management. *Frontiers in Environmental Science*, 6 (43). DOI:10.3389/fenvs.2018.00043.

Ott, K., 2020a. Environmental ethics. *In:* T. Kirchhoff, ed. *Online Encyclopedia Philosophy of Nature*. DOI:10.11588/oepn.2020.0.71420

Ott, K., 2020b. Mapping, Arguing, and Reflecting Environmental Values. *In:* O. Lysaker, ed. *Between Closeness and Evil. A Festschrift for Arne Johan Vetlesen*. Oslo: Scandinavian Academic Press, 263-289.

Ott, K., 2021a. Domains of Climate Ethics Revisited. *In:* T. Matsuda, J. Wolff, T. Yanagawa, eds. *Risks and Regulation of New Technologies*. Kobe: Springer, 173-199.

Ott, K., 2021b. Glanz und Elend des Biodiversitäts-Konzeptes. Eine umweltethische Analyse mit Blick auf das Recht. *Jahrbuch für Recht und Ethik*, 29, 79-103.

Ott, K., 2021c. Waldreichtum. *Zeitschrift für Europäisches Umwelt- und Planungsrecht*, 19 (1), 73-88.

Ott, K., 2023. Gemeinschaft und Gesellschaft, ‚starke' Nachhaltigkeit und Assoziationen freier Menschen. *In:* D. Haselbach, ed. *Ferdinand Tönnies und die Debatte um Gemeinwohl und Nachhaltigkeit*. Wiesbaden: Springer, 143-164.

Ott, K. and Döring, R., 2011. *Theorie und Praxis starker Nachhaltigkeit*. 3rd ed. Marburg: Metropolis.

Ott, K. and Fischer, T., 2015. On a Philosophy of Individualized Medicine: Conceptual and Ethical Questions. *In:* T. Fischer, M. Langanke, P. Marschall, S. Michl, eds. *Individualized Medicine*. Cham: Springer, 115-163.

Ott, K. and Kalu, K.I., 2020. Sustainable Aquaculture Fish Feeding Production – A Perspective for the Niger Delta. *In:* K. Ott, C. Schulz, R. Schulz, eds. *Nachhaltige Aquakultur*. Marburg: Metropolis, 165-172.

Ott, K. and Reinmuth, K.C., 2021. Integrating environmental Value Systems: A Proposal for Synthesis. Transitioning to Sustainable Life on Land. *In:* V. Beckmann, ed. *Transitioning to Sustainability*. Basel: MDPI, 41-73.

Ott, K. and Riemann, M., 2018. On Flight Reasons - Persecution, Escape, Displacement. *In:* G. Besier and K. Stoklosa, eds. *How to deal with Refugees? Europe as a Continent of Dreams*. Berlin, Münster, Wien: LIT, 15-39.

Ott, K. and Voget-Kleschin, L., 2013. Suffizienz: Umweltethik und Lebenstilfragen. *In*: J.-O. Beckers, F. Preußger, T. Rusche, eds. *Dialog. Reflexion. Verantwortung. Zur Diskussion der Diskurspragmatik*. Würzburg: Königshausen & Neumann, 315-344.

Ott, K., Dierks, J., Voget-Kleschin, L., eds., 2016. *Handbuch Umweltethik*. Stuttgart: Metzler.

Ott, K., Kerschbaumer, L., Köbbing, J.F., Thevs, N., 2016. Bringing Sustainability Down to Earth: Heihe River as a Paradigm Case of Sustainable Water Allocation. *Agricultural & Environmental Ethics*, 29 (5), 835-856.

Ott, K., Matz-Lück, N., Negenborn, C. von, 2022. Ethics, justice, and human rights: normative considerations in marine environmental change. *In:* P. Harris, ed. *Routledge Handbook of Marine Governance and Global Environmental Change*. London, New York: Routledge, 299-312.

Ott, K., Potthast, T., Gorke, M., Nevers, P., 1999. Über die Anfänge des Naturschutzgedankens in Deutschland und den USA im 19. Jahrhundert. Naturnutzung und Naturschutz in der europäischen Rechts- und Verwaltungsgeschichte. *Jahrbuch für Europäisches Verfassungsrecht*, 11, 1-55.

Ott, K., Schulz, C., Schulz, R., eds., 2020. *Nachhaltige Aquakultur*. Marburg: Metropolis.

Overmann, K. and Coolidge, F., eds., 2019. *Squeezing Minds from Stones*. Oxford: University Press.

Paech, N., 2014. *Befreiung vom Überfluss*. München: Oekom.

Paillard, E., 2017. *The stage and the city: non-elite characters in the tragedies of Sophocles*. Paris: Éditions de Boccard.

Pape, H., ed., 1994. *Kreativität und Logik*. Frankfurt/M.: Suhrkamp.

Parfit, D., 1982. Future Generations: Further Problems. *Philosophy & Public Affairs*, 11 (2), 113-172.

Parsons, T., 1954. *Essays in Sociological Theory*. Glencoe: Free Press.

Patel, A., 2018. Music as a Transformative Technology of the Mind: An Update. *In:* H. Honing, ed. *The Origins of Musicality*. Cambridge/Mass: MIT Press, 113-126.

Pattoni, M.P., 1987. *L'autenticitä del Prometeo Incatenato di Eschilo*. Pisa: Scuola Normale Superiore.

Peebles, C.S., 1993. Aspects of Cognitive Archaeology. *Cambridge Archaeological Journal*, 3 (2), 250-253.

Pelluchon, C., 2021. *Das Zeitalter des Lebendigen*. Darmstadt: WBG Academic.

Perone, U., 2011. Emotionalität als anthropologische Komponente. *In:* C.F. Gethmann, ed. *Lebenswelt und Wissenschaft*. Hamburg: Meiner, 1277-1286.

Perreault, C., 2019. *The Quality of the Archaeological Record*. Chicago and London: University of Chicago Press.

Petersen, J.W., 1782. *Geschichte der deutschen National-Neigung zum Trunke*. Leipzig: Haug.

Pettit, P., 2014. *Just Freedom. A Moral Compass for a Complex World*. New York: Norton & Company.

Peukert, H., 1978. *Wissenschaftstheorie – Handlungstheorie – Fundamentale Theologie*. Frankfurt/M.: Suhrkamp.

Pfister, C., 2010. The '1950s Syndrome' and the Transition from a Slow-Going to a Rapid Loss of Global Sustainability. *In:* F. Uekoetter, ed. *The Turning Points of Environmental History*. Pittsburgh: Pittsburgh University Press, pp. 90-118.

Pike, K.L., 1967. Etic and emic standpoints for the description of behavior. In: K.L. Pike, *Language in relation to a unified theory of the structure of human behavior*. Berlin/Boston: De Gruyter, 37-72.

Piketty, T., 2022. *A Brief History of Equality*. Harvard: Belknap Press.

Pinker, S., 2018. *Enlightenment Now: The Case for Science, Reason, Humanism and Progress*. London: Allen Lane.

Platon, 1971. *Politeia*. Werke in 8 Bänden (ed. Eigler). Vol. 4. Darmstadt: WBG.

Platon, 1971. *Symposion*. Werke in 8 Bänden (ed. Eigler). Vol. 3. Darmstadt: WBG.

Plessner, H., 1928/2011. *Die Stufen des Organischen und der Mensch*. Berlin: De Gruyter.

Plumwood, V., 1995. Human Vulnerability and the Experience of Being Prey. *Quadrant*, 39 (3), 29-34.

Podlecki, A.J., 2005. *Aeschylus. Prometheus Bound*. Edited with an Introduction, Translation and Commentary. Oxford: Oxbow.

Polanyi, K., 1944/2011. *The Great Transformation*. Boston: Beacon Press.

Pollard, A.M., Armitage, R., Makarewicz, C., eds., 2023. *Handbook of Archaeological Sciences*. 2nd Edition. Hoboken and Chichester: Wiley.

Ponseti, J. and Stirn, A., 2019. Wie viele Geschlechter gibt es und kann man sie wechseln? *Zeitschrift für Sexualforschung*, 32, 131-147.

Popper, K., 1934. *Logik der Forschung*. Tübingen: Mohr 2002.

Pottage, A., 2019. Holocene jurisprudence. *Journal of Human Rights and the Environment*, 20 (2), 153-175.

Preucel, R.W., 1991. *Processual and postprocessual archaeologies: multiple ways of knowing the past*. Carbondale: Southern Illinois University Press.

Preucel, R.W., 2006. *Archaeological Semiotics*. Malden, MA, Oxford: Blackwell.

Pruetz, J. and Bertolani, P., 2007. Savanna Chimpanzees, *Pan troglodytes verus*, Hunt with Tools. *Current Biology*, 17, 412-417.

Quine, W.V., 1948. On What There Is. *The Review of Metaphysics*, 2, 21-38.

Raab, L.M. and Goodyear, A.C., 1984. Middle-Range Theory in Archaeology: A Critical Review of Origins and Applications. *American Antiquity*, 49 (2), 255-268.

Rahnema, M., 1991. *Global Poverty: A Pauperizing Myth*. Montreal: Intercultural Institute.

Rajalla, U. and Mills, P., eds., 2017. *Forms of Dwelling. 20 Years of Taskscapes in Archaeology*. Oxford: Oxbow.

Ranke, L. von, 1922. *Weltgeschichte*. 5th ed., Vol. 1. München, Leipzig: Duncker und Humblot.

Ramachandran, V., 2003. *The Emerging Mind*. London: Profile Books.

Ramsey, C., 2023. Science-based Dating in Archaeology. In: A.M. Pollard, R. Armitage, C. Makarewicz, eds. *Handbook of Archaeological Sciences*. 2nd Edition. Hoboken and Chichester: Wiley, 1-5.

Rappe, G., 1995. *Archaische Leiberfahrung*. Berlin: Akademie Verlag.

Rathfelder, A., 2023. *Auf der Suche nach Zukunft – Das ökologische politische Denken im deutschsprachigen Raum*. Baden-Baden: Nomos.

Rawls, J., 1971. *A Theory of Justice*. Cambridge: Harvard University Press.

Rawls, J., 1988. The Priority of Right and Ideas of the Good. *Philosophy and Public Affairs*, 17 (4), 251-276.

Rawls, J., 1999. *The Law of Peoples*. Cambridge: Harvard University Press.

Rawls, J., 2001. *Justice as Fairness: A Restatement*. Cambridge: Harvard University Press.

Regan, T., 1986. *The Case for Animal Rights*. Berkeley: University of California Press.

Reichert, A. and Ott, K., 2021. A Lockean Perspective on Large-Scale Land Acquisitions. *Modern Concepts and Developments in Agronomy*, 9 (5), 961-963.

Reiter, B., 2021. The African Origins of Democracy. *Academia Letters*, Article 414. DOI:10.20935/AL414.

Reitze, B., 2017. *Der Chor in den Tragödien des Sophokles. Person, Reflexion, Dramaturgie*. Tübingen: Narr Francke.

Reynolds, J., 2021. Earth system interventions as technologies of the Anthropocene. *Environmental Innovation and Societal Transitions*, 40, 132-146.

Ribeiro, A., 2016. Archaeology will be just fine. *Archaeological Dialogues*, 23, 146-51.

Ribeiro, A., 2018. *Archaeology and the Historical Understanding*. Bonn: Habelt.

Ribeiro, A., 2019. Science, Data, and Case-Studies under the Third Science Revolution: Some Theoretical Considerations. *Current Swedish Archaeology*, 27, 115-32.

Ribeiro, A., 2021. Social Archaeology as the Study of Ethical Life: Agency, Intentionality, and Responsibility. *In:* A. Killin and S. Allen-Hermanson, eds. *Explorations in Archaeology and Philosophy*. Springer Switzerland: Synthese Library, 215-233.

Ribeiro, A., 2022. *Intentionality in Archaeology*. New York and London: Routledge.

Ribeiro, A., 2023. Action and narrative in archaeology: a brief outline. In: J. Miera, ed., *Narrating the Past: Archaeological Epistemology, Explanation and Communication*. Budapest: Archaeolingua Foundation.

Ribeiro, A., Lattmann, C., Schlicht, J.-E., Thalheim, B., Sabnis, S., Alliata, V., Ott, K., in press. Conceptualising an anatomy of transformations: DPSIR, theorisation, semiotics, and emergence. *In:* J. Müller, W. Kirleis, N. Taylor, eds. *Perspectives on Socio-environmental Transformations in Ancient Europe*. Dordrecht: Springer.

Richter, H. and Stupperich, R., eds., 1999. *Griechenland und das Meer*. Mannheim: Biblopolis-Peleus.

Ricoeur, P., 1971. *Die Fehlbarkeit des Menschen*. Freiburg: Alber.

Riehl, W.H., 1850/1907. *Naturgeschichte des Volkes*. 10th ed. Stuttgart and Berlin: Cotta.

Risse, M. and Wollner, G., 2019. *On Trade Justice*. Oxford: University Press.

Robb, J., 2013. Material Culture, Landscapes of Action, and Emergent Causation. *Current Anthropology,* 54 (6), 657-683.

Robb, J., 2014. The Future Neolithic: A New Research Agenda. *In:* A. Whittle and P. Bickle, eds. *Early Farmers: the view from Archaeology and Science*. Proceedings of the British Academy, 198, 21-38.

Robb, J., 2015. What Do Things Want? Object Design as a Middle Range Theory of Material Culture. *Archaeological Papers of the AAA*, 26, 166-180.

Robb, J. and Harris, O., 2018. Becoming gendered in the European prehistory: Was Neolithic gender fundamentally different? *American Antiquity,* 83 (1), 128-147.

Robb, J. and Miracle, P., 2007. Beyond 'migration' versus 'acculturation: new models for the spread of agriculture. *Proceedings of the British Academy,* 144, 99-115.

Robb, J. and Pauketat, T., 2013. From Moments to Millenia. *In:* J. Robb and T. Pauketat, eds. *Big Histories, Human Lives*. Santa Fe: SAR Press, 3-33.

Robbins, L., 1932. *An Essay on the Nature and Significance of Economic Science*. London: Macmillan & Co.

Roberts, C., 2012. *Ocean of Life*. London: Allen Lane.

Rockström, J., Steffen, W., Noone, K. *et al.* 2009. A safe operating space for humanity. *Nature* 461, 472–475.

Rohr, S., 1993. Über die Schönheit *des Findens*. Stuttgart: MandP.

Rolston, H., 1988. *Environmental Ethics*. Philadelphia: Temple University Press.

Rosenberg, A., 1935. *Der Mythus des 20. Jahrhunderts*. München: Hoheneichen.

Rosling, H., 2018. *Factfulness*. United Kingdom: Sceptre.

Rosman, A. and Rubel, P., 1972. The Potlach: A Structural Analysis. *American Anthropologist, New Series,* 74 (3), 658-671.

Rostow, W.W., 1960. *The Stages of Economic Growth. A Non-Communist Manifesto*. Cambridge: Cambridge University Press.

Routledge, B., 2021. Scaffolding and Concept-Metaphors: Building Archaeological Knowledge. *In:* A. Killin and S. Allen-Hermanson, eds. *Explorations in Archaeology and Philosophy*. Cham: Springer, 47-63.

Rousseau, J.J., 1755/1984. *A Discourse on Inequality*. London: Penguin.

Ruddiman, W., 2003. The Anthropogenic Greenhouse Era Began Thousands of Years Ago. *Climatic Change,* 61 (3), 261-293.

Ruddiman, W., 2007. The early anthropogenic hypothesis: challenges and responses. *Reviews of Geophysics,* 45, RG4001.

Ruddiman, W., 2014. *Earth Transformed*. New York: Freeman.

Ruddiman, W., Fuller, D., Kutzbach, J., Tzedakis, P., Kaplan, J., Ellis, E., Vavrus, S., Roberts, C., Fyfle, R., He, F., Lemmen, C., Woodbridge, J., 2015. Late Holocene Climate: Natural or anthropogenic? *Review of Geophysics,* 54, 93-118.

Rüsen, J., 1969. *Begriffene Geschichte*. Paderborn: Schöningh.

Russel, K., 1988. *After Eden: The behavioral ecology of early food production in the Near East and North Africa*. London: BAR International Series 391.

Russell, N., 2007. The Domestication of Anthropology. *In:* R. Cassidy and M. Mullin, eds. *Where the Wild Things are Now. Domestication Reconsidered*. Oxford: Berg, 27-48.

Ryle, G., 1949. *The Concept of Mind*. New York: Hutchinson

Sachsse, H., 1978. *Anthropologie der Technik*. Braunschweig: Vieweg.

Sahal, D., 1976. Elements of an Emerging Theory of Complexity. *Cybernetica*, 19, 5-38.

Sahlins, M., 1972/2004. *Stone Age Economics*. London: Routledge.

Sahlins, M., 2022. *The New Science of the Enchanted Universe: An Anthropology of Most of Humanity*. Princeton: Princeton University Press.

Sahlins, M. and Service, E., eds., 1960. *Evolution and Culture*. Ann Arbor: University of Michigan Press.

Sandkühler, H.J. and de la Vega, R., eds., 1974. *Marxismus und Ethik*. Frankfurt/M.: Suhrkamp.

Sanjuán, L., 2005. *Introducción al Reconocimiento y Análisis Arqueológico del Territorio*. (Introduction to Archaeological Reconnaissance and Analysis of the Territory). Barcelona: Ariel.

Sartre, J.P., 1977. *Drei Essays*. Berlin: Ullstein.

Sauer, E.W., 2004. *Archaeology and Ancient History: Breaking down the Boundaries*. London and New York: Routledge.

Schäfer, L., 1993. *Das Bacon-Projekt*. Frankfurt/M.: Suhrkamp.

Schama, S., 1995. *Landscape and Memory. Nature as Imagination*. New York: Alfred Knopf.

Schampel, J., 1982. *Das Warenmärchen*. Meisenheim: Athäneum.

Scharl, S., 2003. Die Neolithisierung Europas – Modelle und Hypothesen. *Archäologische Informationen*, 26 (2) 243-254.

Schellnhuber, H.J., 2021. Die roten Linien. *Frankfurter Allgemeine Zeitung* vom 27. 10. 2021, N2.

Schiffer, M.B., 1985. Is There a "Pompeii Premise" in Archaeology? *Journal of Anthropological Research*, 41, 18-41.

Schiffer, M.B., 1987. *Formation Processes of the Archaeological Record*. Salt Lake City, NM: University of New Mexico Press.

Schleiermacher, D.F., 1838/1977. *Hermeneutik und Kritik*. Frankfurt/M.: Suhrkamp.

Schmelzer, M. and Vetter, A., 2019. *Degrowth/Postwachstum zur Einführung*. Hamburg: Junius.

Schmidt, L., Rutter, A., Käppel, L., Nakoinz, O., ed., forthcoming 2023. *Mediterranean Connections*. Leiden: Sidestone.

Schmitt, C., 1950. *Der Nomos der Erde*. 5th ed. Berlin: Duncker and Humblot 2010.

Schmitt, C., 2006. *The Nomos of the Earth*. New York: Telos Press.

Schmoller, G., 1919. *Grundriß der allgemeinen Volkswirtschaftslehre*. München, Leipzig: Duncker & Humblot.

Schnädelbach, H., 1983. *Philosophie in Deutschland 1831-1933*. Frankfurt/M.: Suhrkamp.

Schneider, H.W., 1963. *A History of American Philosophy*. New York and London: Columbia University Press.

Schneider, H., forthcoming 2023. The Ideology of Seafaring in the Odyssey and Telemachos' Hanging of the Slave Girls (Od. 22,461-474). *In:* L. Schmidt, A. Rutter, L. Käppel, O. Nakoinz, ed. *Mediterranean Connections*. Leiden: Sidestone.

Scholtes, F., 2007. *Umweltherrschaft und Freiheit*. Bielefeld: transcript.

Schrad, M.L., 2014. *Vodka Politics. Alcohol, Autocracy, and the Secret History of the Russian State*. Oxford: Oxford University Press.

Schütz, A., 1971. *Das Problem der Relevanz*. Frankfurt/M.: Suhrkamp.

Schüz, S., 2021. Hegels negative Anthropologie? *In*: H. Bajohr and S. Edinger, eds. *Negative Anthropologie*. Berlin: De Gruyter, 65-102.

Schulz, W., 1934. *Altgermanische Kultur in Wort und Bild*. München: Lehmann.

Schuppert, F., 2014. *Freedom, Recognition and Non-Domination*. Dordrecht: Springer Netherlands.

Scott, J.A., 2009. *The Art of Not Being Governed. An Anarchist History of Upland Southeast Asia*. New Haven and London: Yale University Press.

Scott, J.A., 2017. *Against the Grain*. New Haven: Yale University Press.

Scruton, R., 2014. *How to be a Conservative*. London: Bloomsbury Continuum.

Seboek, T. and J. Umiker-Seboek, 1980. *'You know my method'. A Juxtaposition of Charles S. Peirce and Sherlock Holmes*. Indiana: Bloomington.

Seddon, N., Chausson, A., Berry, P., Girardin, C. A., Smith, A., Turner, B., 2020. Understanding the value and limits of nature-based solutions to climate change and other global challenges. *Philosophical Transactions of the Royal Society B*, 375(1794), 20190120.

Segal, C.P., 1964/2019. Sophocles' praise of man and the conflicts of the Antigone. *In:* C.P. Segal. *Interpreting Greek Tragedy. Myth, Poetry*. 2nd ed. Ithaca/London: Cornell University Press, 137-161.

Segal, C.P., 1981. *Tragedy and Civilization. An Interpretation of Sophocles*. Norman: University of Oklahoma Press.

Segbers, F., 2002. *Die Herausforderung der Tora*. 3rd ed. Luzern: Edition Exodus.

Sennett, R., 2009. *The Craftsman*. Yale: Yale University Press.

Seo, K., Ryu, D., Eom, J., Jeon, T., Kim, J., Youm, K., Chen., Wilson, C., 2023. Drift of Earth's Pole Confirm Groundwater Depletion as a Significant Contributor to Global Sea Level Rise 1993-2010. *Geophysical Research Letters* 50, e2023GL103509.

Service, E., 1966. *Primitive Social Organization*. New York: Random House.

Shennan, S., 2018. *The First Farmers of Europe: An Evolutionary Perspective*. Cambridge: Cambridge University Press.

Shillington, K., 2019. *History of Africa*. 4th ed. London: Red Globe Press.

Shin, J., Price, M.H., Wolpert, D.H., Shimao, H., Tracey, B., Kohler, T.A., 2021. Scale and information-processing thresholds in Holocene social evolution. *Nature Communications,* 11, Article no. 2394. DOI:10.1038/s41467-020-16035-9.

Shott, M.J., 1998. Status and role of formation theory in contemporary archaeological practice. *Journal of Archaeological Research,* 6 (4), 299-329.

Skinner, B.F., 1971. *Beyond Freedom and Dignity*. New York: Knopf.

Smith, A., 1776/1976. *An Inquiry into the Nature and Causes of the Wealth of Nations*. Oxford: Oxford University Press.

Smith, B.D. and Zedar, M.A., 2013. The onset on the Anthropocene. *Anthropocene,* 4, 8-13.

Smith, E.A., 1983. Anthropological Applications of Optimal Foraging Theory: A Critical Review. *Current Anthropology,* 24 (5), 625-651.

Smith, M., 1955. The Limitations of Inference in Archaeology. *Archaeological Newsletter,* 6 (1), 3-7.

Smith, M.E., 2010. The archaeological study of neighborhoods and districts in ancient cities. *Journal of Anthropological Archaeology,* 29, 137-154.

Smith, M.E., 2011. Empirical urban theory for archaeologists. *Journal of Archaeological Method and Theory,* 18, 167-92.

Smith, M.E., 2017. Social science and archaeological enquiry. *Antiquity,* 91, 520-528.

Smith, M.E. and Lobo, J., 2019. Cities Through the Ages: One Thing or Many? *Frontiers in Digital Humanities,* 6, article 12.

Smith, M.E., Engquist, A., Carvajal, C., Johnston-Zimmerman, K., Algara, M. Gilliland, B., Kuznetsov, Y., Young, A., 2015. Neighborhood formation in semi-urban settlements. *Journal of Urbanism,* 8 (2), 173-198.

Smith, M.E., Kohler, T.A., Feinman, G.M., 2018. Studying inequality's deep past. *In*: M.E. Smith and G.M. Feinman, eds. *Ten Thousand Years of Inequality: The Archaeology of Wealth Differences*. Tuscon: University of Arizona Press, 3-38.

Smith, M.E., Lobo, J., Peeples, M., Huster, A., 2021. The persistence of ancient settlements and urban sustainability. *PNAS,* 118 (20), Article no. e2018155118.

Smith, P., 2006. Children and Ceramic Innovation. *Archaeological Papers of the American Anthropological Association,* 15, 65-76.

Snow, C.P., 1961. *The Two Cultures. Rede Lecture 1959.* Cambridge: Cambridge: Cambridge University Press.

Sørensen, T.F., 2017. The Two Cultures and a World Apart: Archaeology and Science at a New Crossroads. *Norwegian Archaeological Review,* 50, 101-115.

Sonnemann, U., 1969. *Negative Anthropologie.* Reinbek: Rowohlt.

South, S., 1978. Pattern Recognition in Historical Archaeology. *American Antiquity,* 43 (2), 223-230.

Spengler, O., 1923. *Der Untergang des Abendlandes.* München: Beck.

Spengler, R., Petraglia, M., Kistler, L., Ashastina, K., Kistler, L., Mueller, N., Boivin, N., 2021. Exaptation Traits for Megafaunal Mutualism as a Factor in Plant Domestication. *Frontiers in Plant Science,*12, Article no. 649394.

Sperber, D., 1989. *Das Wissen des Ethnologen.* Frankfurt/M.: Ed. Qumran im Campus-Verlag.

Spriggs, M., ed., 2009. *Marxist Perspectives in Archaeology.* Cambridge: Cambridge University Press.

Stanton, T.W., 2004. Concepts of Determinism and Free Will in Archaeology. *Anales de Antropologica,* 38, 29-83.

Stegmaier, W., 2008. *Philosophie der Orientierung.* Berlin: DeGruyter.

Stegmüller, W., 1980. *Neue Wege der Wissenschaftsphilosophie.* Berlin: Springer

Steichen, E., 1955. *The Family of Man.* New York: Museum of Modern Art.

Steiner, F., 1949. *A Comparative Study on the Forms of Slavery.* PhD Thesis University of Oxford.

Stocking, G.W., 1966. Franz Boas and the Culture Concept in Historical Perspective. *American Anthropologist, New Series,* 68 (4), 867-882.

Strahm, C., 2006. Die Jungsteinzeit. *In:* Zeitverlag Bucerius, ed., *Welt- und Kulturgeschichte,* Bd. 1. Hamburg: Zeitverlag, 120-168.

Strenz, J., 2001. *Männerfrisuren der Spätarchaik.* Mainz: Zabern.

Takacs, D., 1996. *The Idea of Biodiversity: Philosophies of Paradise.* Baltimore: John Hopkins University Press.

Talesh, N., 1991. Law and Judiciary in Saudi Arabia. *In:* P. Sack, C. Wellna, M. Yasaki, eds. *Monistic or Pluralistic Legal Culture.* Berlin: Duncker & Humblot, 43-72.

Tallis, R., 2003. *The Hand: A Philosophical Inquiry into Human Being.* Edinburgh: Edinburgh University Press.

Tallis, R., 2011. *Aping mankind: Neuromania, Darwinitis and the Misrepresentation of Humanity.* Durham: Acumen.

Tang, A. and Kemp, L., 2021. A Fate Worse Than Warming? *Frontiers in Climate,* 3, Article no. 720312.

Tanner, N., 1981. *On Becoming Human.* Cambridge: Cambridge University Press.

Tarski, A., 1944/1977. Die semantische Konzeption der Wahrheit und die Grundlagen der Semantik. *In:* G. Skirrbekk, ed. *Wahrheitstheorien.* Frankfurt/M.: Suhrkamp, 140-188.

Taylor, P., 1986. *Respect for Nature.* Princeton: Princeton University Press.

Terberger, T., Burger, J., Lüth, F., Müller, J., Piezonka, H., 2018. Step by step – The neolithisation of Northern Central Europe in the light of stable isotope analysis. *Journal of Archaeological Science,* 99, 66-86.

Tetens, J., 1774/2014. Gedanken von dem Einfluß des Climatis in die Denkungsart des Menschen. Reprint in *Zeitschrift für Kulturphilosophie* 8 (2), 373-380.

Thomas, W.L., ed., 1955. *Man's Role in Changing the Face of the Earth*. New York and Chicago: Chicago University Press.

Thompson, M., 1979/2017. *Rubbish Theory*. London: Pluto.

Tietz, W., 2015. *Hirten, Bauern, Götter. Eine Geschichte der römischen Landwirtschaft*. München: Beck.

Tönnies, F., 1887/1979. *Gemeinschaft und Gesellschaft*. Darmstadt: WBG.

Toynbee, A., 1934-1961. *A Study of History*. Oxford: Oxford University Press.

Toynbee, A., 1976. *Mankind and Mother Earth – A Narrative History of the World*. Oxford: Oxford University Press.

Treherne, P., 2017. The warrior's beauty: the masculine body and self-identity in Bronze-Age Europe. *Journal of European Archaeology Archive*, 3, 105-144.

Trentmann, F., 2016. *Empire of Things*. London: Allen Lane.

Trigger, B., 1993. *Marxism in Contemporary Western Archaeology*. Tucson: University of Arizona Press.

Trigger, B., 1995. Expanding middle-range theory. *Antiquity*, 69, 448-458.

Trigger, B., 2006. *A History of Archaeological Thought*. Cambridge: Cambridge University Press.

Troeltsch, E., 1922/1961. *Der Historismus und seine Probleme*. Reprint Scientia: Aalen.

Tugendhat, E., 1994. *Vorlesungen über Ethik*. Frankfurt/M.: Suhrkamp.

Turchin, P., Currie, T.E., Whitehouse, H., Spencer, C., 2017. Quantitative historical analysis uncovers a single dimension of complexity that structures global variation in human social organization. *PNAS, Anthropology*, 115 (2), Article no. E144-E151. doi10.1073/pnsa.1708800115.

Uppenbrink, J., 1996. Arrhenius and Global Warming. *Science*, 272 (5265), 1122.

Utzinger, C., 2003. *Periphrades Aner. Untersuchungen zum ersten Stasimon der Sophokleischen „Antigone" und zu den antiken Kulturentstehungstheorien*. Göttingen: Vandenhoeck und Ruprecht.

Veblen, T., 1912. *The Theory of the Leisure Class*. New York: Huebsch.

Vico, G., 1774/1990. *Prinzipien einer neuen Wissenschaft über die gemeinsame Natur der Völker*. Hamburg: Meiner.

Voegelin, E., 1956. *Order and History* 1. Baton Rouge: Louisiana State University Press.

Vossenkuhl, W., 1982. *Anatomie des Sprachgebrauchs*. Stuttgart: Klett-Cotta.

Wadley, L., 2019. Ensnaring the Mind: Cognitive Implications of Snares and Traps. *In:* K. Overmann and F. Coolidge, eds. *Squeezing Minds from Stones*. Oxford: Oxford University Press, 457-472.

Walker, M., Head, M.J., Lowe, J., Berkelhammer, M., Björck, S., Cheng, H., Cwynar, L.C., Fisher, D., Gkinis, V., Long, A., Newnham, R., Rasmussen, S.O., Weiss, H., 2019. Subdividing the Holocene Series/Epoch. *Journal of Quaternary Science*, 34 (3), 1-14.

Walter, J., 2017. Poseidon's Wrath and the End of Helike. *In:* C. Schliephake, ed. *Ecocriticism, Ecology, and the Cultures of Antiquity*. Lanham: Lexington, 31-43.

Walton, K.L., 1990. *Mimesis as Make-Believe: On the Foundations of the Representational Arts*. Harvard: Harvard University Press.

Walzer, M., 1983. *Spheres of Justice*. New York: Basic Books.

Waters, C., 2022. Eine einmalige Dominanz in der Erdgeschichte. *Frankfurter Allgemeine Zeitung* vom 18. Mai 2022, S. N2.

Waters, C., Zalasiewicz, J., Summerhayes, C., Barnosky, A.D., Poirer, C., Gałuszka, A., Cearreta, A., Edgeworth, M., Ellis, E.C., Ellic, M., Jeandel, C., Leinfelder, R., McNeill, J.R., Richter, D.D., Steffen, W., Syvitski, J., Vidas, D., Wagreich, M., Williams, M., Zhisheng, A., Grinevald, J., Odada, E., Oreskes, M., Wolfe, A.P.,

2016. The Anthropocene is functionally and stratigraphically distinct from the Holocene. *Science,* 351, Issue 6269.

WBGU (Wissenschaftlicher Beirat Globale Umweltveränderungen), 2011. *World in Transition – A Social Contract for Sustainability*. Berlin: WBGU.

Weber, B. and Depew, D., eds., 2003. *Evolution and Learning. The Baldwin Effect Reconsidered*. Cambridge/Mass: MIT Press.

Weber, M., 1905/2001. *The Protestant Ethics and the Spirit of Capitalism*. London: Routledge.

Weber, M., 1921/1972. *Wirtschaft und Gesellschaft*. 5th Edition. Tübingen: Mohr, Siebeck.

Weniger, G.-C., 2007. Von der Entstehung des Neandertalers bis zum Ende des Eiszeitalters. *In:* A. Jockenhövel, ed. *WBG-Weltgeschichte, Band I: Grundlagen der globalen Welt. Vom Beginn bis 1200 v. Chr*. Darmstadt: WBG, 54-91.

Werber, N., 2014. *Geopolitik zur Einführung*. Hamburg: Junius.

Werner, M., 2021. *Einführung in die Ethik*. Stuttgart: Metzler.

West, M.L., 1979. The Prometheus Trilogy. *Journal of Hellenic Studies,* 99, 130-148.

West, M.L., 1990. *Studies in Aeschylus*. Stuttgart: B. G. Teubner.

White, L., 1967. The Historical Roots of Our Ecological Crisis. *Science,* 155, 1203-1207.

Whittle, A., 1997. Moving on and moving around: Neolithic settlement mobility. *In*: P. Topping, ed. *Neolithic Landscapes*. Oxford: Oxbow.

Whorf, B.L., 1956. *Language, Thought and Reality*. Cambridge/Mass: MIT Press.

Widlok, T., 2017. *Anthropology and the Economy of Sharing*. London and New York: Routledge.

Willey, G. and Sabloff, J., 1980. *A History of American Archaeology*. San Francisco: Freeman.

Williams, B., 1986. *Ethics and the Limits of Philosophy*. Harvard: Harvard University Press.

Wilson, E.O., 1975/2000. *Sociobiology: The New Synthesis*. Harvard: Harvard University Press.

Wilson, E.O., 1984. *Biophilia*. Cambridge: Cambridge University Press.

Wilson, P., 1988. *The Domestication of the Human Species*. Yale: Yale University Press.

Wilson, P., 2007. Agriculture or Architecture? The Beginning of Domestication. *In:* R. Cassidy and M. Mullin, eds. *Where the Wild Things are Now. Domestication Reconsidered*. Oxford: Berg, 101-122.

Winch, P., 1958/1965. *The Idea of a Social Science*. 4th ed. London: Routledge.

Windelband, W., 1907. Geschichte und Naturwissenschaft. *In:* W. Windelband, *Präludien 2*. Tübingen: Siebeck.

Wirth, U., ed. 2000: *Die Welt als Zeichen und Hypothese*. Frankfurt/M.: Suhrkamp.

Wittfogel, K.A., 1931. Wirtschaft und Gesellschaft Chinas. Leipzig: Hirschfeld.

Wittgenstein, L., 1958. Philosophical Investigations. Oxford: Basil Blackwell.

Wittgenstein, L., 1969. *On Certainty*. Oxford: Basil Blackwell.

Woodburn, J., 1982. Egalitarian Societies. *Man. New Series,* 17(3), 431-451.

Worster, D., 1979. *Dust Bowl: The Southern Plains in the 1930s*. Oxford: Oxford University Press.

Wright, G.H. von, 1971. *Explanation and Understanding*. Ithaca, New York: Cornell University Press.

Wylie, A., 1985. The Reaction Against Analogy. *Advances in Archaeological Method and Theory,* 8, 63-111.

Wynn, T., 2019. Epilogue: Situating the Cognitive in Cognitive Archaeology. *In:* K. Overmann and F. Coolidge, eds. *Squeezing Minds from Stones*. Oxford: Oxford University Press, 497-504.

Yoffee, N. and Sherratt, A., 1993. *Archaeological theory: who sets the agenda?* Cambridge: Cambridge University Press.

Zabinski, C., 2020. *Amber Waves. The Extraordinary Biography of Wheat from Wild Grass to World Megacrop*. Chicago: Chicago University Press.

Zalasiewicz, J., Waters, C.N., Ellis, E.C., Head, M.J., Vidas, D., Steffen, W., Thomas, J.A., Horn, E., Summerhayes, C.P., Leinfelder, R., McNeill, J.R., Gałuszka, A., Williams, M., Barnosky, A.D., Richter, D. de B., Gibbard, P.L., Syvitski, J., Jeandel, C., Cearreta, A., Cundy, A.B., Fairchild, I.J., Rose, N.L., Ivar do Sol, J.A., Shotyk, W., Turner, S., Wagreich, M., Zinke, J., 2020. The Anthropocene: Comparing Its Meaning in Geology (Chronostratigraphy) with Conceptual Approaches Arising in Other Disciplines. *Earth's Future*, 9. DOI: 10.1029/2020ER001896.

Zalasiewicz, J., Waters, C.N., Williams, M., Barnosky, A.D., Cearreta, A., Crutzen, P., Ellis, E., Ellis, M.A., Fairchild, I., Grinevald, J., Haff, P.K., Hajdas, I., Leinfelder, R., McNeill, J., Odada, E.O., Poirier, C., Richter, D., Steffen, W., Summerhayes, C., Syvitski, J.P.M., Vidas, D., Wagreich, M., Wing, S.L., Wolfe, A.P., Zhisheng, A., Oreskes, M., 2015. When did the Anthropocene begin? *Quaternary International*, 383, 196-203.

Zentgraf, D. and Schmidt, L., eds., forthcoming 2024. Special Issue: Gardens, Human Senses and Eudaimonia. *Studies in the History of Gardens and Designed Landscapes.*

Zerbe, S., 2022. *Restoration of Multifunctional Cultural Landscapes*. Cham: Springer.

Zerbe, S. and Ott, K., 2021. Pesticides, soil removal, and fire for the restoration of ecosystems? A call for ethical standards in ecosystem restoration. *Waldökologie, Landschaftsforschung und Naturschutz*, 20, 59-73.

Ziegler, J., 2021. Was ist so schlimm am Kapitalismus? *Der Blaue Reiter*, 45, 74-79.

Ziegler, R., 2020. Paludiculture as a critical sustainability innovation mission. *Research Policy*, 49, Article no. 103979.

Zimmermann, A., 2003. Spuren der Ideengeschichte in der ur- und frühgeschichtlichen Archäologie Deutschlands. *In:* J. Eckert, U. Eisenhauer, A. Zimmermann, eds. *Archäologische Perspektiven*. Rahden: Leidorf, 3-17.

Zimmermann, A., 2007. Neolithisierung und frühe soziale Gefüge. *In:* A. Jockenhövel, ed. *Grundlagen der globalen Welt. Vom Beginn bis 1200 v.Chr.* Darmstadt: WBG, 95-127.

# Abbreviations

AT: Agricultural transformation
BECCS: Bioenergy and Carbon Capture and Storage
CT: Claiming territory
DMP: Domestic Mode of Production
DPSIR model: "Driver-pressure-state-impact-response" model
EH: Epistemology of History
GDP: Gross domestic product
GHG: Greenhouse gas
GMT: Global mean temperature
HM: Historical Materialism
LBGTIQA: Lesbian, bisexual, gay, transgender, intersexual, queer, asexual
MRT: Middle Range Theory
NCC: Natural Climate Contributions
PA: Prehistoric Archaeology
RTF: Reflective Turn Forum
SC: Set of Concepts
SDG: Sustainable Development Goal
SAI: Sulphate Aerosol Injection
SRM: Solar Radiation Management
TI: Theoretical Investment
TPCL: Transcendental-pragmatic Conceptual Ladder